The Ohio Cultural Alliance: Genius Knows No Boundaries

Other Publications by George D. Beelen PhD

PRINT (available in local public libraries)

Harding and Mexico: Diplomacy by Economic Persuasion
George D. Beelen PhD, 1987

Common Threads In a Diverse World
George D. Beelen PhD, 1990

Guadalajara: A View from the North
George D. Beelen PhD, 1992

Ethnic Encyclopedia
George D. Beelen PhD, 1996

George D. Beelen – An Autobiography
In Context
George D. Beelen PhD, 2019

FILM (available on YouTube)

Peopling of the Mahoning Valley
George D. Beelen PhD, 1997

Going Places
George D. Beelen PhD, 1998

Going Places II
George D. Beelen PhD, 2007

Thirty Years: Peace Through Understanding
George D. Beelen PhD, 2017

The Ohio Cultural Alliance
Genius Knows No Boundaries

THIRTY YEARS OF UNDERSTANDING

AND HOPE THROUGH LOCAL ENGAGEMENT

George D. Beelen PhD

Beelen Publications – Youngstown, Ohio

BEELEN PUBLICATIONS

ISBN Number 978-1-915904-22-5

Supported by the Mahoning Valley Historical Society

To Betty, my wife, mother of my children
and my north star in life for over 66 years.

Table of Contents

THE OHIO CULTURAL ALLIANCE:
A LOCAL MANIFESTATION OF
THE MAXIM GENIUS KNOWS NO
BOUNDARIES

I. Introduction and Prologue

Genius knows no boundary is an assertion that history tells us about ourselves and becomes a reality the more one studies, reads, travels, and interacts with our fellow man. All peoples and all cultures enjoy people who are brilliant, empathetic, artistic, energetic, peaceful, resourceful and express noble ideas and values. Every culture also is made up of those who are dull, violent, anti-intellectual, lazy, and dependent. These traits may not always be manifested at the same time or in the same place. That is to say, not every culture, people, or nation expresses good and bad traits simultaneously.

The Quetzal bird dropping the seed of peace, by Pepin Hernandez Laos

All peoples and races have contributed to the progress and perils of our planet, but not all at the same historical time and in the same ways. Most scientists believe that races are genetically equal but know that there are different levels of development at any given time. Franz Boas, a distinguished anthropologist, argues that "The history of mankind proves that advances of cultures depend upon the opportunities presented to a social group to learn from the experiences of their neighbors." That is to say, the greater and more varied the contacts, the greater the opportunities to learn and grow. A people or nation become great by interacting with others, and conversely, a people begin to decline as they refuse to interact, as they become ultra-nationalist, nativist, and xenophobic. Their fear or hatred or suspicion of others leads to insularity, arrogance, and selfishness that can hasten the decline.

Let us consider some specific examples of successes and declines of civilizations throughout history:

The Egyptians, nearly 5,000 years ago, and the Aztecs about 500 years ago, built their magnificent pyramids to celebrate their great cultures, but they built them on the backs of the poor, the peasants or the masses, and were doomed to fail eventually.

The Chinese, some 3,500 years ago, became masters of a broad area because of their military and naval technology--bronze, war chariots, and ships—made possible by contact with many others. But the peasants failed to share.

The superb accomplishments of the Greeks and then the Romans with their arts, government, and sciences contributed mightily to progress, but the benefits and rewards were not shared by most of their citizens.

The Arab world shone at a time when the Western world experienced the so-called "Dark Ages." Northern Europeans were frequently referred to as stupid and lacking wit and intellect. But the Arabs overextended themselves and eventually fell. Moreover, not all benefitted.

The Ottoman Empire, which began at the end of the 13th century, continued in some form until the early 20th century. Its organization and expansive nature made it one of the largest empires. But ultimately, its bloated bureaucracy and inability to industrialize led to its fall.

The Africans developed many great empires, including Ghana (700-1200), Mali (1200-1500), and Songhai (1350-1600): state building was growing, the University of Timbuktu was world-class, and trade was brisk, but here too the benefits were uneven and not shared by all.

As Western Europeans, including Spain, began their explorations that led to global unity, it was they who dominated what became a rather united world. By the nineteenth century, they controlled the globe politically with their great empires and economically with their joint stock companies and corporations. They also enjoyed cultural domination, so Western culture became the global model. It was assumed, incorrectly, that this was the natural order of things. Today, that notion is being challenged after only a short time of leadership because genius has no boundaries.

Two generalizations apply in each case just described: first, that these great civilizations, as well as others, were successful in direct proportion to their interaction with others, and second, that nothing fails like success. The so-called law of "retarding lead" suggests that the nations in the lead have the most difficulty changing and retaining their lead in a period of transition. So, they falter and fail.

Today it is the United States that takes its turn to lead. That leadership position has been achieved, at least in part, by the continuing contributions of peoples from many lands-by interactions with others—diverse others. We learned from others from other lands. Indeed, many came to the United States. They came before 1776; they came since 1776. And still, they come.

To summarize, we can conclude that all peoples or nations can succeed and prosper because all have the genius capacity, and all succeed in direct proportion to their ability to change and to interact and learn from others. Additionally, success, prosperity, and leadership should be broad-based. Therefore, if we wish to continue to lead, we should acknowledge these special precepts that call for a broad association with all peoples of the world and move toward a more equitable distribution of the nation's and the world's abundance. These are not necessarily new ideas, and they have been offered to the world by more learned people than this author.

What has consumed me for at least four decades is how these ideas can be explored at the local level-very local, at the community level. Some suggestions may include local United Nations Associations, various local and national charitable organizations, Peace Corps types of organizations and cultural alliances are some that come to mind. An organization that I have been a part of is the Ohio Cultural Alliance. The development and potential impact of this organization is the theme of this work.

The Ohio Cultural Alliance (OCA), an incorporated, tax-exempt organization based in Youngstown, Ohio, was founded in 1987. The OCA participates along with other cultural alliances throughout the world to promote world peace and understanding by interacting with people from other cultures, from within and outside the United States. The hope is that such contact will bring about understanding and empathy, which could help lead to peace. While the

OCA was in a nascent state earlier, it was actually formed in 1987, has developed over the next thirty years, and eventually merged with our local Mahoning Valley Historical Society in 2018.

A confluence of events led to the 1987 formation of the OCA. In 1982 I was invited to speak to a group in Middletown, Ohio, who were engaged in a celebration of the culture of Mexico. It was a city-wide activity sponsored by the city and Armco Steel. My talk, "National Identity and Political Themes in the Mexican Arts, "was well received, most notably by participants Jo Ellen Jorde and Pepin Hernandez Laos. Jo Ellen was a benefactor and major player in the Dallas Cultural Alliance, and Pepin, an architect, and painter was a leader of the Guadalajara Cultural Alliance. The two groups had interacted over the years. They invited me to give the same talk at a conference the two groups were convening in a few months. After the conference and several subsequent meetings in Mexico, I was fortunate to meet many other Mexican artists who impressed me. Among them were Carlos de Obeso, a wealthy and politically connected patron of the arts, and Bernardo Colunga, a composer/pianist and well-connected cultural figure in Guadalajara. Fortuitously, Youngstown State University (hereafter referred to as YSU in this work) was interested in my Mexican activity and asked if I could set up a program that would feature Mexicans and their arts. It was proposed by Dr. Larry Looby, Assistant to President Humphrey, and sponsored by the Wean Foundation.

"The Pianist (Bernardo), the Painter (Pepin), and the Patrician Politician (Carlos)" resulted in a six-week program featuring each of the principals. At two-week intervals during spring 1987, each spent the period of time speaking at area schools, cultural groups, and Youngstown State University classes, giving interviews to the local newspapers, television, and radio. All told, during the six weeks, the visitors from Mexico appeared before at least 5,000 people, and who knows how many they reached with their various press appearances and interviews. After the programs were completed, each of the speakers was of one mind that we must effect a permanent organization, and we should call it the Ohio Cultural Alliance.

The die was cast.

Pepin Hernandez Laos

Bernardo Colunga

Carlos de Obeso

II. Origins of the Ohio Cultural Alliance

With the charge to initiate a local cultural alliance, we adopted a temporary name of the Ohio Cultural Alliance. It became permanent. We proceeded to meet and organize with the goal of developing a model to guide us. Meeting in the fall of 1987 in the Dean's Lounge in DeBartolo Hall, YSU, about 15-20 of us met to discuss Mexico and eventually broadened our scope to include other parts of the world. Fortunately, we had among us an inquisitive initial cohort- several members who had traveled to Mexico with me; Mike Adams, a former Peace Corps volunteer; several teachers; and area residents who met our three Mexicans who participated in the six-week program sponsored by YSU in Spring, 1987. In these early years, we maintained contact with Guadalajara friends, having met them at various Empathy Conferences, highlighted by Empathy Essay Contests, won by Janet Greenway (1987), Leslie Chain (1988), and Barbara Kozarich (1990). During this same time period, we elected officers: President, George D. Beelen; 1st Vice-President, Gary Schreckgost; 2nd Vice-President Reverend Jim Ray; Secretary, John Catoline and Treasurer, Dorothy Palguta Tesner.

The OCA had an exciting and productive second year. In addition to the monthly programs and the continued sponsorship of the essay contest, we finally succeeded after months of trying to ship many boxes of books, collected over several months, to Honduras. Mike and Ana Maria Adams provided the Honduran contacts, and the U.S. Air Force Reserve, flying out of the Vienna Air Base, provided the transportation. Porfirio Esparra, a member of the Reserve, facilitated the entire process.

The OCA encouraged the foreign travel experiences of Drs. Melissa Smith, YSU Foreign Languages, to the U.S.S.R.; Mary Beaubian, YSU Economics, to Europe; and George Beelen, YSU History to Mexico, all of whom gave short presentations of their respective trips upon their return. We have also promoted and encouraged the activities of the budding program of peace studies at YSU, directed by Dr. Alice Budge, the International Education Forum, supervised locally by Mike Adams and provided modest financial assistance and abundant encouragement to the Youngstown High School's song and dance group, The Youngstown Connection as they traveled abroad.

Each of the monthly programs provided empathetic insights into cultures mostly different from our own. After an October meeting which was basically organizational in nature, the OCA focused upon Africa in November and December, Asia in January and February, Europe (overview) in March and April, and Mexico in May.

In November and December, Dr. Amos Beyan, YSU History Department, provided a historical overview of Africa, particularly Sub-Sahara Africa, and Dr. Victor Wan-Tatah, YSU Philosophy, shared with us in lecture and movie form important cultural aspects of Africa.

Sister Norma Raupple, Ursuline Order with visiting African students

In January, Dr. Christopher Bache, YSU Philosophy, sensitized us to Eastern thought with a mesmerizing lecture. In February, Dr. Pei Huang, YSU History, spoke to us about modern Japan, with particular emphasis on how traditional Japan co-exists with modern, technological Japan.

In March, Professor Roman Rudnytsky, YSU'S Dana School of Music, shared his knowledge and musical talent with us as he discussed the national music of Ukraine, Spain, and Hungary, after which he played representative selections on the piano. The following month, Dr. Leslie Domonkos, YSU History, dazzled us with lectures and slides as he took us on a vicarious journey through Hungary and its history. A sumptuous dinner of Hungarian cuisine preceded the program. The presenters reminded us of what Plato once said "music is a moral law. It gives soul to the universe, wings to the mind, flight to the imagination, and charm and gaiety to life and to everything."

In May, Dr. George D. Beelen, YSU History, focused through slide and lecture upon our "Distant Neighbor, Mexico", emphasizing that our two countries are so near, yet so far. We met for this program at El Carlos Restaurant, where we ate a Mexican feast amidst a Latin American ambiance.

In sum, the activities of the second year of OCA began to suggest the model we would follow in the years ahead. We had officers, a series of programs under our belt, met at various sites, learned about some of our brothers and sisters "different from us," and ate meals from different lands. Much of our activity during these two years centered around YSU, providing speakers meeting places and mailing salient information to members. Under the leadership of Debbie Markovich, Struthers High School teacher, we began a pen pal relationship between her students and students from other countries. As we grew, we knew we would need to incorporate to enjoy tax-exempt status. Attorney Michael Morley performed this necessary task for us. We were gaining attendance slowly, from 15-20 the first year to 30-40 the second year. We prepared yearly brochures containing relevant information, including a retrospective of the previous year, programming for the coming year, OCA By-laws, and a list of officers. The brochure was graced (in our first year's brochure and our last) with a logo painted by Pepin Hernandez Laos, depicting the Quetzal bird, an ancient Mayan symbol, surrounding the earth, dropping the seed of peace bound for the hearts of humankind to effect worldwide understanding. Pepin also provided us with several of his paintings which we raffled to help us with fundraising.

While much of our daily life is fast-moving and eruptive, peace and understanding are slow, gradual processes. Cultural alliances, including the OCA, can facilitate that process. As President John Kennedy said in another time and place, "The energy, the faith, the devotion which we bring to this endeavor will light our country, and the glow from that fire can truly light the world." Today, cultural alliances, notably the OCA, can serve as beacons to help light our part of the world.

OCA at YSU 1989

Reverend Morris Lee, Edna Pincham and Dr. GDB

Dr. Chris Bache

Dr. Les Domonkos

III. Creating a Model

By the third year of the OCA, we were ready to implement a model, a model we would substantially embrace for the next thirty years. We were established as a social and cultural organization with an international flavor: the main components were a talk, a meal, and cultural enrichment. We addressed "people different from us" with an overarching theme that "genius knows no boundaries". Our streamlined model for the 3rd year included a theme for the year- "Common Threads in a Diverse World" (1989-90); a topic/country speaker within the theme; relevant cultural enrichment; a topic-appropriate site (if possible); a topic appropriate meal (if possible); a brief business meeting; ten meetings per year; meetings on the first Monday of the month, from 6:30-9:00. By any standard the OCA had an exciting and productive year. In addition to the monthly programs, attended by an average of 70 persons at each monthly meeting, we again sponsored an Empathy Essay Contest won by Barbara Kozarich. Ms. Kozarich had all expenses paid for a conference held in Guadalajara, where she read her winning essay and met counterparts from Mexican colleges and several colleges in the United States.

Accomplishments during this year also included financially assisting the Youngstown Connection, which was invited to perform at the Berlin Wall in East Germany, Austria, Liechtenstein, and Switzerland. We publicized a number of travel opportunities (U.S.S.R. with Dr. George Kulchytsky); (Europe with Dr. Mary Beaubien); and (Mexico, with Dr. George D. Beelen). We received a $1,500 grant from the International Institute Foundation and applied for and received tax-exempt status from the IRS.

But the heart of our activity was the attempt to develop an empathetic understanding of others, using the theme "Common Threads in a Diverse World". The speakers focused on the universality of humankind as expressed by an astronomer, an archeologist, a philosopher, a rabbi, two priests, a minister, and two lay religious. Each of the speakers addressed the notion that one cannot really know oneself until one knows others-people, cultures, religions, and philosophies. Most of the meetings were held at a site that added a relevant ambiance. Also, an ethnic meal was usually provided to enhance the flavor of the evening. Thus, sites included a planetarium, a synagogue, several churches, and a mosque; among ethnic meals served were Jewish, Greek, and English cuisine. This combination of oral presentations plus an on-site, ethnic meal appeared to provide an empathetic atmosphere that permitted participants to "drink deeply" of ideas and cultures different from their own. We were interacting with each other, and we were beginning to build community within the Mahoning Valley.

The first three presentations set the stage for the remaining six: the common universe we inhabit, the sameness of humankind, and the universal elements of our philosophies/religions, all pointing to the common threads of the specific religions which were treated.

September - Dr. Warren Young YSU Astronomy in "The Oneness of the Universe" delineated the origin of the universe and the earth as he points out how each of us, as children of the universe, is a beneficiary of phenomena that began about 15 billion years ago. He suggested that our earth is but a minute aspect of the infinite universe that all humankind occupies.

October - Dr. John White YSU Anthropology in "The Oneness of Humankind" told us of the long evolutionary process of homo- sapiens and that every human represents the end product of that evolutionary process. While differences obviously exist among us, Dr. White argues, we are quite simply, much more alike.

November - Dr. Christopher Bache, YSU Philosophy Department, stated in "The Oneness of Philosophies/Religions" that popular (exoteric) religions stress differences, while the deeper, mystical (esoteric) religions stress common themes. Acknowledging the differences that exoteric religions manifest, Dr. Bache argues that esoteric religions teach that we humans make up a single organism. Therefore, we should cultivate toward all other (human) beings the care we spontaneously feel for ourselves.

Having heard Drs. Young, White, and Bache remind us of our common heritage; we then explored some of the universal and unique aspects of several major religions of the world. Each of the speakers explored how religions seek truth, strive for improvement or perfection, pray to a Supreme Being and use many means to help achieve their goals: written and spoken word, music, art, and architecture, among others.

December - In his presentation "The Ideas and Culture of Judaism," Rabbi Mitchell Kornspan, rabbi at Ohev Tzedek Temple, instructed us about historic Judaism and how the Talmud's interpretation of the Torah has been a guide to living Judaism in the present. After tracing the roots of Judaism, he commented on the influence Judaism has had upon Christianity, Islam, and many of the ideas and institutions by which much of the world lives today.

January - Monsignor Michael Cariglio, Jr., pastor of Our Lady of Mt. Carmel Church, in "The Ideas and Culture of Catholicism," grappled with the one and the many as he related Catholicism's development, its impact, and its search for truth. Father Cariglio sees the Catholic Church as a dynamic body teaching and learning during all eras of the two millennia of its existence.

February - "The Ideas and Culture of Islam" was discussed by a lay practitioner, Dr. Ikram Khawaja, YSU Geology, and Imam Munner Sareed, a visiting Imam. They asserted that the proper meaning of Islam is the attainment of peace, both inner and outer peace. Expressing the commonality of our species, they stated that all humanity, in its essential religiousness, is affiliated to each other.

The remaining three religions addressed clearly indicate how the tenets or philosophies of those religions are complemented by art forms—paintings, sculpture, music, architecture, etc. Although these representations are used by most religions, these three were considered by our organization primarily in terms of the significance of music or art and architecture upon Episcopalianism, Third Baptist, and Greek Orthodox religions, respectively.

March - Dr. Ronald Gould, YSU Dana School of Music, in his talk "The Musical Heritage of the Anglican (Episcopalian) Church," sensitively shared his knowledge and enthusiasm for the music of the Anglican Church. Gould argued that "inextricably wedded to the church's theology and polity, the music offers us a rich panoply of styles and has influenced so many aspects of our modern society." He told us that he, as most humans, has been inspired, thrilled, comforted, and moved by the music of the religion. He performed on the magnificent Episcopalian church organ, some of the inspiring music of which he spoke.

April - No less moved by music is Reverend Morris Lee, pastor of Third Baptist Church, in "The Music of the Third Baptist Church", wherein he traced the music of his church. He observed that their church music reflects the sum total of expressions that have evolved since the beginning of the Church, which was in the times of slavery but based upon the Bible, especially the Old Testament. He suggested that the music of his Church acknowledges these varied roots and symbolizes its dynamic nature. He spoke in his church in Youngstown, Ohio, amidst the ambiance and had two of his choir groups grace us with both traditional music as well as gospel music.

May - Reverend George Papas, pastor, Archangel Michael Greek Orthodox Church, in Campbell, Ohio, addressed, among the paintings and icons in the Church, Greek Orthodox Church history and traditions, again reminding us of the commonality of our religions. Dr. Louis Cassimatis' YSU History, in his talk "The Sense of Unity in Byzantine Art and Architecture, "expressed the significance of art and architecture for those of the Greek Orthodox faith as well as for all humankind. "We all pursue ultimate truth", he asserted;" it is this pursuit which gives all peoples a sense of commonality—even as national, cultural, and religious differences serve to generate powerful centrifugal influences. Truth is sometimes sought through art."

Driven home during this year was how religious groups perceive life on earth and in the hereafter, as well as how they perceive their fellow humans. Although one can discern differences among these beliefs and practices, one cannot but be struck by the many similarities "Common Threads in a Diverse World". Perhaps we can conclude this section with the words of St. Francis of Assisi:" the more men seek to know the truth, the more they become brothers."

We traveled throughout the community to sites relevant to each topic. Additionally, relevant cultural enrichment was provided by the ambiance of the religious site and frequent appropriate music, and often, our palates were favored by the various ethnic cuisines. We were on our way to becoming the largest area organization that met on a monthly basis.

Each of the speakers agreed to put his oral comments in written form to be compiled in booklet form and shared with others. This was done within a few months, and the books served as one of our early fundraisers. In sum, the third year of OCA was an outstanding one that helped us to understand our brothers and sisters, whomever and wherever they may be.

GDB (left), Monsignor Michael Cariglio (center) and Monsignor Robert Sifrin (right)

A card from Dr. Kong Oh, reflecting the oneness of the Baha'i faith

The Vindicator

THURSDAY, SEPTEMBER 28, 1989

Jane Tims
Staff columnist

Group hails universality of mankind

The Ohio Cultural Alliance sounds like some multi-branched organization that meets once a year in Columbus to compare who's done the most in which town. It isn't.

It's a single unit founded right here in Youngstown and borrowed, in a sense, from the World Cultural Alliance in Dallas, Texas and Guadalajara, Mexico.

OCA started with Dr. George D. Beelen, chairman of the history department at Youngstown State University. He specializes in Latin America with emphasis on Mexico, has authored a book on U.S.-Mexico relations and takes groups of teachers to Mexico to help widen the scope of their instruction.

So when members of the World Cultural Alliance heard him speak in Cincinnati and asked him to deliver the same speech at their alliance meetings in Dallas and Guadalajara, he jumped at the chance.

He came home from those speeches determined to start a similar alliance here, and in 1987 formed the core.

Now, beginning its third year, the OCA has a mailing list of 300. Although the OCA speaker series, free and open to the public, is not the group's only project, it is perhaps the most visible, and this year's series is already under way.

Universality theme

The theme is universality of humankind. Looking at the schedule, I can imagine the path at the planning session, a path that leads from broad to narrow, from recognition of likenesses to appreciation of differences.

We are all part of the universe, I can hear the planners saying, so let's start with that. We are all members of humankind; let's move to that. Cultures become separated by philosophies and religions, so let's offer an overview and then examine a representative few. Now all we have to do is fill in that outline with dynamic speakers.

So on Sept. 13 Dr. Warren Young, chairman of YSU's physics and astronomy department, started the season with the broadest topic.

The subjects narrow gradually: Oct. 2, Dr. John White on "The Oneness of Humankind," and Nov. 6, Dr. Christopher Bache on "The Commonality of Philosophies/Religions." Each of those is at 7 p.m. in DeBartolo Hall, Room 121-22.

The religions become specific: Dec. 5, Rabbi Mitchell Kornspan on "The Ideas and Culture of Judaism," at Ohev Tzedek Synagogue; Jan. 8, Rev. Michael Cariglio Jr., on "The Ideas and Culture of Catholicism," at Our Lady of Mount Carmel Church; Feb. 5, Dr. Ronald Gould on "The Music of Episcopalianism" at St. John's Episcopal Church; March 5, Rev. George T. Pappas on "The Art and Architecture of the Greek Orthodox Church," at Archangel Michael Greek Orthodox Church; Apr. 2, Mrs. Edna Pincham

As if the speaker series were not ambitious enough, the Ohio Cultural Alliance will again sponsor an essay contest open to any YSU student. Following in the steps of the first two winners, Janet Grenemeyer and Leslie Chain, the winner will deliver his or her essay at an international conference, probably in Guadalajara, expenses paid.

Last year the OCA decided to send books to schoolchildren in Honduras. It sounded simple enough. Indeed, collecting the books was no problem, but working through the Pentagon and the Agency for International Development required patience.

Undaunted, local people including Porfirio Esparra, Ana Maria and Mike Adams and the Air Force Reserves at Vienna persevered until the books finally were sent.

Gratitude expressed in letters from the young Hondurans convinced the OCA its efforts were worthwhile. This year the group may collect simple medical supplies to send to another country south of the border.

Farther down the road, OCA would like to send a local contingent to Mexico, the trip designed so that each member spends a few days with his counterpart — U.S. doctor with Mexican doctor, U.S. teacher with Mexican teacher.

The subsequent step, then, would be to have the Mexican group come here, and after that, to replicate the program in additional countries.

To institute a program of such complexity takes time; likewise, goodwill among nations. It takes people learning about people, one step at a time, and the Ohio Cultural Alliance is part of that process.

Dr. John White, Dr. Louis Cassimatis

Rabbi Mitchel Kornspan

IV. Themes

We selected themes relating to a country, region, or ethnic group: most of the themes fit this category. We were, after all, dealing with people like us and different from us. The few exceptions included topics that were enriching elements of life. The OCA hit its stride during the fourth year of our existence. In addition to the ten monthly programs, attended by an average of 115 persons each meeting, the OCA sponsored a two-phased cultural exchange program between artists (art, literature, music) of Youngstown, Ohio, and Guadalajara, Mexico; co-sponsored several programs with the Youngstown Chapter of the United Nations Association (UNA) and edited a 110-page booklet, "Common Threads in a Diverse World", which is a written version of the OCA 1989-90 program. We sold several hundred copies of this work as one of our fundraisers.

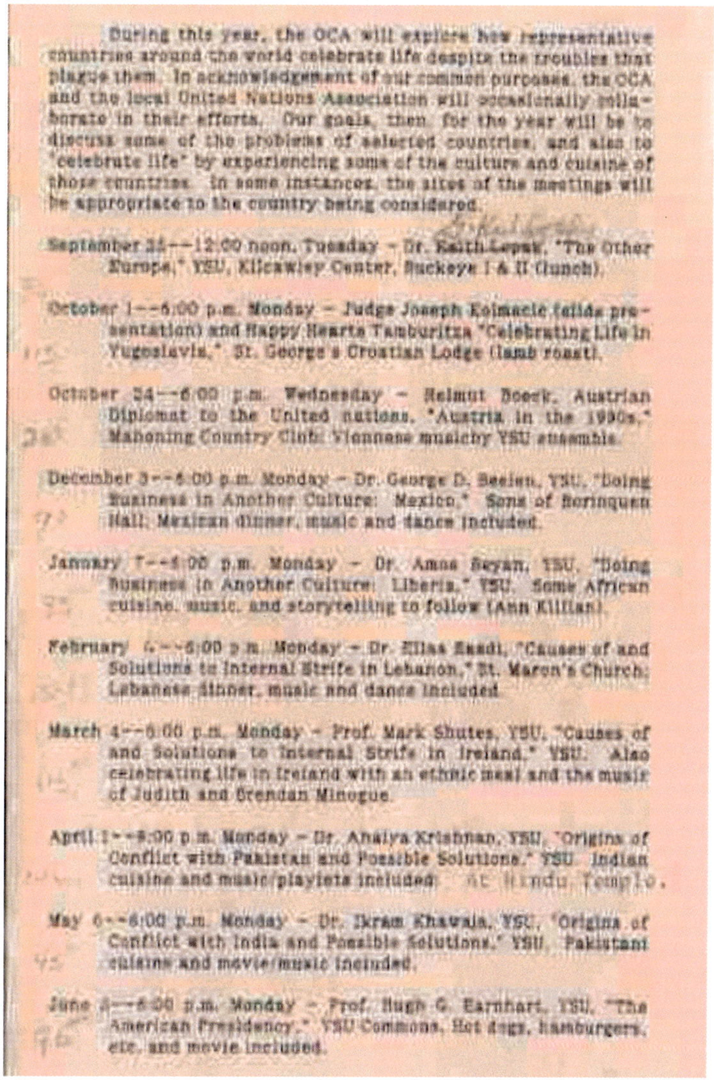

During this year, the OCA will explore how representative countries around the world celebrate life despite the troubles that plague them. In acknowledgement of our common purposes, the OCA and the local United Nations Association will occasionally collaborate in their efforts. Our goals, then, for the year will be to discuss some of the problems of selected countries, and also to "celebrate life" by experiencing some of the culture and cuisine of those countries. In some instances, the sites of the meetings will be appropriate to the country being considered.

September 24--12:00 noon, Tuesday - Dr. Keith Lepak, "The Other Europe," YSU, Kilcawley Center, Buckeye I & II (lunch).

October 1--6:00 p.m. Monday - Judge Joseph Kolmacic (slide presentation) and Happy Hearts Tamburitza "Celebrating Life in Yugoslavia," St. George's Croatian Lodge (lamb roast).

October 24--6:00 p.m. Wednesday - Helmut Boeck, Austrian Diplomat to the United nations, "Austria in the 1990s," Mahoning Country Club: Viennese music by YSU ensemble.

December 3--6:00 p.m. Monday - Dr. George D. Beelen, YSU, "Doing Business in Another Culture: Mexico," Sons of Borinquen Hall: Mexican dinner, music and dance included.

January 7--6:00 p.m. Monday - Dr. Amos Bayan, YSU, "Doing Business in Another Culture: Liberia," YSU. Some African cuisine, music, and storytelling to follow (Ann Killian).

February 4--6:00 p.m. Monday - Dr. Elias Saadi, "Causes of and Solutions to Internal Strife in Lebanon," St. Maron's Church; Lebanese dinner, music and dance included.

March 4--6:00 p.m. Monday - Prof. Mark Shutes, YSU, "Causes of and Solutions to Internal Strife in Ireland," YSU. Also celebrating life in Ireland with an ethnic meal and the music of Judith and Brendan Minogue.

April 1--6:00 p.m. Monday - Dr. Ahalya Krishnan, YSU, "Origins of Conflict with Pakistan and Possible Solutions," YSU. Indian cuisine and music/playlets included. At Hindu Temple.

May 6--6:00 p.m. Monday - Dr. Ikram Khawaja, YSU, "Origins of Conflict with India and Possible Solutions," YSU. Pakistani cuisine and movie/music included.

June 3--6:00 p.m. Monday - Prof. Hugh G. Earnhart, YSU, "The American Presidency," YSU Commons. Hot dogs, hamburgers, etc. and movie included.

V. Celebrating Life in a Troubled World

The theme selected for the 1990-91 year was "Celebrating Life in a Troubled World," wherein we explored some of the real problems of the representative countries, but we also learned something about how they celebrate their heritage amidst their troubles. Significant changes were occurring in Eastern Europe during this time period, particularly in U.S.S.R. and the former Yugoslavia.

September - Accordingly, we heard Dr. George Kulchytsky, YSU History, discuss Eastern Europe with particular emphasis on the breakup of the Soviet Union and Ukraine. The evening included a modified Russian ethnic meal and appropriate piano music performed by Professor Roman Rudnytsky (YSU Dana School of Music).

October - Judge Joseph Kolmacic, Campbell Municipal Court Judge, whose ethnic roots are Croatian, spoke of the current troubles in the former Yugoslavia, with a specific focus on Croatia, which he recently visited. His slides and music provided an atmosphere conducive to understanding the culture, and the food, highlighted by a lamb roast, really helped us to feel the culture. Adding to the cultural enrichment was a concert provided by the Happy Hearts Tamburitza group.

Judge Joseph Kolmacic and wife Josephine

November - In conjunction with the local UNA, the OCA hosted Dr. Helmut Boeck, First Secretary of the Austrian Mission to the United Nations, who addressed the topic, "Austria's Role in the New Europe". Cuisine, provided by the Mahoning Country Club, and cultural enrichment by Roman Rudnytsky, offered a Viennese touch to the evening.

December - Dr. George D. Beelen, YSU History, addressed the topic "Doing Business in Another Culture: Mexico," which is robust but does have its knotty problems. The program was held at the Sons of Borinquen Hall, which provided an ethnic meal and appropriate music and dance.

January - Dr. Amos Beyan, YSU History, also addressed the same topic regarding Liberia, indicating that this country founded by former slaves engages in more limited, but growing business with the U.S. Modified Liberian cuisine, appropriate music, and storytelling by Ann Killian added the cultural enrichment. The meeting was held at YSU.

February - Dr. Elias Saadi, local cardiologist, spoke at St. Maron church hall on the topic "Causes of and Solutions to Internal Strife in Lebanon". Clearly familiar with his ancestral homeland, Saadi spoke of the beauty of Lebanon but also of the acrimony of the various factions. Problems, yes, but he and we celebrated the culture with an authentic Lebanese dinner, followed by a troupe performing typical music and dance.

March - Professor Mark Shutes, YSU Anthropology, similarly spoke of "Causes of and Solutions to Internal Strife in Ireland". Tracing the origins of the problems of Ireland and

Northern Ireland and the involvement of England, Shutes also proposed some possible solutions to those difficulties. An Irish ethnic meal was provided by the caterers at the Croatian Lodge, the site of the meeting, and relevant music was provided by Judith and Brendan Minogue, complementing the evening.

April/May - Another two-part program featured Dr. Ahalya Krishnan, YSU Psychology with ancestry from India, and Dr. Ikram Khawaja, YSU Geology Department, with Pakistani origins. Since the partition of British India in 1947 and the subsequent creation of India and Pakistan, the two countries have been involved in a number of conflicts and military stand-offs. They each discussed the origins and possible solutions between India and Pakistan as they saw it. In each case, we were treated to an ethnic meal and music from each of the cultures. The former was held at India Palace Restaurant in Liberty and the latter at YSU.

June - For our final meeting of the 1990-91-year, Professor Hugh Earnhart, YSU History, focused on The American Presidency. He discussed how several of those presidents dealt with troubles during their respective administrations. Despite these obstacles and troubles, the United States always found ways to celebrate, as did we in our June meeting, complete with flags, patriotic videos, buntings and hot dogs, hamburgers, beans, potato salad, apple pie, and ice cream-a fitting conclusion to our quest to celebrate life in a troubled world.

During this season, the Ohio Cultural Alliance had an opportunity to try to experiment with a "Walk in Their Shoes" exercise. This venture was made up of local artists who interacted with counterparts in Guadalajara, Mexico. This Guadalajara Exchange represented a continuing effort to engage in cultural contact with Mexico. Bernardo Colunga, Youngstown State University Wean Lecturer, Spring, 1987, proposed the cultural exchange of visual art, literature, and music from residents of the Youngstown area to Guadalajara during the week of December 6-11, 1990, and for reciprocity during April 1991, to correspond with YSU's Hispanic Awareness Week (see below).

Colunga's proposal called for a one-day focus on each of the arts mentioned, plus one day when I would talk about YSU. The idea was to exchange ideas through culture, whether or not every one of the authors was present. Thirteen of us did attend, and more than forty items of art were represented. The works were sent to Mexico well in advance of the program and were shared as follows:

Day 1-The visual arts were tastefully displayed. Attached to the works were a picture and a short resume of each artist. A brief statement regarding each work accompanied the picture and resume.

Day 2-The literary works were read aloud to the audience. And here, too, a picture and a short resume of each author were displayed.

Day 3-The compositions were performed by accomplished musicians-guitar, piano, flute or violin, or any combination of these instruments.

Day 4-I gave a speech about the Youngstown area and Youngstown State University specifically.

The Exchange was an overwhelming success in terms of artists "walking in others" shoes and also in learning about some people "different from us". We also learned there were some real geniuses in Mexico - "genius knows no boundaries".

During these early days of the OCA, we operated out of and with YSU; thus, we used the resources of the university: secretaries, students, and colleagues. Mary Bellotto, the History Department secretary, was vital to our success during the first three years by typing, organizing, and even making cookies for the first few meetings. Later, Bonnie Harris, who replaced Mary upon her retirement, did the typing and mailing. Once we incorporated, we did not operate out of the History Department. For the remainder of OCA's history, it was Betty Beelen, my wife, who did the typing, preparation of the yearly programs, the monthly letters of meeting notices, the maintaining of the mailing list, and the mailing, among other details that an organization with a mailing list of 600 entails.

VI. The Making of America; A Land of Hope

"The Making of America" was our focus for 1991-92 and 1992-93-a two-year program where we considered the arrival of many ethnic groups to the United States, including the Youngstown area; their problems while here and their various legacies as we explored how all these groups contributed to the making of America. In most instances, typical meals, aspects of culture, and appropriate sites complemented the programs.

Most immigrants reported that the decision to leave their homeland was the hardest thing they ever had to do: the leave-taking; the journey; the farewells to home and relatives, in all likelihood never to be seen again; the last lingering looks at things and places and the traditions of their beloved homeland. It was usually a final farewell—they were emigrating.

At the opening meeting in September, held at the Arms Museum, Dr. George D. Beelen introduced the two-year program with comments and videos which suggested the varied and heterogeneous peoples that constitute the people of the United States. Beelen offered comments in response to Alexis de Tocqueville's query, "What then is an American, This new man?" Complementing these comments was a film regarding immigrants entering the U.S. through Ellis Island, "Island of Hope; Island of Tears".

Dr. John White, YSU Anthropology, captured the attention of the group that attended the October meeting held at the Butler Art Institute as he spoke of the Native Americans. With Native American music in the background, Dr. White spoke of the earliest settlers in the Americas, particularly in northeastern Ohio, and of the varied cultures which they developed. Dr. White said, "the influences on modern American culture by our Native American brothers and sisters are already well-documented: in drama, theater, music-the arts in general; in sports-lacrosse, ice hockey, snow showing; in clothing-moccasins, parkas, anoraks, mukluks, and chaps; in foods-the tomato, potato, maize corn, beans, squash, chocolate, vanilla, and peanuts-to list but a few; and in the pleasant music of our well-known and lyrical place names-Susquehanna, Massachusetts, Dakota, and Mississippi. Locally, in addition to the Mahoning, we have Ashtabula, Shenango, Pymatuming, Allegheny, and Ohio. The nearly 400 years of cultural contact and its accompanying acculturation, assimilation, and, yes, even annihilation, has made the Native American an integral part of the fabric of American culture", White said. The cuisine, prepared by Eberth Catering, bore some resemblance to what Native Americans may have eaten centuries ago. We also enjoyed the ambiance of The Butler Museum of American Art, including a large collection of Native American works.

In November, Mrs. Annette El-Hayek, a former YSU graduate student, spoke at St. John's Episcopal Church in Youngstown of the migrants from various sections of Great Britain. With a special emphasis on Scotland (her native land), she indicated the difficulties encountered by the immigrants' arrival in the new land and their subsequent contributions to the nation and the Mahoning Valley. The first settlers with ties to Britain, including Scotland, generally came from other parts of America. Stories of economic opportunities from other immigrants and direct recruitment brought others with skills needed for the young mining and steel industries directly from England, Scotland, and Wales. Each of these groups left a mark and played a vital role in the development of the Valley. The English meal prepared by members of the congregation and the Scottish dancers (two of whom were her two sons) were great complements to the evening.

Professor Alfred Bright, YSU Art, captivated the group in December as he narrated a visual slide presentation regarding the African American migration to America. He shared with us his insights into the great civilizations of Africa and how they became part of the American experience. Coming to America as slaves in 1619, to the Youngstown area as early as the mid-19th century, and with significant migration from the South to the North in the 1920s and 1930s, Professor Bright spoke of the continuing and growing number and influence of African Americans in the nation and the Youngstown area. The evening was hosted by New Bethel Baptist Church, whose pastor was Reverend Lonnie Simon, who spoke about the importance of the Church in the Black community and some personal experiences in living in Youngstown. Members of the congregation prepared a delicious "soul feast" for us.

January's meeting focused on French immigrants. Our speaker was Dr. George Gauthier, Hiram College Language Department, who traced the early (18th and 19 centuries) French immigration to America and to northeast Ohio. With slides, he showed examples of their continuing legacy. Although persons of French ancestry are a small percentage of the population of Mahoning County, the French have a long history here. The YSU chefs prepared a sumptuous meal that had a distinctly French flavor, and Professor Roman Rudnytsky again played for us the music of French composers.

In February, the focus was the migration from the Scandinavian countries. Short movies about Norway and Sweden were shown during the entire evening, and remarks were made by two foreign exchange students dressed in native costumes as they compared their cultures with life in the Mahoning Valley. A brief talk regarding the Scandinavian presence in the Mahoning Valley was given by Mathew Butts (YSU History Department graduate student). The meal, prepared by YSU chefs, was based on recipes from a Scandinavian cookbook provided by local resident Arlene Anderson. We met at YSU.

Dr. Daniel O'Neill, YSU Speech Department, was the speaker in March. He traced the Irish migration to the United States and to the Mahoning Valley as that group settled here in the mid-19th century and thereafter. Dr. O'Neill spoke of the problems and contributions of the Irish as they became part of this "land of hope." He reported that people who claim Irish ancestry are a dominant cultural group in present-day Mahoning Valley. They have lived in the area since the earliest days of the Western Reserve and continued to be drawn to the Valley throughout the entire 19th century. Their experiences varied, but they contributed strongly to the economic, political, and social life, including the religious life of the community. The meeting was hosted by St. Patrick's Church in Youngstown, whose staff prepared a wonderful Irish meal. The entertainment was provided by a lively children's Irish Step Dance group, which ended the event on a gala note.

In April, German native Hildegard Schnuttgen, YSU Reference Librarian, born in Germany, delightfully shared some of her native culture and history as she narrated the story of the German arrival in America. Her anecdotal research regarding Germans in the Mahoning Valley was well received by the OCA audience, which included a number of members of German heritage. She reported that the Germans were the largest ethnic group in the U.S., whose descendants comprise close to thirty percent of the total population. Germans have played an important part in shaping the development of their new homeland in all phases of social and cultural life, including in the Mahoning Valley. The authentic German meal, prepared by the hosting Saxon Club personnel, was as good as it gets; the melodic voices of the famous Concordia Chorus created a mood of actually being in a German beer garden.

The speaker in May was Mrs. Adrianne Slivkoff, a native of Italy and a teacher of Italian in the Austintown schools. Her presentation of the migration of the Italians to America captured the mood of the problems faced by this "new immigrant" from southeastern Europe and the contributions made by them. Mrs. Slivkoff's look at the Italians in the Mahoning Valley was instructive. They were the most numerous of the immigrants from southern and eastern Europe during the period 1890-1924. And that also included the Valley. While many of them were induced to come to America to work in jobs that the Industrial Revolution created, they were often treated harshly and assigned to the most intensive and dangerous jobs. Early Italian immigrants were often met with racial prejudice, especially those of darker complexion arrivals from Southern Italy who were sometimes described as "subhuman." They worked to assimilate and to make positive contributions, yet were determined to preserve some of their cherished traditions. The Italian cuisine that was served at Mt. Carmel Church Hall, prepared by Lou Fusillo, was a premier Italian meal. Dr. Wade and Rosemary Raridon, YSU Dana School of Music, in full tuxedo and gown, graced us with magnificent Italian opera. They sang arias as lovingly as the stars of La Boehme.

June's meeting focused on Polish immigration. Poland natives Joseph and Judy Magielski spoke poignantly of their Polish roots and of the migration to America of others from their fatherland. The earliest recording of Polish immigrants in the Mahoning Valley was in 1890. During the next few decades, others came to work in the steel mills and in the railroad industry. The legacy of the Polish immigrants is the fraternal organizations, churches, schools, and cultural organizations which have remained. Krakusy Hall was the site of the meeting. We were served a sumptuous meal by caterers of Polish background. A children's group provided music, dance, and playlets that depicted Polish culture.

In sum, the 1991-92 season provided the OCA members with an informative and entertaining beginning to the two-year program whose theme, "The Making of America, A Land of Hope," attempted to consider our common human experiences and allowed us to recognize our diversity. The attendance now swelled to an average of 140-150 members per meeting. During this year, the OCA co-sponsored with Youngstown State University and the Youngstown State University Foundation a Youngstown/Guadalajara cultural exchange. From March 19-28, 1992, twelve Mexicans from Guadalajara came to Youngstown to present their art, music, and literature to the delight of many area residents. From August 28-September 6, 1982, Youngstown residents traveled from Youngstown to Guadalajara. It was a huge success, with thirty- seven area artists (art, literature, music) submitting about 150 works to be displayed, performed, or read in Mexico. Twelve OCA/YSU members actually traveled to Guadalajara. An edited work by each of the exchange members contributed to a work entitled "Guadalajara: A View From the North," which provided a fund-raising opportunity. An added attraction of this exchange was the collecting and delivery of 250 pounds of used football equipment to Guadalajara upon the request of that city. A major contributor of equipment was YSU football coach Jim Tressel, offering used equipment.

The 1992-93 OCA season was kicked off with September's meeting that focused upon the Czechoslovakians (within a few months to be divided into Slovakia and the Czech Republic). Michael Kurilla (a graduate with B.A. and M.A. in YSU's History Department and a doctoral student at Kent State), with grandparents born in Czechoslovakia, brilliantly articulated the emigration story of southern and eastern Europeans, of which the Czechoslovakians were a part. Most of these immigrants came to the Valley during the period 1890-1924, as with others from southern and eastern Europe. There were two important factors that created a cohesive bond for the Czech and Slovak immigrants in developing a sense of identity and security with their fellow new arrivals in dealing with the influences of a new American society: the role of the church in the immigrant's life and the role of ethnic fraternal organizations. Hosted by YSU, an ethnic meal was reasonably authentic, and dancing to the polka band of Steve Garchar (popular during the 1950s and 1960s) concluded the evening.

On October 12 (Columbus Day), Dr. Silvia Hyre, a native of El Salvador, who was currently the Foreign Language Lab Director at YSU, addressed the recent and early migrations of Hispanics to America. Her insightful and humorous remarks were enthusiastically received. The Hispanic presence has been evident in the U.S. for many years, as the Spanish colonized the Americas in the 15th and 16th centuries. But coming to the Valley is a more recent phenomenon. While a handful of Spanish were in the Valley earlier in the 19th century, Puerto Ricans and Mexicans came later in that same century. Like many other groups who came to the area, Puerto Ricans faced many problems, notwithstanding the fact that they had been American citizens since 1917. Ultimately, they were well-accepted in the community. Complementing the evening were ethnic music and dances by Hispanic children and a timely visit by Christopher Columbus (Dr. George D. Beelen) in appropriate 15th-century dress.

Dr. Saul Friedman, YSU History, traced the Jewish diaspora as it related to America, including the Youngstown area, in a poignant presentation delivered in the sanctuary of Ohev Tzedek Temple for the November meeting. He reported that it was German Jews who came to America and the Valley in the mid- 19thcentury, with others from Hungary, Russia, and Romania arriving by the end of the century. Regardless of their nationalities, degrees of orthodoxy, or secularism, Youngstown's Jews have upheld ethical concepts that form the core of Jewish tradition. The evening also consisted of excellent Jewish cuisine prepared by members of the Temple and the singing of retired cantor Lawrence Ehrlich.

Ukrainian and Russian migration to the U.S. was the topic for December, with Dr. George Kulchytsky, YSU History, presiding. His presentation focused chiefly on the Ukrainian's contributions to the U.S. and to the Mahoning Valley, with a truncated consideration of the Russian story in the Valley. Roman Rudnytsky again performed piano selections at the Holy Trinity Ukrainian Hall, in which members prepared a typical ethnic meal and showed off the 1500 loaves of Christmas kolachi, which they also prepared. A special guest who briefly spoke to us was Dr. Leslie Cochran, YSU president from 1992-2000.

The Reverend Remus Bleahu, native Romanian and pastor of Holy Trinity Romanian Orthodox Church in Youngstown, the site of this program, spoke in January of his ethnic group's migration to America and the Youngstown area. As with others from southern and eastern Europe, the Romanians came to America and to the Valley basically from 1890-1924. Pushed out of Romania by bad economic conditions, they were also pulled to the U.S. and our area by jobs in the Youngstown steel mills and coal mines in West Virginia. Although much of the early Romanian immigrants' life revolved around their arduous work, they did find solace in both religion and social organizations. A visit to the iconic church itself was an added feature of the evening. Ethnic "mamaliga si tocana de pui" (corn meal mush and chicken stew) was on the menu this evening, with appropriate violin and pan flute melodies and Romanian doinas (songs) presented by George Bodnar, providing cultural enrichment.

Greeks coming to America was the February topic of Dr. Louis Cassimatis, limited-service instructor in the YSU History Department. Held at St. John's Orthodox Church Hall in Boardman, Dr. Cassimatis employed slides and anecdotal material to weave his story and the contributions of the Greek community to America and the Mahoning Valley. Upon their arrival, the immigrants were sometimes confronted with obstacles and an environment that was frequently hostile. They tended to settle in close proximity to friends, relatives, and others from the same part of Greece. Nevertheless, with the passage of time, those early migrants were able to surmount these obstacles and thus became an integral part of the heritage of the Mahoning Valley. Cultural ambiance and excellent Greek food prepared by parishioners were complemented by native song and dance, including audience participation.

In March, the focus was the Serbian migration to our nation and to our area. Joseph Raysich, a native of Serbia, was the speaker; it was hosted by his church, Holy Trinity Serbian Orthodox Church, in Youngstown. The Serbs came to the Valley in waves, with the number who came difficult to discern because, at various periods, they were part of the Austro-Hungarian monarchy, then part of Yugoslavia, often blurring the ethnicity of the immigrants from the Balkan regions of Europe. His narrative, plus the extensive display of Serbian artifacts, pictures, books, etc., a delicious ethnic meal (served in the church hall), and finally, the songs and dance of two church groups, combined to make an enlightening evening.

April's meeting was held at the Hungarian Presbyterian Church in Youngstown and featured Dr. Leslie Domonkos, YSU History, a native of Hungary who spoke lovingly and articulately of his and other countrymen's migration to America and to northeast Ohio. He cited difficulties adjusting-personally and generally-to, the new customs and schooling as he and many of his countrymen struggled and succeeded in many walks of life in this land of hope. They, too, came in waves to America and to the Mahoning Valley: a few in the 1860s and 1870s, a tidal wave between 1880-1914, following World War II and during the Hungarian Revolution of 1956. Internationally known pianist Roman Rudnytsky, again, performed several of Liszt's works to the 175 members, who sat attentively after eating a typical Hungarian meal of beef goulash, stuffed cabbage, cucumbers bathed in sour cream, and paprika topped off with tasty desserts. Standing ovations were given to Domonkos and Rudnytsky.

The Asian migration to America was discussed in May by Dr. Yih-Wu Liu, YSU Economics Department. Although his major focus was on China, he did make occasional references to other parts of Asia as well. His insightful reflections regarding 19thand 20th century migrations to America and the Mahoning Valley helped us to understand Asians today. Asian nationalities emigrated to the U.S. for a variety of reasons, including education, employment, and safety. Their presence in the Valley has become increasingly vital, providing many of the area's doctors and academics. YSU chefs, aided by local Chinese friends, prepared a sumptuous feast, after which a local youth group performed typical ethnic dances.

With the June meeting's focus on the Arab world, we concluded the OCA's sixth year. Professor Alexia Naff, Ph.D. of the Smithsonian Institute, summarized for us the migrations to America of the varied Arab peoples. With Lebanon as her primary concentration, Dr. Naff poignantly related the contributions and the problems of Arab peoples in America. The Lebanese represent the largest community of Arab-speaking people in our area; the second largest group of Arabs in our Valley is the Palestinian community. The elaborately prepared meal by the Maronite center personnel, led by Mrs. Ray Nakely, the vitality of the dancing performed by a youth group, and the sensitive hymns of the Maronite nuns in the beautiful Maronite church completed a full evening and year.

What can we conclude from the information and insights which we gained from the 20 presentations of speakers from various cultures? While we acknowledge their differences, we also note their areas of commonality. All came from somewhere else: the native Americans came from Asian Mongolia, escaping the harshness of the environment; the northern and western Europeans came to escape persecution and seek a better life economically and socially; the Africans were brought here as slaves in the 17th and 18th centuries and in the 20th century from the South of the U.S. to the North; the southern and eastern Europeans came because of poor economic conditions on the farm, poverty in the cities; concern for the arbitrary nature of the police and army; social discrimination and anti-Semitism. The most recent immigrants who came from Latin America, Asia, and the Middle East were pushed out of some countries and pulled into the U.S. for labor and/ or medical doctors and academics. The Mahoning Valley area reflected the pattern of the U.S. as a whole.

They have been a varied lot. Speaking every language and representing every nationality, race, and religion, these disparate groups have each contributed to the culture and to the economy that has helped us move toward the "American Dream." Each group suffered hardship, humiliation, and discrimination at various times and to various degrees, but each experienced notable success, enjoyed progress, and contributed to the American dream. They came to America and the Mahoning Valley as they initially settled within their own ethnic enclaves but gradually began the assimilation or acculturation process and moved into neighborhoods depending more upon economic considerations rather than ethnic affinity.

Among the world's leading scientific, artistic, political, and economic figures today are Americans whose immigrant ancestors were once dismissed as "beaten people of beaten races". Gershwin, the Kennedys, Ronald Reagan, Andrew Carnegie, Ralph Bunche, Thurgood Marshall, Zubin Mehta, Rita Moreno, Casey Kasem, and many of our doctors with hard-to-pronounce names are Americans rather than ethnic figures. Our culture has been richly enhanced by the progress of ancestors of slaves who have become members of Congress, the Supreme Court, and even the White House. Genius knows no boundaries.

During these last two years, we learned about people like us and people different from us. Locally, those who came to the Valley as laborers often distinguished themselves in fields of business and many professions: Vaschak Funeral Home, Kosko-baseball, Bibo and Rudnytsky-music, Yallech Lumber, Sirbu Market, DeBartolo/Cafaro as businessmen and the many ethnic restaurants in the Valley as a few examples to give further evidence that genius knows no boundaries.

The Ohio Cultural Alliance enjoyed travel-actually and vicariously- during these initial years. In addition to the travel to a different local venue each month and a trip to the Cathedral of Learning in Pittsburgh, some of us traveled to Mexico for cultural exchanges. Plans were made to increase international travel by affiliating with The Friendship Force, which originated in 1976 by Wayne Smith and was endorsed by Jimmy and Rosalyn Carter. The Friendship Force is a friend-to-friend program wherein participants live for 7-10 days in the homes of their "brother and sisters' from other lands-a sort of "walk-in-their-shoes arrangement. My visit to Moscow in March 1992 introduced me to this wonderful program. For several years we kept abreast of The Friendship Force activities; some of our OCA members participated in their travel opportunities during the 1990s.

An added delight for this year's program was the award given to the Ohio Cultural Alliance by the Ohio Association of Historical Societies and Museums. Pat Cummins, current director of the Mahoning Valley Historical Society, prepared a notebook of our two-year program, "The Making of America-A Land of Hope," for submission to the organization. It contained a summary of the OCA, a summary of the 20 programs offered during the two years, the sample talk of a presentation given by Michael Kurilla on Czechoslovakia, news clips from various publications, and accompanying pictures of our various activities. We were honored to accept the award in person in Columbus at the organization's annual conference on November 6, 1993.

Award of Achievement

PRESENTED BY

OHIO ASSOCIATION OF HISTORICAL SOCIETIES & MUSEUMS

To

Dr George Beslen

"The Making of America--A Land of Hope"

on this 6th day of November 1993

Ohio Cultural Alliance, Inc.

PRESIDENT

CHAIRMAN, AWARDS COMMITTEE

An award for the Ohio Cultural Alliance, early in our history

Dr. Les Domonkos

Dr. Saul Freidman

Michael Kurilla

Dr. Yih-Wiu Liu

Judith Magielski

George Bodnar

Hildegard Schnuttgen

Arms Museum of Youngstown

VII. Doing Business in Another Culture

The September 1993 meeting was designed to provide an overview of the theme of "Doing Business in Another Culture". The speakers were Reid Dulberger of the Youngstown-Warren Chamber of Commerce and Dr. George D. Beelen, YSU, History Department, who introduced the year's program, and Dr. Eugene Eshleman, a global businessman from Grove City, Pennsylvania, who offered (on film) insights to doing business with people of other cultures. Eberth Catering prepared a meal, locally referred to as the "Youngstown buffet", which includes pasta, chicken, sausage and peppers, vegetables, and dessert. We ended the evening with a tour of the Youngstown Historical Center of Industry and Labor (aka Steel Museum) as we reminisced about the Youngstown of yesterday, with its good and bad old days. Our program for this year is designed to give us some indication of where we must go tomorrow in this new global society.

In October, at St. John's Episcopal Church, Peter Mitchell, President of Sovereign Circuits, Youngstown, shared his knowledge of doing business with England, his native land. His witty presentation was complemented by an array of British artifacts which he had on display. In general, he reported, England, a major ally, provided robust trade, with few obstacles, given similar language and business history. Dr. Lowell Satre (YSU, History Department) showed fascinating slides from a section of England that he recently visited. The meal, which consisted of beef, mashed potatoes, vegetable, and porridge, was prepared and served by church parishioners.

"Doing Business with Greece" was the November topic, with Attorney Serge Hadji-Mihaloglou as our speaker. He was a member of the New York and Ohio Bars and an International Advisor and lawyer for TRW, Cleveland, Ohio. He said, "Greece has been a popular vacation destination for many years, but corporate investors have been cautious. A common perception is that continuous political unrest and pervasive government controls have held back economic development. The Greek Prime Minister, Constantine Mitsotakis, addressed these concerns...and his comments are encouraging". The speaker answered many preliminary questions that are usually asked by the business community and said, "Greece is worth considering for certain investments provided they are properly researched and managed." He continued with, "As a first step, the Hellenic Industrial Development Bank, or ETVA as it is called in Greek, published a number of useful guides in several languages." And these guides should be consulted by all trade partners, he suggested. Complementing the speaker's presentation and the ethnic meal (including pastichio, souzaoukia, stuffed grape leaves, spanakopites, tiropites, and Greek salad and pastry) were youngsters who sang and danced to traditional Greek folk music. The meeting was held at St. John's Greek Orthodox Church in Boardman.

Slovakia was the focus of December's meeting held at St. Matthias Church Hall in Youngstown. Our speaker was Steve Bacon, a local business and community leader who, since retirement, has devoted much of his time shuttling back and forth to Slovakia, encouraging mutual understanding and economic intercourse between the U.S. and Slovakia. He said that Slovakia is "an ideal place to do business; while business in the country was formerly state-run, Slovakia plans to take six years to privatize". In a word, Bacon said, "the business climate is improving". The meal, prepared by members of the congregation, included boneless pork roast, halushki, pirogi, stuffed cabbage, and kolachi. Adding to the pleasure of the evening were Alex and Teresa Sepesy, who played Gypsy melodies on their harmonicas.

Al Kanetsky of Mitsui, Inc. in Cleveland addressed "Doing Business with Japan" for the January meeting. His insights on doing business in this growing market, for both imports and exports, indicate the importance of this former adversary to the U.S. economy. His important presentation was made more vivid by the interesting Kabuki film that he showed. Also offering some insights into the culture of Japan was Mary Jane Hoder, a local teacher who recently returned from teaching in Japan. Held at YSU, the Japanese cuisine was reasonably authentic.

Tae Sik Ro, a native of Korea, who transplanted to Canfield, where he now is an import/export businessman, spoke in February on the topic "Doing Business in Korea" (really, South Korea). He told of the meteoric rise in business with Korea and the relative ease with which business intercourse operates. A film regarding life in Korea complemented Mr. Ro's talk. We met at the Jade Court in Poland, where we dined on an authentic Korean meal.

In March, three speakers Leo F. Tseng, John Sy Chen, and Shuh-Kuen Chen, all from the Coordination Council of North American Affairs in Chicago, addressed "Doing Business with China". Their seriousness of purpose was made more palatable by their humorous asides. At that time, they were eager to increase their trade (particularly exports to the U.S.) and suggested that China was also eager to accept U.S. exports. Held at Jade Court, again, the meal was authentic (including won-ton soup, sweet and sour chicken, Szechuan chicken, sweet and sour pork, egg rolls, and fried bananas), as was the approach taken by the Chinese spokesmen who captivated the OCA audience. Slides were also shown for additional illustration.

April's meeting was special in that it kicked off a week of activities that dealt with Mexico. Dr. David Decker, YSU, Director of the Williamson Center for International Business, spoke about "Doing Business with Mexico," and the ten Mexican visitors from Guadalajara, Mexico, participating in the Youngstown-Guadalajara Cultural exchange, were introduced and offered a few personal insights. All of us spoke about the need for "distant neighbors" to better understand each other. Too many on each side of the border fail to learn about each other, to the detriment of both countries. The fact of the matter is we each need the other for a variety of reasons-markets, labor, arts, and immigration. We spoke, too, of the new North American Free Trade Agreement (NAFTA) of which both were (along with Canada) a part. We all thought, at the time, that this was a win-win agreement. We convened in the Ohio Room at YSU and enjoyed an authentic Mexican meal. Cultural enrichment was in the form of a visual exhibit of Mexican culture, poetry readings, and remarks from two leaders of the Mexican group-Bernardo Colunga and Eduardo Azuri.

"Doing Business with Argentina" was the topic addressed in May by Norma and Jorge Viana, native Argentines now living in the Youngstown area. Their insights about Argentina helped us to better understand that nation's history and economic development. They understood why the U.S. might be wary of intercourse with Argentina, given its sometimes authoritarian political history. But they suggested that those days are in the past and better things are ahead for their native land and hopefully for better relations between Argentina and the United States. Meeting and dining again in the Ohio Room of Kilcawley at YSU, our chefs promised an authentic Argentine meal, and they delivered. The evening ended with tango dancers from Candlelight Dance Studio performing and teaching all of us to tango!

At the June meeting, Duane Duckworth addressed "Doing Business with Brazil". Mr. Duckworth spent a number of years in Brazil as General Manager and President of both U.S.

and British firms. He also set up foreign operations for Commercial Intertech (a Youngstown-based firm) in Brazil during the 1970s. His engrossing speech was given even more meaning by a multi-media presentation of film, slides, music, and filmstrips relating to the variety of life in the huge country of Brazil. He emphasized the importance of increasing our trade with Brazil (both imports and exports) with this giant country with a burgeoning population. We met again at YSU, Kilcawley Center, Chestnut Room, and Fountain Amphitheater. The meal consisted of American picnic fare, topped off by a Brazilian desert.

Special projects for the 1993-94 year have included sponsorship of Youngstown/Guadalajara Cultural Exchange; a brief attempt to encourage foreign films at the Austintown Theater; OCA Day sponsorship on WYSU; completion of a 15-minute OCA video, entitled, "Going Places with the Ohio Cultural Alliance" (produced and directed by George D. Beelen, Jr.); volunteering for fundraising on Channels 45/49 at their Kent State site and acceptance of the state of Ohio award from the Ohio Association of Historical Societies and Museums in Columbus, Ohio.

The Ohio Cultural Alliance has "gone places" during the last seven years ranging from travel to varied Youngstown venues for monthly meetings to international travel for a few members (grants of $200 for such travel, based on benefit to YSU, Youngstown area schools, area social groups, and/or OCA.) We agreed that the meeting format would be continued in the ensuing years; the theme for the next year was to be "The Family in Another Culture".

Plans were also in motion to increase foreign travel by affiliating with The Friendship Force, the friend-to-friend program where participants live for 7-10 days in the homes of their "brothers and sisters" from other lands-a sort of walk-in-their-shoes arrangement. That is exactly what the OCA tries to do virtually as we engage in the study of varied cultures in our quest to learn about people like us and different from us. We ended this year with a statement: "To the extent that we have 'gone places' and have learned about some of our fellow human beings, we are gratified and thankful; to the extent that we have failed by omission or commission, we are committed to traveling even farther down the road to peace and understanding of all peoples."

Youngstown Steel Museum

Some members of the YSU group on cultural exchange in Guadalajara, Mexico

Entire YSU group on cultural exchange in Guadalajara, Mexico

VIII. The Family in Another Culture

The "Family in Another Culture" was the topic explored for the next two years: 1994-95 and 1995-96. The family has been defined as the nucleus of civilization, as a household composed of parents and children, a group of persons closely related by blood or marriage; a creation of nature that is "never what it used to be". Most families have these definitions in common, yet, as we learned over the last two years, there are enough variations among different people. The status of women and children in most cultures has been that of inferiors, sometimes even property. One of the great achievements of the 20th century has been the elevation of the position of women and children in the American family, but not yet universally. The stern patriarch has been eliminated, and with his passing, the rule of fear based on punishment has disappeared from most families around the world. Women and men share as equals to an increasing extent. Some have embraced these changes, some have accepted them tacitly, and some with fear that the "jury is still out" as to the changes' efficacy. Some cultures covertly or overtly refuse to accept such changes.

The initial meeting of the 1994-95 year held in September at the Arms Museum of Local History served as an overview of the theme for the year. Speakers were Dr. Mary Beaubian, YSU, Home Economics, local coordinator for the United Nations' Year of the Family, and Dr. George D. Beelen. Dr. Beaubian spoke about the importance that the U.N. places on the institution of the family and the various family-focused activities to be held in the local area during this year. Dr. Beelen spoke about the American family from the colonial period to the present and the changes from a basically patriarchal family to a more equitable family structure, with children who were "to be seen and not heard" to one that was more tolerant. His anecdotes regarding the family were pertinent and even impertinent. One of the more cynical versions of the 20th-century family was given by Max Lerner (mid-20th century journalist and educator): the "American family" is an anarchic collection of delinquent adolescents, cacophonous brats, a domineering wife, and a harassed two-timing husband, their discords frequently aired by divorce courts and tabloids, the whole of it watched by Doctor Spock for baby care, Doctor Gesell for child growth, and Doctor Kinsey for the record of erotic successes and failures." The cultural enrichment included a tour of the Arms Museum and a film related to the family. The meal was catered by Eberth Catering, a group we engaged pretty often during our earliest years until they ceased their operations.

In October, we attracted a large crowd of 215 people as we focused on the Amish family. Dr. Thomas Newcomb, a local educator and Amish culture specialist, shared insights regarding the Amish family. Edmund Collens displayed and commented upon his Amish-related artwork, and Amish cooks prepared for us an "Amish wedding feast" that was abundant and delicious. Our interesting dilemma was the dining room at Vienna Presbyterian Church, the site of our meeting, could not accommodate everyone at a single sitting, so we divided the group with one eating and the other with a program in the church proper. Then we reversed the process.

We learned of some of the similarities between the Amish and the Mennonites and some of the differences. The Amish consist of an Old Order and a New Order. The Amish are located locally just north of Warren. While their everyday life is more akin to America's rural agrarian existence with family resembling that of this earlier period, there are some exceptions. While children adhere to these rules, they may leave this type of living at age 16. We also know that they eat well and exercise robustly as they engage in their basically rural-agrarian life.

The Jewish family was the November focus, with Eric Geboff, Assistant Director of the Jewish Community Center, the site of the meeting, as our speaker. Complementing the speaker's presentation were the musical talents of Dr. Robert Rollin on the piano and Gweneth Rollin on the violin (both YSU, Music Department) playing Jewish melodies and a Jewish meal catered and served by the Jewish Community Center personnel.

The focus for December was the Catholic family, with locally-based and nationally-known Pat Vivo as our speaker. Her inspirational presentation was matched by the lively singing of Christmas carols by locally famous Maureen Collins and her accompanist, both principals in the very popular Easy Street Productions. Mrs. Vivo spoke anecdotally of her own family as she took us on an emotional roller coaster of being a teacher, mother of eight children, and the wife of a popular politician and popular speaker in her own right. We met at St. Christine's Church in Youngstown; Eberth Catering prepared chicken marsala, braciole, and pasta as part of the menu.

Neither the snow nor the cold (in 30 years, we never had to cancel a meeting) held back the substantial turn-out in January at Immaculate Conception Church Hall in Youngstown to hear Drs. Mary Bivins, YSU History Department, and Dr. Ndinzi Masagara, YSU Foreign Language Department, address the African family. Using anecdotal as well as scholarly material, the speakers incorporated demographic data via the overhead projector and showed slides to enhance the evening. They also spoke in some detail about the various activities that YSU will sponsor during African American History Month in February. Eberth Catering prepared the meal, which included some items from African cuisine.

Hildegard Schnuttgen retired YSU Research Librarian and native of Germany, shared personal and researched material with us in February as we explored the German family here and abroad. Meeting at the Saxon Club, we were treated to the marvelous singing of the forty-three-member Concordia Chorus and the outstanding ethnic cuisine of the Saxon Club, which included German sausage, potato salad, and chocolate cake.

In March, Dr. James Kiriazis, retired YSU Sociology chairman and professor, addressed in a humorous and sensitive style the Greek family. Typical Greek cuisine, dancing, and music, which included audience participation, provided cultural enrichment, as did the venue for the meeting-St. John's Greek Orthodox Church Hall in Campbell. Our visit to the Church proper was a cultural experience, given the many icons and pictures that are part of Orthodox churches.

Dr. Ahalya Krishnan YSU, Psychology, a native of India, shared personal and professional insights into the Indian family at our April meeting, held at the India Community Center located at that time in Austintown. Dr. Krishnan stressed the importance of strong family ties, with marriage being more of a relationship between two families than between two persons. Marriages are seen as part of the parents' responsibility and are arranged. Young people do have the right to reject an arrangement. She displayed many "ads" seeking suitable persons for matrimonial arrangements. Dr. Krishnan arranged for typical Indian fare prepared by members of the local Indian community. Two brightly dressed and very talented young dancers, Neha Kumar and Priya Kollipara enchanted us with their intricate and spirited dancing.

The Polish family was the subject of the May meeting held at Krakusy Hall in Youngstown. Judith Magielski, a local teacher of Polish history and a specialist in Polish lore, gave a fascinating presentation about her "adopted" culture. Complementing the lively evening was YSU student Mark Leydo playing Polish melodies on the piano and a Polish feast that included breaded pork, sauerkraut, kielbasa, and Polish salad.

The final meeting of the season was held in June at Youngstown State University. Our speaker was Dr. Anne York, YSU History, a French history professor and frequent visitor to France, where she engages in formal and informal studies of French history and culture. Dr. York's fascinating look at the French family was enriched by her multi-media presentation that included her slides, videos, music, and recipes of French cuisine used by YSU chefs to prepare our meals.

Special projects for this year included partial sponsorship of a YSU delegation of students, faculty, and OCA members to continue our cultural exchanges with Guadalajara, Mexico; continued participation in The Friendship Force and continued subsidization of foreign travel of OCA members; special Mothers' Day recognition awards at May meeting; initiated a pen pal program with Hungarian students; tour to the Cathedral of Learning in Pittsburgh (this facility contains about two dozen ethnic rooms that create an ambiance of the culture of these various countries).

At the September meeting, the first of the 1995-96 meeting, we continued with the theme "The Family in Another Culture". John Spencer, YSU, Textbook Coordinator at the Bookstore, and an active member of the area's Italian community, addressed elements of the family here and in Italy. A sumptuous Italian meal was catered by Lou Fusillo Catering and served at Mt. Carmel Social Center in Youngstown. A dance group consisting of 16 participants from Howland, Ohio, entertained us with several lively dance numbers.

In October, the OCA met at YSU to learn about the African family as interpreted this time by Dr. Victor Wan-Tatah, YSU, Philosophy and native of Cameroon. Interestingly, his interpretations were somewhat different from those who spoke of Africa last season. The YSU chefs followed recipes that were given to them by Dr. Wan-Tatah, who assured us they were quite authentic. Storyteller and teacher, Jocelyn Dabney, delighted us with her fascinating African stories; her husband provided background drum music while she spoke.

The November focus was the Hungarian family, with Dr. Stephen Hanzely, YSU Chemistry and native of Hungary as our speaker. Dr. Hanzely fled his country during the Hungarian Revolution of 1956. A delicious Hungarian meal, which included chicken paprikash, beef goulash, and strudel, prepared by Eberth Catering, was served at the site of our meeting, St. Stephen of Hungary Church in Youngstown. To complement Dr. Hanzeley's presentation, Dr. Caroline Oltmanns, YSU, Dana School of Music, and her husband Timothy Ehlen performed, in concert together, beautiful Hungarian melodies.

The Czechoslovakian family was the subject of the December meeting held at St. Matthias Church Hall in Youngstown. Our speaker was Michael Kurilla, a former YSU, History graduate student who traced his own family's experiences in the U.S. and the Mahoning Valley. As a third-generation descendant of Slovak and Ruthenian immigrant grandparents and an active member of the Holy Name Church, he has long had an interest in his ethnic heritage. He spoke of the close connection that he and his family and others of his ethnic background had to their Church. In his day, ethnic parishes, generally begun in the late 19th and early 20 centuries, were closely adhered to. Eberth Catering provided an excellent ethnic meal that consisted of breaded chicken, stuffed cabbage, potato pierogi, and kolachi. St. Matthias Choir, directed by Mark Leydo, sang traditional Christmas carols, with audience participation, concluded the evening.

The January meeting was re-scheduled for the middle of April. Dr. Gail Okawa, YSU, English Department, was our speaker. Her approach to the Japanese family was influenced by her Japanese grandparents, who were interned placed in a camp during World War II. She drew from personal, anecdotal information and researched data. The meal was prepared by the YSU chefs and included a few Japanese delicacies. She showed a movie, "High Tech/High Touch Japan," which presents how Japan has revolutionized the industrial world while retaining most of its traditional customs and values.

The February speaker was Dr. Emil Hernandez, Clinical Director of Eastern Mental Health Center, who considered the Hispanic family, with particular emphasis upon the Puerto Rican family. He spoke of the closeness of the multi-generational family as well as the importance of godparenthood. The meeting was held at St. Joseph's Church Hall, located in Austintown, and was catered by Eberth Catering, who prepared pretty authentic Hispanic cuisine. The evening concluded with a group that sang and danced to traditional Hispanic melodies; they even produced a piñata which several members of our OCA group tried to open with good swings to get the goodies within.

Dr. Paula Pratt, a specialist in Irish women's literature, shared some insights regarding the Irish family, both here and in Ireland, at our March meeting. She has made extensive studies of the Irish family, most notably with her work regarding Irish women in contemporary society; as a person of Irish descent and a frequent traveler to Ireland, her remarks rang true. To complement Dr. Pratt's presentation, Dr. Allan Mosher (YSU, Music Department) sang traditional Irish melodies in his beautiful baritone voice; Country Mayo Band provided additional musical Irish numbers. We met at the magnificently restored Marble Room of Stambaugh Auditorium, with an Irish meal catered by Eberth Catering. The menu included ham and cabbage, Irish lamb stew, and redskin potatoes.

Turkey was our focus in April. Discussing the Turkish family was Dr. Birsen Karpak, YSU, Management Department, who offered thoughtful comments regarding the family structure in her native land. Dr. Birsen spoke of Mustafa Kemal Ataturk, founder of the Turkish Republic. Tracing the long history of Turkey, she interpreted Turkey in the words of Ataturk as a country rich in its own national culture, open to the heritage of world civilization, and at home in the endowments of the modern technological age. She referred to the family as hospitable, educated, and secular. Held at YSU, we were treated to a modified Turkish meal and to beautiful native dances performed by Pinar Ceyhan from Pittsburgh.

In May, the OCA vicariously visited Scandinavian families through the words of Dr. Lowell Satre, YSU History Department. Both he and his wife trace their origins to Scandinavian lands, which they visited a few years ago. His remarks centered on the secular nature of the family relationship and their hospitality to each other and to others. The Scandinavian cuisine prepared by Eberth Catering was quite authentic, and the Scandinavian organ selections of Mary Halewell, organist for Bethel Lutheran Church in Boardman, the site of the meeting was uplifting.

The final meeting of the season, held in June at the Orthodox Social Center on Belle Vista Rd., in Youngstown, treated the Russian family. The speaker of the evening was Dr. Melissa Smith, YSU, Foreign Language, who shared her research and experiences regarding the Russian family. A wonderful Russian meal was catered and served by members of Sts. Peter and Paul Church and beautiful Russian melodies emanated from the accordion of Betty Bannon and the violin of Michael Dolovy as they strolled through the audience.

Special projects for the year included participation in The Friendship Force; continued subsidization of foreign travel of OCA members; planning a special two-day workshop entitled "Traditional and Complementary Health Care: The Best of All Worlds," and the preparing of a publication, "An Ethnic Encyclopedia". (See more below)

Dr. Victor Wan Tahtah

Maureen Collins

John Spencer

Dr. Ahalya Krishnon

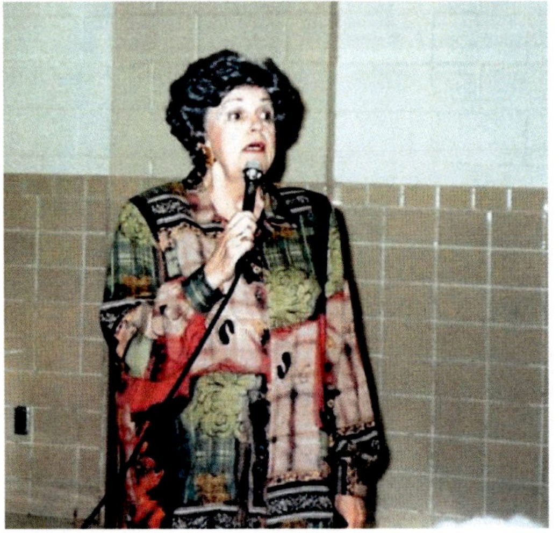

Pat Vivo

Dr. James Kiriazis

Dr. Anne York

Dr. Paula Pratt

Jocelyn Dabney

Dr. GDB with Dr. Lowell Satre and wife Ellen

Japanese dancers

Dr. Caroline Oltmans and Timothy Ehlen

Dr. Gail Okawa

IX. Health and Medical Care in Another Culture

The Ohio Cultural Alliance theme for the 1996-97season (our 10th year) was "Health and Medical Care in Another Culture". Health is primarily a scientific challenge because it depends on how much we know or can find out about preventing disease, improving nutrition, and curing aliments. But a major problem of public health is how to pay for health care in various countries. What are the best ways to accommodate people of different social strata? What are the best methods of healing people? How much should be personal, and how much should be governmental? We tried to discuss some of the questions during the course of this OCA season.

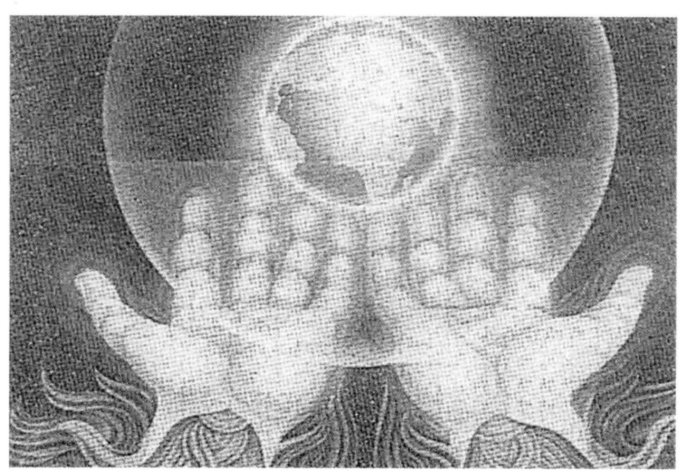

Traditional Medicine and Complementary Therapies: Creating Integrated Healthcare

As a prelude to the regular programming, we sponsored a timely and unique two-day Workshop on Monday and Tuesday, September 30th and October 1st, 1996, dealing with both traditional and alternative / complementary approaches to medical and health care in the United States. Over the two-day period, the Workshop offered continuous sessions addressing the latest thoughts in both modern technical/traditional health care as well as alternative/complementary approaches, including hypnosis, acupuncture, chiropractic, humor, massage, psychotherapy, art, yoga, Tai Chi, imagery, and prayer. We dedicated this Workshop to Jo Ellen Jorde, who inspired me and motivated me to create the Ohio Cultural Alliance and to reflect upon many of the ideas which such Alliances encourage. Jo Ellen also introduced me to Dr. Larry Dossey and thus the idea of the Health Care Conference/Workshop.

We assembled an outstanding group of local specialists as presenters. In addition, several sessions focused upon the role of prayer in medicine, highlighted by the keynote address (one of three talks that he gave) of noted author and physician Larry Dossey, M.D., who traveled from Santa Fe, New Mexico, to be with us. Dr. Dossey, author of the New York Times best-seller "Healing Words" and the just released "Prayer is Good Medicine", has been described by Deepak Chopra, M.D., as "a pioneer in the new medicine of the future...He shows us how we can create a lasting partnership between faith and medicine."

We had an opportunity to interact with medical doctors and a wide array of therapists who helped us explore traditional medicine and complementary therapies-the best of all worlds. Our goal was to try to develop a balance among the various approaches and to feature integrated health care.

Dr. Dossey kicked off the season with a keynote address entitled "Prayer is Good Medicine" at an early breakfast meeting at YSU. He argued that prayer can bring unexplained good to the earth and, even more importantly, that it can serve as an antidote to anxiety and despair, often bringing hope and confidence instead. He challenged us to "regard prayer, with its many inflections, as a common universal tongue", and he asked rhetorically, "Can we not delight in our difference and celebrate our diversity?" Dr. Dossey replicated some of the ideas of his keynote presentation and offered some additional insights in his address entitled "Power of Prayer in Healing" at the OCA evening meeting held again at the Ukrainian Orthodox Social Center. Eberth Catering offered a "Youngstown Buffet". On Tuesday, Dr. Dossey gave his third address," Complementary Cardiovascular Care, "at a luncheon session. This was our largest gathering to date-about 300 people.

Larry Dossey, M.D.

Through the days on Monday and Tuesday, we offered continuous sessions:

- Henrika Fitzpatrick, M.D., "Efficacy of Complementary Therapies"
- William Reeves, M.D., "High Technology Medicine; Cancer"
- Jenny Wang, M.D., "Acupuncture"
- Henry Yoo, M.D., D.V.M.," Pet Therapy"
- Janet Mau, R.N., "Hospice Care"
- Emmanuel Hallaman, "Humor in Healing"
- Maryann Pernotto, M.S., RNCS, LPCC, "Psychotherapy/Positive Thinking"
- Dan DelliQuadri, D.C.," Chiropractic Therapy"
- Karen Holby, M.Ed.," Yoga-The Integration of Body, Mind and Spirit"
- Marsha Kuite, M.A. "Holistic Medicine: What is it and What do I do With it?"
- Master Xiao-Bo Huang La Presta," Tai chi demonstrations and audience participation."
- Mark Reniniga, M.D., "Helping to Integrate Rational and Complementary Therapies"
- Celeste Sinistro, CMT; R.N., "Music Therapy"
- Atef Labib, M.D.," High Technology Medicine: Heart/Stroke"
- Jane Ehrman, M.Ed., CHES, "Hypnosis/Imagery and Wellness"
- Donna Sloan, M.A.," Ethics, Spirituality, and Alternative Medicine"
- Norm Jones, LPC "Cancer and the Mind/Body Connection"
- Alfred Bright, M.A., "Art and Healing"

- George D. Beelen., Ph.D. "Empathy in History: A Road to Understanding"
- Margaret Sandy, L.M.T. and John Chianese, L.M.T. "Alternative Modalities in Massage Therapy"

In November, the OCA met at the Saxon Club to hear Ohio State Senator Robert Hagan and long-time student of the Canadian health care system to speak about their plan as he contrasted it with ours. He explained how the Canadian system of health care is largely government-run, at least basic services. "While some elective services may at times be postponed, Canadians are very happy with their health care and wonder why some U.S. citizens disparage their government plan." As usual, the Saxon Club prepared a delicious meal for us, and Roman Rudnytsky, an OCA favorite, played piano selections to the delight of those in attendance.

The December focus was health care in France, with Salim El-Hayek, M.D., who received his medical education in France, as our speaker. He is a native of Lebanon, married to a native of Scotland, whom he met in France while they were both studying. His analysis of health care in France indicated that it was closer to the state-run Canadian system than to ours in the U.S. Professor Allan Mosher, again, sang French songs and selections from French composers. Eberth Catering served a French dinner, with the Ursuline Mother House in Boardman as the site of the meeting.

Dominican Republic was featured in January with Federico Cano, M.D., as our speaker. He is a native of the Dominican Republic and a prominent doctor in our area today. His slides and narrative clearly showed that the country is still a Third World country with attendant deficiencies in health care. The rhythmic meringue, performed by professional dancers Mr. and Mrs. Kenneth Scavnicky, added cultural enrichment to the evening. We met again at the Saxon Club, who prepared for us an authentic Hispanic meal.

Well-known ophthalmologist Dr. Kong Oh, originally from Malaysia, spoke to us about health and medical care in his native country in February. His observations were that his native land still practices rather basic, if not primitive, medical care. To complement Dr. Oh's presentation, a group of dancers led by Mark Lee provided cultural enrichment by performing the traditional "Dragon Dance". The meeting was held at the Ukrainian Orthodox Center, whose parishioners prepared a delicious meal.

In March, the OCA met at the Maronite Center in Youngstown to hear four Lebanese medical doctors and a nurse-midwife led by Dr. Munir El Hayek engage in a comprehensive discussion of health care and medicine in Lebanon. The specialties included thoracic surgery, pulmonary problems, obstetrics, and gynecology. They concluded that the health care in Lebanon was getting better, at least in some of the areas of the country. St. Maron's Youth dancers provided the cultural enrichment, and a six-course Lebanese dinner was prepared by the Ladies' Guild of the church.

Health and Medical Care in India was the topic addressed in April by the immediate past president of the Mahoning County Medical Society, Chander Kohli, M.D., currently a neurosurgeon in the Youngstown area. Using slides to embellish his text, Dr. Kohli shared health care insights regarding his native land. The meeting was held at the Ursuline Mother House, with the meal prepared by Eberth Catering, which included several items of Indian cuisine. Miss Pavana Bhat, a senior at Lisbon High School, performed authentic Indian dances from the land of her ancestors.

The Philippines was our focus in May. Discussing health care and medicine in his native land, Escarlito U. Sevilla, M.D., offered fascinating insights using slides to complement his presentation. He, too, argued that his native country, even though once a territory of the United States, was behind in the health care of their people. As an added attraction, Dr. Seville was joined by his wife, Lita, and by Rea McClain in several native dances performed with native costumes and music. We met at the Saxon Club, who prepared the meal, which included a few Philippine items.

The final meeting of the season was held in June at YSU and dealt with several Asian countries, primarily Japan and Korea. Speaker for the evening was Dr. Henry Yoo, an area veterinarian, and health care management consultant. He said that while many Asian countries are behind in their progress in health care, Japan and South Korea are making great progress and are led by the government. Cultural enrichment was provided by Anna Korchmaros and her cultural group, performing lively and colorful Japanese dances dressed in native costumes and employing appropriate props.

OCA's two special projects for the year were the Health Care Workshop, "Traditional Medicine and Complementary Therapies: The Best of All Worlds," and the printing of our third publication, "An Ethnic Encyclopedia: The Peopling of the Mahoning Valley". Both were unqualified successes that proved to be fitting capstones to the first decade of our existence.

In September 1996, the Ohio Cultural Alliance announced the publication of "An Ethnic Encyclopedia: The Peopling of the Mahoning Valley", an edited booklet commemorating the 200th and the 150th anniversaries of the City of Youngstown and of the Mahoning County, respectively. Over a year in the making, thirty authors wrote essays depicting some of the varied ethnic groups that make up the population of the Mahoning Valley, arranged alphabetically, beginning with the African-American and ending with the Welsh. The work is complemented by flags of each nationality and by more than 100 photos, some dating to the early 1900s.

The articles discuss some of the earliest immigrant groups that came to this Valley more than 200 years ago, the subsequent waves that came during the mid-1800s, the late 1800s, and the early 1900s, and those that have come most recently. One can read poignant, sometimes very personal, descriptions of the hardship each had to endure and the significant contributions they made. We learn of the important role of the churches, the families, schooling, work, food, customs, and much more. Most importantly, we learn not only the uniqueness of each group but also what they had in common. From this diversity, the Mahoning Valley has developed its own proud and distinctive personality.

Our first decade-1987-1997 could be considered a real success. We were beginning to represent a presence in the Mahoning Valley. We were beginning to develop a sense of community. Our hope was that we could continue to develop programs that relate to the disparate peoples of the Valley and to continue to learn about the people, the talents, the sites, the religions, the food, and the geography of the Valley in our quest to understand how we were similar and different and yet respect each other.

Dr. Salim El Hayek

Honorable Robert Hagan

Dr. Lito and Lita Sevilla

Dr. Chander Kohli

X. Expressions of Culture: The Arts in Other Nations

The Ohio Cultural Alliance started its 11th year by introducing a two-year topic, "Expressions of Culture: The Arts in Other Nations". It has been said that there are many routes to truth and understanding. President John F. Kennedy once said, "We must never forget that art is not a form of propaganda; it is a form of truth." An anonymous speaker said, "Art is what separates man from beast." And Franklin D. Roosevelt once said, "The arts cannot thrive except where men are free to be themselves." Through the last decade we embarked in a search for truth by speeches, entertainment, travel, food, and discussion; we now proposed to focus primarily upon the arts in the nations which have been selected. We have already used the arts as complements to speeches that have been given during the last ten years. But, for the next two years, we gave the arts a primary focus.

The OCA kicked off the 1997-98 year in September with a thoughtful look at the arts in general by way of a talk given by YSU's Dean of the College of Fine and Performing Arts, Dr. George McCloud. His specific title, "In Search of a Civilization: America Through a Chinese Looking Glass," provided ample reflection regarding the importance of the arts in our own society as well as worldwide, contrasting America and China. Dr. McCloud argued that China is a culture trying to become a nation; the United States is a nation trying to become a civilization." John Mancino, a YSU music student, rendered a wide array of international music selections. Eberth Catering served dinner reflecting the cuisines of several different nations. Before and afterward, we toured the site of our meeting, the Butler Institute of American Art, known the world over as home to one of the finest collections of American art anywhere.

Lamb on a spit

In October, the OCA met at St. George Lodge #66 to explore the arts in the Croatian tradition. Maria J. Leskur of the Croatian Consulate in Cleveland helped us to understand the arts in Croatia through her words and a large number of handmade items from the land of her husband and parents. She spoke of beautiful music, poetry, and art as she wove stories of the arts through many decades. We were honored to have with us the Consul General of Croatia, Domagoj Sola, who brought special greetings. Cultural enrichment was provided by the Veseli Tamburitza Orchestra, led by Rose Husnick, all of Farrell, Pennsylvania. The very ethnic Croatian meal was abundant and delicious and included barbecued lamb, breaded chicken, Croatian potato salad, and stuffed cabbage. It was an evening to remember.

The Italian arts were featured in November with Florence DiRienzo Sneider as our speaker. Love for her parents' native land and her vivacious nature sparked her presentation. She spoke of the beautiful music, specifically opera, the many Italian composers, the magnificent sculpture, and the popular Italian food. The site of this meeting was St. Lucy Church Hall in Campbell, whose parishioners prepared a meal that included two pasta dishes, chicken parmigiana, among other Italian delicacies. The evening concluded with excerpts from the Italian opera, Pagliacci, sung by Dr. Allan Mosher (YSU Dana School of Music) and his students, James Matranga and Michael Black.

Dr. George Kulchytsky, YSU, History, shared his enthusiasm for the arts of his native land Ukraine, at our December meeting. He highlighted the tender music, Orthodox art, and architecture, in addition to the multi-colored eggs. We met at the Ukrainian Orthodox Center in Youngstown, whose congregation offered us a wonderful ethnic meal consisting of stuffed cabbage, honey-baked chicken, and halushki. One of the highlights of this year was the Karavan Ensemble from Sharon, Pennsylvania, led by Carol Novosel. The troupe, numbering more than 25 people, performed Ukrainian dances with high energy and amazing talent.

January's focus was the arts in Germany. Dr. John Boehm, YSU, limited- service instructor at YSU, traced, with wit, wisdom, and knowledge, the arts in his native land. The music, he said, is melodic, arousing, and given to percussion sounds. But he added opera and German composers certainly provided much of the art of the Germans. Dr. Melissa Tosh-Matranga and her husband Jim Matranga sang beautiful German music. And, once again, the Saxon Club served up their wonderful fare: pork chops, baked chicken, sausage w/peppers, and onions, among other items.

In February, Dr. James Kiriazis, a retired YSU professor of sociology, shared his excitement about the arts of Greece. He traced the magnificent Greek culture of the period of the early 5th century B.C. and beyond-it was "gay, spontaneous, and full of rhythmic motion." He reminded us of literary works, such as the Iliad and the Odyssey, and other epic works, including lyric poetry and drama. Held at St. John's Greek Orthodox Church Hall in Boardman, the Philoptochos Ladies' Guild prepared a sumptuous meal, and a local children's dance group provided the cultural enrichment.

The March meeting was one of our largest gatherings, owing either to the great interest in the Irish arts, the culinary talents of Eberth Catering, or the curiosity of members to see the view from the new DeBartolo Stadium Club on the YSU campus. Joan Reedy, a former YSU graduate History major, offered a sensitive look at the arts of Ireland, and the Step Dancers displayed their talents and energy as they emulated their internationally acclaimed Riverdance brethren.

Dr. Saul Friedman, YSU, History, favored us with his interpretation of the arts in the Jewish tradition at our April meeting. "Learning is an essential element in success," Friedman remarked as he went on to discuss Jewish music, art, architecture, and drama, most notably in the form of movies (particularly focusing upon the Warner brothers of Youngstown.) His poignant reflections were also mirrored in the violin and piano selections performed by Drs. Gweneth and Robert Rollin, also of YSU. The ethnic meal, under the direction of Florine Rusnak, was prepared by members of the Ohev Tzedek Temple in Boardman.

The May focus featured the arts in Poland, with Jacek and soprano Dorota Sobieski sharing their musical talents and knowledge of Polish arts. Mr. Sobieski, former director of the National Theater in Warsaw, Poland, and his wife, were both featured in the New Music Festival at YSU and in the local Opera Circle. Piano selections and reminiscences were also offered by James Tavolario, a noted area musician and active member of the Polish Arts

Society. The excellent Polish dinner consisted of breaded pork chops, stuffed cabbage kielbasa and kraut, and pierogies, among other items, and was provided by Lilak Catering at Krakusy Hall in Youngstown, the site of our meeting.

Our season finale focused on the arts in the African tradition as the June meeting took us to the Third Baptist Church Fellowship Hall for a presentation by well-known YSU art professor Alfred (Al) Bright. His comments and slides were thought-provoking, instructive, and sensitive. The church, he reminded us, was vital to Africans, as well as to African Americans. And the music was absolutely vital to the success of the church. "Symbolism, religious and otherwise, was typical of African music, especially of drum rhythms and dance; this is manifest in the local area, as well," he said. "Many Africans were remarkably skilled artists, particularly in sculpture," Bright added. Third Baptist's inspirational choir provided cultural enrichment in the form of several gospel selections, which elicited a standing ovation at their conclusion.

As a special bonus to paid-up members, OCA purchased and distributed a limited number of copies of the multi-faith calendar, "Spiritual Sounds". We continue to maintain contact with The Friendship Force and encourage that organization, as well as other groups that promote understanding of people "different from us". Our movie project, "The Peopling of the Mahoning Valley," continues to move forward slowly but surely as we develop funds and assistance to bring the project to completion. It had been a good year-with still more to come.

Maryann Senediak and Ann Thompson with speaker, Halim El-Dabh

"I take vibrations in everything around me and make music," mused Halim El-Dabh, the September kick-off speaker for the Ohio Cultural Alliance's 12th year, continuing the topic, "Expressions of Culture: The Arts in Other Nations". El-Dabh is a world-renowned composer who addresses the rhythm of life from the "Mideast to the Midwest." A native of Egypt, El-Dabh has traveled the world teaching and learning from the well-known to the less known. He has worked with composers Leopold Stokowsky, Irvine Fine, Leonard Bernstein, Aaron Copeland, and Igor Stravinsky and has collaborated with dancer/choreographer Martha Graham. Publishing dozens of works, his music has been showcased on venues such as Broadway and PBS's Great Performances. He taught at Kent State University from 1969 to 1998, when he retired to devote more time to composing and lecturing. He was the first in Fine Arts at Kent to achieve the designation of University Professor. El-Dabh said he sees music as energy. "It is a physical thing that should engage listeners totally. The purpose of my music is to find yourself," he says. "It's about giving back to the people around me. Music is the life of people." El-Dabh tries to help people tap into their unlimited potential by making use of his infectious energy-not only for music but also for language, culture, art, and people. "I want them to learn to use their bodies, their voices, and their knowledge of design and sculpture to open the visions of learning". Although he has made music his life, it seems more accurate to say music has made him. A professor at Kent State said of El-Dabh, "He brings people of all races and backgrounds together with his music."

We met for this 1st meeting of the season at the Butler Institute of American Art with the meal catered by Eberth Catering. In addition to the stimulating lecture, El-Dabh also played one of his compositions on a drum, after which he invited some of those in the audience to join him on another drum. What an evening El-Dabh treated us to! As if not enough stimulation for one meeting, we also were able to peruse Butler Art Museum before and after the meeting.

In October, the OCA heard Ann Maigetter and John Raycich (both active in the local Serbian community) discuss the arts in the Serbian tradition. We met at the Serbian Holy Trinity Orthodox Church Hall in Youngstown and were served a traditional ethnic meal consisting of kolbassi, stuffed cabbage, and chicken paprikash, among other items. Our cultural enrichment was provided by the Avala Tamburitzans, a Serbian folklore dance group comprised of members of the three local Serbian Orthodox churches. A fine cultural display of artifacts provided additional aspects of Serbian culture. We dealt with many of our senses as we sampled Serbian culture- we tasted, smelled, heard, saw, and learned.

The Russian arts were featured in November with Dr. Melissa Smith, YSU, Foreign Languages as our speaker. Her capacity as a professor of Russian literature and her frequent travels to Russia gave her a currency that few local people have. Her talk and slides gave witness to the Russian "love of literature, classical music, ballet, and drama and architecture." "Wall and panel painting is a form of art that decorated churches from the Middle Ages to this day," Dr. Smith reported. Her talk and slides, the wonderful Russian meal prepared by Livosky Caterers (borscht, chicken Kiev, beef stroganoff, etc.), the beautiful melodies sung by the Men's choir of St. John's Russian Orthodox Church in Campbell (the site of the meeting), and the striking artifact display made for a memorable evening.

Annette El-Hayek shared her knowledge and enthusiasm for the arts of the Arab world at our December meeting. She spoke considerably about the Arab world during the European "Dark Ages" (Middle Ages), at which time the Arab world shone-in art, architecture, and music especially. Our ethnic meal was prepared by members of the congregation of the Maronite Center; it included traditional favorites such as kibbee, humous, and lamb. The evening concluded with the professional Middle Eastern "belly dancing "of Sherena.

January's focus was the arts in the Scandinavian tradition. Dr. Martha Pallante, YSU, History, whose ancestry includes Norwegian, sketched key contributions of Norway, Finland, Denmark, and Sweden as she spoke to us about the arts in those countries. We met at the Ursuline Mother House in Canfield. Eberth Catering prepared an ethnic meal that featured chicken w/celery sauce, Norwegian meatballs and noodles, Danish carrots, and Copenhagen carrots. The talented and popular Roman Rudnytsky regaled us with relevant piano selections, for which he again received a standing ovation. All of this was our reward for coming out in the season's largest snow fall.

In February, Monsignor Peter Polando, Judge John Leskovyansky, and Thomas Hricik, President of the Catholic Slovak Union of North America, offered varied comments regarding the arts of Slovakia. They spoke of the Slovak folk songs, Slovak folk dance, Slovak bands, particularly polka bands, and shared artifacts that each brought with them. The meal was another "Youngstown buffet" prepared by the caterers of the Saxon Club, the site of our meeting. The Pittsburgh Slovakians dance troupe delighted us with some lively folk dances.

The March meeting focus was the arts in the Welsh tradition. Dr. Marcelle Wilson (YSU, History Department) offered an informative and delightful look at Welsh arts. She told of the Welsh love of music in the form of Eisteddfod, Gorsedd, and Gymanfa Ganu. Welsh Eisteddfods, musical and literary contests, brought prominence to Youngstown in the 1860s and were popular in the Youngstown area until the early 20th century. A Gorsedd is an ancient Welsh Druid rite and institution popular among the early Welsh settlers to Youngstown. And the Gymanfu Ganu is an expression of the Welsh soul that gives an outlet to deep religious beliefs through song, sung in harmony by persons in all stations of life-thus a democratic institution. We met at the Ursuline Mother House with Eberth Catering serving some Welsh cuisine that included Brunswick stew, roast beef, and colcannon. Dr. Allan Mosher stirred the crowd as he sang beautiful Welsh melodies, including the Welsh national anthem.

The Ohio Cultural Alliance held its April meeting at the YSU DeBartolo Stadium Club, at which time Claudia Corbe addressed the arts in the French tradition. Both Claudia and her husband, Dr. Herve Corbe, are well-known in the local French community. Claudia is the Co-coordinator of the Northern Trumbull County Gifted and Talented Program. She discussed some of the important music of French composers, as well as important art and architecture, and how some of the local organizations, such as Le Cercle Francais, strive to promote French arts and culture generally. Appropriate French music provided by YSU's Early Music Ensemble, led by Dr. Laura Buch, was a great way to end our evening. An additional touch to our senses was the beautiful sunset and an overview of Youngstown from high above at the YSU DeBartolo Stadium Club.

The May focus featured the arts in the Hispanic tradition. Drs. Silvia Hyre and George D. Beelen, both of YSU, shared historical and personal perspectives of the arts in Latin America. Dr. Hyre, an El Salvadoran native, is the Director of the Center for International Studies at YSU, and Dr. Beelen has been a retired professor of Latin American history for more than three decades at YSU; both are frequent travelers to various parts of Latin America. Lively, music and art were cited as vital to Hispanic peoples locally and in countries to our south. The site of the meeting was the Ukrainian Orthodox Center; cultural enrichment was provided by a Latin American youth dance group directed by Marie Silva. We were even invited to try a meringue or a tango step or two.

Our season finale in June dealt with the arts In Hungary, with YSU professor Dr. Leslie Domonkos as our speaker. His informative and delightful remarks clearly show the love that Dr. Domonkos has for his native land. The wonderful ethnic meal of beef goulash, stuffed cabbage, and Hungarian dessert was prepared by the Calvin Center congregation, which was the site of this meeting. How great it was to hear the talented Todd Cuttshaw, a student of the YSU Dana School of Music, play Hungarian melodies on the piano.

In sum, OCA's 12th year was a huge success. Indeed, a feature article in the suburban weekly, Town Crier, written by Sharon Mika, noted the exciting, informative, and entertaining agenda we have pursued and OCA's contribution to the local community. There was still more to come in the new millennium, including the completion of our long-awaited movie, "The Peopling of the Mahoning Valley."

Dr. Melissa Smith

Florence DiRienzo Schneider

Ann Maigetter

Serbian dancers

Monsignor Peter Polando

Dr. Silvia Hyre

Jacek Sobieski

Dorotea Sobieski

XI. Reflections on the Millennium

The Ohio Cultural Alliance kicked off the 1999-2000 season in September with Dr. George D. Beelen introducing the topic for the next two years, "Reflections on the Millennium." We met at the Pilgrim Collegiate Church (razed several years later), located just across the street from YSU's Jones Hall. Eberth Catering served another festive meal. I started with some thoughts about the 2nd millennium and ended with a peaceful meditation as we entered the 3rd millennium. At the ending of the millennium, we wondered what the new millennium portends. A thousand years ago, when the earth was "reassuringly flat and the universe revolved around it", the ordinary person had no last name, let alone any claim to individualism. The self was subordinate to the church and the king. What followed was the Renaissance explosion of scientific discovery and humanist insight and, as both cause and effect, the rise of individual self-consciousness. All at once, it seemed, man had replaced God at the center of earthly life. And perhaps more than any great war or invention or feat of navigation, this upheaval marked the beginning of our modern era. There are now 20 times as many people as there were in the year 1,000. Most have last names, and many of us have a personal identity or a reasonable expectation of acquiring one. And nowhere has this individualism become more apparent than in the United States. Has this individualism gone too far? Is it time to move toward a more community relationship? What will the new millennial hold for us? For the next two years, we tried to gain some perspective as to how a number of countries welcomed the new millennium.

A peaceful meditation was written by Robert Muller, Chancellor of the University for Peace and former assistant secretary-general of the United Nations:

"I dream that in January 2000, the whole world will stand still in prayer, awe, and gratitude for our beautiful, heavenly earth and for the arc of human life.... I dream that the third millennium will be declared and made humanity's First Millennium of Peace." And we all say Amen.

Finally, to help us kick off our 13th year, we were fortunate to host the talented musical group, The Youngstown Connection. They are under the leadership of Dr. Carol Baird, music director in the Youngstown schools. This diverse group from the Youngstown schools sang and danced their way into our hearts.

Throughout our OCA history, we have drawn upon YSU for speakers, cultural enrichment, and meeting sites. And we continued to do so in the years ahead. Our speaker in October was Dr. Les Domonkos, YSU History, cultural enrichment by Dr. Kevin Orr YSU, Music, and our site was at YSU. Dr. Domonkos offered insights into Y1K (year 1,000 A.D.) as he discussed the world in year 1,000, where he said, "Year 1,000 was a leap year starting on a Monday of the Julian calendar. This year fell well into the period known as the Middle Ages (Medieval Period) in Europe. It was a world without buttons, which had yet to be invented. Clothes were still fastened with clasps and thongs. Life was short. A boy of twelve was considered old enough to swear an oath of allegiance to the king, while girls married in their early teens, often to men who were much older than they were." "The year 1,000 came and went", he said," with a huge, collective sigh of relief across Europe. Most people had expected that the end of the first millennium would be accompanied by the end of the world.

Yet, most of the history we know and most of the way we live our life occurred in the second millennium." Dr. Orr placed us in a wonderful mood as he displayed his piano talents with a variety of selections.

The Scandinavian tradition during the 2nd millennium was featured in November with YSU's Dr. Martha Pallante as our speaker. We met at the Sts. Peter and Paul Ukrainian Orthodox Social Center, whose parishioners catered the meal that included a few items of Scandinavian flavor. Dr. Pallante spoke of the incredible progress that the Scandinavian countries made during the 2nd millennium, particularly in the area of developing a social contract with its citizens. This made for a very high "happiness quotient" for those countries. Dr. Tedrow Perkins (oboe) and Diane Yazvac (piano), both from YSU's Dana School of Music, performed appropriate musical selections.

In December, Dr. Mustansir Mir, Director of Islamic Studies at YSU, shared the accomplishments of Islamic peoples during the last millennium, particularly during the middle part of the millennium, when Europe was somnolent. Jasmin Rashid displayed and described a host of artistic items reflecting the Islamic tradition. Dr. Mir reflected upon the extent of the Islamic world-from the Atlantic Ocean to the Pacific, in a broad band that reached across North Africa, the Middle East, Central Asia, and down to Indonesia. Islam retained much of its original vigor to 1900 and continues today to be one of the fastest-growing religions in the world. Events of worldwide significance, like the Iranian Revolution of 1979, partly account for this phenomenon. Dr. Mir also shared, "that interest is manifested in the increasing number of papers, studies, and research projects on Islam and the Muslim world and the establishment of Islamic studies world-wide, including YSU." The meeting was held at the Presbyterian Church in Youngstown, with Eberth Catering serving up a meal that had some suggestions of Muslim cuisine.

John Axe YSU, History Department, a scholar of Spanish history and language and frequent traveler to Spain, was the speaker who shared his knowledge of Spain during the 2nd millennium. Mr. Axe is the author of innumerable books and articles dealing with collectibles from Spain and the United States. As a member observed, Mr. Axe was irreverent and interesting. We met at the Ursuline Mother House, with Eberth Catering serving a delicious meal that contained some Spanish items. Cultural enrichment was provided by Jim Ferris and Suzanne Gelinas of Always Dancing Dance Studio, who demonstrated several exciting Spanish dances.

The February meeting focus was Italy, with Monsignor John Ashton, Pastor of St. Lucy Roman Catholic Church, as our speaker-an Irishman speaking knowledgeably and sensitively about Italy! His Italian credentials come from his frequent travels and study in Italy and his pastorate at a basically Italian church. Monsignor Ashton, with his stentorian voice and his knowledge of the history-good and bad-of Italy, made for a fascinating speech. Betty Bannon performed delightful Italian melodies on her accordion, and Georgetown Catering served a wonderful Italian meal.

In March, YSU's Dr. Yih-Wu Liu spoke of China during the last millennium as we dined at the Golden Hunan Restaurant in Liberty. Dr. Liu is a professor of Economics at YSU and a frequent traveler to both Taiwan and mainland China. He covered the long history of China, its ups and downs, and their more recent history of the fall of the last dynasty, the rise of nationalism, the institution of communism, and the U.S. renewal of relations under the Nixon presidency. Cultural enrichment was provided by talented soprano Dr. Mei Zhong, Professor of Voice at Idaho State University and performer in both China and the U.S. The Golden Hunan prepared an extensive Chinese buffet for our traditional ethnic meal.

Dr. Warren Young (YSU Astronomy Department) again spoke to us, this time about the greatness of Mexico during the Mayan/Aztec eras, at our April meeting held at YSU's new Beeghly Education Building. His remarks focused on the mathematical, astronomical, and cultural advances of the extensive Mayan civilization, as well as the political and cultural aspects of the Aztecs. Adding to the evening was the movie "Sentinels of Silence," showing and discussing the great Mayan pyramids. The Casa Ramirez Restaurant staff prepared and delivered our authentic Mexican meal that was both abundant and sumptuous.

The May meeting featured France as interpreted by Dr. Anne York (YSU History Department). Her teaching, studies and travels to France render her credentials outstanding. Dr. York spoke of the early European history that included France, the French Revolution and its aftermath, and the more modern democratic France. We met in the Marble Room of Stambaugh Auditorium in Youngstown with Eberth Catering serving a wonderful French-like meal. Dr. Allan Mosher and a few of his students offered beautiful French melodies to complement Dr. York's sensitive and humorous exploration of France through the 2nd millennium.

Our season finale in June featured the Polish tradition and its development during the last millennium. Our speaker was Eric Lewandawski (YSU Director of Grants and Sponsored Programs), who is of Polish ancestry. He related to us the strengths and weaknesses of Poland as it emerged as a discrete country during the 2nd millennium. Complementing the insightful comments of Mr. Lewandowski was the excellent cuisine prepared by Kathryn Pozzuto and the Polish National Church, the site of the meeting. Professor Roman Rudnytsky once again performed Polish numbers for us, which set us in a mood of happiness. (Indeed, he performed for us just about every year of OCA's existence.)

In sum, Ohio Cultural Alliance's 13th year was a resounding success, with ten fine programs and dinners, a record number of paid memberships, growing attendance at meetings, and the completion and distribution of our video, "The Peopling of the Mahoning Valley". The 45-minute film was a few years in the making. My writing of the script was a testimony of my love and long interest in the Mahoning Valley. My son, George D. Beelen, Jr., refined the script to make it more flowing for a film, and he did all the technical and cinematic work necessary for a professional piece. After some months of tweaking until he and I were satisfied that it was a real contribution to the Mahoning Valley, we "took it to press". The film chronicles how the Valley was populated, beginning with the Native Americans as they settled along the Mahoning River and the diverse people who came to the Valley-the Northern and Western Europeans, the Southern and Eastern Europeans, and the most recent immigrants from the South of United States, Puerto Rico, Latin America, Asia and the Middle East and how each group, in succession, struggled to adjust to a new environment and ultimately had many successes. We sold (or contributed to all the area schools and libraries) at least 3,000 copies of the video.

OCA film prepared for the Bicentennial of Mahoning County

Post Card of Steel Valley In its prime

Downtown Youngstown in the 1950's

Rare image of Edward DeBartolo (left) and William Cafaro (right)

Hard and hot labor built Youngstown

The OCA kicked off the 2000-2001 season in September with Dr. Lou Zona, YSU Art Department and Executive Director of the Butler Museum of American Art, the site of the meeting. He captivated the audience with highlights of the many rich cultures as he offered thoughts related to our continuing theme, "Reflections on the Millennium". He pointed out the diversity of the museum in terms of holdings and how it has grown in quantity and quality over the decades of the last millennium. His talk and visual presentation were complemented by tours of the galleries preceding and following dinner, which was provided by Eberth Catering.

In October, Dr. John Boehm YSU, Foreign Languages, addressed the German accomplishments of the last millennium-including their emergence as a nation, their leadership in science, medicine, and the arts, their failures in the Nazi era, and their remarkable come- back, particularly the re-unification of their country, after several decades of division into East Germany and West Germany. Dr. Misook Yun, YSU, Music, and several of her students enthralled us with fascinating melodies of the Saxon culture. The Saxon Club, the site of our meeting, provided the usual wonderful ethnic meal.

The English were featured in November, with Dr. Lowell Satre, YSU, History, as our speaker. He spoke about England's social contract with its citizens, including socialized medicine and education for all. He compared England's parliamentary system with our federal system in the U.S. His comments about the recovery of England after World War II and the close relationship that developed with the U.S. during the war and afterward were codified with North Atlantic Treaty Organization (NATO) which signaled permanence in the ensuing years. Dr. Ronald Gould (YSU Dana School of Music) gave us a tutorial on English music and performed beautiful music on St. John's Episcopal Church organ. It was also the site of our meeting, whose parishioners prepared an English meal. The number of attendees was growing, and once again, this necessitated two sittings for dinner.

December marked our largest attendance ever, and our most ambitious undertaking as OCA sponsored a performance of "Christmas in Croatia" by the 60-member international music and dance group ZIVILI, which is a Croatian word meaning "To Life!" It was a heart-warming, brilliantly theatrical holiday production of singers, dancers, and musicians, dedicated to the preservation and presentation of the colorful old traditions of Slavic nations. "Christmas in Croatia" takes place in a small village in Croatia. It begins with the more solemn choral works that are a part of Croatian Midnight Mass church services, but the mood becomes more lighthearted and spirited as the piece moves to a village home where various customs and traditions are observed. As is typical of most gatherings in Croatia, high-spirited dancing and singing took place. The story is seen through the eyes of an immigrant as he reflects on his childhood Christmases in Croatia. Held at Canfield High School, the performance attendance was nearly 1,000, and dinner attendance numbered 380-both virtual sell-outs. A traditional Croatian ethnic meal prepared by Livosky Catering included breaded chicken, leg of lamb, kolbassi and kraut, halushki potato salad, and strudel. To top it all off, Libby Fill and her Tamburitza group of five entertained us through the dinner. Betty Beelen was honored for organizing so much of this event.

Reverend Alexander Goussetis of Archangel Michael Orthodox Church in Campbell was the January speaker. Reverend Goussetis shared insights regarding the Greeks during the 2nd millennium, which focused on progress and regression. He noted that Greece reached its apogee in the period before the beginning of the Christian era and has often struggled since. From the 15th to the 19th centuries, the Greek peninsula was under the domination of the Ottoman Turks. During those centuries, a fundamental cohesive element that sustained the Greek people and preserved their heritage was the Church, which was Reverend Goussetis' primary focus. We enjoyed a typical Greek meal served by the parishioners of Archangel Michael and enjoyed the young dance group, who were talented and delightful.

The February meeting focus was Africa as Dr. Daniel Ayana YSU, History, presented significant accomplishments of several African nations and Africa as a continent. After brief comments about past significant African civilizations, he homed in on Africa today (early 21st century) that he argued a compressed change was going on. "Africans are in the process of regaining ancient heritage for a renaissance, adopting new ones and finding new challenges; Africa has fifty-six countries. Of these, less than ten have conflicts of various types…The other forty-five or so are managing. Some, such as Botswana, are registering miraculous economic growth and stability." Dr. Ayana offered two characteristics of Africa: the sense of community that extends to all aspects of life and the belief that nature's resources are not limitless. He was most prescient when he concluded his presentation with, "To make this planet habitable and bequeath to the next generation, we need a sense of understanding nature as a limited resource. And such notions can be retrieved from the Africans, and in these two ways, Africa is both the past and the future of humanity." The meal was prepared by the parishioners of the Presbyterian Church in Youngstown, the site of our meeting. The YSU Full Gospel Choir provided rousing music that had our members enthusiastically humming, singing, clapping, or tapping.

In March, Dr. Alexander Pantsov, a Moscow native teaching at Capital University in Columbus, spoke about the vertiginous nature of Russian development as it evolved/devolved through the 2nd millennium. He traced with passion and humor the Russian desire to expand; the rivalry with the Turks and the English, among others; the Tsarist years, and the Russian Revolution. He spent some time with the on-again-off-again relations with the Western powers, including the United States. St. John's Russian Orthodox Church was the site of our meeting. They provided the Russian ethnic meal and entertained us with their Men's choir, led by local Dr. Nicholas Nicholoff.

Michael Kurilla was our April speaker, held at the Polish National Church. His talk was carefully researched and peppered with personal and family memories. He offered an informative look at the Slavic tradition, particularly Slovak, in the latter days of the last millennium. The end of the Russian despotism in Czechoslovakia and the break-up into Slovakia and the Czech Republic, as well as their move into the orbit of the Western powers, were some of his main points of emphasis. The ethnic meal was again prepared by parishioners of the church. Betty Bannon charmed us with her Slavic melodies played on her accordion.

The May meeting featured Dr. Saul Friedman, YSU, History, who spoke of Jewish traditions, their religion, their triumphs and struggles of the last millennium, and their diaspora, including the U.S. and the Zionist movement. Dr. Friedman, always the passionate, compassionate, and insightful speaker, did not disappoint this evening. His talk was complemented by Lawrence Ehrlich, former cantor of Rodef Sholom Synagogue, the venue for our meeting. His chanting and remarks were inspiring and complemented Dr. Freidman's powerful address. Synagogue members prepared and served a typical ethnic Jewish meal.

In June, our season finale featured YSU's sixth president, Dr. David Sweet, who addressed the topic of "American Diversity and Its Implementation at YSU". He said that we were moving in the right direction with staff and faculty but still not where he wanted us to be. The remarkably talented Youngstown Connection consisting of twelve high school students of diverse backgrounds once again sang and danced their way into our hearts. We again met at the Sts. Peter and Paul Ukrainian Center to enjoy their usual delicious ethnic meal.

Ohio Cultural Alliance enjoyed another stellar year-our 14th. We hosted ten fine programs and dinners, a record number of memberships, more than 300, with a mailing list of nearly 600 names. We were now averaging between 225-250 people at each meeting, with the largest ever, 350 for dinner and nearly 1,000 for the program "Christmas in Croatia". We continued the sales of our film "The Peopling of the Mahoning Valley" to locals and those who were locals, now living elsewhere. Our newest endeavor was to co-sponsor and participate in the Festival of Nations, a component of the 2001 Summer Festival of the Arts on the YSU campus.

Part of dancing group particpating in "Christmas in Croatia

Dr. Mustansir Mir

Eric Lewandowski

Monsignor John Ashton

Dr. Daniel Ayana

John Axe

Dr. Mei Zhong

Dr. David Sweet

Dr. Alexander Pantsov

Dr. Ted Perkins

Nicholas Nicholoff Singers

XII. Monuments, Memories and Milestones of the World

On September 12, 2001, Ohio Cultural Alliance's kick-off for the 2001-02season (our 15thyear) was just one day after one of America's most tragic days. Dr. George D. Beelen was to offer an introduction to the two-year theme of "Monuments, Memories, and Milestones of the World" and give a lighthearted look at love and marriage in the United States. Instead, the evening was somber and patriotic, with Dr. Beelen reflecting upon America with a short talk entitled "Dynamic Symbols of American Democracy" and many OCA members offering their own heartfelt reflections regarding the implications of the previous day's events. Held at the beautiful D.D & Velma Davis Education and Visitor Center at Mill Creek's Riverside Gardens, the evening ended with horn selections of a YSU Dana Quartet.

In October, Attorney Joseph Schiavone entertained members by giving many pertinent (and impertinent) remarks regarding Italy. In keeping with the theme, Atty. Schiavone shared some of his travels and memories as he took us on vicarious trips to Rome and the Vatican, Venice, Milan, Florence, and Pisa, and the wonderful countryside of various parts of the country. He reminded us of the wonderful cuisine in all parts of the country. Area musician John Gabriele delighted us with Italian melodies with his one-man "band" accordion, playing during and after dinner. The Italian meal was provided by Georgetown Catering, the site of this meeting. Some of our meetings this season were co-hosted by travel agencies; Burger Travel served in that capacity this month. Debra Burger spoke about their agency for a few minutes and offered a $150.00 discount on their next trip to one of our members.

Costa Rica was featured in November with Dr. John White, YSU, Sociology/Anthropology, as our speaker. Having just returned from a forty-day anthropological dig in Costa Rica, Dr. White spoke glowingly of the people of this country, many of whom are "geniuses" and hospitable. Costa Rica is a country without an army and is among the best off in terms of their standard of living, their democratic political policies, and degree of "happiness". Meeting at the Ursuline Mother House, Casa Ramirez catered a wonderful Hispanic meal that was abundant and tasty. Graduate students from YSU, Pierre Van Der Westhiezen and Sophia Grobler, delighted us with their Hispanic piano selections.

Our December speaker was Dr. William Greenway, YSU, English Department. He spoke of Wales, the country of his ancestors and the subject of much of his prose and poetry. Dr. Greenway's many trips to Wales have inspired a rich store of published articles and poetry, for which he has been generously awarded. A feel for his work can be gleaned from one of the poems, "Pit Pony": "There are only a few left, he says, kept by old Welsh miners, souvenirs, like gallstones or gold teeth, torn from this 'pit', so cold and wet my breath comes out a soul up into my helmet's lantern beam, anthracite walls running, gleaming, and the floors iron-rutted with tram tracks, the almost pure rust that grows and waves like orange moss in the gutters of water that used to rise and drown...." Dr. Allan Mosher, again, and one of his students completed the evening by singing emotional Welsh selections, which included the Welsh national anthem. We met at the Polish National Church in Youngstown, whose parishioners served a meal that had Welsh items that the Welsh members among us testified to their authenticity.

Brenda Chadambura, a university student at YSU, was OCA's January speaker, addressing the country of Zimbabwe, her native land. She had distinguished herself at YSU and had become active in the community. Brenda spoke with great insight and humor about the potential of Zimbabwe and its beauty, with beautiful waterfalls such as Mosi-o-Tunya and their potential as a country, including potential for tourism. Her address referred to such monuments as the ruined city of Great Zimbabwe, which was built in the 11th century and inhabited for over 300 years. Among the notable elements among the ruins are soapstone bird sculptures that are unique to Great Zimbabwe. Indeed, the stone-carved Zimbabwe bird is the national emblem of Zimbabwe, appearing on the national flags and coats of arms of both Zimbabwe and Rhodesia, the former name of the country. The caterer was Mrs. Jennie Lott's Food Service, who served a typical African ethnic meal with items such as fried chicken, African bobtie (meatballs), beans w/rice pilaf, and sweet potato. We met at Tabernacle Baptist Church in Youngstown. Jocyln Dabney, an accomplished storyteller, offered insights into Africa through her fascinating stories, told in an animated fashion.

The February meeting focus was Australia, as Sandy Ferguson, a travel agent for Pan Atlas Travel, informed us of the enchantment of that land. Films regarding Australia visually enhanced her talk, which detailed some of the iconic examples of the country: the modern cities, the backlands, which still have natives living there, and the Opera House in Sydney. The meeting was held at YSU's DeBartolo Stadium Club and catered by Livosky Caterers, who served: Aussie lamb kabobs, Sheppard pie, kiwi cheesecake, etc. Sandy also provided the $150.00 travel voucher for one member for future travel.

In March, Attorney Robert Casey presented colorful, instructive, and humorous memories of Ireland and some of its iconic features. He included a look at the many churches and taverns that he remembers from his many trips to Ireland and his considerable studies and discussion with Irish natives. A Riverdance film was shown during dinner-corn beef, cabbage, and potatoes, of course, which was prepared by the chefs at the Croatian Lodge, Lodge #66 in Youngstown. They have been preparing such a meal at the Lodge on or about St. Patrick's Day for years. And the Irish among us said that the meal was authentic and delicious. Mike Cervone and Megan Morris sang their hearts out with a program of Irish music. Sponsoring the $150.00 travel voucher was Cheryl Hudak of Travel dimensions.

Dr. Stephen Hanzely, recently retired from the Physics Department at YSU and a native of Hungary, spoke of his homeland in April. His power point presentation and an accompanying film captured much of the beauty of Hungary. Betty Bannon, again, on her accordion, accompanied by Susan Breneis-Fisher on violin and Jeff Bremer on bass, graced us with enchanting Hungarian melodies. We met at the familiar Saxon Club, who, once again, served up an ethnic meal that Dr. Hanzely attested to its authenticity. A couple of surprises were the $150.00 travel voucher presented to one of our members by John Kropolinsky of Progressive Travel Agency and the sample of Hungarian wine donated by Dr. Hanzely.

The May meeting featured Switzerland, with Gloria Gloor Atwell as our speaker. Her parents were born in Switzerland; she herself is a frequent visitor to her parents' native land and is active in Swiss-American affairs in the Akron-Canton area. She complemented her remarks with interesting slides. Her address and the slides gave evidence of the beautiful landscape and the industriousness and hospitality of the Swiss. We met at the Churchill United Methodist Church in Liberty; the dinner was prepared by the Methodist Church Women's Club and included Zurich geschnetzeltes, Swiss steak, risotto ala Milanese and chocolate mousse, etc. The AAA provided the travel voucher to one member for international travel. Once again, a standing ovation was given to Roman Rudnytsky, who "tickled the ivories" with his beautiful and inspirational music on the piano.

In June, we visited the Philippines vicariously, with OCA member Estrellite (Lita) Sevilla as our speaker. Mrs. Seville is a native of the Philippines, a frequent visitor, the recent president of NEO Filipino-American Organization, and OCA Trustee. Her love of her homeland shone through with her inspiring talk, her slides, and her dancing. She was joined in the bamboo dancing by her husband and several others of the local Philippine community. We met at The Georgetown in Boardman, who prepared the meal that included a few surprises that suggested the Philippines and their cuisine.

In sum, the Ohio Cultural Alliance's fifteenth year was again a success and growing with each additional year, with ten programs and dinners, plus the attendant activities at each meeting, a record number of memberships and attendance, and the sale and distribution of our video "The Peopling of the Mahoning Valley" now complete. Members of OCA and local press were invited to a preview of the film at a press conference and reception held at YSU; the film was well received, with many present buying DVD copies and taking others to sell. Later in the year, the film was telecast on the local PBS station located in Kent, Ohio. It was repeated on three occasions during the next year or so. We also participated for the second year in the Festival of Nations component of the 2002 Summer Festival of the Arts on the YSU campus. We were learning about people like us and different from us as we increasingly concluded that "genius knows no boundaries."

Our successful fifteenth season gave us reason to believe that a continuation of the theme, "Monuments, Memories, and Milestones," would result in similar interest and success during our sixteenth year. In September, we kicked off the year with France as our focus. Our speaker was Dr. Paul Dalbec, YSU Professor Emeritus, who has been teaching French for more than three decades at the university and long been a leader in the area's French organization, Le Cercle Francais. As a frequent traveler to France, he also had many memories of the people, sights, landmarks, and culture of the French, which he shared with us in his address and appropriate slides. The meeting was held at the Polish National Church, whose parishioners prepared their usual good meal that included a few special French delicacies. A woodwind trio, under the leadership of Dr. Ted Perkins, performed French selections to complete our program for the evening.

Our speaker for October was Reverend Ashwin Kumar Welch, born to missionaries in India, where he lived until the age of sixteen. His mother was from Gujrat, India and his father was from Louisiana. He returned to India with his wife to work as lay missionaries until he went back to the U.S., where both he and his wife became ministers. They were currently co-pastors at Boardman United Methodist Church. He spoke of the land of his birth with love and respect--and considerable humor. His reflections of India included comments about the emerging democratic government that followed English colonial rule. Today, he said, India was the largest democracy in the world. Dr. Julia of YSU's Psychology Department and native of India, delighted us with colorful Indian classical dances. Her performance was thematic: it started with a prayer to Lord Ganesha (the God with the elephant head), after which the first item performed was Kautam, which is an item that praises Lord Ganesha; Alaripu in Mishra was the next item that literally means flowering; the final item was Jatisvaram into which intricate rhythmic variations are interwoven. She dedicated her performance to Lord Nataraja so that true peace and harmony may be reawakened around the globe. We met at St. Nicholas Activity Center in Youngstown with a meal prepared by Peppers' Catering (not very Indian) but included several Indian items.

Well-known ophthalmologist Dr. H.S. Wang, a native of Taiwan (born in North Korea), and his wife Florence are both active in the local Asian (Chinese) community and frequent travelers to Taiwan and mainland China were our November speakers. His beautiful slides complemented his and his wife's narrative on China and Taiwan. They spoke about early dynasties in China, the Revolution, the political breakoff of Taiwan, long-range planning, and such sites as the China Wall. The meeting took place at the Grand Buffet, a Chinese Restaurant in Boardman, and concluded with a colorful and exciting Dragon Dance organized by Mark Pringle. Many of us wondered, along with the Wangs, what the future held for the unification of Taiwan and China was and how it would impact the United States.

One is reminded of Sung Tzu, Chinese philosopher, c.350 B.C. speaking of peace:

"Constantly rebuffed but never discouraged, we went around from state to state helping people settle their differences, arguing against the wanton attack and pleading for the suppression of arms that the age in which we lived might be saved from its state of continual war. To this end, we interviewed princes and lectured the common people, nowhere meeting with any great success, but obstinately persisting in our task till kings and commoners alike grew weary of listening to them. Yet, undeterred, we continued to force ourselves on peoples' attention." How prescient was this!

In December, Reverend Jim Ray, Sue Anzellotti-Ray, Jake and Lotte Erhart, Rob Anzellotti, and Barbara Berger shared fascinating personal travel to Germany. After a brief discussion about many changes in Germany during the last century-some good and some disastrous, they homed in on their enchantment with the many sights they visited on their recent visit to Germany. They marveled at the cleanliness of the cities and the countryside, the friendliness of the people, and the sights such as the falls at Thuringia, the beauty of Bavaria, the castles in Saxony, and the rebuilt areas of Brandenburg and Berlin. Our meal at the Saxon Club included baked chicken, breaded pork chops, and German potato salad. The piano artistry of Roman Rudnytsky was featured again as he delighted an appreciative audience with melodies from German composers.

Michael Benz, president of Kollander Travel Agency in Cleveland, spoke of Croatia in January. His valuable insights gained from study and innumerable trips to Croatia helped introduce the OCA-sponsored trip to Croatia in August 2003. He started with a quote by Bernard Shaw, "Those who seek paradise on Earth should come to Dubrovnik and see Dubrovnik" that set the stage for Michael's panoramic visit to Croatia, which took us (virtually) to Dubrovnik, one of the sites of the movie, "Star Wars"; Zagreb, the historic capital with the city's historical center, St. Mark's Church, with its multicolored roof, the historic Cathedral, and the university, one of the region's oldest; and the beautiful Plitvice Lakes, a natural wonder of sixteen terraced lakes (a UNESCO recognized preserve) and Split, the oldest Slavic city on the gorgeous Adriatic Sea. The site of the meeting was the Croatian Lodge # 66 in Youngstown, where the sumptuous meal included breaded chicken, stuffed cabbage, and Croatian potato salad under the direction of Fran Piersante and Nada Bada. To top off the meeting, Libby and her Tamburitza group entertained us through the evening. What fun she was!

The February meeting focus was England. Dr. Barbara Brothers retired from YSU Arts and Sciences Dean at the end of her career and long-time chair and professor of the English Department before that. A frequent traveler and an avid student of English literature and history, Dr. Brothers shared her personal and vicarious experiences with a receptive audience. She spoke of the glory of England over many centuries, particularly the nineteenth century, the role of their royalty, the importance of English law and literature, the landscape of the countryside, and the iconic sites such as Windsor Castle and Buckingham Palace, and the Parliament building. The site of the meeting was Poland Methodist Church in Poland, whose caterers prepared a pretty typical English meal. Cultural enrichment was provided by an OCA favorite, Dr. Allan Mosher, and Jennifer Davis, who sang beautiful works with an English flavor.

Egypt was featured in March, with Dr. Atef Labib as our speaker. A noted cardiovascular surgeon and native of Egypt, Dr. Labib used beautiful slides to complement his knowledgeable narrative. He spoke of the ancient heritage of the country, remembered for its papyrus and pyramids, as well as the current political situation as it tries to establish its current role in world affairs. A film about the country created vivid images of the old and new in Egypt. The Georgetown was the site of the meeting; they served a meal that had some elements of Egyptian cuisine, highlighted by Egyptian desserts from Goussains' Mid-East Bakery.

In April, Attorney Edwin Romero, local attorney and native of the U.S. Commonwealth of Puerto Rico, spoke passionately of his parents coming to the Valley but also of the beauty of the island that they left behind. However, I am told that both he and his family have visited Puerto Rico frequently. Attorney Romero related to us the ambivalent relationship that exists between Puerto Rico and mainland U.S. They are citizens of the U.S. but cannot vote for president of the U.S. They participate in the U.S. armed forces but pay no U.S. taxes and are among the curious relationships between the two entities. Attorney Romero related how they are a great tourist attraction, particularly for cruise ships. Filipe Gonzalez' Trio moved around the room, serenading with lively Latin melodies members at each of the tables. Our meal was prepared by the YSU chefs who promised and delivered an authentic Hispanic meal.

The May meeting featured Greece with our speaker, Konstantine Georgiadis, a native of Greece, owner of a Washington D.C. travel agency, and frequent traveler to Greece. He was brought to us (literally and figuratively) by Luba Horsky of AAA Travel. He spoke of the glories of Greece, the economic and sometimes military difficulties of modern Greece, as well as the beautiful landscape of the countryside, the luscious islands, and the memorable ruins of "yesterday" in Greece. There is no doubt that one of the current advantages of Greece is its tourist trade. Traditional Greek food and music completed the evening. The meal was prepared and served by Balaci Kristan and her staff at Archangel Michael Church Hall located in Campbell; it was truly a Greek ethnic feast. Cultural enrichment was provided by Georgio Theofilos and Sotiri Tsourekis, who sang and played guitar and bouzouki, which introduced many of us to a new musical experience. An additional surprise was Mr. Georgiadis' generous contribution of a trip for two to Greece and the Greek Islands awarded to the lucky winner of our evening raffle.

After two years of "visiting" eighteen countries within our theme, "Monuments, Memories and Milestones of the World", we focused on the USA at our June meeting with Harry Meshel as our speaker. One of the premier community leaders, active political figures, and sought-after speakers in the Mahoning Valley, we were fortunate to host him for this final OCA meeting of the season. His leadership at the local, state, and national levels gives Harry a unique perspective on our nation. Known for his candor and wealth of experience as a respected public servant, he shared with insight and passion his view of America. Harry showed his love for our democratic institutions and how dearly we have paid to "try to make a perfect Union." He admonished us and challenged us to be more alert to those who would tear down what Americans have accomplished over the generations and to be active and involved in all aspects of life as we make us even better. We met at Mill Creek Riverside Gardens Banquet Center with Peppers' Catering, an all-American meal that featured many regional dishes. Another local leader from the world of art, Al Bright, provided cultural enrichment by creating (live) a beautiful painting to the accompaniment of a jazz quartet. He mesmerized us all as he seemingly created this art effortlessly. The resultant painting was auctioned off to Dr. Warren and Sandy Young; Professor Bright donated one-quarter of the proceeds to the OCA.

By any measure, this year, the Ohio Cultural Alliance again enjoyed a successful year; we increased our paid membership for this year to 300 and continued to grow our mailing list. The ten outstanding programs, dinners, and cultural enrichment were at ten different sites, which is in keeping with the OCA "going places" with sponsoring an actual thirteen-day trip to Croatia and continuing participation in the Festival of Nations at YSU. We are also fortunate and grateful for the talent and generosity of those who participate in our programs. Happily, no one has refused our invitation to participate, either this year or all the previous fifteen years. We were embedded in the Youngstown area.

Dr. William Greenway

Brenda Charambura

Dr. Paul Dalbec

Dr. Stephen Hanzely

YSU Dana String Quartet

Dr. Martha Pallante

Dr. H. S. Wang

XIII. The Immigrant Experience: From the Old World to the Mahoning Valley

The peopling of America is one of the greatest stories of human history. Some 50 million immigrants have come to our country-some to the Mahoning Valley. We dealt in our 18th year with some of the people who came to the Valley, what their experiences were upon leaving their homelands, how they were treated upon arriving in the new land, and how they fared in the Valley. So, our theme for the 2003-04 year and the 2004-2005 year was "The Immigrant Experience: From the Old World to the Mahoning Valley". Sometimes they were encouraged to come; sometimes, they were prohibited from coming. At times they came for but a short time; others determined to come and stay permanently. And something happened to them. They became Americans by way of a "melting pot", a "new race", a "smelting pot", an "ethnic synthesis," or a "patchwork quilt". They were responding to the invitation from the lady with her outstretched hand saying, "Give me your tired, your poor, your huddled masses yearning to breathe free, the wretched refuse of your teeming shore. Send these, the homeless, tempest-tost to me; I lift my lamp beside the golden door." We devoted two years to the theme of this diaspora of people.

In September, the Ohio Cultural Alliance kicked off its 17th year with a focus on Italy. Our speakers were Drs. Martha Pallante and Donna DeBlasio, professors in YSU's History Department. Both offered experiences of their families that came to the Valley in the 1890s. Italians were the most numerous of the immigrants who came to the U.S. in the latter part of the 19th century-some four million during the years 1890-1924. And many came to the Mahoning Valley. Mostly, artisans and peasants came from all regions of Italy but mainly from southern Italy. While many of the Italian immigrants were induced to come to America to work in jobs the Industrial Revolution created, they were often treated harshly and assigned to the most labor-intensive and dangerous jobs. Early Italian immigrants were often met with racial prejudice, especially those of darker complexion arrivals from southern Italy. The largest number of Italian immigrants came to the Valley after 1890, although a few came earlier. Some found jobs in the coal industry of Brown-Bonnell Company, some in the blast furnaces in Girard and Brier Hill, and others in the nascent steel industry. The vast majority settled in the Brier Hill and Smoky Hollow areas, near their jobs. Corner groceries, tailor shops, cobblers, and dry goods shops emerged to service these growing enclaves, sometimes referred to as "Little Italy". They worked to assimilate yet were determined to retain some of their cherished traditions. They established ethnic newspapers and churches. They brought with them a passion for art, music, dance, and food. Many became successful in industry, business, education, the arts government, and sports.

We met for this meeting at Mt. Carmel Center in Youngstown, with Fusillo Catering preparing a genuine ethnic Italian meal that everyone raved about. Music wafted through the hall as John Gabriel treated us to another musical montage of Italian music as he moved through the audience with his "one-man accordion band".

I was the speaker for October, addressing the topic of Romanian immigration to the Valley, focusing particularly on the Kosa family and my maternal grandparents. The Romanians came to America impelled by both "push" and "pull" factors. Pushed by depressed economic and social conditions of a pretty primitive society, coupled with little desire to serve in the Austro-Hungarian military and pulled by letters and other news from the U.S. which said unskilled workmen could earn $200.oo a month and that $3.00 a day wages were theirs for the picking. Despite the stress and uncertainty of leaving the familiar and arriving in a strange place, this America, so alien and far removed from the Old World; they settled in New York, Cleveland, Akron, and Youngstown; an example was John Kosa (father of 10) who lived in New Jersey and then Zelienople, Pennsylvania before settling in Youngstown. He married Mary Ungurean in 1905, and they would have a total of ten children, including my mother, Rosalie. Similar experiences marked the development of the Balomirean (Beelen) family. The meeting was held at Holy Resurrection Romanian Orthodox Church in Warren, with Caesare Catering serving a Romanian meal. Betty Bannon led a trio to perform appropriate music.

Kosa Family circa 1920

A large group of 250 attended the November meeting with Alexandra "Sandy" Vansuch speaking to us about the Russian immigrants to the Valley. A long-time director of the Oakland Center for the Arts, and daughter of an Orthodox priest of Russian ancestry, she was steeped in local Russian history. Her father served as pastor of St. John's Russian Orthodox Church in Campbell, the site of this meeting. While some Russians came to the U.S. in the 1880s, more came in several waves, often seeking political asylum, depending upon the international situation between America and Russia. Among these waves was the period of the Russian Revolution in 1917, the period following World War II, the period of the cold war, and the period of glasnost and perestroika, with a thaw in relations between the two countries. During some of the waves, local churches sponsored Russian immigrants, as did the Hebrew Immigrant Aid Society and the Youngstown Area Jewish Family and Children's Service. Locally, Russian ethnic identity has been largely centered in the churches and synagogues. Indeed, several Russian Orthodox churches and several Jewish synagogues were established early in the 20th century. Culturally, Russians have exerted an influence beyond their few numbers. These influences are noted in the Russian language being taught at YSU, with guest lecturers in the Valley, a classical radio station at YSU that plays music by Russian composers regularly, Russian festivals, and the theater scene which was partly because of Ms. Vansuch's prominence in the Valley. In addition to the usual sumptuous meal that Livosky Catering prepared for us, we had a special treat from the Style of Five musical groups from Russia (arranged by YSU professor Dr. Howard Mettee). They performed many Russian selections on their traditional folk instruments, along with some modern synthesizers. They received a protracted standing ovation.

In December, Dr. Leslie Domonkos, an OCA favorite, spoke personally and poignantly of his (plus his mother, father, and two siblings) flight from Hungary during the 1940s. His personal journey to America and ultimately to Farrell, Pennsylvania, was long and arduous, including stays in displaced persons camps for several years. But Hungarians were already in the Youngstown area, having arrived during the Great Hungarian emigration from 1890 to 1914. An obvious loss to Hungary, it was good for America to gain the workforce they needed to help build the industrial might of this new land. Although the greatest number of Hungarian immigrants who came to America in the early years were peasants, few of them continued in agriculture. Rather they settled in the industrial centers of the northeast and mid-west, many working in the coal mines and steel industry; as the years went by, Hungarians established churches, societies, and newspapers to remember the homeland and to maintain parts of that culture as they assimilated into the new culture. As with other immigrant groups, Youngstown's Hungarian-Americans assumed positions over time in Youngstown's business, political, civic, and intellectual life.

The meal was prepared by the Saxon club chefs, who served up a meal consisting of stuffed cabbage, chicken paprikash, buttered noodles Viennese cream cake. To add to the favorites of the evening, Roman Rudnytsky brilliantly favored us with Hungarian selections to the delight of all present. Both Dr. Domonkos and Professor Rudnytsky received standing ovations.

Jeanne Ann Garver Macejko, an active member of Welsh organizations and frequent visitor to Wales, spoke in January of the Welsh arrival to the Valley, which included her maternal and paternal great-grandparents. She has had a long love affair with Celtic culture, has visited Wales six times, and is an active member of Youngstown's St. David's Society and the Calon Lan Welsh Club.

The Welsh came to the Mahoning Valley in pretty significant numbers during the early and middle of the 19th century as Youngstown began to develop as an industrial powerhouse. Although many left Wales to escape poverty and some were farmers, many proved to be suitable workers in the iron and steel plants in the Valley, particularly in the smelting furnaces of Mineral Ridge and the rolling mills of Youngstown and Niles. Thomas Davis, among the first Welshmen known to have settled in the Valley, was credited with the discovery of coal on the property of Governor David Tod in Brier Hill. He and Morgan Reese were the first to cut the famous Brier Hill block coal. Other Welshmen came to mine coal here and in other sections of the Mahoning Valley. Welsh blended in well with others in the area and quickly moved into management and entrepreneurial positions, again in the coal and steel businesses. Welshmen founded a Congregational church in Brier Hill in 1845, but significant growth prompted members to construct in 1861 a new building near downtown at its present site. The building soon became an ethnic community center as well as a house of worship. The building is in disrepair today and will soon be removed. Among notable Welshmen in the area was John D. "Bonesetter" Reese, whose common touch of working on rich, poor, common, and famous endeared him far and wide. The meeting was held at Western Reserve United Methodist Church in Canfield, whose parishioners, led by Darlene Wells, served a pretty authentic ethnic meal that included roast beef and mashed potatoes, and Welsh cakes. Cultural enrichment was provided by John Tamblien, who recited Welsh poetry, and Megan Morris, who sang Welsh melodies.

The February meeting focus was Poland, with Reverend Joseph Rudjak as our speaker. He is the pastor at Sts. Peter and Paul Catholic Church in Youngstown. Father Rudjak, a dynamic priest of Polish ancestry, who frequently visits Poland, spoke lovingly and humorously about the Polish arrival to the Mahoning Valley. While Poles had some history in America early in our history, the earliest recording of Polish immigrants coming to the Valley is 1890, as many came to work at the Valley's iron and steel companies and railroads. Most settled near their place of employment, specifically in Brier Hill, on the northwest side of Youngstown and the lower south side. Churches were immediately built, with Catholic schools accompanying them. Fraternal organizations were also established to help immigrants in their struggles with their identities, values, and traditions as they were engaged in the acculturation process of a new land. The network of family, friends, and associates also helped to find housing and employment. As they became proud Americans, they also kept alive the spirit of their homeland: the traditions of blessing Easter baskets of food, of celebrating with the Polish language in song and prayer, of keeping alive foods such as pierogis, and celebrating Pulaski Day, Polish Heritage Day and Christmas Eve "Wigilia" with family and friends. The very talented musicians Jacek and Dorotea Sobieski performed beautifully; he was on the piano, and she was a marvelous opera singer. Their music wafted through the Polish National Church, to which we retired after a delicious meal (in the church hall) prepared by the parishioners of the church, the site of this meeting.

Featured in March was Ireland (of course), with Attorney Richard McLaughlin as our speaker. His talk included Irish history, Irish immigrants' arrival to the Valley, and some personal notes about his parents, who raised ten children, with Attorney McLaughlin the youngest. People who claim Irish ancestry are a dominant cultural group in the Mahoning Valley. The Irish have lived in the area since the earliest days of the Western Reserve with such names as Daniel Shehy, who accompanied John Young in a surveying expedition in the 1790s to mark the founding of Youngstown. They continued to be drawn to the Valley in subsequent years, particularly during the potato blight in Ireland in the 1840s and the resultant starvation of the mid-19th century. The Irish immigrants and their descendants who followed tended to cluster along the Shehy neighborhood, off Albert Street, in Smoky Hollow and Kilkenny, on the south side of the river along Poland Avenue, and in Coitsville. By 1860, they were among the most numerous foreign-born group-more than 15%. Their occupations included laborers, coal miners, and servants, as well as smaller numbers in the growing Youngstown economy. Additionally, they participated in the many trades and occupations of a growing Youngstown. A few were well off among those who arrived in the Valley during this famine migration to the area, but most of these young, laboring people fared slightly worse than the earlier Americans but about average for the other foreign-born. By 1900 the Irish were doing better economically. While most wage earners were still mostly laborers, others were advancing in industry and business. And increasingly, there were Irish among the professional classes, teachers, doctors, and lawyers, and many were homeowners. After 1921, Irish emigration to America dropped significantly, but the enthusiasm of the Irish for their ancestral homeland did not diminish. They were Irish Americans. And one no doubt heard Celtic music, step-dancing, and Irish stories in the Kensington Avenue McLaughlin home in the early-mid-20th century and similarly in the Colonial Drive home in the late 20th century and the early 21st century. Someone who could tell such stories and sing such songs was our cultural enrichment guest, Attorney Vincent Gilmartin, who waxed eloquently with both; Jackie Bibo accompanied him on the piano. The site of our meeting was the beautiful Youngstown Club, once a premier venue but now closed. They served a fine meal that had some Irish elements. We had one of our largest crowds, some 280 people.

In April, Sarah Brown-Clark, clerk of courts in Youngtown, a long-time professor at YSU, and area activist spoke of the Black Experience in America, with special emphasis upon the African American emigration from the U.S. South to the Mahoning Valley. The institution of slavery in America is as old as our nation, with the largest number living in the South. Some emigrated to the North, either by being manumitted then moving North or later by the "Underground Railroad" to escape from bondage. While some traveled to the Youngstown area via local "railroad stations", most continued their travels to Canada. Blacks came to the Valley in modest numbers until 1918, when a heavy migration from the South brought many to the city to work in the steel mills. Despite the fact that Blacks were often not welcomed by city natives, last in line for the best jobs, and limited in where they could live, many left an impressive mark on the community. While ultimately, some Blacks did become members of the professions, most worked at one form of labor or another. Increasingly through the 20th century, Blacks attended schools and colleges, became teachers and administrators, and even Board of Education members. Additionally, by the last third of the 20th century, YSU had become integrated, employing a number of Black professors; several Board of Trustees members were also appointed. Eventually, the Black community contributed to health care professionals, funeral directors, small businesses, such as barbers, beauty schools, utility and government employees, political leaders, artists, and musicians. Probably the most visible are the pastors of the Black churches, about which the social organization of the African American community is largely centered. Today, the African American community has grown in numbers and influence, providing a much more diverse choice of careers.

We met at The Georgetown, which was becoming one of our favorite venues. The meal contained some "soul" food items and special desserts by Marcella Allen. The evening concluded with Sophia Brooks singing sensitive spirituals that were both hopeful and mournful.

The May meeting featured the Arab World, with specific emphasis on the Lebanese, the most numerous of Arabs in the Valley. Our speaker was Ray Nakely, of Lebanese descent, who has visited Lebanon and has been an advocate for American understanding of the Arab world. Mr. Nakely has long been active in international affairs while at YSU and continued as president of the United Nations Association, Youngstown chapter. He has also been active with St. Maron's Church, where he is a member. He began his address with prose written by Kahlil Gibran, which starts with: "I believe that you are contributors to this new civilization. I believe that you have inherited from your forefathers an ancient dream, a song, a prophecy, which you can proudly lay as a gift of gratitude upon the lap of America." It was in the late 19th century that the first Arab settlers came to the Valley; they hailed from the area now known as Lebanon. Many Lebanese in the community, although proud of their native language, do not necessarily consider themselves Arabs. Although Lebanese came in small numbers during the 20th century, they assimilated well and became contributing members of the community. Major accomplishments of the Lebanese community were the construction of the present Maronite Church and the National Shrine of Our Lady of Lebanon, which had as additions the Antonine Sisters' Adult Day Care facility. During the last half of the 20th century, a number of Lebanese began their own successful businesses, namely in the area of wholesale and retail food services, building and painting contracting carpet retailers, real estate, and bars and restaurants; others entered the professional world as doctors, educators, and lawyers. In a word, the Arabs/Lebanese in the Valley have managed to integrate rather well and have reached prominent positions in the community.

The site of the meeting was The National Shrine of Our Lady of Lebanon Social Hall, whose caterer, Mike Varga, served up an outstanding Middle Eastern meal. Cultural enrichment was provided by the singing Antonine Sisters of Lebanon and the lively young adult dancers from St. Maron's Church.

The final meeting of OCA's 17th year focused on the Czech Republic and Slovakia, with Michael Kurilla serving again as our June speaker. His well-crafted presentation addressed his family's arrival to the U.S., then to Pennsylvania, and finally to the Mahoning Valley. He has done considerable research on the country of his ancestors. Mr. Kurilla earned his B.A. and M.A. degrees from YSU and considerable doctoral work at Kent State.

Czechoslovakian emigration to the Mahoning Valley was basically the settlement of Slovaks and Ruthenians, thousands of them during the period of 1890-1924, but only a trickle of Czechs. Those thousands came, as with others from southern and eastern Europe, to work in the steel mills, and they tended to live near where they worked. The two largest areas of the population were in East Youngstown (now Campbell) and the Steelton area. During the course of the 20th century, a plethora of clubs and societies were formed, and six Roman Catholic nationality churches were established in the Valley, reflecting the large streams of incoming immigrants. The contributions of and the legacy of these Slavic groups have been significant. They provided the labor pool of the blue-collar steel mill workers, who did so much to build Mahoning Country. After a short period of assimilation, they developed all types of businesses-doctors, dentists, lawyers, grocers, taverns, insurance men, banks, and more to provide services for a segment of the population. They also made contributions in local government service and politics, as well as significant contributions in the social, cultural, and musical organizations of the community and, finally, in the area of sports.

We met at St. Matthias Church Hall in Youngstown with Carolyn Catering preparing an abundant and very ethnic Slavic dinner. To conclude this evening, YSU Professor John Wilcox, on violin, and his daughter Julia, on piano, entertained us with lovely Slavic selections.

Dare I say we enjoyed another successful season with more than 300 paid memberships, meeting attendance averaging about 225-250 people, with one at 280 attendees, with ten outstanding programs and dinners, each at a different venue-including several new ones: Youngstown Club, National Shrine of Lebanon, Western Reserve United Methodist Church and St. Matthias Church. OCA also sponsored another actual visit- to China, with several members joining an AAA tour. A special follow-up meeting to discuss the trip was held in August

For its 18th year, the Ohio Cultural Alliance continued with the theme of "The Immigrant Experience: From the Old World to the Mahoning Valley". In September, Dr. John Boehm was our speaker again. He is an active member of the Saxon Club, the site of the meeting, a German language instructor at YSU, and a frequent visitor to Germany, but most importantly, he spoke about his leaving Germany in the 1940s. His memories were bitter-sweet as he recalled his youthful years as the Nazis were becoming dominant. Germans were among the earliest settlers in the Western Reserve, including the Youngstown area, but they came to the Mahoning Valley in large numbers during the years 1850-1870. While many were farmers, others distinguished themselves as bankers, educators, architects, physicians, merchants, contractors, and engineers, among other occupations. While assimilating, German ethnicity was kept alive by various cultural organizations such as churches, singing societies, gymnastic societies, and social clubs such as The Mannerchor and The Saxon Club. While Germany produced many of the leaders of the Valley, perhaps four families have cast the broadest net: the Deibels, the Renners, the Maags, and the Stambaughs.

Germans continued to arrive in Youngstown through the 19th century, diminishing in the 20th century, with German influence significant in the earlier period but damaged by the first and second world wars. However, throughout, the Germans had been considered to be energetic, professional, and strong people. Their contributions and the legacy of so many leaders have been legion. Assimilation and world events have not diminished the appreciation that German-Americans have regarding their heritage and the part they have played in developing the Mahoning Valley. Examples of those characteristics are the very site in which we met, The Saxon Club, the very ethnic German meal which we were served, and the music of the large aggregation delighting us with German music, the Concordia Chorus.

Our speakers for October were Dr. Martha Pallante, chair of the History Department at YSU, whose ancestry is part Norwegian, and her daughter Sarah who studies that culture and presented aspects of Norwegian life during History Day at YSU and at the state level. They spoke of their Scandinavian descendants who emigrated to the valley in the late 1800s and early 1900s, although some came in smaller numbers in the 1870s, settling in the Hazelton area of Youngstown. Among those early arrivals from Sweden were Gustave and Alfred Hammar. From the 1880s through the 1920s, Scandinavian immigrants joined the Valley's growing industrial force, where they engaged primarily in the making of steel and the construction trades. Most of the Scandinavians that came to the Valley during these years joined their kin who settled on the Southside of Youngstown. Unlike some of the other immigrants who came to the area, Scandinavians attracted relatively little notice; they were, after all, white. Fair skin and hair, these immigrants blended easily into the fabric of the community. The majority of Scandinavians found employment with the burgeoning steel mills, with local construction companies, or in a variety of small commercial enterprises such as Alfred Hammar and Sons, a furniture and carpet retailer on the Southside.

The Scandinavian immigrants easily transitioned into the main street of American life as they made their contributions to education, religion, and reform movements. They were predominantly literate and valued access to schools, and they enthusiastically practiced their faiths and participated in their fraternal organizations. Initially living and working in the heart of the city in its industrial core, they moved to more prosperous areas north and south of the city by the mid and late 20th century. As they advanced through the economic and social strata of the Valley, they were absorbed by the majority population. Aside from a few church affiliations, Scandinavians have largely disappeared as a distinct ethnic population in the region.

The meal was prepared by Darlene Wells and staff, who are all parishioners of Western Reserve United Methodist Church which was the site of this month's meeting. We were once again treated to the beautiful music by Betty Bannon of the accordion, Sally Dolovy on the violin, and Jeffrey Bremmer on the base. They included music that was peaceful and reminded us of the long dark nights that our speakers reminded us of. Their very appropriate music included compositions of Grieg and Sebelius.

Greece was our focus in November. Dr. James Kiriazis spoke of his native country and some of his early successes and failure as a Greek in the Mahoning Valley. He was with YSU for over fifty years, including in the 1950s when I had him as a student. His activities on campus and off are legendary: as a professor, a chairman of the Sociology and Anthropology Department, a host of a radio program, and an avid promoter of Greek activities in the area. The ambiance of the evening was captivating, from Dr. Kiriazis' talk to the authentic Greek meal served at St. Nicholas Greek Orthodox Church Hall in Youngstown, the site of the meeting, and the beautiful music of Georgio and Stefanos Theofilis playing traditional Greek string instruments.

Greek migration to the Valley began in 1888 when George and James Chelekis arrived, who, along with those fellow Greeks who came later, worked with the other new immigrants at the laboring jobs. Their appearance, language, religion, food, and their overall culture appeared exotic and mysterious to Americans, so they had some serious obstacles early on. They were also willing to take work with low wages and often dangerous. (In a personal note, when I was working at the Campbell works of the Youngstown Sheet and Tube, Open Hearth, Greeks had advanced to one of the most dangerous jobs there, as second helpers who had to tap the furnaces bare-chested, poking the furnace with a rod until the molten metal started to ooze out!) Greek immigration into the Valley came in three waves: 1890-1924, 1950-1960, and after 1965. The more recent ones bore almost no resemblance to the earliest immigrants in their acceptance and their acclimation to the American culture. But through their church community, the social organizations, and family, they retained some of their culture. They, as with other ethnic groups, eventually moved into the professions and business. Their entrepreneurial spirit is manifested clearly in that as early as the 1920's Greek-Americans owned outright or were partners in some 400 businesses within the city limits of Youngstown.

In December, the focus was Croatia, with Jamie Marich speaking and performing. Of Croatian ancestry, she also spent two and one-half years in Croatia/Bosnia-Hercegovina teaching and learning. She sang for us beautiful ethnic melodies, and she played the guitar, violin, and mandolin. We again were treated to an authentic meal organized by Francis Piersante and staff, who are the caterers for Croatian Lodge #66, the site of our meeting. Ms. Marich offered fascinating reflections of her grandfather, who immigrated to the Valley early in the 20th century and delighted us with music in his memory.

Following the pattern of the other Slavic countries, Croatian emigration to America and to the Mahoning Valley began in the 1890s with the push of conditions in the homeland and the pull of good employment here. The young men usually emigrated first and took the more menial jobs. They often lived in crowded boarding houses until they saved enough money to send for family. Landlords and tavern keepers were usually the first to learn English and often acted as welcome confidents, interpreters, bankers, and intermediaries in a new world that offered the opportunity but also a dependable supply of charlatans. Their numbers probably peaked during the years 1915-1918, ostensibly to avoid the war, then tapered off after World War I. These early immigrants have been described as laboring people, some of whom helped lay the first pavement and streetcar tracks on Federal Street and cut down corn and wheat fields to make way for the imposing steel mills.

As families grew and finances improved, the newcomers organized activities: Sunday picnics featuring traditional barbecued lamb and apple strudel; athletic events; ethnic plays; and dances with Tamburitza music, polka and kolo dancing, and singing of traditional songs. The Croatian presence in the Valley could best be recounted via the establishment of fraternal organizations, churches, political groups, and newspapers. Education was revered by these immigrants; it was the road to success. They saw their families grow and contribute to the Mahoning Valley with businesses such as Yallech Lumber; John Borak, businessman and mayor of Campbell and George Vukovich, mayor of Youngstown; many teachers, athletes, such as Leo Mogus (basketball) and Frank Sinkowich (football); and judges Joseph Kolmacic and Robert Kalafut, all part of a dream which started somewhere in Croatia and became a reality in Mahoning County.

The January focus was Turkey. St Michael's Church Hall in Canfield was nearly converted into a Turkish interior as Gular Koknar, national executive director of the Turkish Cultural Foundation, spoke. The meal, very authentically Turkish, and the music complemented the ambiance. The music was performed by Ali Ihsan Karamavruc and his wife Mukaddes: he played a string instrument called saz or baglama, and they both sang. Ms. Koknar spoke to us about her organization which was founded to promote and preserve Turkish cultural heritage. She and Dr. Birsen Karpak of YSU School of Business addressed the country of Turkey, indicating the Turks are typically Moslem but that Turkey has been officially secular since President Mustafa Kemal Ataturk. Therefore, Turks living in the Valley are Turks first and Muslims second.

The first Turks came to the United States around 1900. The Mahoning Valley has a small Turkish community, with the first Turks coming to the Valley in the mid-1950s. Some came for post-graduate studies, while others came for improved economic opportunities. Unlike many of the earlier immigrant groups, those from Turkey usually had some education, even professional and graduate degrees. Another reason they immigrated to the U.S. and the Valley was for better education and better opportunities for their children. Although immigration to a foreign country is never easy, almost all the Turks spoke English upon arrival and had some advanced education. So, most were well received in the communities where they settled; most chose Boardman and Canfield. Although there are but a few Turks in the valley, they are well-represented as medical doctors, university professors, architects, economists, and restaurant owners. They are Turkish Americans.

The Carpatho-Rusyn tradition was the focus in February, with our speaker, John Righetti, president of the Carpatho-Rusyn Society, based in Pittsburgh. He was a knowledgeable, passionate, and entertaining speaker. The Carpatho-Rusyns are a distinct Eastern Slavic people who lived for more than a thousand years in remote villages scattered along the foothills and valleys of the Carpathian Mountains of East Central Europe. These villages were located mostly among those Western Slavs (Slovaks and Poles), Hungarians, Romanians, and Ukrainians. Although they have been known by a variety of other names, they typically referred to themselves as Ruthenian, Rusnaks, or Lemko for those who settled on the northern slopes of the Carpathians. They generally worship at a Byzantine Catholic Church/ Russian Greek Catholic, unlike most of the other Slavs. The Ruthenian migration patterns closely shadowed that of the Slovaks, given their close proximity and the interrelationships of Ruthenians and Slovaks in Europe. Thus, it was difficult to differentiate one from the other. Indeed, the Ruthenians were often misidentified as they settled in America and the Youngstown area. By the mid-20th century, there were 4,000 foreign-born and next-generation Ruthenians in Mahoning County as they made their contributions to the Valley. Today, the name is hardly known by the average resident of the Valley, usually subsumed by the Slovak people. The meeting was held at St. Matthias Church in Youngstown; Carolyn's Catering prepared a sumptuous ethnic Slavic meal. The evening concluded with a quartet from Pittsburgh. Making up the group were Dean Poloka, Mike Liberatore, Robert, and Brian Barko, who played Rusyn melodies on traditional instruments.

OCA's vice president Mary Ann Senediak was the speaker in March. She spoke of her own ethnic background, Ukraine. Dressed in native ethnic costumes, she also displayed a host of ethnic items during her presentation. The meeting was held at the Ursuline Mother House in Canfield; Livosky Catering served a wonderful Slavic meal. Ukrainian immigration to the U.S. took place in three waves: the late 19th century, the interwar period, and the post-World War II period. The first Ukrainians arrived in Mahoning County and settled on the west side of Youngstown. As with most of the immigrants from southern and eastern Europe, they worked in the steel mills and labor-intensive jobs. The Ukrainian churches are at the heart of Youngstown's thriving Ukrainian community. However, Ukrainians had difficulties with their religious affiliation. Ukrainians, associated with the Roman Catholic Church for centuries in Ukraine, ran into difficulty with the Irish-dominated Catholic hierarchy, which insisted upon celibate clergy, but Ukrainians were accustomed to having married clergy. As a result, many turned to the Byzantine Rite of the Roman Catholic Church. Many also practiced the Orthodox faith.

As with most of the immigrants from southern and eastern Europe, the Ukrainians initially had problems with a new language and a new culture. They, too, had menial jobs and blue-collar jobs because of their limited education. An additional problem from Europe, which is reflected in America and the Valley, is the relationship between Russia and Ukraine, with the latter having a strong belief in democracy. While the Ukrainians of the Valley have striven to retain much of their heritage through their churches, festivals, dances, and songs, they are well assimilated as they became Ukrainian Americans. As an example of their culture, the

Ansembel Karavan, a talented dance group from western Pennsylvania, provided our cultural enrichment.

The April meeting featured Puerto Rico, with local businessman Flor "Shorty" Navarro as our speaker. He spoke about his (and other Hispanics) coming to the mainland U.S. and the Mahoning Valley and how he came to epitomize the "American dream". In telling his story, he related that he was fourteen in the 1950s when his family emigrated from Puerto Rico so his father could get a job in the steel mills. He said he always liked automobiles, so much so that when he was 15-16 years old, he would take engines apart and put them back together. As a student at East High School, he went to work in a gas station which increased his interest in automobiles. Thereafter, he joined the Marine Corps, where he honed his skills. Starting with $600 after the military stint, he bought a couple of junkers, which he repaired and cleaned up and sold them for a profit. He repeated this process, increasing the number of vehicles each time, and ultimately, he opened a dealership and became one of the largest in the area.

Hispanics overall and Puerto Ricans, in particular, are among the latecomers to come to the Mahoning Valley and, as such, started at the bottom. Only a few were in the area before the 1940s, coming in larger numbers into the early 1960s. Most of them came from Puerto Rico when the local mills were flourishing. Typical of these immigrants were Rafael Romero and Porfirio Esparra, both of whom took jobs at the Youngstown Sheet and Tube. Mr. Romero married and raised a family and became an influential leader in the community. He and his wife were instrumental in establishing the first Hispanic church in the city, St. Rose of Lima. Mr. Esparra came to Youngstown as a musician, but the job at the Sheet and Tube was more-steady. He reared a family of ten children, all of whom earned YSU college degrees; they all served the community well. Dr. Alfonso Garcia, a long-time faculty member of YSU, and Henry Guzman worked to set up Organization Civica y Cultural Americana (OCCHA) that helped immigrants to acclimate to America. Mexicans were the second largest group to come to the Valley, with smaller groups coming from other parts of Latin America.

The meal was prepared by the chefs at the Youngstown Club, who included in the menu some Hispanic cuisine. Music by Filipe Gonzalez and Mary Ann Santiago, playing their guitars, wafted through the Club as the musicians moved from table to table to the delight of the large crowd.

Dr. Y.T. Chiu spoke of his native China at our May meeting. His remarks were incisive and passionate as he spoke about his coming to the Valley and his impressions of the U.S. from a "new American's point of view. Born in Hong Kong, Dr. Chiu moved to China during World War II, then to Taiwan. He emigrated to Youngstown in 1962, where he has engaged in his practice of plastic surgery ever since.

Asians are among the most recent immigrants to the Valley. Although some Chinese came during the mid-20th century to establish Chinese restaurants, their descendants soon joined the professional cohorts who came as professionals, basically in medicine and education. Among those are Drs. Kong Oh, Hai Shiuh Wang, Yih-Wu (Andy) Liu, Pei Huang and Dr. Chiu. There are fewer Japanese and Koreans in the Valley. The men came seeking political asylum or a better education; women came as G.I. brides. YSU helped some of them, notably Dr. Gail Okawa of the English Department. Koreans came in the 1970s for business and professional opportunities; among them are Tae S. Ro, an import/export businessman, and Dr. Hyun W. Kim, a YSU professor of Mechanical Engineering. Although only a small number live here, they have established several small churches.

The ambiance could not be better, in that the site of the meeting was the Grand Buffet in Boardman that offered an extensive buffet of Asian delicacies, and the magical voices of YSU professors Drs. Allan Mosher and Misook Yun, who sang excerpts from Madame Butterfly.

The June meeting featured a film, "Island of Hope, Island of Tears", which focused on immigrants coming through Ellis Island. The film complemented our review of eighteen countries during the last two years by showing how many who came to the Mahoning Valley first passed through Ellis Island. The documentary vividly depicted what we have been addressing for two years, indicating the joy and sorrow of those who emigrated from their homelands. We noted many commonalities of people like us and different from us; we learned that all ethnic groups have genius within them- genius knows no boundary. We heard many poignant stories of those leaving their homelands and arriving in their new milieu, with welcoming greetings to fierce enmity. Most had a difficult time leaving, getting here, and those early years of acculturation while here. Most had virtually nothing in the way of financial wherewithal upon arrival. All groups had some very successful immigrants and descendants who contributed significantly to America and the Mahoning Valley.

We met at St. Matthias Church Hall in Youngstown with a meal prepared by Carolyn Catering, now one of our favorite caterers. She prepared a variety of ethnic foods, representing Slavic, Italian and German cuisine. At this final meeting of the season, we celebrated all of the ethnic groups of the Valley. Cultural enrichment abounded: with beautiful music through dinner by Betty Bannon on accordion, Sally Dolovy on violin, and "The Youngstown Connection," who thrilled us with their singing and dancing, which stressed inclusion and patriotism. What a fitting conclusion to another wonderful year.

In a footnote to this theme of immigration, I offer a summary of an article from the Cleveland Plain Dealer, entitled "Immigrants' Kids: Nation's Brainy Superstars" (July 20, 2004), "The children of immigrants are becoming the top math and science students in the United States, dominating academic competitions and representing the strongest hope the nation has of keeping an edge in high-tech and biomedical fields. ...and that their children are the nation's rising intellectual superstars. If opponents of immigration had succeeded over the last 20 years, two-thirds of the most outstanding future American scientists and mathematicians would not be here today because U.S. policy would have barred their parents from entering the U.S".

My Paternal Grandfather (left), my Uncle John, my father George and my Paternal Grandmother (right).
The Balomirean (aka Beelen) family emigrated from Romania in the early 1900's

Style of Five

Dr. Allan Mosher

Alexandra "Sandy" Vansuch

Jamie Marich

Sophla Brooks

Flor "Shorty" Navarro

Ray Nakely

Attorney Richard McLaughlin

XIV. Enriching Elements of Life

Inspiring discourse, rousing music, delicious cuisine, and fragrant scents welcomed the Ohio Cultural Alliance members that met in September 2005 to commence our 19th year. We met at D.D. Davis Friends Riverside Gardens at Mill Creek Park almost exactly one year after the horrific events of 9/11 and in the wake of the natural disaster of hurricane Katrina. So much of our life at that time was, in one way or another, related to both of those tragedies. We needed, I thought, to find ways to deal with these problems. We surely could not ignore them, nor could we will them away. But we can consider balance to our sentiments and place these and other problems of our times in perspective. To make our local contribution to this more positive perspective, the OCA offered for the next two years topics that we called "Enriching Elements of Life". There are activities and/or disciplines that tend to enrich, to ennoble, or to move humankind to a higher purpose. These are elements that also create attitudes of creativity and insights that move us to those higher purposes. The topics we came up with were religion, music, drama/theater, art, literature, film, dance, journalism, philosophy, nature, history, poetry, humor, education, architecture, politics, and law.

Of course, we know these enriching elements do not always lead to a "higher purpose". Sometimes they are perverted: music that led Jews to the gas chambers; film that is used for propaganda; art that tends to demean; religion that justifies war; journalism that serves up lies. But our approach in the Ohio Cultural Alliance envisions the positive side of these enriching elements of life. We started this journey over the next two years.

Dr. Chris Bache introduced the theme of "Enriching Elements of Life" in that September meeting by suggesting that "doing nothing consciously" can lead to a state of mind which often inspires us. He wondered if there is any one activity that enriches us, ennobles us, moves us to a higher purpose, stimulates creativity, awakens altruistic thoughts and actions, or inspires our ethereal selves. He concluded that there was only one activity that could fuel all of these undertakings at the same time, and that is the art of doing nothing. "In fact, it's an essential activity. It is so essential, in fact, so much an assumed part of the rhythm of our lives that we tend to overlook its significance entirely." Dr. Bache argued, too, that "every religion he has studied has valued silence and practiced meditation which gives credence to the importance of doing nothing consciously. Art, music, dance, poetry, etc., can be created and appreciated in such a milieu," Dr. Bache suggested.

A YSU jazz quartet (part of the famous YSU Jazz Ensemble), led by Seth Rogers and advised by Kent Engelhart, put us in a state of mind that stimulated and inspired us. This is yet another example of the multi-faceted and multi-talented people that make up Youngstown State University. The meal was prepared by Catering by Robynn.

Our speaker for October was Monsignor John Ashton, who spoke of the enriching nature of religion. Pastor of St. Lucy's Catholic Church, biblical scholar (having spent several years in such study in Rome), and an excellent speaker (his stentorian voice, itself, is enriching), he adroitly addressed the major religions of the world and their collective effect on humanity. He stressed the centrality of religion, stressing that "religion has had an incredible influence on our existence, albeit an enriching one. From prehistoric times to the present, we have looked to religion to alleviate the problems and enrich the joys in our lives."

Monsignor Ashton discussed in some detail the religions which have the greatest number of adherents, beginning with Christianity with the most followers. He related how those early Christians popularized the Hebrew teaching that every human being is created in God's image and all human beings are created equal. The religion with the second largest number of followers is Islam. For Muslims, confessing the proper fundamental beliefs is the basis from which all actions flow. The religion with the third largest number of followers is Hinduism. Its goal is to offer attractive paths of devotion for every type of personality at every social level. The fourth religion with the most followers in the world today is Buddhism which holds to a middle path of living that avoids extremes in pursuit of pleasures or the denial of necessities. In Monsignor Ashton's judgment, "religion is the penultimate enricher of the elements of life because it includes a sense of duty, a sense of righteousness, and the belief that there is more in our world than science and technology." He ends with a reaffirmation of the preeminence of religion with how he began: a quotation of Scottish author Muriel Spark, "Religion and art first; then philosophy, lastly science. That is the order of the great subjects of life; that's their order of prominence."

Cultural enrichment, facilitated by OCA member Warren Harrell, was provided by Phillips CME Chapel Church male chorus, who performed several religious selections that were reverent and upbeat. Meeting in St. Lucy's Church Hall, the dinner was prepared by Monica's Catering, one of the primary caterers for St. Lucy's functions.

Music was the focus in November. Dr. Ronald Gould, YSU Dana School of Music, spoke of and provided examples (on the organ) of the enriching nature of music. He set many moods with a variety of types of music, which he said is the universal language of mankind, or as Shakespeare declared, "the food of love". Giving witness to the importance of music and its enrichment nature was Martin Luther: "Besides theology, music is the only art capable of affording peace and joy of the heart like that induced by the study of the science of divinity. This is why the prophets preferred music before all the other arts, proclaiming the Word in psalms and hymns." Dr. Gould argued that psychologists tell us that music is the most emotional of all the arts. Its sound world immediately envelops us and demands our attention as perhaps no other art form does." In keeping with the closeness of religion and music is Robert Browning's observation, "God has a few of us whom He whispers in the ear; the rest may reason and welcome; 'tis we musicians know." Dr. Gould spoke of these aphorisms and the joys of timeless music and of new musical discoveries, as he spoke and regaled us with some of that timeless music. We met at the Canfield, Western Reserve United Methodist Church, whose caterers, organized by Darlene Wells, served the usual wonderful meal.

In December, the focus was drama/theater, with an OCA meeting at the Youngstown Playhouse in Youngstown. Dr. George McCloud, YSU Dean of Fine and Performing Arts, spoke briefly of the excitement and wonder of the theater, after which he and Joseph Monda, YSU student and veteran actor in the local Youngstown Playhouse; and Walter Ulbricht, Executive Director of Marketing and Communications at YSU did humorous, thoughtful and enriching excerpts from a variety of plays. Running through the evening in the theater proper, we showed some video examples, "Julius Caesar" and "Tony Awards," when members were not seated for dinner and/or after dinner but before the live program. Dr. McCloud began his comments by distinguishing drama from the theater. "Theater is a form of performance in which the audience is asked to participate with its imagination to complete the experience of some story or some other form of reality. The type of theater we will offer this evening is sometimes called 'readers' theater' because all the performers do is read, and most of the work is done by the audience. What kind of work is required of the audience? It is the work of imagination." He also introduced to us the epic mode, which is a combination of the lyric (the mode in which a world is being described rather than shown) as opposed to the dramatic (where the audience is having a world demonstrated or actually shown to the audience. They performed for us an adaptation of William Goldman's novel, "Boys and Girls Together," which Dr. McCloud called "The Nose is for Laughing." The readings were thoughtfully done, the wisdom shone through and ended with "The ears are for hearing, The lips are to smile. The nose is for laughing, The tongue is for guile."

All of the various forms of drama and theater offered this evening exhibited how these elements of life could be enriching. Suggesting such positive attributes is the comment of Henry James, "The anomalous fact is that the theater, so called, can flourish in barbarism, but that any drama worth speaking of can develop but in the air of civilization."

Our meal was prepared by Livosky Catering, now becoming one of OCA's favorites. This particular meeting was a bit chaotic in that the large crowd could not all eat at the same time. So, we needed to eat during two sittings. In all, we were reminded of the wonderful world of drama and theater, adding to our lives as being enriching leading to understanding and empathy.

The January meeting focus was art, with Dr. Lou Zona, YSU Art Department, and Executive Director of The Butler Institute of American Art, the site of this meeting, as our speaker. He shared his enthusiasm and knowledge for the discipline in general and with The Butler in particular.

Ralph Waldo Emerson defined art as "silent poetry and speaking painting". A painter was once asked by a viewer to explain his painting. The artist responded: "If I could have explained it orally, I wouldn't have painted it." President Lyndon Johnson once said: "Art is not a tender or fragile thing. It has been kept alive in the habitations of cruelty and oppressions. It has struggled toward the light from the manifold darkness of war and conflict, and persecutions. Yet it flourishes most abundantly when the artist can speak as he wishes and describes the world as he sees it without any official direction." We saw varied expressions of art in the wonderful Butler Museum of American Art. Some anonymous wisdom I have read: "Great art is precisely that which never was nor will be taught; it is preeminently and finally the expression of the spirits of great men and women, and Art is what separates man from beast."

In addition to the entrancing and enriching works of art at The Butler and the mellifluous words of Dr. Zona, we were also privileged to hear the dulcet tones again of Dr. Allan Mosher and Jennifer Davis as they sang beautiful melodies, including excerpts from "Porgy and Bess". Talk about an enriching evening. Who could help being uplifted by the many ways in which our senses were affected? Our meal was prepared by Chapters Thymely Events/Winslows Café, who was then the official caterer for The Butler.

Literature was the topic in February with our speaker Dr. Sherry Linkon, YSU, English Department. Samuel Johnson wrote that "The glory of every people arises from its authors", a sentiment Dr. Linkon would certainly affirm. She argues that "stories help us to make sense of the truth. Yes, they make the truth more palatable, but they also make it understandable. The first way that literature enhances our lives, then, is by helping us understand the world around us. The human mind seeks order and reason. We want things to make sense, so we turn to stories because narrative provides a sense of cause and effect." Dr. Linkon said that "one quality that sets literature aside from other forms of story, like theater or film, is its portability." Yet another quality that sets literature apart from other forms of storytelling is that it provides special enrichment in its attention to perspective, which thus gives us access to someone else's version of the story. "Finally," she asserts, "our literature gives us the gift of language in rich and enjoyable ways." She shared her enthusiasm and the many rewards of literature and ended with another reward of literature in that "it's just plain fun."

We met for this meeting at The Georgetown in Boardman and again enjoyed their usual excellent and varied buffet. Keeping with the mood of enrichment in our lives, Corrine Morini sang with the accompaniment of Diane Yasvek on piano, melodies that were beautiful and helped conclude a fulfilling evening.

Dr. Rick Shale, YSU English Department, was the speaker in March. His focus was film, which he said was a synthesis of most of the other enriching elements which we had addressed during the year. The Production Code of the Motion Picture Association of America in the early 1960s set forth the following: "Most art appeals to the mature. This art appeals at once to every class, mature, immature, developed, undeveloped, law-abiding, criminal…." Dr. Shale traced the history of film development and reported that "the early movies were not only an entertaining diversion; they were seeds for social and cultural change." He continued with the statement, "movies matter because they are the mythology of the modern era." And as such, the films were produced in and featured American matters, which were shown worldwide. These films exported our culture, our image, and our values all over the world. "Movies, especially American films, promote the idea that one can change in positive ways. American film audiences are addicted to happy endings. The American dream is grounded in the notion that we are a classless society where upward mobility is not only possible but also probable, where wrongs can be righted, and justice can triumph." Dr. Shale showed clips of films of several of the most memorable movies of all time, which described how the movies enriched, challenged, and enlightened our lives and how they provide memories not only of the films themselves but of the movie-going experience itself. We met again at the Saxon Club and were served their usual outstanding meal.

The April meeting featured dance with Anita Lin as the speaker and the choreographer of dance selections performed by her students. Ms. Lin had been Artistic Director of the Ballet Western reserve from 1982 to 2009. She has danced professionally with the Cincinnati Ballet Company, the New Orleans Ballet Company, and in London, England, where she studied under the Royal Academy of Dance technique. She danced as principal with the University of Louisville Preparatory Dance Company. An anonymous observer offered the comment: "When you get a chance to sit or dance, I hope you dance." A popular song by Lee Ann Womack by the same title has captured that mood also. "I hope you never lose your sense of wonder, You get your fill to eat but always keep that hunger, May you never take one single breath for granted, God forbid love ever leave you empty-handed, I hope you still feel small when you stand beside the ocean, Whenever one door closes I hope one more opens, Promise me that you'll give faith a fighting chance, And when you get the choice to sit out or dance, I hope you dance…I hope you dance." Ms. Lin gave us a brief look at the history of ballet which began in 15th-century Italy, where lavish royal banquets were held. They included food, music, storytelling, traditional dances, pantomime, and eventually ballet. It soon became international, with four distinct teaching methods emerging: French, Danish, Russian, and Italian/English. Ms. Lin added, "The style of American teachers tends to reflect our culture: a melting pot of various techniques and styles to create something uniquely our own." After riveting comments on her and her family coming to the Youngstown area, she and several of her students demonstrated intricate steps and movements of ballet. The meeting was held at Our Lady of Mt. Carmel Social Hall in Youngstown, where we enjoyed another culinary experience directed by caterer Lou Fusillo.

Andrea Wood spoke of journalism as an Enriching Element of Life at the May meeting. Ms. Wood is the founder and editor of The Business Journal, a former investigative reporter for WYTV, and a local resident since 1974. She doubtless would agree with Thomas Jefferson when he uttered the words, "were it left to me to decide whether we should have a government without newspapers or newspapers without a government, I should not hesitate a moment to prefer the latter." We are enriched by what we read; we can hold more intelligent discussions with friends, family, or acquaintances. "The enrichment is emotional as well as intellectual", Ms. Wood asserted. "Journalism, in all its forms, enriches our lives as it helps us to see the world more clearly."

She actually began her talk with, "Journalism has enriched her life, but it certainly has not made her rich." She cited other noteworthy comments made by individuals from different eras: "A good newspaper, I suppose, is a nation talking to itself", wrote Arthur Miller, and "I fear three newspapers more than a hundred thousand bayonets," bellowed Napoleon. Indeed, our very Constitution contains the Bill of Rights as Amendment I, Freedom of the press.

This meeting was held at St. Matthias Church Hall in Youngstown with a meal prepared by Carolyn Catering, serving her really delicious and abundant ethnic food. Cultural enrichment was provided by Roman Rudnytsky, who took time out from his teaching at YSU and his wide-ranging travels at sites around the world and on innumerable cruises. He was becoming our most frequent guest artist and the most enthusiastic responses from his audiences.

The final meeting of the season was in June; it featured Dr. Thomas Shipka, who addressed the Enriching Element of Life: Philosophy. Dr. Shipka, YSU professor and chairman of the Philosophy Department, author, WYSU contributor, and activist on and off campus. After he set the stage for philosophy with a definition, he stated: "Literally, philosophy means the love of wisdom, from the Greek words philein (to love) and sophia (wisdom or knowledge or truth). Technically, we can define philosophy as the evaluation of beliefs to determine whether they are true, and the evaluations of practices-customs-to determine whether they are sensible and ethical." Dr. Shipka said that John Stuart Mill's work, "On Liberty" could be used as a model for the value of philosophy and the value of individuality and toleration and is "at once a masterpiece of writing and a pillar of individual liberty in modern civilization". He asked us to reflect on the lessons which Mill offers in "On Liberty" to help us in today's troubled world. Dr. Shipka chronicled many of the world's ills-both at home and abroad-and how Mill's philosophy could ameliorate many of them. "What John Stuart Mill offers to the modern world is hope", Dr. Shipka concluded. We met at the beautiful Youngstown Club (now closed) in downtown Youngstown and were served an elegant dinner prepared by the Club chefs. Cultural enrichment was provided by the Wade Raridon Singers, who concluded the evening and the 19th year with beautiful selections that also evoked hope and understanding. Among the varied works sung were "In These Delightful, Pleasant Groves" (1690), "Bring Him Home" (Les Miserables), and Selections from Carousel (1945). What a good ending to the first half of our theme, "Enriching Elements of Life," to be followed next year with the second half of the same theme.

Having been enriched by the various "Elements of Life" during the ten meetings of last year, we launched our 20th year (2006-07) with ten more topics, beginning with nature. In September, Sue Dicken, Executive Director of Mill Creek Park, and Carol Potter, Development Director, were our speakers, continuing our theme, "Enriching Elements of Life: Nature". Charles Kingsley's reflections are certainly in keeping with those of our speakers: "Beauty is God's handwriting. Welcome it in every fair face, every fair sky, every fair flower". Our speakers explained how Mill Creek Park's Fellows Riverside Gardens gave credence to Kingsley's reflections: The twelve-acre display garden features a landscape of remarkable beauty with diverse and colorful plant displays, roses of all classes, seasonal displays of annuals, perennials, flowing bulbs and scenic vistas. The natural habitat is enhanced by the careful plantings to grow from young plants and seedlings to burst forth in brilliant colors. Each year more than 40,000 bulbs announce the arrival of spring. Crocus, tulips, narcissus, and other bulbs give forth their joyful colors in abundance. Annuals by the thousands replace the bulbs as they subside. Old favorites and new varieties are skillfully blended to produce a show that certainly enriches each of us. The settings of the trees, mixed with flowers and man-made metal statuary and other items, create spaces that tend to ennoble us all and enrich us. The site of the meeting, of course, was at D. D. Davis Fellows Riverside Gardens, Mill Creek Park, a jewel of the Mahoning Valley. The cultural enrichment was provided by the gardens themselves, as many strolled the area before and after the meeting. The meal was prepared by Peppers Gourmet Foods and Catering Company.

Our speaker for October was Dr. Alexander Pantsov, professor of history at Capital University and adjunct professor at Ohio State University. He is a native of Russia, a specialist in Sino-Russian relations, and the author of several historical monographs. History is more than "bunk" or "one damn thing after another," as Henry Ford once said. Rather, history is a human and humane inquiry that deals with people and their varied personalities by chance or individual choices. It gives us perspective and balance in our judgments and actions. Dr. Pantsov reviewed the role of history and humanities in general, then, with great passion, humor, and knowledge, he traced the evolution of Russia. He skillfully moved from Russia's beginnings to its feudal period, the Mongol conquest, the Tsarist period, the Russian Empire, the Russian Revolution, the Soviet Union, and finally, the Russian Federation. While the political development may not have always represented progress, one can always admire their development in the arts-literature, music, and art with names such as Leo Tolstoy, Alexander Pushkin, Peter Ilyich Tchaikovsky, Fyoder Dostoevsky, and Alexander Solzhenitsyn, Michael Baryshnikov and the Bolshoi Ballet to mention a few. Dr. Pantsov also spoke of the folk arts, including the matryoska, dolls within dolls. He was certainly in sync with the notion that if we lose our capacity to understand the past, or to read and write poems or to listen and compose music, we shall find ourselves closer to the animals and much further from the truths that we seek. Our venue was The Saxon Club, again with their gourmet meal of breaded chicken, pork chops, parslied potatoes, green beans, etc. Our world traveler and performer Roman Rudnytsky again graced us with his beautiful Russian piano selections.

Poetry was the focus in November. Dr. William Greenway, YSU English Department, prolific poet and veteran of our cultural exchange to Guadalajara, Mexico, is thus also an author of one chapter of our OCA book entitled, "Guadalajara: A View from the North". William Hazlitt once said, "Poetry is the universal language which the heart holds with nature and itself. He who has contempt for poetry cannot have much respect for himself or for anything else." Dr. Greenway loves poetry and has received many honors for his efforts. He has said poetry should strike the reader as a wording of his highest thoughts, which one can easily discern from his own works. He often writes about his Welsh ancestry. About his work, William says, "Two things are obvious to me about my poetry. One is that, perhaps because I was raised in the South, which has a rich verbal tradition, I care about the way real people talk, the colorful ways they express themselves, and the images they use. The other thing I notice about my work is that it is nourished by my dreams...." Dr. Greenway draws his inspiration from the greats...Robert Frost, Ralph Waldo Emerson, and William Stafford, saying, "All these writers urge me to do all I can to spread the word that poetry is a way of living more fully...poetry is a way to make and keep ourselves whole, as individuals, as communities, as a world". What is more in keeping what we have been about in the Ohio Cultural Alliance, indeed with the theme this year, "Enriching Elements of Life." We were enriched also by the meaningful dances of the Red Hawk Native American group, who interpreted segments of their ancestors' lives. We met at the Immaculate Heart of Mary Social Hall in Austintown. Rachel's Catering prepared the meal that had some Welsh selections.

In December, the focus was religion with Reverend Morris Lee, long-time pastor of the Third Baptist Church in Youngstown. For this meeting, we convened at the Maronite Center in Youngstown, whose caterers included some "soul food" as part of our meal. His knowledge of his faith and his beautiful, distinctive speaking voice always captivated his listeners; he did not disappoint this evening. The premise of Reverend Lee was that though many have eschewed and/or denounced religion over the years, and although sometimes religion is perverted to gain control over a "malfunctioning brain", religion is infinitely more beneficial. Reverend Lee argues that "from religion has come to the glue that holds people together," and it "gives humankind its essence and the will to go on". He discussed three main religions: Judaism, Christianity, and Islam. He contends that when one follows the commandments given in both the Hebrew Scriptures and in the New Testament, one's life is enriched. And Islam deals with the subjects that concern all human beings: wisdom, beliefs, worship, and law. It provides guidelines (through the words of the Koran) for a just society and equal division of power. On the last day, the dead will be resurrected, and judgment will be pronounced upon every person according to his or her deeds. He concludes that part of any religious system is its moral values which regulate human life. It is the religion that tells us what is right and what is wrong, what is just and what is unjust, what is virtue and what is vice. Religion has many moral values within the family and within the community. Religion enriches morals, and morals build relationships between people and the world around. This enrichment is contagious. The Harambee Dancers displayed their remarkable talent, energy, and excitement with their costumes and dance selections based on African culture.

The January meeting focus was humor, as expressed by local comedian Sue Soller. We met at Our Lady of Mt. Carmel Social Center in Youngstown, with caterer Lou Fusillo serving up another "Youngstown buffet". Washington Irving is quoted as saying that "honest good humor is the oil and wine of a merry meeting, and there is no jovial companionship equal to that where the jokes are rather small and the laughter abundant." Ms. Soller wondered just what humor is but could not imagine facing life without a sense of humor. She offered as a definition that a sense of humor is the quality of being laughable or comical or funny or something designed to induce laughter or amusement. "In another word, I think we all agree, humor is something that makes us laugh. However, what makes us laugh is a whole new ball game." She said that could include "marriage, men, women, husbands, wives, kids, politics, sports, mothers-in-law, theater, senior citizens, blonds, religion", etc., nothing is sacred. She went on to tell a few stories, which really gave us belly laughs. Continuing, she said there here are hundreds of comedians but did not think all of them were funny, particularly those that were "dirty" or contained foul language. She cites some of those that she liked: Bob Hope, Jack Benny, Red Skelton, Lucille Ball, among others. She used a quip of Red Skelton: "I'm nuts, and I know it, but so long as I make 'em laugh, they ain't going to lock me up". And she told a few of these types of stories. Other kinds of humor, like limericks, editing errors even greeting cards, can bring a chuckle to us. One of the most popular types of humor is self-deprecating, even in our daily lives. No one has been any more successful at this kind of humor than Erma Bombeck, whose columns were carried in the local newspaper, The Vindicator, three times a week up until her death in 1996. Erma Bombeck speaking about mothers: "When the Good Lord was creating mothers, He was into His sixth day of overtime when the angel appeared and said, 'You're doing a lot of fiddling around on this one'" Ms. Soller concluded with a favorite quote of Erma's, "I would rather laugh to forget than forget to laugh." There is no doubt that laughing with some regularity, seeing the humor in much of life, and not forgetting to keep humor in life, gives life some balance and could certainly be an enriching element in life. In keeping with the tenor of the evening, Dr. Allan Mosher and Jennifer Davis, his wife, sang duets and solos, some with a suggestion of humor.

Education was the topic in February with our speaker, Dr. Philip Ginnetti, YSU School of Education Dean. He shared with us the enriching nature of children's literature. I am certain that Dr. Ginnetti agreed with the statement made by President John F. Kennedy, "A child miseducated is a child lost." Indeed, he said at the meeting, "...children's books are written to present information in an esthetically pleasing way, stimulate creativity and add to the knowledge base of the reader." Dr. Ginnetti traced the beginnings of children's literature with storytelling by storytellers who traveled from village to village and beyond. Often details of stories were changed to adapt to the audience, keeping the core of the story the same, an example of which is the Cinderella story, which has more than 500 versions. As storytelling became more sophisticated and as people became more literate, stories were written down and passed on-village to village, city to city, continent to continent. Among the reasons for teaching children literature are that it fosters literature, it enhances language development, it aids in the development of comprehension, it inspires inquiry which sparks the imagination.

Dr. Ginnetti discussed the huge sales of children's literature and the wide variety of people who write them, citing such names as Paul McCartney, Caroline Kennedy, Marlo Thomas, Lynne Cheney, and our own Professor Hugh Earnhart, YSU History Department retiree. "The genre that is the most challenging for children is nonfiction. However ... nonfiction that is presented in an interesting way could be informative and even fun. The real benefit of nonfiction is that it gives the children a chance to learn about real things, and it stimulates a higher level of creative and critical thinking, all of which is enriching." Dr. Ginnetti provided a lengthy list of children's books representing a host of categories: history, science, mathematics, and vocabulary development. There is no doubt that Dr. Ginnetti has left a legacy in the Mahoning Valley that mirrors Alexander Pope's admonition, "Tis education forms the common mind, Just as the twig is bent the tree's inclined." Dr. Ginnetti passed away in 2012, a genuine loss to YSU and to the entire community. The meeting was held at St. Matthias Church Hall in Youngstown, with Carolyn Catering serving an abundant and delicious Slavic meal. The Seraphim Singers regaled us with inspirational folk and African-American spirituals.

Gary Balog, a local architect, was our speaker in March. He has worked in his profession for several decades and has become active in local, state, and national professional organizations. His PowerPoint presentation displayed how architecture enriches our lives. Architectural history encompasses the ideas, philosophies, and discourse that molded the architectural praxis. An efficient architect needs to observe, analyze, interpret and evaluate the building blocks of his craft. Mr. Balog said that different styles in architecture mark different periods in history. He continued with a narrative and slides that showed architecture through the various civilizations of Greece, Rome, and the Middle Ages, to the skyscrapers of Chicago and New York to the iconic buildings of the Youngstown area. He spoke of the Ohio One Building, the Stambaugh Building, Jones Hall, YSU to the early buildings built by P. Ross Berry, among others. The site of the meeting was Holy Trinity Church Serbian Hall in Youngstown; parishioners prepared a wonderful ethnic meal again. Dr. Ted Perkins, YSU Dana School of Music, and his horn quartet shared delightful melodies with us.

The April meeting featured politics, with Ohio State Senator Ken Carano as our speaker. His long tenure as a teacher in Austintown, his stellar career as a speech coach, his many civic contributions to his community, and his outstanding and honorable service in the Ohio State Legislature qualified this particular "politician" to address this difficult topic. Politics is more often referred to in a disparaging way rather than as an enriching element, but

Mr. Carano, by his life and his presentation, was an example of the latter. He stressed the need for all citizens to take an active interest in politics and government, from running for office at any level to the very least, keeping informed and voting. This is necessary because if the best of us do not get involved, the least of us will, and they make the laws for all of us. His serious yet humorous presentation was so well received that I think he even made a few converts.

The meeting was held at Western Reserve United Methodist Church Hall in Canfield, whose parishioners prepared and served the usual good meal. Cultural enrichment was provided by Thomas Solich, a popular local pianist (who happens to be blind) who delighted us with varied selections.

In May, Attorney Ronald Slipski spoke of the enriching elements of the law. He dispelled some of the negative ideas that many have of law and lawyers and spoke of many of the noble and enriching aspects of the law. He had just recently become the recipient of the Ohio Bar Association's Eugene R. Weir Award for Ethics and Professionalism. The award recognizes the demonstration of exceptional professional responsibility among Ohio lawyers. He was cited as "developing professionalism for himself and for other members of the bar; he had also acted as an advocate for the client side of the grievance process." As chair of the Mahoning County Bar Association's Grievance Committee for a number of years, he revised the grievance bylaws and the grievance application to make it more accessible to complainants and worked to provide the grievant with a full explanation of the process and the rationale for granting or denying a grievance. His talk gave credence to what he was feted for above as he showed reverence for the law and the equitable distribution of the law. When the enforcement of the law is committed to those who revere it, the law merely deters some human beings from offending and punishes other human beings for offending. Attorney Slipski also agreed with Thomas Jefferson when he uttered, "a strict observation of the written law is doubtless one of the high duties of a good citizen, but it is not the highest. The laws of necessity, of self-preservation, of saving our country when in danger, are of higher obligation." Attorney Slipski said, "lawyers have to seek to raise and hold a high level of public respect. If a society loses trust in lawyers, society as we know it would collapse." The law and lawyers must strive for the highest morality and fairness, he concluded in a robust and credible manner. We met at The Georgetown in Boardman, where we were treated to a fine "Youngstown buffet". The Struthers Community Show Choir, led by Bob Noble, completed the evening with a medley of popular tunes.

The final meeting in June featured comments from the author who reviewed the theme of the last two years, "Enriching Elements of Life," coupled with a brief address regarding what is arguably the quintessential enriching element of life-love. George D. Beelen, Jr. showed his 23-minute video that reviews the 20-year history of the Ohio Cultural Alliance. Our goal during the last two years as we addressed certain enriching elements of life was to focus on how these selected elements tend to ennoble us, to make way for our wiser selves, to propel us toward the better angels. And love can be an integral part of each of these elements.

Although the major portion of my talk related to human love, particularly between man and woman, with some comments about men, some about women, some about what women think about men and what men think about women, some discussion about various kinds of courtship, and some discussion about marriage, I said some pertinent things about each and even some impertinent remarks. Even though my major comments related to love of man and woman, I allowed that there are many kinds of human love: love of children, parents, relatives, etc.; love of man for man; love of woman for woman. I ended with, "Love is patient; love is kind; love is not envious or boastful or arrogant or rude; It does not insist on its own way; it is not irritable or resentful; it does not rejoice in wrongdoing, but rejoices in the truth."

I suffer under no illusions that all of these elements are always used positively; they can be perverted: religion has at times led to hate and war; music can be cacophonous and disturbing; theater and film can be vile; art and architecture can be ugly; literature and poetry can be pornographic; journalism and history can be fake, inaccurate and misleading; philosophy can be insincere; nature can be violated; humor can be depraved and hateful; education can be proselytizing; law, government, and politics can corrupt and non-inclusive to mention some possibilities of such negative interpretations.

But we chose to stress how these selected elements can be used, and usually are, to enrich, ennoble and enhance one's life. George D. Beelen Jr.'s film recounted in about 20 minutes, visually and with narrative, much of the flavor of what the Ohio Cultural Alliance has done in promoting peace and understanding in our community.

OCA Video Title Page

Michael Kurilla

Andrea Wood and husband Dennis LaRue

Sally Dolovy, Betty Bannon & Jeffrey Bremmer

Warren and Iva Harrell

Dr. Sherry Linkon

Attorney Ronald Slipski

Anita Lin

Ballet Western Reserve

Dr. Rick Shale

Dr. Y. T. Chiu and wife Marylin

Dr. Tom Shipka

Ken Carano

John Gabriele

XV. My Story

The Ohio Cultural Alliance began its 21st year with a new three-year theme, "MY Story," during which time we heard thirty citizens from the Mahoning Valley, representing a variety of professions/occupations and a variety of religions and races. What rings true with these disparate people is that their stories reflect some combination of genius, of people like us and people different from us, of love, of service, of compassion, of understanding, and of empathy. For this year, 2007-08, we heard the stories of four members of the clergy, two politicians, a medical doctor, a philanthropist, a journalist, and an Irish activist/organizer, each of whom had a fascinating ethnic and/or religious background that has framed their lives and impacted many others. We continued our pattern of "going places" in terms of virtually traveling to various sites around the Valley and were treated to cultural enrichment in the form of ten different persons/groups to entertain us. In general, attention was devoted to these local citizens of the 20th century because of their unique stories and/or their contributions to the community and how they were representatives of the best of us.

In September, Reverend Joseph Rudjak, a Catholic priest of Polish and Ukrainian background, became pastor of two churches, one Croatian and the other Hungarian, who shared his rich and varied background with us. He not only cherishes all of the ethnic backgrounds that he represents, but he also strives for all ethnic people to remember their ethnicity as they hold dear their American status.

Father Rudjak was born in 1944 in Youngstown. The heart of Father Rudjak's home and family was the Catholic faith expressed in the Polish American community and burnished by attending St. Casimir's Grade School and Ursuline High School, both in Youngstown. His Catholic faith and Polish identity were strengthened by influence from the Polish Legion of American Vets, the St. Stanislaus Club, and the Polish Arts Club. After studying at the seminary in Cincinnati, at Kent State University, and at Catholic University in Lublin, Poland, he was ordained to the Diaconate in 1970. As a deacon, he ministered at churches in Cincinnati, Ashtabula, at St. Luke's in Boardman, St. James in Warren, St. Rose in Girard, Sacred Heart in Youngstown, and in Campus Ministry at Youngstown State University and Kent State University. He was ordained as a priest in 2000. After a short assignment at St. Paul's parish in North Canton, he was assigned as pastor at Sts. Peter and Paul in Youngstown (2003) and Our Lady of Hungary in Youngstown (2004), as said above, positions he still holds.

Father Rudjak is an exemplary human being as personified by his namesake Joseph, the earthly Father of Christ. Both Josephs reflect integrity, righteousness, kindness, and sensitivity. He ministers to the needs of his parishioners in two churches (at one time three). We know that he makes attempts to speak in his native Polish, as well as in Croatian and Hungarian, and encourages the preservation of the traditions of each of these cultures. Among Father Joe's initiatives have been improvements in both churches: among them are a ramp and an elevator for the elderly and physically challenged, razing of the old and abandoned school for creating a shrine with Stations of the Cross, and improvements in both social halls. Under his leadership, parishioners volunteer with Catholic-based social programs, including Dorothy Day House, Beatitude House, and St. Vincent de Paul kitchen. The parish's Holy Name Society, Altar and Rosary Society, and Daughters' Club have participated in community ministries. He is most welcoming at each of the churches with such comments as, "when you're here, you're family". He has also hosted at Sts. Peter and Paul (partly because of the unusually good acoustics in the church) musical programs, among them several performers for the YSU New Music School.

If there is any way to define Father Rudjak's contributions to the larger community, it is his tireless efforts to urge his church congregants and others in the larger community to celebrate and preserve their ethnic identities and share them with others. Indeed, that philosophy was the impetus to initiate the Ethnic Heritage Society, which was spearheaded by Father Joe. Tony Lariccia, local philanthropist and future speaker for the OCA and the Ohio Cultural Alliance, provided some of the initial funds for seed money. Father Rudjak also encourages ecumenism with many non-Catholic denominations, including Ambassadors for Christ, which is a local group that brings together people of different religions and races and who share a unifying bond of Christianity. Pastors, including Father Rudjak, describe the group as a blessing to the East Side congregations and community. Father Joe has said, "When people get together and pray, music is part of the healing. He added, "when church members sit with people they don't know, that builds fellowship, friendship, and understanding." Another group, the Father Joe, participated in is the Society of Saint John Chrysostom, which encourages Orthodox/Catholic dialogue. Other activities that Father Joe is actively involved with are blessing of animals and blessing of the bikes and bikers. He has certainly been an "apostle" of Pope Francis's comments he made in Rio de Janeiro in 2013, "Do not be afraid to go and to bring Christ into every area of life, to the fringes of society, even to those who seem farthest away, most indifferent." This meeting was held at the Croatian Lodge #66 in Youngstown, where we were treated to an abundant and sumptuous ethnic meal prepared by the Lodge caterers. Libby Fill and her Tamburitza musical group thrilled us with their lively and toe-tapping Croatian music.

Father Joseph Rudjak

Libby Fill (left) and her Tamburitza Group

Dr. Rashid Abdu, in October, mesmerized us with his story, summarized from his book, "Journey of a Yemeni Boy". He recalled his journey that started as a child in Yemen "when that country was still frozen in the dark ages." It followed a long, uncharted, rough, and tortuous path that was certainly circuitous. Children were married young; childbirth deaths were common; most of the people were illiterate, and most believed the world was flat. At age nine on barefoot and at times on a camel, young Rashid left his little village to travel to Aden, about eighty miles away, where his uncle was working. He got a job in a coffee shop, working eighteen hours a day (every day), cleaning floors, serving food (at noon carrying bowls of food to laborers working one mile away), and washing pots and pans. He earned $1.50 a month, which went to his poor family at home. He often slept in the dirt streets among the roaming goats. This was all taking place during World War II while the Italians were dropping bombs on Aden, a British protectorate. At one point, his father took him back home, but Rashid shortly returned to Aden. He continued to work at various menial jobs for the same pay and the same terrible living conditions.

An event changed his future. His uncle's son contracted yellow fever, and Rashid was tasked with becoming his cousin's bedside nurse. He was to feed him and keep him clean and dry. It looked hopeless, but the doctor who saw the cousin every day also performed surgery on the patient, removing many kidney stones. After one month, the cousin improved and lived. When the doctor left the house, Rashid said to himself, "I want to be like that doctor." From then on, Rashid was laser focused on school in addition to his work. He got a job with the American Red Cross on the Air Base, where his uncle worked as a chauffeur. The job this time was as a messenger boy, added to another job to help make and distribute donuts to the soldiers throughout the camp. School was two miles away and through the desert, which he walked every day. Always hungry, he depended upon the garbage for simple sustenance until nurses made sure he had one good meal a day.

Another fortuitous circumstance was his introduction to Harlan Clark, American Consul in Aden, who was originally from Brookfield, Ohio. Starting as a houseboy for the Clarks, he eventually became their cook, did laundry, tilled the garden, cleaned the house, etc., and helped care for the Clark's two little children. In his "spare time," he fit in a lot of schooling. He even served as a junior interpreter. From Aden, the Clarks were transferred to Saudi Arabia, then to Beirut, with Rashid following on a cargo ship to Egypt, a train to Haifa, then to Beirut. At the American University of Beirut, he was given a placement exam and was placed in the 8th grade, the appropriate chronological grade for a 14-year-old. He had "fit in" a lot of schooling-genius knows no boundaries. When the Clarks left for the U.S., they asked Rashid to accompany them. His family opposed this; he went anyway. He discovered America and realized how lucky he was to be here. Continuing his work with the Clarks, he was enrolled in Falls Church High School in Virginia. This first and only foreign student became president of his class, a member of the National Honor Society, won first place in "I Speak for Democracy" contest, and even spoke on the Voice of America network. Following high school, he was offered a scholarship to Lafayette College, Pennsylvania, in competition with sixty others. He still had to work for his room and board, books, and other expenses. Once during this time, he said that he had exactly one penny to his name. Medical school was still his goal, but how to get there was the question.

So, this was yet another unbelievable situation. Getting accepted into medical school was and is always difficult. But he was accepted at George Washington Medical School, his first choice; of 3,000 applicants, Rashid was among 100 who were accepted. Thereafter, he returned to Yemen to celebrate with the family. They were happy to see him but unhappy that he was going to continue his education. They wanted him to stay in Yemen, get a paying job, get married to his first cousin and start a family. During that same visit, Rashid said he was not yet ready to marry, convinced his father that his eleven siblings (at least the seven boys) should go to school (at his expense), and convinced the king of Yemen to give him a scholarship to medical school. By this time, Rashid had become something of a famous Yemeni-little Rashid, consorting with educated and upper-echelon people.

After graduation from medical school, he visited the Clarks again, meeting a physician from Sharon, Pennsylvania, who suggested that Dr. Abdu check out St. Elizabeth's Hospital in Youngstown, Ohio. He did and served the following five years at St. Elizabeth's. He said he "was so impressed with St. Elizabeth's, especially with the nuns and the way they take care of the poor." This left a lasting impression on him. He had a fifty-year career as a surgeon, mostly at St. Elizabeth's, now Mercy Health, St. Elizabeth's Hospital in Youngstown, and St. Joseph's Hospital in Warren.

During this time, he developed a reputation as an outstanding surgeon, acknowledged as a leader in his field. His award as an Arab American of the year recipient in 2017 was announced with these words: "He embodies the spirit of leadership, ingenuity, and compassion ...and exemplifies the perseverance and humbleness at the heart of the immigrant contribution to the American success story."

He married Joanie, with whom they were blessed with four children. In addition to his excellence as a surgeon, he was a dear husband and father. It was one of his daughters that introduced him at the event where he was honored as Arab American of the year in the U.S., and each of them is successful in their own life. Upon his wife's death of breast cancer in 1994, he became the driving force behind the establishment of the state-of-the-art Joanie Abdu Comprehensive Breast Care Center affiliated with Mercy Health of Youngstown. Dr. Abdu's hard and determined work and his love for his wife resulted in a facility that is among the best in the nation and widely acclaimed by locals and nationwide.

Dr. Abdu has become something of an iconic figure in the area. He has told his story in his book and has retold it widely in the local area and elsewhere. He has been honored for his medical work and his compassionate care (just ask my wife, Betty, who was one of his patients). He has also been honored, even revered in Yemen, where he has returned on many occasions. Most importantly, he returned to operate on his mother when no one else would; they said she was too old and near death anyway. The surgery was successful, and she enjoyed 28 more years after the operation. Over the years, he served in Yemen as a teacher, consultant, and visiting professor. On one trip, he went back to inspect a new medical school and a new hospital which he helped to design. By this time, even his father was beginning to acknowledge the importance of education. Suddenly everybody wanted their sons to be like Rashid. Now there are more than 20 physicians from the local area, including four doctors and three engineers in his own family. Dr. Rashid Abdu has been a credit to his family, his native country, his adopted country, and to all that know him. He ended one of his talks with an Arab saying that is one to live by: "If a day passes without extending a helping hand and learning something new, that day will not be considered a part of your life." Education and helping one's fellow man are certainly the hallmarks of Dr. Rashid Abdu's life. As a retiree, Dr. Abdu is a friend to many, an amateur photographer, and a painter. What an inspiration his talk to the OCA was. Genius knows no boundaries.

We met for this meeting at The Georgetown, whose caterers prepared some Arab ethnic items. The cultural enrichment was provided by Angela Prato, a professional belly dancer from Canton, Ohio.

Joanie Abdu Center affiliated with Mercy Health of Youngstown

Dancer Angela Prato flanked by Dr. Abdu, speaker and Dr. Beelen

The story of an African American Bishop coming to Youngstown was the theme of Bishop George Murry for our November meeting. It was held at St. Charles Church Hall in Boardman, with Livosky Catering preparing the sumptuous meal. The cultural enrichment we enjoyed came in two forms: the beautiful St. Charles Catholic Church proper, where the program was held, and the enchanting and passionate operatic music selections sung by Dorota Sobieski, who was accompanied on piano by her critically acclaimed husband, Jacek Sobieski. The attendance for the evening was 330 people, one of the largest ever for OCA.

To meet Bishop Murry, one is immediately taken to this imposing, ebullient man, who engages his audience from the moment he walks into the venue. He is usually early to arrive, and within minutes, he is pleasantly "working" the audience as well as the best politicians. This was true at every event when I was fortunate to hear him speak, including the one on this evening. To speak to him for even a few moments or from the first few moments of his talk, one is assured that this bright, Jesuit man of God has much to offer his fellow human beings.

Bishop Murry's propensity for faith-sharing had its origins early in childhood. He was born into a family of Methodists, but his parents enrolled him in St. Bartholomew Catholic School in Camden, New Jersey when he was in third grade. The family began to attend both the Methodist Church and the Sunday morning children's Mass at the Catholic Church. As little George learned more about the Catholic faith in school, he became interested in becoming a Catholic officially. He was fascinated by the Catholic Church and said he came to believe it was where he belonged. "It was my home". When he was 9 years old, in 1958, George Murry was baptized into the Catholic Church. His younger brother later followed his example, and eventually, his parents also became Catholics.

George served as an altar server at St. Bartholomew Parish and stayed after school to help the sisters. He always planned to become a priest, and he told anyone who asked that he would be entering the seminary. Even more ambitiously, when asked by an associate pastor what he was going to do when he grew up, young George said, "I 'm going to be the pope." That was only a childhood dream. Bishop Murry did not live long enough to accede to the papacy. His achievements, though-both in education and in the clerical sphere, were substantial. At schools where he led, he advocated for a strong Catholic education, resisting efforts to water down the Church's consistent teaching to make them more palatable to society. Notwithstanding that last statement, he always made a thorough and logical case for the basic tenets of the Church.

After graduating from Camden Catholic High School, he went on to do undergraduate studies at St. Joseph's College in Philadelphia, St. Thomas Seminary in Bloomfield, Connecticut, and St. Mary's Seminary in Baltimore, earning a Bachelor of Arts in Philosophy in 1972. In that same year, he was admitted as a member of the Society of Jesus (Jesuits). After completing his period of the novitiate, he went on to obtain a Master of Divinity degree from the Jesuit School of Theology at Berkley and a Master's and Doctorate in American Cultural History from George Washington University in Washington, D.C. In 1979, George Murry was ordained to the Catholic priesthood in the Jesuit province of Maryland.

Father Murry started his educator's whirlwind in 1986, beginning as an assistant professor of American Studies at Georgetown University and teaching there for four years. He also served as the President of Archbishop Carroll High School in Washington D.C. from 1989 to 1994, when he was appointed Associate Vice President for Academic Affairs at the University of Detroit Mercy.

Kathy Schiffer was assigned as assistant to Father George when he came to the University of Detroit Mercy. She remembered when he arrived that, he quickly became one of her favorite people: "he had a leadership style that was strong, yet warm, and his laughter could be heard down the hall. He was a tall and imposing figure and was, according to campus rumors, likely to be named president of some Jesuit university in the future. He loved God, he loved the Catholic Church with its rich traditions and art, and he loved the field of education." During the five months that Schiffer was with Father George, she had the opportunity to help him when Pope John Paul II called on Father Murry to become auxiliary bishop in Chicago. She helped with arrangements for his send-off to Detroit by working with the artist to design an Episcopal coat of arms and compiling a guest list for his reception in Chicago. She was present for the ordination ceremony in 1995, where apostolic pro-nuncio Archbishop Agostino Cacciavillan celebrated the liturgy and read the special message from the Holy Father, and when Cardinal Joseph Bernardin consecrated three bishops for the Archdiocese of Chicago, including Bishop Murry. For the next three years, Bishop Murry served the people on Chicago's south side (1995-1998). Mrs. Schiffer was also invited to the Virgin Islands in 1998 to attend the installation of Bishop Murry as coadjutor of the Diocese of St. Thomas. He was to serve here from 1998 to 2007. She always enjoyed conversations with her boss-his energy and his openness to sharing his vision for Catholic higher education. Bishop Murry loved the Catholic Church, including the simplicity of the cathedral where he was installed in the Virgin Islands. He didn't appreciate the modernized architecture of recent decades. "The Church has been a repository of great beauty", she reported Bishop Murry saying, and that he hoped that "the Church's appreciation for beauty would continue in the future. He loved classical art and architecture, stained glass windows, and the great sculptures and paintings of the medieval masters which glorified God in a unique way."

In 2007, Pope Benedict XVI appointed George Murry as the fifth Bishop of Youngstown, the first African American to serve in that capacity. Youngstown welcomed him warmly and increasingly so as he served his first Masses, visited many of the Catholic churches and schools in the diocese, and accepted lecture invitations in the area and elsewhere. Here and at other positions where he served with predominantly white priests and colleagues, there could be some unique challenges, such as where to get a haircut. But with his magnetic smile and calm presence, he met the challenges with equanimity. Indeed, as many of us feared, this brilliant Jesuit and humble man of God would probably not be with us for long. The year he came to Youngstown, he was elected Secretary of the United States Conference of Catholic Bishops (USCCB) and was re-elected to a three-year term the following year. But that was not all: Murry served on numerous boards, including those of the University of Detroit, St. Joseph's University, Mount St. Mary's College, Loyola Academy in Detroit, and Catholic Relief Services. He was a trustee of Loyola University Chicago and Fairfield University and was chairman of the Committee on Domestic Policy of the U.S. Catholic Council of Bishops. He was also appointed Chair of the National Catholic Educational Association in 2015, where he served until the end of 2017. But there was still more. In 2015 Pope Francis appointed Murry a member of the Synod of Bishops that met to discuss family life. At that meeting, he said he supported the view that church practice toward the divorced and remarried could change without altering doctrine. He also supported greater participation from theologians, cultural historians, and other experts and that the Synod needed to find a way to hear the voices of the people who were the subject of its discussions. He supported the creation of a commission to consider allowing women to serve as deacons, saying, "It would be a wise idea to look into it, to learn more about it, and then to present it to the Pope to say there either are theological problems or not. And, if not, let's move forward." It is clear that this convert to Catholicism was moved to bring God to his fellow man, using every waking moment and every ounce of strength to do just that. Can the reader understand why we often wondered how long he would stay with us in Youngstown?

In 2018 Bishop Murry was a keynote speaker at the Ignatian Family Teach-in for Justice, where he drew attendees into envisioning a more just world through reform within the Catholic Church, drawing from his role as former chair of the U.S. Conference of Catholic Bishops Committee Against Racism, a position he held briefly. "While racism is America's most persistent sin, it appears as if the American Catholic Church has been virtually silent about it", he said. He grounded his call to action in personal relationships as a starting point, urging attendees to "make an effort to know someone of a different race, to listen to their story, to walk in their shoes, then to use the gifts that you have been given…to offer people on the margins an opportunity." The Ignatian family described Bishop Murry's address as humble and impactful for those in attendance. "He challenged us but also gave us hope." His last official statement, released on June 1, 2020, was a response to the May 25th killing of George Floyd, where he, along with brother bishops, stated "that the fight to eradicate racism is a pro-life issue. Racism is not a thing of the past or simply a throwaway political issue when convenient. It is a real and present danger." May I offer as an editorial note that those are the very sentiments that we have tried to convey with the Ohio Cultural Alliance, particularly with the theme of "My Story" studying people like us and different from us with the overarching notion that "genius knows no boundaries." He spoke a second time to the OCA, again to an overwhelming crowd.

As we all know, Bishop Murry died after several bouts of leukemia. Although he did not serve us long enough, he served us well. He not only served us, but he also made friends with us. And educated us. And inspired us. And gave us hope. Father/Bishop George Murry made friends everywhere he went. He made and kept in touch with friends he had made in Archbishop Carroll High School and with others from Washington D.C., This was true of everywhere he served, according to Kathy Schiffer, his assistant at the University of Detroit Mercy. In his thirteen years ministering to us in the Diocese of Youngstown, he loved us, and we loved him. His fellow priests admired him, the community was grateful for his guidance, and his illness and ultimate death were stunning. Youngstown Mayor Jamael Tito Brown said Bishop Murry "was a true friend, always looking out for the wellness in the community". U.S. Representative Tim Ryan offered that "his voice will be deeply missed." Mary Fiala, superintendent of the Diocesan schools, recalled that the students and faculty were always thrilled when Murry came to visit because he always was supportive and affirming of the work they were doing. He so loved the Youngstown area that he had determined to be laid to rest at Resurrection Cemetery in the local community. May he rest in peace.

Bishop George Murry

St. Columba Cathedral Diocese of Youngstown

In December, Reverend Cosmin Antonescu shared his Romanian story with us. It is a beautiful story that is encapsulated in his utterance that he is proud to be a Romanian, his native land, and is "grateful to God for his blessing of bringing me to this blessed country (America) where I can become what I wish and want". He continued, "Each one of us is a micro-universe, as Saint Maximos said, with his own aspirations and dreams, with his own ups and downs, but whose aim is still the same with all mankind: happiness and fulfillment." He invited us into his own micro-universe.

He divided his story into three parts: his time in Romania under the communist regime until 1989; the time from1989 to 2003 while still in Romania; the short time in America since 2003. After a brief historical look at Romania, he related his life in this beautiful yet troubled country. Born in 1979 in Sibiu, as the middle child of three, he lived a simple life with his family, which included his grandfather, who lived in a shepherd's cabin in the mountains where Cosmin visited every summer. There he learned the deep connection between man, nature, and God. Here also, he reflected, "I learned what it means to depend on rain or on the sun in order to have the daily bread. I also learned what the Bible said that the man should eat his bread and, in his face, sweat." Cosmin remembered good memories and bad from the early formative years. Good memories were the Sunday church service, standing for the entire time, but then the reward of a wonderful chicken meal and the peace that was brought to the whole family. But the bad memories were always the tension and fear in the air, the inability to express oneself, and the everyday poverty and misery which they had to endure.

The second part of his story started in the winter of 1989 when the people of Romania rose to end the communist regime under Nicolae Ceausescu. After some time of adjustment to the new political situation, Cosmin's parents tried to improve their economic situation and raise their standard of living. When he was 14, he was permitted to go to a theological high school in Alba Iulia, 30 miles away. It was a good life; he learned a great deal, all on a very tight schedule, and met many good friends. The most special person that he met was his future wife, Camelia, whom he married in his home city, Sibiu. Within a year, they had the first of their three children. This part of the story covered the years 1989-2003.

In 2003 Cosmin fortuitously became a choir director to an acapella theological choral group who were invited by the Romanian Orthodox Church of America to sing at the installation of a dignitary of the church. After one month in the U. S., they returned to Romania, much to the consternation of those who thought he should have remained in America. He said he needed to finish his last year at the theological college. The following year the choral group was invited again; this time, Cosmin stayed. In 2005 Cosmin's wife and son joined him. "In the winter of 2005, His Eminence Archbishop Nathaniel decided to send me to serve the Romanian Orthodox Church of Youngstown, Ohio, and here I am with you today, sharing my story." This was the chronological story to the time of his arrival in Youngstown, and two years later, he spoke to the Ohio Cultural Alliance. I met him a few times during these two years and a few times more before he left for his new assignment at Saint Andrew Romanian Orthodox Church in Potomac, Maryland.

While in Youngstown, in America generally, he had to decide what he was really about: what do I want? What can I do? How do I do it? Am I happy with what I am doing? This private discussion with himself was significant; this was his first obstacle. "In America", he said, "you can have whatever you want as long as you are healthy, as long as you are working, and as long as you use your brain." One has the freedom of many choices. He was really saying in America; one has unlimited possibilities. "This evening, I can be here as an Orthodox priest; tomorrow, I can be in California as a truck driver. America gives us a new kind of freedom: the freedom not just to express ourselves, but also the freedom to become what and who we want," he said.

He also spoke about how he liked American diversity: "diversity of culture and different religious ideas; this enriched me." Elaborating, he said, "Here in America, you have the possibility to interact with different religions daily. If I want to understand better a Muslim, a Buddhist, or someone who is not like me, I can do it in a matter of minutes: there is a mosque around the corner, a Buddhist temple across the street, a synagogue 20 minutes away.... I understand better the others, their way of thinking, and I also understand and define myself better and deeper." Could we, who are OCA members, define any better what we believe America is and/or can be and what our mission is? He ended his talk with a statement that he is still proud to be a Romanian and that feeling will always be in his soul, but he is "grateful to God for his blessing of bringing me to this blessed country where I can really become what I wish and want".

While in Youngstown, he helped to organize the 100th anniversary of the founding of Holy Trinity Romanian Orthodox Church; he enriched the Carmen Sylva Ladies' Auxiliaries, the AROY Chapter of young adults, and the choir. He dedicated time and resources to repurposing the basement into a functioning part of the church, and he actually did work repairs in the church and on the church grounds. (I saw him at work with trees and leaves outside.) He well represented the Romanian Orthodox Church in the community. He ended his story in 2007, but I feel the story of Reverend Cosmin Antonescu if far from over. The event was held at St. John's Greek Orthodox Church in Boardman, but the Romanian meal was prepared by members of the Holy Trinity Romanian Church. A very talented Romanian folk dance group from Canton, Ohio, thrilled us with dances as they shared their vigorous moves and colorful costumes with us.

Since he left the Youngstown area, he has continued to serve in many capacities. In tracking Father Antonescu, I found that his story is far from over. On November 1, 2014, he was invited to become part of the Romanian Orthodox community in Washington, D.C. He was called to serve the needs of Saint Andrew Mission in Potomac, Maryland. He wrote, "This much larger venue was difficult at first, but at the same time, was somewhat expected, having known the particular situation of the Romanian Orthodox community, which I continue to discover and try to understand day by day."

Recently he has entered into the discussion of the status of the Orthodox Christian Church. Some scholars have argued that Orthodox Christians exist in greater numbers today, yet they represent a diminished share of Christians worldwide. Confined primarily to an aging Europe and strongly tethered to tradition, Orthodox Christians may need to change their ways to remain relevant. Reverend Antonescu contributed to the discussion, "People are sending out a signal that they don't identify with structures of the past anymore and look for new forms of spirituality. We were the most constant church in Christianity but failing to respond to ever-changing needs made us lose ground in society."

Most recently, Father Antonescu has become a counselor in training after completing a Master's degree in Clinical Mental Health from Loyola University's Pastoral Counseling Department. He has been described as having a passion for understanding human nature, being eager to be a healing presence and creating an open, safe environment, helping to open one's heart with a desire to promote self-awareness and fulfillment. In the therapeutic dialog, Father Antonescu has a special interest in facilitating a deeper understanding for couples and families, as well as for individuals in any stage of their lives. He uses an integrative approach, creating a welcoming space, unconditional positive regard, and respect for the uniqueness of each individual and relationship. He has a special role in helping new immigrants adjust to new cultural roles. We saw suggestions of these traits when he served the Youngstown community ever so shortly. We wish him continued success in various ministries.

Reverend Cosmin Antonescu

Romanian dance group

The January meeting focus was the African Indian background of Bertram de Souza, a Youngstown Vindicator journalist. He was a long-time writer for the Vindicator as an editorial contributor and a political writer. Bertram had considerable influence in the Valley and was viewed with approbation or disdain where residents swore by him or at him. At this OCA meeting, the keen attention to his story and the standing ovation after his talk clearly indicated how this cohort viewed him.

Mr. de Souza has at times considered himself as "a man without a country" and at other times a man who is part of many cultures: "I am Indian by ancestry, Portuguese by religion and culture, African by deeply rooted geography and American by citizenship." He explained that in 1915 his grandparents and a granduncle left Goa, a Portuguese colony on the west coast of India, for Uganda. Bertram's mother, along with her two brothers and three sisters, were born in Uganda. His father was born and reared in India and relocated to Uganda after he married Bertram's mother. Uganda and India were both British colonies; therefore, both of his parents were British citizens.

Bertram was born in Uganda. When he was 7 years old, his father sent him to a Jesuit boarding school in Bombay, India. "It was a life-changing experience-and, not necessarily for the better", he said. In 1977, he returned to study with the Jesuits, where he studied at Marquette University for his master's degree. Notwithstanding the fact that his mother and other family members had a long history and deep affinity for Uganda, Asians were expelled in 1972. Bertram, at this time, was a student at Kansas State University working on a bachelor's degree in Journalism. He had come to the United States on a foreign student visa because he was a Ugandan citizen. Upon completion of his education, he was to return to Uganda. Of course, this didn't happen because of Idi Amin's edict in 1972 to expel Asians. Thus, his parents went to Britain because they were British citizens.

Shortly after Amin's edict, the Uganda government reviewed Bertram's status and concluded that Uganda no longer considered him to be a citizen. So, he and his brother settled in Canada. He became a man without a country. Neither the British government nor the Indian or Portuguese would accept him and the U.S. government "was hamstrung because of immigration laws." After graduating from Kansas State, he went to work for a newspaper in Selma, Alabama, where he got to know the area's, Congressman Walter Flowers. The Congressman offered to sponsor special legislation to make him a citizen, but Bertram declined "because, as a journalist, he could not accept such a favor." He ultimately received American citizenship after spending five years as a permanent resident. "Indeed, that is the most memorable event of my 29 years in the Mahoning Valley."

Bertram concluded his story by saying he "was acutely aware of the ongoing debate in the United States and around the world over the issue of immigration and cultural diversity. The Ohio Cultural Alliance and other organizations must be heard, if for no other reason than to serve as a counterpoint to the arguments being put forth by those who choose to ignore that this country's strength is in its diversity."

This well-attended meeting was held at Antone's Banquet Hall in Boardman, whose caterers prepared a wonderful meal that included some Indian and African items. The cultural enrichment was provided by the Seraphim Singers, who offered folk and African American selections.

Bertram de Souza

Harry Meshel in February shared his reflections on his prolific array of public activities and how his Greek background helped to frame his life. How does one write of a true icon of the Valley and beyond? We all know of his outstanding array of plaques, commendations, awards, and honors by virtually all of the social, political, and cultural organizations of the Valley and the State. One only needs to visit Meshel Hall on YSU's campus to view some of the tangible manifestations of these honors, occupying an entire first-floor wall.

These awards have been given to Harry because he has worked hard to promote these organizations. And in any organization in which he was a member, he was not an apathetic or uninvolved follower; he played a leading role. Until his very last days, when Harry was invited as a speaker, he always had a plaque or a commendation for that organization or the person being honored. He was an intelligent, articulate, and often outspoken advocate for the Valley and the many components which make up the Mahoning Valley. Harry knows the importance of one's roots. He knows where he came from. On his way to becoming a great American, he always urged others to remember their roots also. Remembering one's ethnic background and acknowledging the importance of other ethnic groups as well both important in that quest to become a complete American, is important to Harry. Perhaps all of these attributes can be summed up in one word-empathy. Harry can walk in someone else's shoes; he understands many points of view; he can "feel your pain."

Harry Michelakis Meshel was born in 1924, in Youngstown, to Evangelos Michelakis and Rubin Markakis Michelakis Meshel. He was not born into power and influence, nor were these attributes bestowed upon him. He had to work for them. Growing up in the Great Depression, in an industrial city, he had fewer of the common measures of wealth. His family lost his boyhood home because his parents could not afford the $12.00 per month rent. The Depression made him self-reliant and mindful of the conditions of others, never losing sight of where he came from.

He was a graduate of the original McGuffey Elementary School in Youngstown and an honor graduate of East High School. After graduation, he was eager to serve in World War II but was ineligible because he already had two brothers serving. In trying to enlist in the Marines, he was urged to join a new unit of the Navy called the Seabees. The mission of this new unit was to secure landing sites for disembarking soldiers and Marines, build runways and build and repair bridges. While in the South Pacific theater, he earned two Bronze Stars with Battle Stars in the Battle of Leyte Gulf. The hardships endured during the Depression and serving in the War without familiar family and friends honed a will that served him well after the military, driving him to be the first in his family to attend college- Youngstown College. And he did it in three years. Afterward, Harry braved New York City as he earned an MBA from the prestigious Columbia University. This academic work was accomplished in the late 1940s.

Returning to Youngstown in the early 1950's Harry worked in the steel mills as an open-hearth laborer and a press and furnace operator. In the late 1950s and early 1960s, he worked as a division manager of an investment firm, as a real estate salesman and broker, and as a business and social science adjunct faculty member at YSU and at Ohio University, teaching political science. During this era (1964-1968) he became the executive assistant to Mayor E.B. Flask, after which he was Urban Renewal director for the city of Youngstown and trustee for the Mahoning Valley Health Planning Association. In 1971 Harry was elected Ohio State Senator, serving until 1993. During this period, he ran for U.S. Congress, winning the primary by a huge margin but losing the general election, ostensibly because he was doing such a great job as State Senator. Ever the renaissance man, he was also the International

Supervisor for 15 years of the International Boxing Commission, organizing the first Showtime televised fight in China and several fights in Israel. He was Ohio Democratic Party Chairman from 1993-1995, president for five years on the Board of Commissioners for Mill Creek Metro Parks, and served a nine-year term as YSU Trustee. To honor his parents, siblings, and YSU, he has established several endowments to show his gratitude to the members of his family and the institution that served him well and that he continued to serve for many years.

While State Senator Harry wielded significant power and influence, often fighting from a minority position, he won leadership roles in the Senate and beyond, always doing what was best for his constituency and leading with strength and intelligence. He sponsored and followed through with major legislation: the creation of economic development program providing dollars for business expansion and job creation is unmatched anywhere in the nation; his bill dealing with regulation and control of hazardous material was a model for the nation. He was a strong supporter of workers, consumers, senior citizens, infrastructure legislation, collective bargaining, and the handicapped bill of rights, with successful legislation in all of these areas. In his indefatigable way, Harry also represented the State of Ohio on trade missions over the globe to create markets for goods made in Ohio. Recognized nationally by his peers, Senator Meshel was called upon to participate in seminars and panels all over the country and to appear on national news programs.

Senator Harry Meshel spoke extemporaneously at our OCA meeting as he usually did; he even helped select the dinner items that the caterers at Archangel Michael Church Hall in Campbell prepared for us. A movie about Greece was shown during the dinner hour. Afterward, a dance group of church members delighted us as they danced in their lovely costumes. Harry died on September 4, 2017, at the age of 93.

The Honorable Harry Meshel

Greek dance group

Archangel Michael Greek Orthodox Church in Campbell

In March, Reverend Kathryn Adams spoke of her route to her life's work, focusing on her several missions to Russia. The meeting was held at Western Reserve United Methodist Church, where her husband, Reverend Russ Adams, is pastor. The meal was prepared and served by members of the parish. The world-trotting Professor Roman Rudnytsky graced us again with his piano talent, playing popular Russian melodies.

Reverend Kathryn was born and reared in the Cleveland area. She graduated from Bedford High School, Scarritt College for Christian Workers (Bachelor of Arts), and Vanderbilt University Divinity School (Master of Divinity). Reverend Kathryn has been a United Methodist minister since 1982, during which time she served 18 years as the Protestant Campus Minister at Youngstown State University and 13 years in pastoral ministry. She is married to Reverend Russell Q. Adams, who is the pastor at Western Reserve United Methodist Church, the site of this meeting, as well as many others through our OCA history. The Adams family lives in Canfield; they have two grown daughters-Sarah and Anna, and one granddaughter-Pippa. Reverend Kathryn has volunteered as a docent at the Butler Institute of American Art and currently serving as pastor of a small Lowellville United Methodist Church.

Reverend Kathryn Adams has spent a significant part of her adult life preparing for and leading since 1996 some 16 volunteer-in-mission teams to orphanages in the former Soviet Union, mostly in Dmitrov, Russia. She has called these trips "To Russia with Love", responding to Corinthians 13:1, which reads, "If I speak in the tongues of men and angels, but have not love, I am only a resounding gong or a clanging cymbal." Located in Dmitrov, about an hour and a half north of Moscow, the orphanage is home to 60 children. Most of the children are severely physically handicapped, trying to be children despite braces, crutches, walkers, and wheelchairs. There were numerous illnesses and deformities among them, plenty of crooked spines, missing fingers, missing hands, and twisted feet. In one instance, Reverend Adams was instrumental in bringing 3 Russian orphans to the Youngstown area to be fitted for and receive prosthetic legs. "And yet precious souls are trapped inside these broken bodies, yearning to be known, wanting to be acknowledged, hoping to be loved." Reverend Adams reported that these are throwaway children abandoned by parents who are ashamed of them and unwilling to raise them. Some of the parents are addicted to drugs and/or alcohol. Most of these conditions of youngsters could easily be treated here in the United States.

She and her Team distributed to the orphans blankets, clothing, socks, gloves, hats, toiletries, school supplies, toys, flashlights, and playing cards. The Team members also distributed glow sticks and glowing necklaces, sidewalk chalk, and bubble-blowing items along with crafts with which the children were able to make bracelets, decorate a cross and make frames for their individual photos that the Team took with instant cameras. The Team took children on excursions to a zoo park where they were able to feed and pet a variety of animals, to a McDonalds, and to a Russian Orthodox monastery. Often, for those youngsters who were able, they played soccer with Team members in addition to just walking and running around.

As a result of fundraisers at home, the Team had money to buy for the orphans, new shoes for each child, new carpeting for bedrooms and hallways, embroidery thread, patterns and cloth, computer programs for speech therapy clothing for older teens, and hearing aids for some. The Team also made contributions to the United Methodist Seminary in Moscow.

Every night at the orphanage, the Team gathered for devotions. One evening, a Team member shared words from Max Lucado: "Servanthood requires no skill or seminary degree. Regardless of your strengths, training, or church tenure, you can love the overlooked." Here were people from the Mahoning Valley helping "the least of us". They said it was an intense experience and "inspiring to see how these young children responded to us with love, affection, and a passion for living". It was reported that the children "continually rose above their disabilities and used every ounce of their energy they had to share in the joy of the moment." Team member Shirley Merritt wrote about one of the trips, "It was good to hear the children's sweet voices and see the smiles that would melt your heart.... The world has somehow allowed these special kids to slip through its fingers." Reverend Kathryn Adams and the various Teams that accompanied her were beautiful examples of learning about people "different from us." Here were area residents not only learning about such people but also, they were moved to do something about empathizing with them and doing something to ameliorate their conditions.

Reverend Kathryn Adams

Roman Rudnytsky

The April meeting featured Tony Lariccia, a local philanthropist, who shared his Italian background and his philosophy on wealth sharing. Tony is a small man in physical stature (by his own admission 4' 9") but a man large of heart. Indeed, his kindness, generosity, and colorful personality have made him a giant among men in the Mahoning Valley. Born in1945, Tony was the grandson of Italian immigrants, son of Anthony D. and Laura M. DiCioccio Lariccia with lineage back to the mid-1700s in the village of Montelongo near Campobasso, Italy. He was a 1963 graduate of Struthers High School and earned a bachelor's degree in Business Administration from Youngstown State University. (In fact, he was a student of mine when I was yet only an adjunct faculty member; I take no credit for his success in the stock market.) He has shown his loyalty and gratitude to both institutions: he regularly referred to himself as a "just a kid from Struthers." Through all of his success in the stock market and his career, Tony never forgot his humble roots and his sharing attitude. Tony tells the story of a lesson in giving, learned from his father: "Having just unwrapped a Twinkie (cupcake) and about to take his first bite, Tony's father admonished him stating, 'Don't put that into your mouth without offering it to someone else first. Break it in half and share it'." His working-class beginnings honed the advice his father gave him as he tried a number of jobs. As a teen, Tony somehow accumulated $10,000 by investing his pool and poker-playing winnings in the stock market. Instead of pursuing a career as a gambler, he earned his bachelor's degree and, in 1966, started a job as an accounting clerk for U.S. Steel. When that work proved unsatisfying, Tony began making monthly trips to Merrill Lynch and finally asked the manager for a job. After repeated rejections, he was hired as an accountant trainee. None of this came easily. He was rejected more than once in job hunting, as we have mentioned, and he was rejected by girls in his youth. But ultimately, he was successful in both.

For four decades, he enjoyed a stellar career at Merrill Lynch, where he became known as a brilliant stock analyst and investment advisor. Tony worked hard to achieve success. But he also was not afraid to take chances. He had confidence in himself, and he focused on the big picture. He was disciplined; he had a vision, and he was persistent. This persistence paid off in terms of his huge success in the stock market and also in finding a wife. In 1972 he finally got a date with Mary Olenick, a pretty divorcee who caught his eye while she was working as a receptionist for an ophthalmologist client. They married a year later. By 1977 Lariccia became vice president at Merrill Lynch and was borrowing millions of dollars to buy stocks on margin. "I died a thousand deaths because of it, Lariccia recalls." But his wife said during these tough times that things would get better, and they did. He, in fact, became a multi-millionaire.

Lariccia made his first big charitable donation-$10,000 to Tod's Children's Hospital in 1984 after his second child died from a rare birth defect, just hours after he was born. And he was not yet a millionaire. Mary Lariccia admits that she was not prepared for her husband's first acts of generosity. But in time, Mary became accustomed to his writing these big checks to various organizations. A year or so after the baby's death, the Lariccia's adopted an infant girl that they named Dana to join sister Natalie.

Despite his growing wealth, the Lariccia lifestyle was relatively modest. They still lived in the same $150,000 colonial house in Boardman, built when they were first married. Tony lived a modest lifestyle and taught his own family the importance of humility. He never forgot the dark days of his career, including the 1987 stock market crash and the 2008 financial crisis. He refuses to buy a foreign car; he owns a Cadillac DTS. And they spend their two-week vacations at American resorts "instead of a second home in some exotic, sunny locale". "Mansions, Mercedes, Florida condos, country clubs-I'm scared to death of them", he said. "I know many people who went down that road. Instead of happiness, it brought them misery. It's unsatisfying, empty, and unfulfilling. Happiness begins where unselfishness ends." He used as another model for life, Bruno Papalia, a well-to-do man from the hometown of Struthers. Tony remembered fondly of Papalia buying uniforms for Little League baseball teams in the area, including his own, and taking local children to see Cleveland Indians baseball games. Lariccia vowed, "If God ever gives me wealth, I want to be just like Bruno Papalia."

Tony believed in sharing his success and found this through his philanthropy to the community. He was always proud of Struthers, Youngstown, and the surrounding area and enjoyed helping organizations that improved the community. He also enjoyed motivating children and helping them reach educational goals, as well as helping the underprivileged and animals. He found satisfaction in helping those who could not speak for themselves. Tony Lariccia was a model philanthropist who many in the area said we should all follow his lead. He was the leading light not only of the Mahoning Valley's Italian American community but also of the community as a whole. He never abandoned the Valley even as his fortunes rose. In times of growing disparities between the wealthy and those not so fortunate, Tony's dedication to the Valley stands as an example for the entire nation.

The Lariccia family generally supported causes that benefit large numbers, but there were exceptions to that generality. Gifts made for local high school stadium renovations have been made with the stipulation that the fields be named to honor deserving members of the community. An example of such a gift was the $100,000 donated to refurbish the Struthers High School with the understanding that it would be renamed Laddie J. Fedor Field, after a former typing teacher of Lariccia's who went on to become the Struthers school district's superintendent. This was only one of his contributions to his hometown. He regularly helped to finance his class reunions, which included meals and help with apparel that some classmates could not afford. In fact, when he would see classmates, community members, or friends, he often "picked up the tab."

Tony was also fond of immortalizing everyday heroes in bronze to help people remember how much one person could contribute in life. Examples of these acts of generosity are seen in his contributions of two $100,000 gifts to YSU to commission two statues: one to honor former legendary basketball coach Dominic Rosselli and one to honor the first president of YSU, Howard Jones. At about the same time, he contributed another $100,000 to the nursing department.

These are far from the only gifts the Lariccia's gave to YSU: he gave a $100,000 check (which ultimately led to $750,000) to President David Sweet, just "out of the blue," the president said, toward the school's $12,000,000 campaign to build the Andrews Student Recreation and Wellness Center; he was then tapped to chair the university's $43,000,000 Centennial Campaign in the early 2,000's-an effort to which he pledged $4,000,000, the largest donation by a single individual in the school's history. For this latter gift, a wing of YSU's School of Business has been named in his honor. In 2006 he gave a gift of $100,000 toward the Watson and Tressel Indoor Training Building. By this time, he had given at least $5,300,000 to YSU.

The organizations the Lariccia's supported over the years are almost too numerous to name, but include, besides YSU, Angels for Animals, Animal Charity, the Boardman YMCA, Goodwill Industries, Boardman Park, St. Charles Church, Basilica of Our Lady of Mount Carmel. This last gift came in the form of an impressive statue dedicated to Youngstown's Italian immigrant heritage on the grounds of the basilica adjacent to Smoky Hollow, one of the first neighborhoods where Italians settled in Mahoning County. In 2008, the National Ethnic Association awarded Tony Lariccia with the prestigious Ellis Island Medal of Honor.

In a few side notes, I would add that Tony saw an article in the local newspaper indicating that the Shrine of Mt. Lebanon in nearby North Jackson needed repair. He immediately sent a check to cover the costs. His reason was that before he and Mary were married, they went to those grounds to "make out". Another personal note: during the preceding meetings of OCA and the one to which Tony spoke, I talked of a new organization that was forming; it was to focus upon Ethnic Heritages (the name finally chosen for the group). The generous Mr. Lariccia whispered to me after the meeting to come to his office in the morning, where he had a check of $2,000 for the new group. Accompanying his check was a beautiful note that ended with "P.S., You're super duper." At this April 2008 OCA meeting, we convened at Our Lady of Mount Carmel Social Hall with one of our largest crowds-more than 330 people. Lou Fusillo Catering prepared for us a generous Italian meal; we were also thrilled with the Italian vocal selections of Dr. Allan Mosher and his wife Jennifer, plus two students.

Speaker, Tony Lariccia and wife Mary

This generous good man Anthony "Tony" Lariccia, 71, died on September 20, 2017, with his family by his side. He used to say, "God gave us all of this goodness. If we don't pass it along, something is wrong." Tony Lariccia did indeed pass it (goodness) along. This man, small in stature, had a large, bursting heart, and he will be well remembered. Aphorisms that apply to Tony Lariccia are: "Extraordinary things sometimes do come in small packages" and "It is easier for a camel to go through the eye of a needle than for the rich man to enter into the kingdom of heaven."

YSU singers Dr. Allan Moser and wife Jennifer

In May, Mary Boyer Smith reminisced about her long association with Youngstown State University and how her background prepared her for the many ways she served the University. She had more information regarding YSU and more stories (some apocryphal, some even true) than anyone. The very names of her husband, Dean Joseph Smith, and President Howard Jones were just waiting for laughter-Jones and Smith!! In May 2008, when Mary B. (which everyone affectionately called her) spoke to the OCA, she was 96 years of age. Some were fearful that she could not engage an audience for 30 minutes or so. How wrong they were; she even exceeded that time frame as she continued to be engaging. The Youngstown Club arranged for a high stool beside the lectern and had water available with a few friends close by. The Youngstown Club, in such a beautiful setting, provided and served a wonderful meal; the Wade Raridon Singers again delighted us with their beautiful and varied program. Wade Raridon devoted 41 years at YSU, teaching thousands of students. Many of them wanted more after Wade retired and they graduated. Thus, the formation of the Wade Raridon Singers was born.

Mary Boyer was born in 1911 in Pittsburgh, Pennsylvania, at a time when streetcars and fire engines were horse-drawn. Her family moved to a Cortland, Ohio, farm at age 6, along with 3 brothers. While attending high school, she graduated as class salutatorian, played basketball, and participated in track and field, despite working at a few part-time jobs. After high school, she met Howard Jones (later to become president of Youngstown College) at Hiram College, who helped Mary B. to get a scholarship to Hiram. After Hiram, she found a job teaching at Mecca, Ohio grade school, teaching 4th,5thand 6th grades history, English, and geography. She also got involved in coaching athletics while in the Mecca system. For a period of time, Mary B. was a semi-professional basketball player in Warren. She was hired as an alumni secretary at Hiram, 1936-39, while she was finishing her college studies and dating Joseph Smith, whom she married in 1939. Over the years, Mary B. served as vice president of the Hiram Alumni Executive Board, organized many class reunions for the class of 1939, and created a scholarship in her late husband's name. Most recently, she has served as co-chair and chair of the Hiram College Golden Terriers.

After graduating from Hiram College in 1939, she headed to Youngstown College, hired by President Howard Jones, where she taught biology and served as an admission counselor. Mary B. mused, "I remember I was teaching biology and also pushing doorbells to recruit students. I tried to convince everyone that college might be a way out of the Great Depression. Boys were enrolling, but few girls. At that time, our rate was eight men to one woman." "Working with Bucky Gillespie, they covered the areas of Campbell, Bessemer, New Castle, among other outlying communities." What a role model Mary B. was to those women who enrolled. And that was to continue over the next four decades-she was "breaking the glass ceiling" repeatedly. Amid this activity, Mary B. finished a Master of Arts in Physical Activity from The Ohio State University in 1947.

Mary B. served in these two capacities of teacher and counselor until 1944, when she became an assistant registrar and recorder. During this same time period, she served as department head and professor of the physical education department and coordinator of the health and physical education department from 1947-1957. Initially, the building behind the Main Building (Jones Hall) was to serve as the gym. Eventually, she arranged to have physical education classes at the YMCA for boys and the YWCA for girls. In the process, she worked with football coach Dike Beede, hired basketball coach Dom Rosselli and hired Bill Carson to replace her. For 22 years, she was the assistant registrar before taking over as YSU's registrar in 1966, during which she served until 1971 when she was moved to the position of dean of admission and records. After two years in that role, she became the Director of Planning and Placement until her retirement in June 1980. When Mary B. joined Youngstown College in 1939, the enrollment was 723 students; when she retired, Youngstown State University's enrollment was 15,000.

During Mary B.'s reminiscences, she had stories of the various people she worked with, including Bill Livosky and Jim Scriven, whom she hired to replace her at Admissions; Peg Hendricks, Pauline Botty and she, who started a course in Marriage Psychology that attracted 150 students; the many she worked with in athletics, such as Ed Murvis, a "brilliant rascal". She reflected on women's involvement, Black involvement and civil rights, faculty/staff/administration relations, the "hippies" era, registration and the coming of the computer age, and the successes of many students "who passed her way." We know, too, that Mary B. has contributed generously to departments at YSU, to athletics and has given significantly to fund student scholarships.

For her efforts, Mary B. has earned many awards. In 1977 she was granted a Lifetime Leadership Award from Hiram College. At the 11th annual YWCA Woman of the Year banquet, she was one of the 11 women honored as Woman of the Year. A scholarship at YSU is in her name, presented by the Youngstown Educational Foundation. In 1990, she was inducted into the YSU Athletics Hall of Fame; in 1981, Mary B. Smith was a recipient of a Doctor of Humanities Degree at YSU, and in 1983, she was honored with the prestigious Heritage Award at YSU. In 2001, Mary B. was honored along with Paul McFadden and Jeff Wilkins as the Penguins of the year; Smith Hall, on the YSU campus, was named in honor of Mary and her husband, Joseph.

Mary B. Smith has also been involved and honored by many organizations besides her beloved Hiram College and Youngstown State University: she has served in various positions, including President of the Board of Trustees for McGuffey Center, President of the Youngstown Chapter of the United Nations Association, Cooperative Campus Ministry, Youngstown Branch of the American Association of University Women and the Family Life Education Council. She has also given her time and talents as President of the Board of Trustees for the Society for the Blind and Disabled, coordinator of the Diamond Jubilee of YSU, and is a charter member and past president of the Altrusa Club of Youngstown, as well as President of the Youngstown Federation of Clubs, Inc., an organization of more than 30 women's clubs throughout the Valley; she also played an active role in the development of a Youngstown United Way chapter. In addition, she was active in the First Christian Church in Boardman. In her younger days, she was an avid golfer.

Mary B. Smith

Mary B. Smith has been honored abundantly for the cumulative impact of her lifelong dedication, not only to her academic roots but to the branches of all of society. One of the last honors after her death on September 28, 2012, was a recital tribute by members of the Warren-Youngstown Chapter of Sigma Alpha Iota Alumnae shortly after her passing. The organization is an international music fraternity whose mission is to encourage, nurture and support the art of Music, and encourage women musicians of all ages, races, and nationalities. The concert celebrated Mary B. Smith's long and active life and dedication to SAI and to spur additional contributions to the YSU Scholarship fund named in her memory. We also honor this large woman with a large heart who devoted so much of her life to our area-to, its people, its institutions, and its vitality. In the way of a couple of personal notes I offer: in the last decade or two of her life, she always said that she liked the smell of my Aramis after shave lotion; and secondly, owing to her abundant bosom, while eating, she sometimes dropped things "on her shelf". In the course of the OCA evening, we enjoyed this icon of the Valley; everybody knew and loved "Mary B."

The June meeting featured Sally Pallante, who spoke of her Irish background and the many ways she has contributed to the Irish legacy in the Mahoning Valley. Sally characterized her story as one who was "Called not to do great things but to make a difference." Her story "begins with family and evolves into a passionate dedication to ancestral research and promoting cultural enrichment in the American-Irish community."

Born in 1940, Sally's parents were Anthony and Betty Murphy. "As a baby, my maternal great-grandmother, born in County Donegal, Ireland, would rock me to sleep. That was my first connection to Ireland." Several generations of Murphys lived in Youngstown in the Kilkenny neighborhood homes and along Poland Avenue. When Sally's father went to the Navy during World War II, she and her mother moved in with her grandparent's home on the site where the YSU football field now stands. After the war, Sally characterized her family as "a typical first-generation Irish family of the era." She attended St. Columba church and grade school and participated in various Irish programs: St. Patrick's Show, learning Irish poetry, songs, and dances, and May Crowning. On her birthday, September 2, 1954, lightning struck St. Columba rendering a total loss; her father, then a fireman, was among those who fought the blaze. The new St. Columba, the fourth, was dedicated in 1958.

Sally met the "love of her life", Martin Pallante, while a student at Ursuline High School. They both attended YSU, with Martin continuing his education, earning a Doctorate in Business. They married in 1959 and had four active children who gave them 10 grandchildren; all rocked to sleep as babies "to the strains of Toora Loora Looral, an Irish lullaby. Even our dog has Irish roots!" Faith and traditions are important to the Murphy/Pallante family; the children and grandchildren share Sally's keen interest in the Emerald Isle. They actively participate in St. Patrick's Day activities, wearing something green, eating corned beef and cabbage, listening to Irish music, learning to Irish step dance, etc.

Sally discussed her first trip to Ireland, traveling with her father, who, despite his pride in his Irish roots, had never been to the country either. This trip was to buoy her father, who had recently lost his wife and was experiencing health problems himself. "That first trip to Ireland in 1978 had a profound impact on me and was the origin of my research for our family roots that grew into a passionate interest to preserve Irish culture." She detailed the beauty of the island with forty shades of green that one sees as they approach the Emerald Isle, the interesting coastlines and cities, the historical background of Ireland, the emigration of Irish to America, and talking to the locals about the" troubles" with Northern Ireland. These experiences were the impetus "for me to devote years and energy initiating the Ulster Project that builds bridges of friendship" between the youth of Ireland and Northern Ireland.

Sally said that the search for her heritage began at the Youngstown Library Reference room and "took 28 years and 10 trips to Ireland and countless hours to trace my family to England's Midlands, a district rich in deposits of coal, iron, lime, and fireclay." She traced the Irish from this area to America and to the Mahoning Valley, with the assumption that some of them were her ancestors. "My dedication to preserve Irish history, primarily the stories of the families of our community, is the basis for founding the Irish American Archival Society (IAAS)". She really got started with these projects in 1986 since her children were in college or medical school by this time.

As a member of the Canfield Junior Women's League, she was chairperson of the International Department, which had the task of finding a program that would help children on an international level. Sally read an article in the Catholic Exponent regarding the Ulster Project (a program that brought teens from Northern Ireland together to travel to the U.S.). She contacted people from the Canton/Massillon area that had an Ulster Project and subsequently contacted the appropriate people in Ireland and initiated a project locally in 1988. Sally was co-director of the project undertaken under the auspices of the Canfield Junior Women's League. Because of her work with the Ulster Project, Sally was honored as the YWCA's Religious Woman of the Year in 1988. Twenty years and some 250 Northern Irish teens later, the initiative has expanded to be the Mahoning Valley Ulster Project. The idea is to bring together the youth of Northern Ireland to America to interact with the Irish in the Valley for the fostering of tolerance, understanding, and friendship between these groups. The American host teens gain a broad understanding of another culture, which certainly excites us at the Ohio Cultural Alliance.

In 1992, Sally participated in the Irish Institute, a 2-week educational, ecumenical study trip focusing on the North of Ireland. Present at the Institute were Mary Robinson, President of Ireland, John Hume, a key figure in the original talks with Sinn Fein and the winner of a Noble Peace Prize. In Belfast, they met with clergy, educators, and government leaders and with representatives of Sinn Fein and Loyalist parties. She also participated in several other meetings of a similar nature, including the Ulster Project International Conference in 1993 and the 10th anniversary of the Peace Agreement in 2008 in Belfast. The Mahoning Valley Ulster Project hosted the International Conference in 2009.

In 1996, Sally invited a group of the Valley's Irish Americans to gauge their interest in forming a group committed to collecting, preserving, and presenting the history of the Irish in the Valley. The Irish American Archival Society (IAAS) was the result. Their first project, the "Irish Oral History Project", produced in cooperation with YSU History Department, resulted in a number of Irish histories being preserved in YSU's Maag Library. IAAS members prepared lesson plans, Irish Cultural Suitcases, and other hands-on educational materials to be used in local schools. They are available at the Mahoning Valley Historical Society and the Warren Arts Council. The largest undertaking was the preparation and publication of "The Irish in Youngstown and the Greater Mahoning Valley", with a committee led by Sally and several YSU History professors. The IAAS has also sponsored a variety of seminars and a series of Irish language lessons, they participate in the yearly Festival of Nations at YSU, they set up a yearly display for Ireland in the International Building at the Canfield Fair, and they publish The Harp, a quarterly newsletter that is mailed out to more than 1,000 area homes.

Sally has been a member and leader of the Ireland Ladies Ancient Order of Hibernians (LAOH) and was honored as the LAOH Irish Woman of the Year in 1999. She has worked with Junior Hibernian girls, working on various service projects, including sending homemade gifts to little girls in Northern Ireland and cards to the hospitalized military. In the late '90s, Sally Pallante chaired a meeting with leaders of all area Irish leaders to sponsor a family-oriented Irish Festival in the Mahoning Valley. It was done, and for ten years under Sally's presidency, The Gathering of the Irish Clans grew to two days of "family-oriented culture with Irish music, dance, and the "Land of Leprechauns" for wee folk. Molly's kitchen has home breads and foods, or visit the Pub or shop in the Irish marketplace." After the tragedy of September 11, 2001, Sally requested that the Gathering of the Clan sponsor a Memorial Service on Veterans Day to honor those victims and others who participated in the events of that horrific day.

Sally Pallante ended her heartfelt talk with thoughts that could resonate with us all: "I live by something I read years ago, and that is...I shall pass this world but once. If there be any kindness I can show or any good thing I can do, let me do it now...For I shall not pass this way again" and "While we celebrate our cultures and honor America's rich diversity differently, let's never lose sight of the commonalities that make us human. We are called not to do great things but to make a difference." Sally Pallante has made a difference, and the Ohio Cultural Alliance applauds her.

This June meeting was held at The Embassy Banquet Center in Youngstown. Our meal certainly complemented the theme as we ate roast beef, cabbage, and onions over noodles, redskin potatoes, green beans, and salad. The cultural enrichment was provided by a talented and lively group of Irish step-dancers taught by Theresa Burke, who has been teaching Irish dance for more than 40 years.

Sally Pallante

Irish Step Dancers

Wade Raridon Singers

"MY STORY" was the second year for the theme of the 2008-2009 Ohio Cultural Alliance season. It was again a stellar year. The stories of the varied and informative speakers are indicative of the rich culture of the Mahoning Valley. Included were a Puerto Rican public organization administrator, a Native American, a clergyman, a congressman, a medical doctor, an educator, a mission organizer, a Black entrepreneur, a Jewish activist/organizer, and a businessman. In addition to the speakers, the different venues, the sumptuous meals, and the variety of cultural enrichment, the past season had a few other highlights: the creation of a website, the "adoption" of the Ethnic Heritage Society, the initiation of a "question of the month" and monthly donations (non-perishable food, paper products, personal care items, etc.) to donate to several local agencies.

In September, Henry Guzman, whose parents and he emigrated from Puerto Rico, spoke of his ethnic influences, which led to the many executive positions he has held, including a cabinet position during Ohio Governor Ted Strickland's term of office. His Story, "I Could Never Have Imagined," was one that followed his life from an immigrant child to a series of administrative offices at the State level. He reported that his life seems to divide itself into segments: early years on the east side of Youngstown, working his way through school, his time in the military, his early years in community service, and his time with local and state governments.

At five years old, he, his parents, and two sisters emigrated from Puerto Rico to Youngstown. His father said he was seeking a better life for the family at a time when the Valley needed labor. He credits his family for inculcating the values of family, community, education, and hard work. "I think getting to where I am today started with my family's commitment to our religion and a strong work ethic." Henry contends that the church (Roman Catholic) has long kept his family grounded and continued to remind him of the core values his parents taught him. The church was the center of the Hispanic community, where the planning of community gatherings, picnics, and programs revolved.

Education came a little more slowly, partly because of his lack of English and his coming from a different culture. Henry attributed getting over the humps to his third-grade teacher, Miss Olga Kragel, who had an understanding of the difficulties one might face as a newcomer. Even with her help, school was still a constant struggle in those early days. But with his older sister helping him, the continuing encouragement of his father, and his penchant for reading comic books, he eventually overcame his problems. His several jobs and contact with others helped him to adjust.

In 1965, Henry received a notice from the Draft Board. On advice from his recruiting officer that he voluntarily joined the Army to possibly get more favorable treatment, he signed up for three years. His life was changed dramatically. "Before I knew it, I found myself in the jungles of Vietnam." It was a turning point for him and not just because of the terrors of war, "but because it gave me a profound understanding of how short life really is. I realized that it is what you do while you are here that will define your life and make the mark that you leave behind." He vowed that if he got through the war, he would "make sure I leave something behind not just for my family, but for our communities, cities, and towns, and for the families of those who didn't make it back from Vietnam." He himself was wounded in Vietnam and spent 11 months recuperating in hospitals. He credits all of his family for writing letters to him to keep the faith and to apprise him of what was happening at home.

In 1970, shortly after his return, he married his long-time friend, Nydia, who helped guide him through his next life-changing decisions. (At the time of his appearance at the OCA, they had been married for 38 years and had 4 children and 10 grandchildren.) At about this time, a fledgling organization called Organization Civica y Cultural Americana (OCCHA) was being formed, and Henry was asked to be its first director, where he served for 12 years. And I know he served well because I was on the board of directors for most of those years. There was a period of time when the funds were so low that he served for no pay. Over the years, OCCHA became the focal point for civic, cultural, and social events for the Hispanic community and beyond. Henry had an opportunity to serve as a policeman, but instead, he focused on continuing his education at YSU (he was one of my students), where he was preparing to make a difference. "I could visualize the things I could do and achieve with a college degree. For me, that degree meant I would be able to make a difference for my family and community that I could never have imagined."

Henry ran for the Youngstown Board of Education twice before he was appointed to fill an unexpired term. He was ultimately elected as the first Latino to serve on a school board in the state of Ohio. With growing numbers of Hispanics in the Valley, it was the right time to have someone in that position who understood the needs of that cohort. "As it turns out, being the first director of OCCHA and the first Latino to be elected to an Ohio school board were only the beginning in a series of firsts for me."

His work in these capacities was recognized by Governor Dick Celeste, who chose his first city for "Capital for a Day" to be Youngstown. Henry was asked to discuss the needs of the Latino community with the Governor. Six months after this meeting, Governor Celeste asked Henry to join his staff in Columbus to serve as the Deputy Director of the State and Local Government Commission. After consultation with his family and remembering the words of St. Francis of Assisi, who wrote: "Start by doing what's necessary; then do what's possible, and suddenly you are doing the impossible." With that thought, he started the chapter in his life in state and local government.

For the next 25 years or so, he worked for the government, working for Governor Celeste, then in the Attorney General's Office and the Division of Liquor Control. Afterward, he worked for the city of Cleveland as the Public Service Director, then as the Public Safety Director (a position held by the famous Elliot Ness). He was now in a position to help protect the safety of the public and to help the city of Cleveland's police, fire, and EMS forces. "My little dreams were ending up larger than I could have imagined." It continued when he was called back to Columbus in 2004 to work with Mayor Coleman to serve as Service Director and Acting Mayor. His latest first was to accept Governor Ted Strickland's invitation to be the first Latino cabinet director in Ohio, to serve as the Director of the Ohio Department of Public Safety, a department of more than 4,000 employees, consisting of the Ohio State Highway Patrol, Bureau of Motor Vehicles, Ohio Homeland Security and the Ohio Emergency Management Agency.

Through all of these firsts, Henry Guzman has tried to broaden his understanding of all communities, of all peoples, and all cultures, following the strictures of a writer by the name of Jesus Colon: "To deserve a peoples' love, you must know them. You must learn to appreciate their history, their culture, their values, their aspirations for human advancement and freedom". He concludes with, "My story should serve as an example for anyone, that you SHOULD reach high, HAVE lofty goals, and NEVER give up because you can never imagine what can happen." Quoting Martin Luther King, Jr., Henry advised, "Take the first step in faith. You don't have to see the whole staircase, just take the first step." Surely, Henry Guzman's aspirations and story enhance us all as we follow the path of peace and understanding among peoples.

Felipe Gonzalez walked through the audience singing Hispanic melodies as we enjoyed the fine cuisine provided by Monica's Catering. We met at St. Rose of Lima / St. Lucy's Church in Campbell.

Felipe Gonzalez Trio

Henry Guzman

Tom Netz, in October, spoke of his American Indian heritage with his words and demonstrations. His simple and basic explanations of the world we live in were revealing. Tom Soft Shell Turtle Netz is of Native American and European descent. As the keeper of a tradition, he is an inspiration and a source of knowledge for those Native American families who seek the lost teachings and art forms of their ancestral past. Through spiritual healing and plant medicine healing and walking a good pathway of peace, Tom is able to bring a balance through the teachings of those people who look for oneness between Creator and Earth Mother. Tom spoke of the Indians of the Great Lakes region. His storytelling of area Native Americans was fascinating, and suggested historic sites and museums we might visit. As an Indian activist, he said Ohio's sometimes contentious tribes and nations call on him to overcome differences. He and his group also provided cultural enrichment in the form of music with a drum, flute, and chanting as they danced.

The late Dr. John White, YSU Anthropology Department, in his article, Native American that appears in OCA's "An Ethnic Encyclopedia," writes about the Native Americans that lived in the Mahoning Valley that Tom Netz spoke about. White writes: "The earliest cultural period documented in Ohio is labeled the Paleo-Indian, about 15,000-8,000 B.C. A possible Paleo-Indian encampment, the Erskine site, was discovered in 1971 on the Middle Fork of the Little Beaver Creek about seven miles north of Salem, Ohio, just inside Mahoning County. The occupation of terraces near the Mahoning River during at least the late stages of this period has also been substantiated by the McKibben site excavations in Trumbull County. The Middle Woodland Period, about 1-500 A.D., is primarily noted for its elaborate and widespread trade networks and is labeled Hopewell. Elaborate earthworks became the hallmark of the Hopewell; there is scant evidence to date of such development in Mahoning County. The Boarts site near Lowellville, Ohio, excavated by archeologists from YSU, represents the closest demonstrated Middle Woodland occupation."…as well as with other

Other Native Americans that had some presence in our general area were the League of the Iroquois. After conflicts with several other groups/tribes, the Iroquois laid claim to most of the land from the south shores of Lake Erie to the mouth of the Mahoning. However, by the time the earliest European settlers entered the Mahoning Valley in the latter 19th century, even these Native Americans were moved westward. Tom Netz spoke of the importance of many modern terms that have Native American origins, including the very name of the local salt springs, Mahonink, which we call Mahoning.

This meeting was held at St. Matthias Church Hall and was catered by Carolyn Catering, who prepared a meal that had some Native American items. This was also the first meeting that members brought items to be donated to a charitable organization-this month; it was for Second Harvest Bank.

Speaker Tom Netz with his dance group

Reverend Jim Ray was our speaker for November. He spoke of how he became a minister and how that decision influenced many of his subsequent decisions in his life. Jim Ray was dramatically moved by his attendance at the March on Washington on August 28, 1963, where the Reverend Martin Luther King uttered those "I have a dream" words that changed all of our lives, including the life of Reverend Jim Ray, who was just three years out of seminary.

Jim was the oldest of three children, born in 1929. His parents, Charles Ray and Margaret Ream were married at the start of the Great Depression; his mother had a degree in Library Science, and his father had a degree in Business Administration. The Depression wreaked havoc with his parents' dreams as they searched for a job that was not to be had. With no permanent job, they moved, always into a poorer section of whichever city they were in. His father got his first real job in 1941 in the Columbus area as a life insurance salesman for 26 years; Jim's mother read to the children every night, was active in PTA, and became involved with Church Women United, which brought her in close touch with African-American women.

The Ray family joined Kohr Presbyterian Church, and there began an important faith-building time for him. He said, "I did it all, Sunday school, Sunday worship, and Sunday evening youth groups." He did well in high school; the only option for college was the hometown of Ohio State, where he could live at home and work part-time. He spent two years at OSU studying radio announcing but did not do very well, so he decided to join the ROTC. This planted a seed in his mind, which came to fruition years later as he became a nonviolent peacemaker. College life was diverted when he was drafted into the Army during the Korean War. "This was the first of a number of interventions that would continue to change my life forever," he said.

Inducted in 1951, he did basic training at Fort Riley, Kansas, where he concluded he was not cut out to be a combat soldier. Another intervention that changed his life during basic training was developing a foot infection which put him in the military hospital for seven-and-one-half weeks. During this time, his company shipped out to Korea into severe combat; many of his friends were killed. He wondered why he had not been with them. Was God telling him, "I want you to have this experience but not that one." After his hospital stay, he went home on leave for a week, was shipped out on a troop ship to Korea, and was put into the prisoner of war command. While here, Jim saw the results and the horrors of war, including the illegality of most of our wars. During his 16 months of this duty, he had an opportunity to work more closely with a few of the North Korean prisoners, which broadened his perspective of God's people. "They were, indeed, a lot like me, though from a very different culture", he said.

Jim left the Army in 1953, took a job in Columbus, returned to OSU to graduate in 1956, and soon entered McCormick Theological Seminary in Chicago. He was married during seminary to Barbara Gerlach, graduated in 1960, and took a position as assistant minister at the First Presbyterian Church in Galesburg, Illinois. Their two sons were born there. After several years another intervention occurred in his life whereby a colleague from the seminary invited Jim to replace him in campus ministry at McKinley Foundation because he was taking a pastorate. In 1963 he took the position, which he said was an exciting place to be, in that there were many programs aimed at students, faculty, and staff to provide a Christian faith perspective on the many facets of life. Things were changing on campus as hints of the Viet Nam conflict arose, and the struggles in the South over civil rights became more strident and visible.

Dr. James Hine was the director of the McKinley Foundation for over 20 years; by 1963, things were certainly changing. Dr. Hine was supportive of the epic trip to Washington, D.C., that Jim and another colleague were to make. Reverend Jim Ray's life would never be the same after those days in Washington. When they returned, each of them was involved in the civil rights struggle on campus and in the community. "I found myself walking a picket line in front of the university president's home to protest the very poor record of hiring Black workers on campus at every level." He also became chair of the local war on poverty board. He and other colleagues held workshops on nonviolent tactics for students who were going to Mississippi for Freedom in the Summer of 1964. "I went with a local pastor friend to Hattiesburg, Mississippi, during Holy Week of 1964." A national call had gone out for clergy to demonstrate for civil rights so persons of color could register to vote without being hassled. In March 1965, Reverend Jim participated in the Voting Rights March from Selma to the state capitol in Montgomery, Alabama. In the summer of 1965, he directed a group of ten college students from around the nation doing voter education, registration, tutoring, and helping with a weeklong health clinic.

In August 1968, Reverend Jim received a Danforth Campus Ministry grant for a year of graduate study on "Higher Education and the Urban Crisis". His focus was and continued to be to help the university to humanize the city in which it is located. Subsequently, he served for eleven years on the staff of University and City Ministries (UACM) in Pittsburgh, where there was an Urban Campus Ministry at the University. Within a week of arriving, "I was in the streets with the Black construction coalition because African Americans were not being hired on two major construction projects. While there, he became active with a local community organization called 'Peoples' Oakland.'" While at UACM, he was a key person in The Community of Reconciliation (COR), a multiracial congregation, and one of the seven ministry parts of UACM. "I learned much from being part of a very diverse racial and religious Christian fellowship." By this time, Reverend Jim and his wife had two boys, and she was pregnant with their daughter. His time away was a difficult time for them, and their growing estrangement ultimately led to divorce in 1975.

At one point during these years, Reverend Jim answered a national call to go to the agricultural fields of the San Joaquin Valley in central California to stand in support of farmers as Caesar Chavez was forming a union of migrant workers. In August 1980, he left his position in campus ministry and joined the staff of "The Program for Female Offenders" in Pittsburgh. The human service agency worked with women who were being released from the Allegheny County jail or the state prison, providing them with job training skills and helping them find employment. During his time at UACM, he had also begun a large citizen coalition that sought a humane change in the criminal justice system by pressing for alternatives to incarceration.

By July 1983, Reverend Jim Ray returned to his career in the campus ministry by becoming the director of the Cooperative Campus Ministry at YSU. "I began working with an African-American YSU staff person in a Racial Awareness Program (RAP). This was a weekly dialogue group that brought various racial/ethnic persons together for personal sharing and to focus on common problems and concerns. That weekly program evolved into The Coalition for Diversity ... which helped pave the way to a more affirming climate for persons of any color, culture, gender, or sexual preference." During these years at YSU, he began a silent vigil for peace, standing by The Rock in the core area of the campus. He later led an effort to place a peace pole on the campus core. An integral part of his work was the free clinic where students could receive some basic medical treatment. During the dozen or so years at YSU, Ray was a constant presence with activity in areas of civil rights, peace, and cross-cultural understanding. He retired in 1995 from campus ministry but remained as part-time pastor of the Lowellville Presbyterian Church until it closed, after which he became minister of visitation at Westminster Presbyterian Church in Boardman. He married Suzanne (Sue) Anzellotti in June 2000, and that brought together a blended family of six. Jim continues with many volunteer efforts in areas of peace and justice, with a particular interest in the Palestinian-Israeli struggle. He also has been a valued member of the Ohio Cultural Alliance, where he regularly offers a generic prayer of peace at the beginning of our meetings.

In conclusion, Reverend Jim shared his faith perspective, believing that Jesus came into our midst as a "now person rather than a hereafter person." He quotes Jesus from the Book of Isaiah: "God's spirit is on me. He's chosen me to preach the message of good news to the poor, sent me to announce pardon to prisoners and recovery of sight to the blind, to set the burdened and battered free, to announce this is God's year to act." Reverend Jim argues that "Jesus was not pointing to some distant future. The kingdom of God is here—now! Jesus came to speak truth to power." Martin Luther King, Jr. reminds us that "our lives begin to end the day we become silent about things that matter!" Ray closed with these words of Emile Zola, "If you ask me what I came into the world to do, I will tell you, I came to live out loud!" Reverend Jim Ray may not always live out loud be he certainly has been on the side of the angels who stand for peace, justice, and love.

The dinner was served in the Fellowship Hall of Western Reserve United Methodist Church, with Reverend Jim Ray's talk given in the church proper. The globetrotting Roman Rudnytsky performed beautiful and thoughtful music that complemented the talk.

Reverend Jim Ray

Dorothy Palguta Tesner and my sister, Gloria Dragus checking in guests

In December, Congressman Tim Ryan was our speaker. He concentrated on his paternal Italian background and how it helped to frame his life and how it aided him in public service. Meeting at The Georgetown Banquet Center, Congressman Tim Ryan spoke to a capacity crowd, weaving a story of his Italian Catholic background. "I have an Irish last name, but I was reared Italian." He shared with us family values, his ethnicity, and his faith and how they helped him in life and in government service.

Tim is described in Wikipedia as an American lawyer serving as the U.S. Representative for Ohio's 13th congressional district since 2013 (before the district change, he was elected in 2002 in the 17th district.) Born in Niles, Ryan worked as an aide to U.S. Representative Jim Traficant after graduating from Bowling Green State University. He served in the Ohio Senate from 2001 to 2002 before winning the election to succeed Traficant. In November 2016, Ryan launched an unsuccessful challenge to unseat Nancy Pelosi as party leader of the House Democrats. He was a candidate for the 2020 Democratic presidential nomination before ending his campaign in October 2019 to run for reelection to Congress.

His focus for his presentation to the Oho Cultural alliance was how his rearing in Niles, Ohio framed his life. Born in Niles, the son of Rochelle Maria (Rizzi) and Allen Leroy Ryan, he is of Irish and Italian ancestry. Ryan's parents divorced when he was seven years old; Tim was raised by his mother and grandparents, who lived only two blocks away. He graduated from John F. Kennedy High School in Warren, where he played football as a quarterback and coached junior high basketball. He was recruited to play football at YSU, but a knee injury ended his playing career. He transferred to Bowling Green University, graduating in 1995 with a bachelor's degree. It was after college that he joined the staff of Congressman Traficant, and during this time, he earned a Juris Doctor degree from Franklin Pierce Law Center in Concord, New Hampshire.

These early years of his life left guiding principles for Tim's future. His chief influencers were clearly his mother, his grandmother, and his grandfather. As he reminisced with us, he shared the life values of his Catholic faith, his Italian heritage, and his family. He became aware of having a personal relationship with God, of learning that there is something bigger in life than oneself, of toleration of those "different from us", of helping one's fellow man, of service to others, of the importance of shared rituals, such as Veterans' Day, reverence for the American flag, attendance at Sunday Mass, of Christmas Eve, of sharing at mealtime, laughter, and fun in life. His mother instilled many of these values, despite raising the children alone. Education was a valued goal toward achieving a good and full life.

The Congressman spoke warmly and with admiration about his maternal grandfather, John, whom Tim described as a big man and the family disciplinarian, but he loved him dearly. John would merely give a stern look which would suffice to settle down rambunctious boys. Some of his first examples of service to the community came from observing his grandfather meeting the needs of his extended family and the church they belonged to, Our Lady of Mt. Carmel in Niles. His grandfather is pictured in a photo helping to dig the footer in the same church, where he served in many ways: maintenance of the church, working festivals, and serving as an usher.

His grandmother Ann was a loving and welcoming force in his life. He told of the joy of walking into her house after school, greeted by the smell of mouthwatering tomato sauce or freshly baked pizza in the oven. She also provided a lot of fun and laughter in the house. She was often seen at home and church praying the rosary, showing the personal relationship she had with God. And they both took time to help others, from the church and outside the church. Tim learned plenty from both grandparents, including stories of his great-grandfather, who frequently went to New York to greet newcomers and help them settle. From all of them, young Tim was imbued with an optimistic outlook on life and with the notion that life is to be enjoyed despite setbacks.

Now serving in his tenth term in Congress, Ryan currently serves as a member of the powerful House Appropriations Committee, which controls the expenditure of money by the federal government. He also serves as co-chairman of the Congressional Manufacturing Caucus and remains a leader in the fight to strengthen America's manufacturing base and reform U.S. trade policies. The above caucus examines and promotes policies to help American manufacturers find trained, educated workers, continue to lead the world in developing new industrial technologies, operate on a level playing field with their foreign competitors and obtain the capital they need to thrive. Ryan's primary focus is on the economy and quality of life in Northeast Ohio. He works closely with local officials and community leaders to advance local projects that enhance economic competitiveness and help attract high-quality, high-paying jobs. He is a dynamic leader and speaks out on issues of particular concern in Northeast Ohio. He is a champion of efforts to make college more affordable, revitalize America's cities and improve the health and well-being of American families and children. He is the author of several books: "Healing America: How a Simple Practice Can Help Us Recapture the American Spirit" and "The Real Food Revolution: Healthy Eating, Green Groceries, and the Return of the American Family Farm." Much of his thinking, as revealed in his legislative priorities and his published works, are reminders of his family background and his overall milieu. His most recent work, "A Mindful Nation, "is a manifestation of the thoughtfulness that comes from reflection and consideration of others. Congressman Tim Ryan has been a man on the go, revealing his early influences, his education, and his service to his fellow man. He wants to serve man and his maker as well as he can during his time on earth. He ended his talk with a poem: "I am only one, but I am one. I cannot do everything, but I can do something. And that which I can do, I ought to do. And that which I ought to do, by the grace of God I shall do." The evening concluded with rousing songs and dance routines performed by the talented Youngstown Connection.

Youngstown Connection

Congressman Tim Ryan

Dr. Kong Oh, of Malaysian/Chinese background, used a PowerPoint presentation to give glimpses of his life and how it led to his profession as an ophthalmologist and to his Baha'i religion for our January presentation. The meeting was held at Mr. Anthony's in Boardman, and the cultural enrichment was a return of Mark Lee Pringle's Lion Dancer.

This much we know about Dr. Oh: he is an outstanding doctor with excellent professional credentials and a demeanor that is reassuring; he is generous in his humanitarian activity and in his appreciation for former patients. Whether it is his family background, his education, or his religious convictions, Dr. Kong Oh has left a legacy in the Mahoning Valley and beyond that is incalculable.

Dr. Oh grew up in a traditional Chinese family in Malaysia, as have several generations of his family. His mother and father were highly respected in the community: father was a businessman, and mother, despite having but three years of formal schooling, ran a household with nine children, was a local consultant for weddings and engagements and was a wonderful cook. Parents encouraged children to work hard, practice Chinese calligraphy, not waste food and refrain from spending beyond one's means and save for a "rainy day". "We were always reminded to be kind, courteous, and respectful, especially to elders."

Kong attended the elite Chung Ling Chinese High School in Penang Island, Malaysia, where he did well in mathematics and science but not as well in English and literature. So, he transferred to St. George's School, a Catholic school, for the last two years to improve his English. It was here that he met his wife, Gim. Afterward, he attended and graduated from the Singapore College of Medicine (1969), turning down a government scholarship to study veterinary science at the University of Cambridge in the United Kingdom.

He was recruited in 1971 by the Ventnor Foundation in Atlantic City, New Jersey, to meet a shortage of doctors in the U.S. He interned at Memorial Hospital of Burlington County for one year (1971-72). Following this year, Dr. Oh was offered a three-year residence (1972-75) in ophthalmology at the University of Pennsylvania, Scheie Eye Institute in Philadelphia. And over the years, he has become certified in an untold number of categories, which certainly enhances his ability to provide the kind of medical care we all wish to enjoy.

Dr. Oh moved to Youngstown, Ohio, in 1978, taking over the practice of Dr. Charles Stertzbach. He and his wife Gim raised two children in the Mahoning Valley, where Gim earned a master's degree in Business Administration from YSU, and their two children earned degrees from the Northeast Ohio College of Medicine. For nearly forty years, Dr. Kong Oh served the Valley as a leading ophthalmological surgeon completing more than 20,000 cataract surgeries alone. In addition to serving us in the Valley, Dr. Oh has served as a humanitarian missionary in Dominica, China, Albania, and Mongolia. But that does not tell the whole story because that factual information does not indicate the nature of the man. Dr. Oh is truly a man who is technically capable but also is attentive to the needs of his patients, is calm in his demeanor, has a good "bedside manner," and remembers his patients afterward.

For a number of years, he held seminars relating to Health for Humanity, wherein he assembled specialists in various fields to urge healthy diets, to urge non-smoking, to encourage healthy mental living, among other guidelines for living good lives. Additionally, for several years he sponsored elaborate dinners at Mr. Anthony's Banquet Center for former patients-more than 800 people at each of these gatherings.

In the above paragraphs, we have seen the beautiful standards achieved by his family background and the outstanding education he brought to the Valley. Let us now consider the influence of his chosen faith-the Bahai religion. "We practiced the traditional Chinese-Buddhist culture in school in Malaysia, which is a Muslim country. In our class, we practice various religions: Christianity, Buddhism, Islam, and Hinduism. We had the unique experience of learning in a multiracial and multi-religious school under the guidance of the Irish Catholic Brothers who were dedicated to the education of humanity." Dr. Oh added that he and Gim were introduced to the Bahai faith in 1970 while still in Malaysia. They embraced the teachings of Baha'u'llah, after considerable research and reflection. They came to "believe in the three Onenesses - the Oneness of God; Oneness of religion; and Oneness of humanity. Baha'u'llah taught "that the earth is but one country, mankind its citizens." The Ohs asserted that they "are guided by the spiritual principle of the Baha'i faith-that work, in the spirit of service is worship. We are empowered to strive for excellence and to serve the people in the community with a pure motive." And as Baha'u'llah said, "Let deeds, not words be our adorning." Bahai's believes that God periodically reveals his will through divine messengers, whose purpose is to transform the character of humankind and to develop, within those who respond, moral and spiritual qualities. Therefore, religion is seen as orderly, unified, and progressive from age to age. The existence of God and the universe is thought to be eternal, without a beginning or end. Though inaccessible directly, God is nevertheless seen as conscious of creation, with a will and purpose expressed through messengers called Manifestations of God. Baha'i teachings state that God is too great for humans to fully understand or to create a complete and accurate image of by themselves, so human understanding of God is achieved through his revelations by way of his Manifestations. According to the teachings of the Baha'i religion, the human purpose is to learn, to know, and to love God through such methods as prayer, reflection, and being of service to others.

Dr. Kong Oh

Dr. Kong Oh represents a race, religion, nationality, and culture "different" from most of us in the Mahoning Valley. Through his family background, his education, and his religious faith, he represents the best of humanity. He personifies a "genius" that so many of us have come to appreciate-some directly and others tangentially. Genius knows no boundaries!

Baha'i Temple in Haifa, Israel

Mark Lee Pringle performing Lion Dance

Pakistan was our focus for February. Dr. Ikram Khawaja explained his philosophical journey to the U.S., his college preparation, his teaching, and his rise to the provost at Youngstown State University. A fashion show organized by local artist Tazim Jaffer of nearly 20 people of all ages wonderfully complemented the evening. The venue for the meeting was the Saxon Club in Austintown. We had some authentic ethnic items from Alladin Middle Eastern Restaurant in Boardman.

Dr. Khawaja came to us at YSU in 1968 after earning degrees from the University of Karachi in Pakistan, B.A., Southern Illinois, M.A. and Indiana University, Ph.D. He began teaching as a geology professor at YSU in 1968, then chair of the geology department before retiring in 2002. But after three years, he was asked to return to YSU as the dean of the arts and sciences. After two years as dean-2005-2007, he was asked to temporarily fill the provost position while the university went on a search-a search that resulted in failure. So, Khawaja was asked to accept the position as provost, which he held from 2008 until 2014, also serving as interim president for a short time. The role of provost is to head the academic affairs division of a university. Typically the largest division at any university, academic affairs provides leadership for academic activity and initiatives at a university, including library, research, and international programs. Khawaja said that "the job at this office is to have a vision and to have an agenda, but it is also to encourage people to think creatively." Khawaja left a palpable and lasting impact on the university, even outside his role as provost. During his time in the geology department, he facilitated the donation of $1 million worth of minerals that led to the founding of the YSU Clarence R. Smith Mineral Museum on campus. He also played a pivotal role in the founding of the YSU Center for Islamic Studies. During his "retirement periods" in 2003, 2004, and 2005, Dr. Khawaja volunteered at the first university established for women in Pakistan.

After speaking/writing about some of the tenets of the Muslim faith, he and his colleagues gave examples of that faith. The adherents to the Muslim faith express: the uniqueness of the One and Only god; the Revelations of the teachings and commandments of God to Prophets which make the way of peace of the whole universe and all mankind; the day of judgment which inaugurates the afterlife. Islam establishes a code of conduct that outlines human responsibilities to God, to oneself, to the family, and to humankind. Muslims believe that God is universal, just, and loving. God is not partial to one race or one group of people; God sent His prophets and messengers among all people.

For the cultural enrichment, members of the congregation did the following: set up a table of artifacts, including some pillow covers and saris, some brassware and marble artifacts; displayed a Dholki (musical instrument); displayed several relevant paintings; did a recital of a Quran selection (Surrah/Fateha); recited an Iqbal poem and a Suffi poem; sang three short songs and put on a fashion show with about 20 participants. Once again, members of the Ohio Cultural Alliance enjoyed an experience of talented people displaying their "differences" yet showing common humanity.

Dr. Ikram Khawaja and wife Suzan

Participants in Pakistani fashion presentation

The March meeting featured local Black restaurateur Charlie Staples, who displayed his magnetic personality and how he succeeded in his chosen field. We met at St. Matthias Church Hall with caterer Carolyn preparing part of the food and Charlie Staples providing his sumptuous ribs. Julius Veal, the local guitar acoustic soul balladeer, graced us with music appropriate to the evening.

Charlie Staples is loyal to Youngstown, Ohio. He believes in the Valley and is pleased to serve local residents who have supported him from the beginning. "I really just feel it was my purpose to do what I'm doing: to bring good to the community, to be a role model to younger people, and to show that there is a way out. You don't have to sell drugs and those types of things. Be willing to work hard," he said. Good people come in many forms, as does genius. While Charlie may not put himself up as a genius, he is indeed a role model, not only for the Black community but for us all. The publication "Mahoning Matters" considers Charlie Staples one of the "Movers and Makers" of the Mahoning Valley.

For more than four decades, Charlie has tempted our palate that begins with the sauce. The special sauce is the same recipe that has not been changed since 1911. The barbecue sauce recipe's original owner sold the recipe to Bill Robinson in 1939, who owned Bill Robinson's Bar-B-Que for 35 years before selling the establishment to Charlie Staples. Robinson was not willing to give up the barbecue sauce recipe to just anyone, though. So, he took Staples under his wing for a full year before selling him the recipe. Robinson wanted to make sure that Charlie had what it took to run a successful barbecue restaurant. Charlie renamed the establishment C. Staples Bar-B-Que'd Restaurant, which was then located across the street from the current location. Later, the restaurant was relocated to 372 W. Rayen Avenue in Youngstown and was renamed Charlie Staples's Famous Bar-B-Que.

After the initial success of the restaurant in Youngstown, Staples and his wife Margaret moved to Columbus in the 1980s to open additional restaurants. Later the couple relocated to Houston for 25 years to try their hand at the beauty industry. They sold a variety of health and beauty aids, including shampoos, conditioners, and relaxers. During that time, Staples handed over the restaurant to business partner Carl Young and his wife Emma, who ran the operation until their deaths in 2003. When his other business ventures were not doing as well as he had hoped, he sold out in Houston and moved back to Youngstown in 2003 to refocus his attention on the restaurant.

Upon their return, the Staples tore down the original building, reopened across the street in 2005, and made major renovations to the dining room in 2009. Upon entering the new 3,000-square-foot restaurant, one walks into a serene atmosphere that takes you way down to New Orleans and into a French Quarter type of milieu. In a family environment with plenty of space for groups upstairs and on the main floor, one finds a place to relax, unwind and enjoy companionship with mouth-watering food. On the menu, on any given day, Staples serves up Charlie's famous barbecue chicken, a slab of ribs, or pulled pork smothered with that delicious sauce. And there is Big Bertha-an overstuffed loaded baked potato that lives up to its name. You can dine in, carry out or sit outside on the rooftop patio on a warm summer evening.

But Charlie said that there is still another secret ingredient to his success, and that is "a cup of love", which is in the restaurant's logo. He started joking around with customers when they inquired about the recipe for the sauce, so Charlie responded with, "in every batch, I take a full cup of love, and I pour it in there." Customers who want Charlie Staples' barbecue sauce at home can buy it in original and hot flavors by the bottle in local stores and online. Recently, Charlie introduced a new Texas-style sauce called Cowboy Sauce that is now on store shelves.

From politicians to entertainers, people visit from near and far to taste the "cup of love". It is a place to go for those from Youngstown and the surrounding area, even though it's off the main downtown commercial route. When visitors come to town, the word is you gotta go to Charlie Staples Restaurant before you leave. With faith in himself and his work ethic and with confidence in the Valley, Charlie Staples is here to stay. Indeed, Staples is hopeful his daughter will be the next to take ownership of the restaurant. "She came into the company a few years ago, and it looks like she will carry on. If she can continue to carry on with the Charlie Staples magnetic personality and continue to dispense the "cup of love" to the sauce, she is sure to succeed.

Charlie Staples

Julius Veal

In April, Kathy Price selflessly described how she saw poverty while on vacation in Mexico and was moved to establish the "Mission of Love" which collects food and other necessities, then delivers truck and plane loads to the needy in the U.S. and abroad. Kathy shared what motivated her to initiate the program and how her life has been affected by her efforts in the program. We met at Mt. Carmel Hall, where Lou Fusillo Catering prepared a "Youngstown Buffet". Cultural enrichment was provided by Betty Bannon, accordionist, and Susan Brenneis on violin; they played songs of love.

Love and service most assuredly have been hallmarks of most of Kathy's life. Now in her early 70s, Kathy grew up in Austintown, attending Immaculate Heart of Mary Grade School, then Ursuline High School, where most students did a certain amount of charitable and service-oriented work as part of their studies. While she did not attend college, Price did say she has a degree in human nature. "I have a master's in it", she said. "It's not my mission; it's everyone's mission in life to be of service." Kathy and Robert Price have been married since they were 19. She always dreamed of joining the Peace Corps, while Bob wanted to be an attorney (he ultimately earned a law degree). They have four daughters and six grandchildren. While their children were young, Kathy owned and operated Something Special, a florist shop in Austintown, partly to teach their daughters about responsibility and business. Although Kathy did not officially join the Peace Corps, her dream was still fulfilled. "I have my own Peace Corps, Mission of Love", she said.

A simple vacation in Mexico turned into Kathy's passion. While celebrating their 25th wedding anniversary, Kathy and Bob visited the Mexican Isla Mujeres, where she noted the poverty and the need for school supplies and medical supplies. "I had more (medical supplies) in my cabinet at home ...than the doctor did, servicing 16,000 people on the island," Kathy noted. That did it. She had to do something to mitigate such conditions. The result was the establishment of the Mission of Love Foundation in 1989 as a non-profit organization that provides humanitarian aid to those in need worldwide, especially children. Beginning with financial aid from local businesses and individuals and with local volunteer assistance, the Mission eventually enjoyed a broader scope of contributions and volunteers. Learning of national and international needs was not the problem, nor was the securing of aid from various sources. What was needed was to find a way to distribute the aid. Enter the Denton Program.

The Denton Program was the brainchild of U.S. Senator Jeremiah Denton, who established the program in 1984, just a few years before Kathy launched "Mission". Prior to the program's start, Air Force cargo crews and ground support used to train by flying sandbags around. The Denton Program made for a win-win situation by using crew training as part of delivering humanitarian aid around the world at no cost to the donor. It gave Air Force crews live training during a real mission. For the Mission of Love, the Denton Program has enabled aid to be sent to the poorest of the poor throughout the world. Most of the supplies and items Price coordinates to send around the world are things that would often go into landfills. To be able to use these items productively is something that Kathy believes is "awesome".

"Mission" has served the indigenous people of Mexico, Guatemala, Honduras, Peru, Africa, and Asia. On the home front, they were there to help the victims of Hurricane Katrina and the 9/11 disaster. It also assists in helping the Native Americans on the Pine Ridge Indian Reservation in South Dakota. One of the first was to India to help Sister Teresa of Calcutta, sending medical supplies and materials to make saris. Examples of their work are innumerable. As "Mission" reached 20 years old in 2009, it had just sent its 50th shipment of humanitarian aid under the Air Force Denton Program. The number 50th mission went to Martha Betty in Peru. Betty is the South American version of Price. She has dedicated her life to helping the poor in thc mountains and jungles of the Peruvian rainforest. This airlift contained medical and dental supplies, furniture, educational materials, clothing, nonperishable food, construction materials, and household items. Shortly thereafter, she was joined by 10 local volunteers and 5 from California to fly to Guatemala to help build a greenhouse at an orphanage that serves about 250 children. Price said that the orphanage grows its own food for the children, so a greenhouse was needed. One volunteer who made the trip, Dr. Rashid Abdu (whom we know as one of the subjects of this book) also watched as the crews loaded and unloaded the plane. He noted, "I expected to see a few boxes bundled together for the shipment only to find 13 pallets, 10-by-10-10 feet. Each pallet weighed 2,500 to 3,000 pounds". Added to the shipments made to Peru about a month before brought the total amount of aid to more than 50 tons.

At this 20-year milestone for "Mission" Kathy reported that over 3,000 people from all walks of life have joined them as volunteers. "They willingly gave of their time to help others. I have given a third of my life to the Mission of Love, but I don't regret one second of it. It is good to set an example to my children and grandchildren of how one person can make a difference." That was at 20 years, but Mission goes on. In 2017 alone, the "Mission" made 14 trips to Guatemala, Aransas Pass, Texas, Gatlinburg, Tennessee, two Native American Indian Reservations, and the island of Dominica, some more than once. Among the items delivered were wheelchairs and walkers, distribution of countless comfort quilts, an ambulance, a bus, 139,000 pounds of medical, educational, and building supplies, corn, and provided surgery teams to work on cleft palates, lip and facial deformities to countless indigenous children, therapy for elderly. The enormity of the undertakings and the amounts of material contributions is unbelievable.

Kathy constantly remarks about the people she has met over the years of the Mission-from those that are well-known to those who are not. Andrea Thome and former Cleveland Indians player Jim Thome teamed up with Mission of Love and eQuilter, an online quilting company, to send handmade comfort quilts to victims of the recent Tennessee wildfires. The Thomes and Kathy Price, along with several other volunteers, personally took the quilt to people affected by the fires. Kathy told us that Andrea Thome's deceased mother had served as a volunteer for Mission of Love.

Jane Goodall and her Institute worked with Kathy and the Mission to bring hope to the young people of the Pine Ridge Native American Reservation because those young people "need every tiny bit of help they can get, they've had such a raw deal, and it's about time we began to do something a little bit more than to feel sorry for them," Goodall said.

Eddie Morris had to pick a service project for kids, particularly for kids like his cousin who had brain cancer. He met Kathy, talked about the project, went to the Mission warehouse, and picked out baseball gear, medical supplies, clothes, and furniture for a Guatemala trip. Eddie and his mother served as volunteers on that Guatemala trip.

Debbie Houk, a friend of Kathy's for years, is a retired nurse who has been sorting medical supplies to go to Honduras, as donations are accepted oftentimes in bulk shipments. Houk's children and grandchildren are among the many volunteers who go on mission trips with Mission of Love. And apparently, the work goes on even during the pandemic. I have read that early on, with the Covid-19 virus, Kathy and Bob distributed discretely to hospitals and nursing homes n95 masks, gowns, gloves, safety glasses, etc., when the medical facilities had none or very little. Just this past Christmas week, food bags were distributed to the Indigenous Maya of the Yucatan and Tecpan of Guatemala and the rainforest in Honduras.

Kathy Price and the "Mission of Love" have done remarkable things for more than 30 years. She observes that "our mission in life is not merely to survive, but to thrive and to do so with some passion, some compassion, some humor, and some style...you are not here to save the world but to touch the hearts and hands that are within your reach."

Kathy Price

Betty Bannon on right and Susan Brenneis on left

Suzyn Schwebel Epstein of the Jewish faith shared with us in May the story of her grandmother Schwebel and how the various Schwebel descendants contributed to the richness of the Mahoning Valley. We met at Ohev-Tzedek Temple in Boardman, with our ethnic Jewish meal prepared by Kravitz Catering. Cultural enrichment for the evening was provided by a three-piece Klezmer band led by Jeffrey Bremer. We also took a tour of the sanctuary, with questions answered by Rabbi Joel Berman.

Suzyn comes from several generations of businesses, specifically Schwebel's Bakery, a regional producer of bread and baked goods that was established in 1906 by her grandparents, Joseph and Dora Schwebel. Suzyn has used her heritage well by dedicating her life to service her Jewish faith and to the community of Youngstown. Anyone who knows or reads about Suzyn is soon struck by her heartfelt leadership in religious and secular activities in the Mahoning Valley.

The Schwebel brand was created by Suzyn's grandparents, Joseph and Dora, a married couple that started baking bread in the kitchen of their Campbell, Ohio, home in 1906. They eventually began to sell bread to customers in Youngstown, an event that marks the official beginning of the Schwebel's Bakery. In 1914, Dora and Joseph entered the world of retail sales by working out agreements with several local "mom and pop" grocery stores-a move that opened up new and more profitable sales channels for their young business. To ensure that fresh bread was in the stores when customers asked for it, the young couple added more bakers to assist the family. Eventually, Schwebel's expanded its distribution to areas beyond Youngstown and relied upon horses and wagons to transport their products.

By 1923, Schwebel's secured its first fleet of trucks, with six vehicles on hand. That same year the company invested $25,000 to build a small bakery establishment, complete with a storefront for retail business. At this time, the family could bake and deliver 1,000 loaves a day using the new trucks. The bakery was improving, but in the 1920s and 1930s, they had setbacks. In 1928, Joseph Schwebel died at the age of 46, leaving Dora with six children and the family's business to run alone. It is here that Suzyn shared the trying experiences of her grandmother and the admiration she had for her.

Many people believed the baking business was no place for a woman with young children. Dora was urged to sell and stay home with her children. To make matters worse, the stock market crashed just a year after Joseph died. Suzyn told us her grandmother was determined to carry on, telling us that Grandmother Dora said she would meet her obligations by working all day and night if necessary. She even built a new bakery in 1936 and added to it in 1938 and again in 1941. By the late 1940s, with soldiers returning from World War II and the subsequent baby boom, the company grew significantly. By 1951, Dora and her children built a new facility on Youngstown's Midlothian Boulevard, now outfitted with new equipment and baking processes. It still stands today as an important landmark.

The 1960s marked the beginning of the third generation's active participation in the company. Over the next few decades, with new vitality, new ideas, and a quest to expand outside of Youngstown, the company secured national licensing and became a key player in many cities in Ohio, Pennsylvania, and New York. Schwebel's was becoming a regional force in the baking industry. To complement this expansion, the company developed special baking agreements with Stouffer's, Pillsbury Company, and Disney's Epcot theme park. By the 21st century, the company employed about 1,000 employees. Suzyn was so proud of the family, most notably Grandmother Dora. I believe Dora would also be proud of Suzyn.

Dora's granddaughter, Suzyn, has enhanced the Schwebel name for some years as she distinguished herself in religious and secular activities. Suzyn Schwebel Epstein (married to

Bruce Epstein) has been involved with the Youngstown Area Jewish Federation and its agencies for 53 years. Her first role was at the age of 13 as the very first "volunteen" for Heritage Manor, an agency of the federation. Schwebel has served on the board of the Jewish Family and Children's Services, which is now Jewish Family Services; on the human services board; on the steering committee for the creation of Levy Gardens Assisted Living; the Russian resettlement committee; the Federation's young leadership committee; the Holocaust commemoration and education task force committee and the Jewish community relations council board. In 2020, Suzyn was named the Youngstown Area Jewish Federation board president, becoming only the third woman to be president in the organization's 85-year history.

Suzyn Schwebel Epstein was honored by B'nai B'rith as the 2008 Guardian of the Menorah. This award is presented to outstanding members of the community who have demonstrated, through service and commitment, their devotion to the cause of youth and the Jewish and general community. She was also honored as a recipient of the Esther Marks Volunteer Award in 2004. Other activities in the Jewish community include writing and producing a musical about Heritage Manor, spearheading the appropriation of Holocaust Torahs from Kent Gardens, England, for two synagogues, and serving as an advisory board member for the Kent State University Hillel. She serves on the YSU Judaic, and Holocaust Studies Program Committee, was the coordinator for the Oskar Schindler Program in 2008, is on the board of the Youngstown Zionist Organization of America, and has been a docent and coordinator of five Holocaust exhibits at the Butler Institute of American Art.

Suzyn has displayed her leadership qualities in the secular world, too. She has been president of the Junior League of Youngstown, a Foundation Trustee of Planned Parenthood of the Mahoning Valley, president of the Youngstown Symphony Guild, a graduate of Leadership Mahoning Valley in the class of 2000, president of Youngstown Hearing and Speech Center, and outstanding president of Friends of the Youngstown Historical Center of Industry and Labor and on the board of directors of the Henry Stambaugh Auditorium Association.

I am certain that Dora Schwebel would be pleased with the range of ways that her granddaughter has carried on the Schwebel name-Suzyn, Schwebel Epstein, devoted to service in the community.

Speaker Suzyn Schwebel flanked on right by me and Maryann Senediak and on left by Suzyn's husband and my wife, Betty

Schwebel advertisement from the 1950's

In June, Joseph Nohra explained his Lebanese roots and how they led to a successful career as a husband, father of eight children, a businessman with the Cafaro Company, and deacon in two local churches. We met at the Maronite Center in Youngstown, with a largely ethnic Lebanese meal prepared by Mr. Anthony's Catering. The cultural enrichment for the evening was provided by the voices of the Antonine Sisters of Our Lady of Lebanon Shrine. Joe was a capable, friendly, and religious man of Lebanese ancestry. Knowing of him as an acquaintance in college, in community activities, and of his active children, notably his daughter, Elizabeth, who was a student of mine, one is aware that he was a deeply religious man, dedicated to his family, his work, and his community. He was a tremendous leader and an inspiration. "My" Betty and I really got to know each other, Joe and "his" Betty, while we were in Rome together in the year 2,000.

Joseph Nohra was born in 1935 in Youngstown, the son of parents of Lebanese ancestry. He graduated from Ursuline High School in 1953 and proudly accepted the first Distinguished Alumni Award given by Ursuline many years afterward. He went on to graduate from Youngstown State University in 1957 with a bachelor's degree in Business Administration, majoring in accounting. He was awarded the YSU Pin, which was an honor bestowed upon only five students each year who excelled academically and in extracurricular activities.

Nohra joined the Cafaro Company in 1956, even before he graduated from college; he worked for them until his retirement in 2,000. While with the Cafaro Company, he served as vice president of finance and chief financial officer, as well as a member of the Board of Directors. Joe believed that his career and Catholic vocation was a testament to the strong relationship between the Lebanese and Italian communities in Youngstown. Following his retirement from The Cafaro Co., Joe served as the treasurer of JJC Investment Trust from 2009 to 2014. He also practiced as a Certified Public Accountant briefly after his initial retirement. Throughout his professional life, he maintained a reputation as a person of trust and dedication.

Joseph and Betty were married in 1960 at St. Maron Parish in Youngstown. They met, he told us, when Joe hired Betty as a private nurse to care for his ailing father. He was often heard telling his family and friends that he "first fell in love with her ankles," which is often all that he saw of Betty while she cared for his father. He affectionately referred to Betty throughout their 45-year marriage as his "Mestidda" (beloved wife). While Betty passed away in 2,006, he always referred to her as the love of his life and his soul mate. This loving marriage produced eight children and 24 grandchildren, with Joe and Betty doting over them always and so very proud of them.

Until his death in 2015 (some six years after he spoke to OCA) Joseph served for 34 years as a Permanent Deacon in the Catholic Church. He served both St. Maron and Our Lady of Mt. Carmel parishes in Youngstown. For three years after his retirement, he also served as the Administrator of St. Maron Parish. His faith in his religion and Christ was palpable and genuine, as any who knew him would attest.

Joseph Nohra was active in many aspects of the community besides his churches, and he received many awards for his service. Among the long list of organizations were: the Board of Directors of the Youngstown Diocese Endowment Fund, the Diocesan Board of Education, the Distribution Committee of the Youngstown Foundation, the Board of the Hine Memorial Fund, the Advisory Board of the Antonine Sisters Adult Day Care (including serving as chair), the Board of Trustees of Our Lady of Mt. Carmel Education Foundation (including serving as president), the YSU Board of Trustees (including serving as chair), the Youngstown State University Foundation, the Higher Education Funding Commission of the Board of Regents, the Juvenile Justice Center Community Advisory Board (including serving as chair), the St. Elizabeth Development Foundation Board, the Board of Directors of Stambaugh Auditorium, the Board of Trustees of Villa Maria High School, the Board of Directors of Assumption Nursing Home, the Board of Trustees of Millcreek Child Development Center, the St Maron's Education Foundation, among others.

For this dedicated service and leadership, he received many awards. Among them: the Heart of the Community Award (American Heart Association), an honorary Doctorate of Humane Letters from YSU, the Distinguished Citizen Award from YSU, the Distinguished Alumni Award from the Williamson College of Business Administration at YSU, and the Massabke Medal, the highest award given to a Maronite Catholic for distinguished service.

This outstanding list of awards bestowed on Joseph Nohra for his faith and his community service indicates again what one person can do. In his obituary upon his death in 2015, one reads, "If you knew Joe, you know how strong his faith in Christ was, how much he loved his immediate and extended family and friends, and how much he cherished our community...He was a loving and devoted father, grandfather, brother, and friend."

The 2009-2010 OCA season witnessed another outstanding year. The stories of our speakers were varied and informative, indicative of the rich cultures of the Valley. In addition to the speakers, the different venues, the delicious meals, and the often unique but always entertaining cultural enrichment, the past season had a few other highlights: "adoption" of the Ethnic Heritage Society, the continuation of our "question of the month" and the monthly donations (food, paper products, toiletries, etc.) to local charitable organizations.

Joseph Nohra

Several of the Antonine Sisters

For the Ohio Cultural Alliance's 23rd year, we continued the theme of "My Story". We heard the varied stories of a prominent Protestant family of industry, a Greek immigrant labor leader, a Black American artist, a Zimbabwean immigrant educator, a Catholic nun, a priest of French ancestry, an Italian-American disabled war veteran, an Indian-American doctor, a priest of Lebanese ancestry and a judge of Croatian/Serbian descent. Each one has distinguished himself/herself, and each has an ethnic and/or religious background that has helped to frame their lives.

In September, Reverend Gary George, pastor of St. Maron's Church, thrilled our group with the story of his life in South Africa, Lebanon, and the United States. We learned how, despite many obstacles, he had enriched thousands of lives. His name was recommended by members of St. Maron parish in Youngstown, whose church hall was the site of this meeting. Mr. Anthony's Catering prepared a delicious ethnic meal. OCA member Don Barry played beautifully appropriate music on his keyboard.

Father George was born into a Maronite family in Johannesburg, South Africa; both of his grandparents were from the north of Lebanon. Each Sunday, "we would attend the local Maronite Church as a family, and I was influenced by our spirituality and singing." He painted a picture of struggle, yet one of perseverance, while growing up as a Maronite in a foreign land. "While in high school, I attended a Parish Mission and felt a call to join the Redemptorist Congregation." He studied in South Africa at a local seminary and later received an honors degree from a university in Rome. As a Monk, he took his first vows in 1984 and his final vows in 1987. He was ordained a priest in 1992 by his Redemptorist Bishop and celebrated his first Mass the day after at the Maronite Church he attended while growing up. He arrived in the United States in 1998 to visit his family and accepted a position as the National Maronite Youth Organization (MYO) director for the two Eparchies (there are two Lebanese districts/dioceses/eparchies in the U.S.) He was later assigned as vocation director for the Eparchy of Our Lady of Lebanon, serving as both priest and vocation director. He has served as pastor in several parishes in the ensuing years, including St. Maron's in Youngstown (1999-2010) and as rector of the Maronite Cathedral in St. Louis. Father George led St. Maron's congregation with the help of three sub-deacons and Deacon Joseph Nohra. Simultaneously, Father Gary served the Maronite youth of the country in the two eparchies by leading retreats and workshops. He had done parish missions, retreats, and youth conferences before he came to St. Maron's, and in following his career in subsequent years, he has continued this very important work. In his talk to the OCA, he said, "I hope to bring a message of joy, faithfulness, and excitement into the community through my dedication and perseverance. I pray the youth will respond to the call to build a great parish, and as we build, we will extend this hospitality to everyone around us."

I have followed his career through Google and YouTube to learn of additional evidence of his excellence and commitment. His bishop wrote of Father Gary:" What has Father Gary George packed in the suitcase he has lugged during his years of constant travel for the Eparchy of Our Lady of Lebanon in Los Angeles? ...he brings leadership, enthusiasm, joy, and holiness to the young people across 34 states who flock to his retreats, workshops, and service events for youth. Often isolated in an increasingly secular society, young Maronite Catholics find community at Father Gary's national, regional, and parish retreats. The deeply spiritual, sacrament-centered approach reignites their commitment to Christ and the church. His work as vocation director has doubled the number of young men interested in the priesthood, and as an administrator, he has inspired hope and confidence at Saint Sharbel Parish in Baton Rouge, Louisiana."

Father Gary frequently speaks of the church he attended as a youngster, where he was influenced by the spirituality and singing of the priest and the congregation. At our OCA meeting, we noted his genuine spirituality, his almost poetic speaking delivery- very conversational, and his ability to pull you right into his spiritual world-each of us felt he was speaking to us. And he accomplishes this without the benefit of notes. He encourages one to speak to God and to thank God regularly as He hears you better that way. He uses the speaking tools of anecdotes, such as the reason he has a ponytail. He said his hair had been longer, but he cut it to help the mother of one of his altar servers, who had cancer. The hair was used at an auction to raise funds for her and her children. He said he would do it again.

Father George also uses "props" such as a handheld cross; his garments range from a simple cassock to beautifully ornamented clothes, complete with a colorful cloak. In his workshops, he uses eye-catching pictures, ornaments, books, and other religious symbols. He smiles a lot. He brings the Gospels to life. No wonder he is so good at reaching young people and has been so successful in bringing them to religious life. This sounds like a reincarnation of Bishop Fulton J. Sheen, who was so popular that he was featured on his own radio and television programs for a number of years, from the 1930s to the 1960s.

Father Gary George

Father George's presentation to the OCA was ever so meaningful: he preaches hope "for a better tomorrow, as sincere love drives out fear and we can develop love through having a grateful spirit toward God." We were greatly moved and entertained by this good man who exudes the love of which he speaks. We were told by members of his congregation in Youngstown that he has a reputation for delivering trenchant sermons and speeches. We were not disappointed, and I believe, based on my follow-up research, that he continues to teach, inspire, and bring joy to many. We were blessed to have him in our midst for a while.

Don Barry

Father Gary George and Joseph Nohra

In October, Youngstown Municipal Judge Robert Millich told his story of growing up in a Croatian/Serbian family. We met at Holy Trinity Serbian Hall, where we were treated to some wonderful ethnic Serbian food and to music by the Kosovo Men's Choir from Cleveland. Judge Millich began his talk to the OCA with an anecdote: "When three Croatians get together, you have a Tamburitza musical group; when three Serbians get together, you have a war!" Certainly, an exaggeration, but Millich pulls it off since he has dual ancestry. The differences are real and, at times, devastating. Croats and Serbs speak basically the same language, but they have different religions due to different histories. Croats are Catholic because they used to be part of Austria. Serbs are Orthodox because they used to belong to Ottoman Empire. Although there was relative peace between the two groups during a good part of the 20th century, under the leadership of Marshall Tito, there was actual war in the late 1980s and early 1990s.

Bob Millich was born to a Croatian mother and a Serbian father. His father came to Bethlehem, Pennsylvania, before moving to Youngstown-the Northside. Bob's grandparents were not happy that their daughter was going to marry a Serbian, but once they were married, there was not much of a problem as long as the children were reared Catholics. That apparently was acceptable since Bob's Catholic mother took the children to St. Matthias Catholic Church, and their father rarely attended a church. At times mother and the children went to Sts. Peter and Paul Catholic Church, but that was quite a distance to travel without a car, and St. Matthias was nearby. The family attended lamb roasts at Catholic events, even the father. Bob says that his father liked lamb, and he liked to make political signs. Did that help propel Bob Millich into politics and government service?

Born and reared in Youngstown, Bob said he never envisioned going into the legal profession. He said, "when I was growing up in Youngstown, you were taught that you had two choices, go into the military or work at the mill." He said it was his exposure to the unions while working at the Youngstown Water Department, as well as his father's history of union membership, that led him down the path to a legal career. He started work at the Youngstown Water Department after graduating from Wilson High School and continued work here until he graduated from YSU with a degree in business administration. After a short period at Ohio University, he joined the U.S. Air Force during the Vietnam War. He served active duty as a logistics officer at Hill Air Force Base in Utah (where he earned a master's degree in industrial relations) and later in military intelligence in Germany. From 1972 until 1995, he was a member of the U.S. Air Force Reserve's 910thAirlift Wing in Vienna, Ohio. Bob served as administrator to the medical squadron, doing active duty in 1991 during Desert Storm. He retired as a lieutenant colonel. Millich completed his juris doctor at The University of Akron Law School in 1978. He began working for the Youngstown Law Department in 1980 as first assistant and later as deputy law director, and afterward as law director from 1994 to 1997. Attorney Robert Millich was appointed as judge of the Youngstown Municipal Court when an opening occurred. He took his oath of office in April 1998 and retired on the last day of 2017.

When Judge Millich took the bench, two judges had gone to jail, and another resigned. There was a lot of dysfunction in the court: there was no system to facilitate the transition for new judges, and security for the building was provided by "rent-a-cops who did not carry weapons. Judge Millich changed both of these shortcomings. But his service to the community included much more: he started the misdemeanor veterans' docket, working with an Ohio Supreme Court Justice, Evelyn Lundberg Stratton; he served as presiding judge of the Youngstown Municipal Veterans Treatment Court; he developed the court using counselors, mentors, and community social workers to assist veterans in meaningful rehabilitation; he served as a mentor to other judges; he helped spearhead an effort for a new and improved court building and meted out justice in a largely Democratic community, as a Republican, who was elected twice after his initial appointment.

Service to his community and to his country is certainly a hallmark of this ethnic Croatian/Serbian American. He has led an exemplary life dedicated to making life better for those like him and different from him. Judge Millich was appropriately honored: he was inducted into the Ohio Veterans Hall of Fame and has received plaudits from veterans, judicial colleagues, and individual citizens. He has been a credit to the community.

Judge Robert Millich

Kosovo's Men's Choir from Cleveland

Sister Regina "Gina" Rogers, Ursuline Sister and former General Superior at the Ursuline Mother House in Canfield was our speaker in November. She spoke of her Italian heritage and family traditions. Her talk was followed by soprano Jennifer Davis Mosher who treated us to beautiful Italian selections. We met at St. Patrick's Church Hall in Hubbard, Ohio, with the event being catered by Frankie's Restaurant Caterers, who gave us a chance to dine on excellent Italian fare.

Sister Regina is the daughter of Philip and Caroline, with four siblings. She attended Catholic grade schools but graduated from Poland High School, where I taught during her high school years. In fact, Gina was in my Advanced Placement American History and Speech classes in the mid-1960s. And, of course, she was an outstanding student. She graduated from LaSalle College in Philadelphia and joined the Ursuline Order in 1967. Her work with the Ursuline Sisters has been extensive, as has her work as a teacher at St. Patrick's Grade School and Ursuline High School, both in Youngstown. In addition to Sister Regina's intelligence and teaching acumen, she was always fun-loving-and still is.

For more than 50 years, Sister Regina has been an active Ursuline nun. "I always knew that I wanted to be a teacher. I decided I wanted to be a nun during my senior year in high school. The major motivation to join the community was what I saw in the nuns at Holy Family (where the Rogers Family attended Mass). I loved being around them and used to help them get ready for school. They were always so kind to me and encouraged me to think about a vocation as a sister." She never regretted her choice to become a nun to be devoted to her fellow man, particularly to young high school students. "I love working with high school students. They are always challenging yet sincerely searching. Every day is a new experience. They really do keep me young and on my toes."

In considering her personal life and her values, Gina attributes her Italian heritage to be one of her greatest blessings. Specifically, she talked about the primacy of family. "I don't ever remember an event, a celebration, a time of sadness when I would not be surrounded by family. Every one of these events, holidays and most Sundays were spent with nuclear and extended family. I grew up believing that everyone came from large families-that everyone had cousins they were close to. Didn't everyone eat meals together? Didn't everyone have to go around and kiss all their relatives? But it isn't just the companionship-the being together that is important." As an Italian, she believed that she had a very deep and personal responsibility to and for her family. She offered anecdotal instances of this responsibility.

In thinking about the value of family, Sister spoke of two gifts that she received because of her family. The first is the prevalence of strong women. "The source and fountain of strength in my family are the women-my mother, grandmother, aunts, and sisters. For all of my father's bluster-and that is what it was-my mother ruled our home in her quiet way." The girls were always encouraged to be active, inquiring, and involved convincing them that they could be whatever they wanted to be. But Sister Regina added that the second gift was that in an Italian family, all children were important. "We were never raised to believe that children should be seen and not heard. My grandmother, who had 22 grandchildren, always had time for us. When we were at her house, we could do whatever we wanted... jump on the beds, play with her jewelry, speak our mind, take turns leading grace before eating and drinking wine at dinner."

Sister Regina said that another value that has influenced her life and had come directly from her Italian heritage is her faith-the Catholic faith. "Being Catholic was just who we were." She reflected prayer was a routine part of the day; grace came before every meal; we knelt down to say prayers before bed; often prayed the rosary; home was graced with crucifixes and statues; we went to Mass every Sunday as a family, and wore holy medals.

After she quit working, mother went to daily Mass. Indeed, it was she that taught the children about faith. "We saw in her faith in action. But we also talked about Church. Even when we grew older, my mother never hesitated to ask if we had been to Mass. We saw my mother and grandmother say their prayers. When we went on vacation, the first order of business was to find a church. After my brother was ordained, his job was to have Mass for us." Sister Regina recollected that her mother's faith got her through some very difficult times: when Sister's brother died after an illness with bone cancer, her mother let go of her unshakable belief in God. And when a younger sister died, her mother held tight to her belief in the goodness of God. "My mother's faith is also what moved my brother to enter the seminary. Rather than railing at God for taking his brother, my brother gave himself to God, too."

Another value that influenced Sister Regina is food-or more accurately, she said, the kitchen table. "It is not the food itself...but it is the symbolic value that eating together holds in an Italian family." They enjoyed homemade wedding soup, homemade spaghetti, and some kind of meat. Fortunately, both sets of grandparents were Italian. "It was at the table that we all shared. It was at the table that we all laughed and argued and prayed (and never in whispers-usually in shouts-and always at once.) It was at the table where we truly became family."

Sister Regina concluded her fascinating reflections on the values she gained from her ethnicity with: "From my ancestors of long ago, I inherited the belief that life is filled with goodness and beauty. The art of Italy, the music of the great masters, speak of the graciousness of life. In order to wake us up on Sundays for Mass, my father had an album called Marches from the Opera. He would play it very loud. It was our form of an alarm clock. I still wake up to music...Music is one of my passions. My big question for God, when I get to heaven, is why God didn't give me a good singing voice. I love to sing. That belief in the graciousness of life is also seen in the outward expressions of affection. We kiss; we hug; we touch, all in ways that bespeak love. We are a warm people, be that from the climate or the culture. I am very proud of my roots and the gifts that have come to me because I am Italian." To bolster these reflections, she quoted Sister Rita Costello, a Humility of Mary Sister, with a poem entitled, "An Italian Blessing". The three stanzas end with: "May the land sing songs of blessing to you"; "May the artists sing songs of beauty to you"; May the people sing songs of love to you."

Sister Regina Rogers has developed values through her family, her ethnicity, and her faith. We are blessed that she has been among us in so many capacities, including her presence in November 2009, speaking to the Ohio Cultural Alliance. She has spoken to some of us who have had experiences similar to hers and to some of us with different experiences. But we have more in common than we have differences.

Sister Regina Rogers

Jennifer Davis Mosher

In December, acclaimed artist and YSU Professor Emeritus Alfred (Al) Bright shared his experiences as an African American growing up in Youngstown in the 1950s. Reverend Amariah McIntosh enthusiastically sang moving soul music for us. We met at the Western Reserve United Methodist Church, where we enjoyed a meal prepared by Darlene Wells, heading up the Church caterers.

Bright was born in Youngstown, Ohio, on January 9, 1940, the son of Henry Evans and Elizabeth Daniels Bright. Youngstown, during the mid-20th century, did not officially sanction segregation, but the Valley clearly embraced "segregation-like" conditions. Neighborhoods were segregated (rendered more so with the new circle of freeways around the city of Youngstown), schools were mostly separated by race, teachers and professors were nearly all white, the Youngstown Vindicator newspaper included a section called "news of local colored folk", venues such as the Palace Theater had separate upstairs seats for Blacks, restaurants were usually segregated, and public swimming pools were segregated.

Al told a story of the 1951 winning Little League team in Youngstown. The coaches decided that a fitting way to celebrate this accomplishment was a trip to the local swimming pool. When the coaches, players, and their families arrived at the pool, one player was not permitted to enter. He was asked to sit on the lawn outside the pool area. Several parents took issue with the lifeguards who were enforcing the pool's "no-negro" policy. The lifeguards finally agreed to a concession. Everyone else was to get out of the pool. The little Black boy was to be put on a rubber raft, and a lifeguard pulled him around the pool on the raft. He was specifically told not to touch the water. The little boy who was a key player of this winning team; the little boy who interacted so well with his teammates; the little boy who was excited to celebrate with those teammates was now isolated, embarrassed, and hurt. Al said, "that little boy was me! Who knows how much that incident affected Al's future; he certainly never forgot it. How could he not? Despite (or perhaps because of) this incident and other incidents and conditions he experienced in mid-20th century Youngstown, Ohio, Alfred Bright acquitted himself well, becoming one of the Mahoning Valley's most talented and well-known citizens.

Al earned a bachelor's degree in Art Education from YSU in 1964 and a master's degree in Painting from Kent State in 1965. He quickly became a trailblazer in the local African American community by becoming the first of his race to become a full-time faculty member at YSU and eventually became the founding director of the African Studies program, which he led from 1970 to 1987. He became well-known locally, nationally, and internationally.

For more than 40 years, Professor Al Bright has directly influenced thousands of YSU students by teaching or mentoring their careers and lives. The direct impact of his teaching of art, while great on the students enrolled in his classes, extended far beyond his classroom. He influenced the artistic careers of many local and non-local artists with his teaching, knowledge of and passion for art, moral support, and nurturing. His external activities of art exhibitions and artistic performances had a direct impact on his teaching. The exposure and ability to practice his craft made him a more consummate professional, a better teacher, and a more dedicated advisor to his students. Students greatly benefitted from his consistent and persistent honing of his skill of the art. Among them was Lou Zona, who studied under Bright as an undergraduate art education major. "I always found appealing in Professor Bright's work a dedication to the people he cares about." Jason Lee was another student who was urged to study under Bright. Lee said, "I fell under Bright's wing and studied the same things that gave Bright passion." Lee became an accomplished and worthy professional in his own right.

Professor Bright, who was the first director of the Black Studies Program at YSU, said, "The Black Studies Program sought to infuse the systematic study of African people into university curriculum and to do that in a way that provided exposure to a wide range of what we would call the Black experience, including music, art, history, politics, and education. The original vision was to build a program that offered that kind of global awareness to our students." Among his first students, Marvin Haire reported that "You came away from his courses with a sense of dignity and unique sense of pride of accomplishments of your ancestors that had been pretty much hidden from you your whole life." YSU professor Dolores Sisco, professor in the English Department and director of American Studies, has taught classes specializing in the literature and culture of the African diaspora and believes that she understands Professor Bright's vision about African Studies and how it fits in the Youngstown community. She said that she "discovered early in her YSU career that the Africana Studies program doesn't just interest students coming in. It also interests older community members who were skeptical of what YSU did for the Black community before the start of the program." She added, "she liked the idea of teaching the community about the Black experience through Black History Month, the Youngstown African Marketplace and other local events."

His career started in times of very strong racial bias where there were not many opportunities for minority artists, let alone acceptance in instructing at the college level. During his lifetime Bright had more than 100 solo art exhibits across the country, including at Stanford University, Kent State University, and the Canton Art Institute. His work is a part of multiple permanent collections, including at the Butler Institute of American Art, Kent State University Gallery, the Harmon and Harriet Kelly Collection of African-American Art, Canton Museum of Art, Roanoke Museum of Fine Arts and Northeastern University in Boston, Forum Health Care in Youngstown, Pope and Associates in Cincinnati, Microcomputer, Inc. in Chevy Chase in Maryland, Trumbull Art Guild in Warren, Trumbull Memorial Hospital in Warren and IBM Corporation, First Federal Savings and Loan Co., The Ohio Heart Institute in Youngstown. And untold numbers of paintings in personal collections on sites around the country and even on international sites.

Perhaps his most unique contribution as an artist were his performances as an abstract painter alongside jazz musicians as their music accompanied each stroke of his brush on a canvas. His first such performance was in 1976 at the Trumbull Art Gallery, where he continued to paint to the rhythm of the soulful sounds of Art Blakey and the Jazz Messengers. His audience was always engaged in the creative process with him. He conducted a notable performance in 2012 at the Akron Art Museum for Super Bowl Sunday, where he painted "Portals in Time" to live music by The Jesse Dandy Jazz Trio. He performed similarly at Antioch University, the University of Savannah, and nearly two dozen venues in the Mahoning Valley and surrounding area, including two for the Ohio Cultural Alliance. He usually contributed his time and talent to the sponsoring organization as his finished painting was auctioned off, with the proceeds going to that organization.

Professor Al Bright received numerous local, state, and national awards, including the Reverend Dr. Martin Luther King, Jr. Diversity Award for Lifetime Achievement for his leadership and service to Youngstown, Ohio, three Distinguished Professor Awards from YSU, and was honored at the Who's Who in Black America and Who's Who in American Art. He was a member of many professional organizations and was honored by many of them for his distinguished service.

Al Bright was not only a teacher and artist but also a friend, mentor, and inspiration to those that had the privilege of learning from him or watching each stroke of his brush on his "canvas of life." He was also the consummate gentleman whose life belied the shameful act of the Youngstown community to the young Little Leaguer, which was not very gentlemanly. He was able to rise above those who would present obstacles in the path and vision of this good man. He met life head-on and lived it with joy. Indeed, he had developed a delicious sense of humor, able to tell more consecutive jokes/stories than anyone I know. His legacy is firm, and his works are permanent. This man was "different" from many in the community, but his heart, his talent, his humane nature, and his joy for life vie with the best we have.

Professor Al Bright and his wife Dr. Dee Banks Bright

Reverend Amariah McIntosh

Joel Beeghly, representing the industrial and philanthropic Beeghly family, shared, in January, some significant history of his extended family. A talented young man, Nathan Stephens, received a standing ovation for his beautiful piano performance. We met at the Saxon Club with their catering service preparing a "Youngstown buffet", which all enjoyed.

Joel began with a history of the Beeghly family in Youngstown. The Beeghly family's history in the region began with Leon A. Beeghly, Joel's grandfather, who moved from Toledo, Ohio, to Youngstown in 1918. He was born in 1884 near Bloomfield, Ohio, where he worked on the family farm and spent Sundays at the Methodist Church. He finished high school first in his class of nine, giving a valedictorian address entitled "Charity and Civilization". Afterward, he studied accounting briefly at Oberlin Business College before becoming a teacher in a one-room school. In 1904, Beeghly took a job with a quarry company. He helped the company market flux stone, an important resource as the steel industry grew. On sales trips, Beeghly noticed large piles of blast-furnace slag waste from iron ore, coke, and limestone processing. The slag was typically hauled away by train, but Beeghly recognized that it could work like quarry rock if it were crushed and screened like stone.

After abortive attempts to participate in a slag business in Toledo in 1908 and another in Buffalo, New York, in 1912, Beeghly traveled to Youngstown in 1914 to start, with two partners (William Bliss and William Kilcawley) the Standard Slag Company. The slag was widely used in highway construction in the Midwest. Beeghly realized that with few limestone deposits and thriving steel industry, eastern Ohio was an ideal market for slag. He was right; standard Slag dug in and expanded aggressively; they soon had 25 plants. Joel said the "times were tough in the 1930s, and his grandfather was even turned down for a bank loan by an officer who said that his product was useless since all necessary highways were already built." Despite the Depression, the company continued to grow and acquire sand plants and limestone quarries to feed the business even as some steel plants closed.

Leon Beeghly also earned a reputation for helping local inventors market their industrial ideas. An example is the Steckel mill, a steel-rolling process created by Abram P. Steckel and patented in 1932 but endured rounds of patent litigation to actually develop the Steckel mill; once successful, it experienced its greatest popularity and use in the last decades of the 20th century. Beeghly helped to develop the cold forming of metal, resulting in the Cold Metal Products Company, where his son Charles was involved before becoming president and chairman of Jones and Laughlin Steel, at that time the fourth largest steel company in the country. Sons James and Thornton and later-born John all were involved in Standard Slag. Beeghly also embraced a Cleveland area invention: the industrial-engine-ignition system with continuous sparking. The idea reached the market slowly but ultimately became Altronic Inc. of Girard, which grandson Bruce operated for many years. Beeghly's other business interests included Metal Carbides, which produced machine tools and dies for more than 50 years. He also served as director of Youngstown Sheet and Tube C. until 1958 and remained chairman of the board of Standard Slag until his death in 1967.

For all his professional successes, Beeghly is equally remembered for his community involvement. He served three terms as president of the Youngstown Chamber of Commerce and 41 years as a trustee at Mount Union College. Often described as a "teetotaler", Beeghly was concerned about the effects of alcoholism and quietly backed organizations dedicated to this cause. He also formed a foundation in 1940 that supported churches, missions, medical organizations, and colleges such as Mount Union, Ohio Northern University, and American University, with contributions in excess of $35 million over the next 50 years. In an early connection with Youngstown College/YSU, he once received a phone request from President Howard Jones for a large donation, to which Beeghly called back asking Jones to stop by to pick up a check. This was the beginning of a long multi-generational program of financial assistance to YSU.

Leon Beeghly's humble giving style is legendary, and his family has continued his philanthropic tradition, with YSU being one of the most significant beneficiaries. The Beeghly Physical Education Center opened in 1972, and Beeghly Hall became the home of YSU's College of Education in 1998, both with substantial Beeghly family funds. Seven additional colleges around the country bear the Beeghly name.

Second and third-generation Beeghlys have also been generous stewards of the Valley community in terms of business and philanthropy. The Beeghly family's philanthropic work was continued by sons James, Thornton, and John making contributions to more than 140 organizations over a half-century. Grandson Bruce Beeghly and his wife Nancy have pledged $1.5 million to YSU's most recent "We See Tomorrow" fundraising campaign. The gift will be used for continuing support of the Beeghly College of Education and for two new graduate fellowships. The family also donated its homestead on Market Street in Boardman to Western Reserve Care System in 1965. Formerly known as Forum Health's Beeghly Medical Park, the site is now home to Akron's Children's Hospital-Mahoning Valley, Beeghly Campus.

Joel told of his cousin's work as president of Altronic Inc., on the YSU Board of Trustees, on the Ohio Board of Regents, and on the YSU Foundation, among other activities, as well as his own work as a member of the Friends of the Mahoning River and other organizations that deal with conservation. Working with local organizations and the USDA's Natural Resources Conservation Service, he has made genuine contributions to protecting and preserving our natural resources.

To know some of the Beeghly family is to be certain that the humility of the founding antecedent, Leon Beeghly, has continued through generations. Such humility could be expected with his prescient title to his high school valedictory address, "Charity and Civilization" to which he and his family have contributed mightily in both abundant charity and significant contributions to civilization. Reflecting on his adopted hometown after a lifetime of industrial and philanthropic success, Beeghly once said that Youngstown has been good to him. Such humility.

Leon Beeghly

Joel Beeghly

YSU Beeghly College of Education

YSU Beeghly Athletic Center

The February meeting featured Reverend Bernard Bonnot, pastor at St. Nicholas Church in Struthers at the time he spoke to us. He has since retired after more than 50 years as an active priest. Father Bonnot offered a compelling message as he spoke of his family background and his varied positions in the Catholic Church and Catholic organizations. We met at Antone's Banquet Center in Boardman. Our meal was prepared by Antone's Catering, and the Youngstown Connection again performed lively songs and dance numbers to our delight.

Bernard Robert Bonnot was born in 1941 in Canton, Ohio, the son of Dr. Bernard Robert and Mary Elizabeth Bonnot. Reared in a distinctly conservative milieu, Father Bonnot long ago became a Pope John XXIII and Pope Francis progressive. He was educated at Catholic University from 1961-1964, in Rome at Gregorian University in1968 with a Licentiate of Sacred Theology and a Doctor of Philosophy from the University of Chicago, 1973-76.

Father Bonnot has had and continues to have a varied and illustrative career. In listing his impressive career, it is what he thought, wrote, and did with each aspect of his career that is most noteworthy. He was associate pastor at Immaculate Conception Church in Youngstown, 1968-1971; assistant superintendent of schools, Diocese of Youngstown, 1971-1973; director of adult spiritual growth, Diocese of Youngstown, 1976-1980; part-time instructor in Philosophy-Religious Studies at YSU; director of communications, Diocese of Youngstown, 1980-1987; president, chief Executive officer, CTNA Telecommunications Inc. in New York and Washington D.C., 1987-1990; director of community relations, VISN Interfaith Satellite Network, New York City, 1990-1999 and a brief stint as Acting President before VISN merged with the then new hallmark and Henson Channel which evolved into today's Hallmark Channel, serving there as a Vice-President from 1999-2006 in Los Angeles; Pastor of St. Stephen of Hungary Church, Youngstown, 1981-1987. He was Administrator of Mother of Sorrows Church in Ashtabula, Ohio 2000- 2007 and pastor of St. Nicholas Church in 2007 (along with Holy Trinity Church as it merged in 2011) to his retirement in 2016. During these years, he also served as Chair of the Mahoning Valley Association of Churches for a few years; as a Lieutenant Colonel in the United States Army National Guard since 1977; a member of the Catholic Theological Society of America, the Catholic Biblical Association, the Canon Law Society of America and the United Nations Association president, Youngstown Chapter.

Father Bob speaks to his philosophy in his doctoral dissertation in 1976 and later in his two books," Pope John XXIII: An Astute Pastoral Leader and Pope John XXIII: Model and Mentor for Leaders". Bonnot said of Pope John, "He managed a revolution in one of the most conservative of institutions", the Catholic Church. Bonnot writes that the Pope was one of the world's most successful leaders of the 20th century and that he "provides a model for anyone who cares to learn from him." The latter book is set up as a manual with a case study for leaders and managers. Bonnot hopes "this book will lead its readers and others to look at John also as the patron saint of leadership, specifically the managerial kind. His fame rests on what he did in four and a half short years as CEO-Chief Everything Officer of the Roman Catholic Church." Father Bob could be talking about himself when he describes Pope John as providing managerial leadership without dominating, convincing without controlling; he spoke and acted forcefully but always with respect for others. This has always been the approach to Father Bob that I know and saw up close as he led as president of our local chapter of the United Nations Association.

In Father Bonnot's third book, "Jesus as Priest for Our Time: According to the Order of Melchizedek" he furthers his interpretation of the frozen Catholic Church, which reflects the traditional Catholic sense of priesthood since the Council of Trent as further developed by Pope John's Second Vatican Council and reinforced by Pope Francis' emphasis on priestly ministry as a pastoral rather than a hierarchical calling. Throughout his book, Father Bonnot illustrates his interpretations of priestly ministry with the understanding he has gained from his 50 years of parish service to the priestly people of God. He notes the worldwide crisis of fewer men accepting the call to the priesthood, making it more difficult for Catholics to come together to celebrate the Last Supper, the death and resurrection of Jesus. So, he encouraged consideration of the ordination of married men, the ordination of women as deacons, and even the ordination of women as priests since none of these tenets are doctrinally defined. Bonnot believes his book could be read not only by priests but also by lay persons "and could well serve as a text for an ongoing dialogue within parishes. It could also help dedicated lay persons to understand better their priestly role within the community and in celebration of the Eucharist, which was and is a communal meal, not simply the action of a single person."

Father Bonnot has given many seminars and speeches on topics related to the ideas of Pope John. Illustrative is a talk he gave to his hometown of Canton on May 6, 2010, at the Ken Hamilton Luncheon Forum at St. Michael the Archangel Catholic Church, where he addressed the topic, "Whither the Priesthood of Jesus Christ." He had published many articles for Catholic periodicals and newspapers, among them an article in "Today's American Catholic" entitled "Songs by the Hours". In it, he writes, "The Liturgy of the Hours", sometimes referred to as the Divine Office, is a series of prayers, psalms, hymns, and scriptural readings prayed at appointed times throughout the day by members of the church all over the world. There is a total of seven appointed prayer times in the Office, including Lauds (morning), Terce (midmorning), Sext (noon), None (afternoon), Vespers (evening), Compline (night), and Vigils, or the Office of Readings, which can be prayed at various points throughout the day." He proceeds in the article to flesh in details of the three Canticles sung during the morning, evening, and night hours.

A group of 27 priests formed in 2011 the Association of U.S. Catholic Priests (AUSP) to reaffirm their commitment to the values espoused by the Second Vatican Council. The group is now composed of more than 1,000 priests. From 2014-2019 Father Bonnot was the association's Leadership Team/Board Chair and served as its Executive Director from 2019-2021. "When the group was founded," he said, "members felt that some of the council's openness to the world was being closed off." They also have a kinship with Pope Francis and his pastoral approach. Among the topics AUSP has dealt with are migration theology, priest shortage, administering to the LGBT community, gun violence, death penalty, preaching by laymen and women, climate change, and minimum wage. The AUSP has taken a strong stand against those who have engaged in sexual abuse by saying: "We are sad. We are angry. We are frustrated by another wave of shame (of priests) as we acknowledge that even greater pain has been inflicted on children and families and on all of the faithful by our brothers in the priesthood and the hierarchy." At another AUSP meeting, the priests asked the American bishops to discuss and act on four important issues: confront the poison of racism, urge non-violence, and consider ordaining women as deacons and married men as priests, again with Father Bob Bonnot leading the way. The same group sent a Faith in Action letter to the 2020 presidential candidates urging moral leadership on immigration.

Through the years of his priesthood, Father Bonnot has practiced what he preaches in the church world and in the secular world. And he continues to contribute in retirement. Since retiring in 2016, he continues in active ministry, traveling the country in his RV reflecting, writing, serving as a covering priest, and an Apostolate of the Sea Cruise Chaplain. His faith journey was strengthened through seeing the world. He visited a fellow Youngstown priest in El Salvador, traveled to Maryknoll Missions in Panama, Peru, Chile, Bolivia, and Brazil, and had the pleasure of spending a month in 2003 with the bishop of Ngong, Kenya, experiencing the Church in his diocese and celebrating his 50th anniversary as a priest and bishop. The bishop grew his diocese from 300 Catholics to over 100,000. Bonnot continues to support the work of the Ngong Diocese.

"I most especially spend my time, talent, and energy in service to AUSP's mission and vision. With the guidance of the Holy Spirit, we support the efforts of Pope Francis and our bishops to continue the evangelizing of our people and our world through the implementation of Vatican II. Our current challenge is to overcome the persistent clericalism of both the ordained and the baptized, to see ourselves as priests ordained in the service to the baptized, and to foster synodality in the Church's life from top to bottom and bottom to top."

Father Bernard (Bob) Bonnot is a man who has dedicated his life and his talents of service to his Church, his secular community, his country, and his fellow human beings. He certainly is one who took his lead from his Maker and from his fellow spiritual leaders, Popes John XXIII and Francis.

Father Robert Bonnot

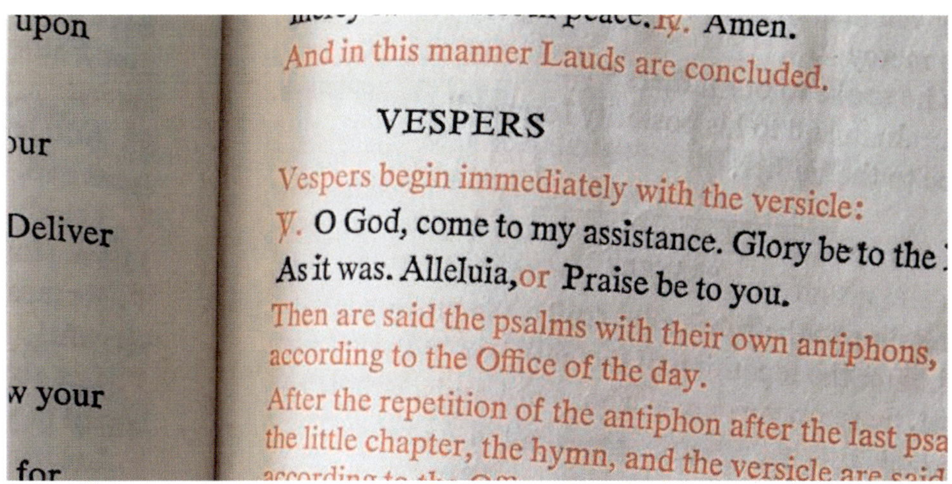

peace. ℟. Amen.

And in this manner Lauds are concluded.

VESPERS

Vespers begin immediately with the versicle:

℣. O God, come to my assistance. Glory be to the

As it was. Alleluia, or Praise be to you.

Then are said the psalms with their own antiphons, according to the Office of the day.

After the repetition of the antiphon after the last psa

the little chapter, the hymn, and the versicle are said

Portion of vespers-evening prayer

The Youngstown Connection

Jim Graham was our March speaker. He shared anecdotal information regarding his Greek birth, his emigration to America, and his activity as a union and community leader. We met at Archangel Michael Greek Orthodox Church in Campbell, whose church caterers prepared a sumptuous Greek meal. Young adult Greek dancers handsomely dressed in their native attire performed lively dances for us.

Jim Graham was born in Piraeus, Greece, in 1947 and emigrated to the United States with his family, entering through Ellis Island. They settled in Warren, Ohio, in 1951. His father was a steelworker, and his mother was a homemaker. He was married in 1970, and they have one son who is a lawyer and an assistant prosecutor in Warren at the time he spoke to us. Jim graduated from Warren Harding High School and continued his education at YSU, earning a B.S. degree in Business Administration. In 2004 Jim was prominently featured as an "Alumnus Success Story for YSU."

Jim began his career at GM Lordstown in 1968, becoming president of UAW Local 1112 in 1995. His greatest passion was to improve the image of the UAW local to the outside community (their generous charitable activities are well known in the Mahoning Valley). His greatest ability is to inspire teamwork and involvement while always deferring credit to those around him. Graham is a dynamic force in the community as well, serving as a councilman and, subsequently, president of the council in Warren. His political leadership has resulted in many personal, local, state, and national proclamations. His activism has also been very instrumental in connecting the local area with Columbus and even Washington.

This kind of activity does not come easily, and not everyone can make such contributions. Jim started his life in the Valley with a culture different from his, but he overcame the obstacles attendant to such differences. In his presentation to the Ohio Cultural Alliance, we were able to feel the nature of the man who achieved such success. He has the temperament, intelligence, and organizational acumen to perform successfully in the labor movement and the political world.

In 1976, Jim was first elected as alternate committeeman; in 1980, he was elected committeeman; in 1985, he was elected zone man; and in 1985, he was elected president of UAW Local 1112. It was a matter of working his way up. He remarked, "You have to deal with everyone in the plant; I enjoy that. My favorite pastime is walking the floor and just talking to people. I think that has a lot to do with my success because I do enjoy that. And that's not something you can fake. If you are talking to somebody, and they know you are talking to them because you have to, they can pick up on it real quick." He spoke about his continuing concerns about the adversarial relationship between the union and management, which he always tried to mitigate. In referring to his predecessors, he said he took some bits and pieces from each of them to model his own approach. Both labor and management concluded that they should not be enemies; rather, they should work together to make a better product and to be competitive with other countries. He also worked toward an increasingly better work life, arguing that a "happy" worker makes for a better and more productive worker. He also spoke against the North American Free Trade Association (NAFTA) because that type of action was always searching for the lowest possible labor rate, regardless of where it would be.

Jim also had the ability to have his mind changed based on experience and more careful observation. An example was his change of heart with the plant manager Herman Moss. Initially, they did not get along until Moss proved to be a manager who believed in communication between labor and management, including suggestions from labor. "He and I...got a joint award from the regional Chamber of Commerce, and it was a great honor." His open mind is evident in his views regarding technology: "technology changes things for the better. I don't like the idea of a robot taking over for a human or the job that the human is doing, but I also know that things change." He also addressed issues that have changed for the better, such as civil rights for African Americans and other minority groups and the increased importance of women in the plant. Graham says that minority groups and women have input and are involved in decisions making a "nice cross-section of the plant serving on committees; I demanded that when I took office." He has thoroughly enjoyed his work at Lordstown. He has had a good rapport with the union members, with management, and with local business and political leaders. "Being brought up in a great home, you can always tell how I feel by looking at me. I can't hide my emotions, and I'm a genuine person. I just enjoy doing it."

Although he did all he could do to keep open the Lordstown Plant and he served in the political world as Warren Councilman and President of Council, these both occurred after his appearance at our OCA meeting in March 2010. We again had evidence of what someone "different from us" could accomplish-starting as this young lad of 4 years old from Greece.

Jim Graham

Greek dance group

In April, former YSU History professor Oliver Musuka spoke to us about his background in Zimbabwe and his deep philosophical beliefs. He and his wife Mildred shared with us several native-Zimbabwean musical melodies, which served as our cultural enrichment. We met at St. Matthias Church Hall, with a wonderful meal prepared by one of our favorites, Carolyn Catering.

Mr. Musuka went to undergraduate school at Morning Side College in Illinois and graduated school at Northwestern University. He taught in the YSU History Department for four years during the late 1970s and early 1980s, replacing a faculty member who was on leave in Africa. We tried to keep him at YSU, but having no opening at the time, he returned to his native Zimbabwe to teach with a goal of someday returning to the United States. By the time he was able to return to the U.S., age had become a factor in securing a teaching position. Between them, he and his wife held four non-teaching jobs in this country they dearly love. Shortly after he spoke to the OCA, he had to return to Zimbabwe to teach in a high school.

Mr. Musuka's talk included a look at the history of the country, its political system, its culture, and religion. Zimbabwe is a landlocked country in southeast Africa, separated from Zambia by the Zambezi River. The Limpopo River in the south forms part of the border with South Africa. It is bordered in the east by Mozambique and the west by Botswana. It is about half the size of Turkey or slightly larger than Montana, with a current population of about 14+ million people. Zimbabwe, formerly known as Rhodesia, was annexed by the United Kingdom (Southern Rhodesia) from the British South Africa Company in 1923. A 1961 constitution was formulated that favored whites in power. In 1965 the government unilaterally declared its independence, but the U.K. did not recognize the act and demanded more complete voting rights for the Black African majority in the country. United Nations sanctions and a guerrilla uprising finally led to free elections in 1979 and independence (as Zimbabwe) in 1980.

Zimbabwe's governmental system is a full presidential republic with a president as chief of state and head of the government. It is theoretically a parliamentary government. The post of prime minister was abolished in 2013 under a revised constitution. Democratic governance deteriorated in recent years. Besides widespread violations of human rights, the independence of the judiciary and the existence of independent media are threatened by the ruling government. The official language is English and Chishona, and Sindebele, with various dialects. Their literacy rate is 90%. Of the 14+ million people, the ethnic groups consist of Shona, 71%; Ndebele, 16%; other African, 11%; white, 1%; mixed and Asian, 1%.

Zimbabwe elected Robert Gabriel Mugabe as the country's first prime minister in 1980. Mugabe became president in 1987 after changes to the constitution created an executive presidency; he remained in power for 37 years. The United States has continually called for political and economic reforms and indeed issued several economic sanctions during Mugabe's tenure. In November 2017, military pressure, public demonstrations calling for Mugabe's removal, the ruling party's vote of no confidence, and impeachment proceedings led to Mugabe's resignation. Former Vice President and Minister of Defense Emerson D. Mnangagwa replaced Mugabe and won the presidency in his own right in 2018. Despite promises of reform, the new government has made little progress in implementing the broad reforms the country needs. The U.S. has made it clear that credible, transparent, and lasting democratic reforms must precede an easing of restrictive measures.

The religions of Zimbabwe are overwhelming Christian at about 84%. Christian denominations in Zimbabwe with significant numbers include Roman Catholicism, Anglicanism, Baptists, Lutheranism, and Methodism. However, over the years, a variety of indigenous Christian denominations have emerged. Charismatic Evangelical denominations, primarily Pentecostal churches, and apostolic churches were the fastest-growing religions in the last couple of decades. While the country is majority Christian, most people practice, to a varying degree, elements of the indigenous religions as well. Mr. Musuka reported that there is an increase in adherence to traditional religion and shamanic healers. It was clear that Mr. Musuka and his wife were dedicated Methodist Christians. It was palpable in the address he gave to us and the music that Oliver and Mildred sang for us. Their music symbolizes much more than simple rhythm, as the folk and pop style music was used as a symbol of hope for Zimbabweans looking to gain independence from Rhodesia. It was Gospel music that became popular in the late 1980s and was the focus of the music the Musuka's sang for us (Zimbabwean and American gospel).

The presentations that the Musuka's graced us with in 2010 clearly gave evidence of their heartfelt Christianity and their humble nature in general. They were not advocates of the Mugabe regime but were not political people. They lived through the upheavals of the end of colonialism in their land, the Mugabe years, and the new Mnangagwa administration. Intermittently, the Musuka's did live in the U.S. but could never receive citizenship. At times during these years, these humble, intelligent Christians wished they could live the remaining years of life in the United States. We again learned of people with different histories from us yet filled with common emotions.

The Musuka's concluded with a song written by Frances R. Havergal, "I Am Trusting Thee". The final stanza is: "I am trusting Thee, Lord Jesus; Never let me fall; I am trusting Thee forever; And for all".

Oliver Musuka

Oliver and Mildred Musuka and daughter Patience

Attorney Carl Nunziato, an Italian-American veteran who was severely wounded in Vietnam, spoke in May. His lifetime stories were informative, poignant, and entertaining. We met at Mt. Carmel Church Social Center with a wonderful Italian meal prepared by Lou Fusillo Catering. Cultural enrichment was provided by Duo Allant-Dr. Kathryn Umble (flute) and Francis Fowler (guitar), both of the Dana School of Music, YSU, performed beautifully melodic Italian numbers.

I doubt that Carl grew up thinking that he was going to be a hero. Suffering horrible wounds in Vietnam and many obstacles, he became one of the leading and most admired citizens of the Mahoning Valley. For some years, I tried to get Carl to speak to the OCA, but he repeatedly said he was not ready. Finally, in 2010 he consented. We learned through previous speakers of the OCA that people could be different from us yet hold many common threads, and we learned that genius has no boundaries. We also learned of people with uncommon courage and valor. Carl Nunziato certainly had experiences that few of us have had, but his core is the same as ours. I am not sure that he would call himself a genius, but what do you call a person who, despite many obstacles, did so much in the aftermath of his war injuries.

Carl Nunziato was born in 1938 on Walnut Street in the Smoky Hollow area of Youngstown. His parents were Thomas and Antoinette, both of Italian nationality. They and others from southern and eastern Europe were often referred to with such appellations as "a beaten people from a beaten race." Nevertheless, Carl said, "we learned a lot of values while growing up in a middle-income, diverse neighborhood, in school and home. Work was one of those values". "I started working when I was 13 and continued all the way through high school and college. I learned to take on responsibility, as well as honesty, and that you have to make it on your own…I had to assume responsibility, be smart and cut my own direction in life."

Carl is a 1961 graduate of Youngstown University (soon to be Youngstown State University), earning a bachelor's degree in English with a teaching certificate. "I thought it would be interesting to try the ROTC program." He earned a commission as a second lieutenant in the Army through YSU's ROTC program. This was the same year that he married his sweetheart, Clara J. Scarpine. He served eight years in the Army, including two tours of duty in Vietnam, where he lost both of his legs in combat. He retired in 1968 at the rank of major. Carl was not certain how long he would remain in the Army. He was officially deployed in 1962, the year of the Cuban missile crisis, but with no immediate threat in Vietnam. "The first time I went to Vietnam, I volunteered. I was stationed in Hawaii as a first lieutenant…I thought it was an opportunity to do something definitive. Communism was still a big issue then, and we were well-trained, so I volunteered for my first tour of duty. It was a short tour, only six months, and I came back fine. We were the only fighting force in Vietnam at that time and spent many hours and days flying machine gunners on helicopters. At night we defended the perimeter of the air bases and some of the smaller camps. I was an intelligence officer and a defense commander. As a senior lieutenant, I was in charge of nine platoons…and was only 24 years old, with nine lieutenants and about 300 men under me. That was a lot of responsibility, but I think my upbringing helped." After his first tour, he returned to Hawaii.

Nunziato was training a unit in Hawaii when the whole division got alerted. He was ordered to go back to Vietnam with his unit, where he was an artillery battery commander and captain with the direct supervision of 200 men. "We left Hawaii by ship, got to Vietnam, and went into an area called Ku-Chi and dug in. We made our perimeter there and set up our artillery to assist the infantry…. We had little water or food. We were lucky to have a gallon of water a day for drinking and washing.... It was hard to get supplies, and it was a really tough three months until supply lines improved."

After about six months into this second tour of Vietnam, he revealed, "we went on Operation Adelborough. It was big; we used two brigades....Ten thousand men made a sweep from east of Saigon all the way to the Cambodian border...which was heavily infiltrated with the Viet Cong and North Vietnamese regulars....The sweep lasted 10 weeks, and I had (control) of the heavy artillery. At the operation's conclusion, we had succeeded in pushing the North Vietnamese and Viet Cong out of the area. In the two or three days before it ended, my unit pulled back. We were around a small South Vietnamese Special Forces camp of about 200 Vietnamese soldiers. They had their families with them. We put our Howitzers to protect them because we had agent information there might be an attack. We got into position...and set up our guns, and dug our foxholes. At about ten that night, the Viet Cong attacked; that's when I was wounded.... There was a lot of gunfire and mortars exploding as I was running across the field (trying to get to my radio equipment). One of the shells landed two feet from me. It blew off my left leg below the knee and injured my right leg and right arm. The medics came and put on a tourniquet. We had a doctor with us who was in a foxhole 20 yards away; he came to put an intravenous in my arm. All the while, shells were exploding, and gunfire continued. After 15 minutes, it subsided. That's when they brought in a helicopter, and I went to a nearby field hospital. I was treated there and ended up spending 23 months in the hospital." Eleanor Roosevelt once reflected on courage with: "You gain strength, courage, and confidence by every experience in which you really stop to look fear in the face. You are able to say to yourself, 'I lived through this horror. I can take the next thing that comes along'.... You must do the thing you think you cannot do." What courage; what strength. Carl Nunziato is a hero in ways few of us can contemplate. But I believe what he did in the aftermath of his injury was even more courageous and took even greater strength and confidence. When asked if he ever felt sorry for himself, he answered, "No, I don't allow that. I certainly have had periods of depression, but I never allow myself to feel sorry because that's the beginning of the end. I have a strong, positive attitude all the time, even when it hurts and even when it's tough. I just make the best of whatever I can. I could have come out of the hospital and sat in the wheelchair and not done anything.... I knew I had to make the best of a bad situation."

With a disability that kept the pain at a high and continuous lcvcl, a disability that necessitated a fitting with artificial limbs, he had to change his whole lifestyle: leave the Army, learn to walk with and then without crutches, could not golf or dance and so many of the things he had enjoyed before. "I made up my mind...that I was going to go on. I figured the best way was with education, so I studied while in the hospital and took the entrance exam for law school. When I left the hospital, I went right to law school (Western Reserve Law School), still walking with crutches and using a wheelchair. I went for three years under rather adverse physical conditions." After he graduated, he worked for a short time in the Cleveland court system, after which he took a job at the Dollar Savings and Trust Bank (later it was National City Bank)-a job he held for 28 years, rising to vice president, as trust attorney and corporation secretary as well as secretary of the holding company of The Dollar Savings and Trust Company.

He has a long list of civic involvement, including the Easter Seal of Mahoning and Columbiana Counties, Youngstown Warren Regional Chamber, Wolves Club of Youngstown, Youngstown Private Industry Council, and Italian Heritage Foundation. Ohio Bankers Association, Stambaugh Pillars Society, Choffin Career Center, Northeast Ohio Legal Services, Amputee Opportunities Foundation, Ohio Society to Prevent Blindness, Ohio Rehabilitation Services Commission, Ohio Governor's Council on Disabled Persons, and Boy Scouts of America. He also has had a lifetime relationship with YSU, establishing the Carl

Nunziato Scholarship at the YSU Foundation, serving on the YSU Alumni Association Board of Directors, membership in the YSU chapter of Phi Kappa Phi, and volunteering on numerous YSU ROTC committees.

Carl took an active role in helping veterans and disabled people through most of his post-Army years. After discovering that there were no barrier-free buildings, "you could not even get into the courthouse," he argued. He and a few other disabled veterans started the Barrier-Free Architecture Committee, working for 15 years to get the courthouse, hospitals, and university barrier-free. Equality for the elderly and disabled became one of his major goals. Carl played a critical role in bringing a VA outpatient clinic to Youngstown and helped build the Veterans Resource Center at Youngstown State University. The facilities have been named Carl Nunziato Youngstown VA Clinic and Carl Nunziato Veterans Resource Center, respectively.

Nunziato has had the accolades of many political and business leaders as well as numerous military honors. He earned the Bronze Star for Meritorious Achievement in Ground Operations Against Hostile Forces, the Purple Heart for Wounds Received in Action, the Air Medal for Meritorious Achievement, the Armed Forces Expeditionary Medal, the National Defense Medal, the Vietnam Services Medal, the Vietnam Campaign Medal with three Battle Stars and Aircraft Crew Gunner Wings.

He received the Disabled Veteran of the Year Award in 1978; he was a recipient of the Ohio Governor's Award in 1980 and the Disabled Citizen of the Year Award given by the Easter Seal Society in 1985. Senator Sherrod Brown said, "Carl served our nation honorably in Vietnam and then continued that in service through his work in the Valley through his advocacy work and philanthropy." Senator Rob Portman declared that "Carl Nunziato is a true son of Ohio and an American patriot," and Congressman Tim Ryan said Carl Nunziato "has dedicated his life to serving our country."

Attorney Carl Nunziato

Yes, Carl Nunziato was a hero in battle and in life; he is an American patriot and a model citizen of the Mahoning Valley. Could we all summon the courage and be as determined as he in the face of so many obstacles? Is he more similar or different from us? Who knows? In the closing advice he gave to an interviewer, he modestly said, "Many people have setbacks and just roll over and kind of quit. It's an attitude thing. You have to make the best of whatever you're dealt in life. Just take a deep breath, count to ten and start over."

YSU Veterans Resource Center named in Carl Nunziato's honor

New, larger and renamed Veterans Affairs Outpatient Clinic named in Carl Nunziato's honor in 2021

The June meeting combined the talents of area internist Doctor Nazim Jaffer and his wife, Tazim, who is an internationally known painter. They shared experiences of their Indian and Tanzanian heritage with us, Nazim, via his talk and Tazim through her artwork. We met at The Georgetown Banquet Center, whose caterers prepared a wonderful meal that was enhanced by ethnic desserts from Zenobia Restaurant in Canfield.

When the Jaffers settled in the Mahoning Valley in the 1970's they were about as "different from us" (in the Valley) as could be in terms of their religion and race. These intelligent professionals, representing the most recent immigrant groups to the Valley, were needed, particularly physicians. But even they were not accepted by some; that was made clear to them when they were denied membership in one of the area's country clubs. Dr. Jaffer is a doctor of internal medicine and had practiced for more than 40 years at the time of their presentations. They travel widely; indeed, their ancestors were part of a diaspora from India to Tanzania. Meeting in Tanzania and marrying there, they ultimately emigrated to America and the Mahoning Valley.

Dr. Jaffer, after graduating from undergraduate school, took his medical degree from the Royal College of Surgeons in Ireland, graduating in 1969. He did his residency at Southside Medical Center in Youngstown. He was affiliated with Trumbull Memorial, Saint Joseph, and Northside Medical hospitals, where he was a primary care physician.

Dr. Jaffer offered a truncated version of Tanzanian history. Indians were part of Tanzanian society long before Tanzania appeared on the world map as a nation in the 1960s. There are today about 50,000 people of Indian origin in Tanzania, probably more when the Jaffers lived there. Many of them are and were traders, and they controlled a sizeable portion of the Tanzanian economy. Indians have a long history in Tanzania, starting with the arrival of Gujarati traders. They came to gradually control the trade in Zanzibar, one of the regions with a significant Indian population. Indians were appointed to key administrative positions like port captains and heads of customs. German rule began in mainland Tanzania during the late 19th century when Germany formed German East Africa. This was followed by British rule after World War I. The mainland was governed as Tanganyika, with the Zanzibar Archipelago remaining a separate colonial jurisdiction. Following their respective independence in 1961 and 1963, the two entities merged in 1964 to form the United Republic of Tanzania. The countries had joined the British Commonwealth in 1961, and Tanzania is still a member of the Commonwealth as one republic. As a result of anti-Indian sentiment in post-independence Tanzania (beginning with the presidency of Julius Nyerere), many Indians migrated to India, Pakistan, the United Kingdom, the United States, and Canada.

As far as its constitution is concerned, Tanzania is a secular state. To this effect, only the main Muslim and Christian holidays are considered public holidays. The Jaffers practiced the Muslim faith. Over 100 different languages are spoken in Tanzania, but English has been the primary language used in foreign trade, in diplomacy, in higher courts, and as a medium of instruction in secondary and higher education. Recent changes discontinued English as the primary language.

Dr. Jaffer spoke of the origin and primary tenets of the Islamic faith. Islam is an Abrahamic monotheistic religion teaching that Muhammad is a messenger of God. It is the world's second-largest religion, with nearly 2 billion followers, or 24.9% of the world's population, known as Muslims. Islam teaches that God (Allah) is merciful, all-powerful, and unique and has guided humanity through prophets, revealed scriptures, and natural signs. The primary scriptures of Islam are the Quran, believed to be the verbatim word of God, as well as the teachings and normative examples of Muhammad. Dr. and Tazim reminded us of the six main tenets of Islam: belief in Allah as the one and only God; belief in angels; belief in the holy books; belief in the Prophets…e.g., Adam, Ibrahim (Abraham), Musa (Moses), Dawud (David), Isa (Jesus); belief in the Day of Judgment and belief in predestination. Such aspects of their faith that God has no offspring, no race, no gender, no body, and is unaffected by the characteristics of human life give credence to the Jaffers' worldview.

Tazim Jaffer depicts the evolving worldview in her art. It appears that Tazim's creativity is in sync with a branch of Shia Islam called the Ismaili. "Just as Ismaili artistic creativity in previous eras reflected the concerns and preoccupations of those times, contemporary cultural production has to deal with those of our times. Whereas the cultural achievements of the past provide sources of inspiration to many contemporary Ismaili artists, their work has to address twenty-first-century issues in order to be relevant to our times and context." (From an article in The Institute of Ismaili Studies, "The Quest for Excellence: Towards a Cultural Renaissance", by Karim H. Karim) Jaffer is cited in the article, "Tazim Jaffer uses innovative ways of combining disparate media such as painting, photography, sculpture, weaving, and jewelry, to explore the complex textures and rich colors of folk motifs."

I quote Tazim with her artist statement made on November 1, 2020, on the opening of her exhibition, Organic Artistry, "Increasingly over the years, I have been photographing when I am not painting and love both mediums. Photography allows me to capture marvelous forms of nature, color, texture, line, shape movement, and energy that are evolving. The act of capturing images with the lens of the camera is a metaphor for my artistic process. It allows me to process the world that I observe, filtering it through my psyche and presenting it to my audience. In creating images, I look for a structure, whether it is abstract, emotive, historical, culturally archival, personal narrative, or an in-depth meditation. In creating my body of work, I am struck by the visual motifs that we find in connection to something primal, elemental, and divine. Though the photographic images in this show are wide-ranging, they all spring from one sentiment-my being intrigued by nature's forms, by human depiction of nature's forms, or by the possibilities of my own artistic juxtaposition of nature's forms."

The worldview of both Nazim and Tazim Jaffer is a clear manifestation of the notion that human beings have more in common than possessing differences. Their varied upbringing, their various cultural influences and philosophies, and their extensive travel are clearly evident in their own philosophies and in their décor, including various works of art, in both of their homes-one in Liberty, Ohio, and another in Bradenton, Florida. They are important citizens of the Mahoning Valley, both making their marks here and are important citizens of the world.

The highlights of the OCA 23rd year were the wonderful stories offered by ten leading citizens of the Mahoning Valley, which concluded the three-year program, "My Story". In addition, we initiated a "Question of the Month" whereby the member that sent in their reservation with the correct answer earned a free meeting; we collected non-perishable food and toiletries for ten charitable organizations in the Valley; we added Frankie's Catering to our list; the Kosovo Men's Choir from Cleveland performed as did a Klezmer Band, and we enjoyed 200+ attendees at eight of our meetings. It was a really good year.

Dr. Nazim and Tazim Jaffer

An example of Tazim Jaffer's Organic Artistry

XVI. Resonating Voices of the World

"Resonating Voices of the World" was the theme for 2010-2011, the 24th year of the Ohio Cultural Alliance. Speakers discussed an historic figure that had a significant, positive influence on the world, using some actual resonating words of the subject's personality. We stated at the outset that the ten people treated were not the only voices of the world but a subjective choice of individuals who represent many countries and many ethnic backgrounds. In addition to learning something and being entertained, we were also able to affirm that "genius knows no boundaries".

In September, Rabbi Joel Berman, recently of Ohev Tzedek Temple, spoke of Moses as an important resonating voice, using some of Moses' words and considerable anecdotal material. The evening was truly multicultural as Teddy Pantelas, of Greek ancestry, played Jewish-themed music on his guitar, and we dined on Serbian food at Holy Trinity Serbian Hall.

A young girl says to her teacher: "Wow, Mr. Daniels, you must be old enough to have known Moses!" Mr. Daniels retorts: "No, young lady, I am not. It wasn't funny when Ben Franklin said it, and it is not funny when you say it." What a way to begin a serious discussion of the iconic figure, Moses. But, many years earlier, before Berman decided to become a rabbi, he was a popular comedian in Los Angeles. He traveled the country and performed at many nightclubs, putting on comedy shows. It was not until later in life that he felt that Judaism had something to say. He went to the rabbi at the synagogue where he grew up to offer to put on a show about Judaism, using old Jewish jokes. The rabbi said it would never work unless you were a rabbi. He studied, traveled to Israel, married, adopted two children from Guatemala, and met with four synagogues before he selected Ohev Tzedek in Youngstown. He led the congregation here for seven years. He encountered many challenges because of the aging population, but he managed to engage the community. He introduced a Torah study class and invited a variety of age groups to a "Rabbi's Tisch", which he felt would help strengthen the youth of the community. He played in a four-rabbi band named "Shalom Rav", and he also led a bi-weekly study group with a Roman Catholic priest for adults of any faith. So, we could be pretty sure that Rabbi Berman's approach would be somewhat unique. He did, indeed, pepper his historic comments with some comedic material.

Moses is the most important prophet in Judaism and an important prophet in Christianity, Islam, in the Baha'i faith, among others. He was the leader of the Israelites and lawgiver to whom the authorship, or "acquisition from heaven", of the Torah (the first five books of the Bible) is attributed. According to the Book of Exodus, Moses was born at a time when his people, the Israelites, an enslaved minority, were increasing in population, and, as a result, the Egyptian pharaoh worried that they might ally themselves with Egypt's enemies. Moses' mother secretly hid him when the Pharaoh ordered all newborn Hebrew boys to be killed in order to reduce the population of the Israelites. Through the pharaoh's daughter, the child was adopted as a foundling from the Nile River and grew up with the Egyptian royal family. After killing an Egyptian slave master who was beating a Hebrew, Moses fled across the Red Sea to Midian, where he encountered the Angel of the Lord, speaking to him from within a burning bush on Mount Horeb, which he regarded as the Mountain of God.

God sent Moses back to Egypt to demand the release of the Israelites from slavery. Moses said he could not speak eloquently, so God allowed Aaron, his elder brother, to become the spokesperson. After the Ten Plagues, Moses led the Exodus of the Israelites out of Egypt and across the Red Sea, after which they based themselves at biblical Mount Sinai, where Moses received the Ten Commandments from God, written on stone tablets. However, since Moses remained a long time on the mountain, some of the people feared he might be dead, so they made a statue of a golden calf and worshipped it, thus disobeying and angering God and Moses. Moses, out of anger, broke the tablets and melted down the golden statue. He then wrote the Ten Commandments on a new set of tablets.

Rabbi Joel Berman

After 40 years of wandering in the desert, Moses died within sight of the "promised land" on Mount Nebo. Scholars hold varying opinions on the status of Moses in history. The modern scholarly consensus is that the biblical person of Moses is largely mythical while holding that a "Moses-like" figure may have existed in the mid to late 13th century B.C. and that archeology can do nothing to prove or confirm either way. In any event, the members of the Ohio Cultural Alliance were treated to an evening of history (or legend) in a serious, albeit, at times, humorous look into an iconic figure special to the religious life of many people.

Teddy Pantelas offering guitar selections

Our October "resonating voice" was Christopher Columbus, as depicted by the author, Dr. George D. Beelen, dressed in authentic period apparel. Several members of the Opera Western Reserve presented lively music from their upcoming opera, La Traviata. We met at St. Patrick's Church Hall in Hubbard. Our meal was catered by Frankie's Restaurant. Special guest for the evening was YSU President Dr. Cynthia Anderson. She gave an update on activities at YSU.

Speaking in the first person as Christopher Columbus, I wondered out loud whether I was still relevant: What shall I do? Whatever shall I do? They call me a villain, a rogue, a lothario, even a murderer. I thought my deeds of more than 500 years ago, in the name of the Spanish crown, rendered me a hero, a discoverer, and a great mariner. I ask you, citizens; let me make my case.

After discussing my parents, my birth, and the place of my birth, Genoa, Italy, I discussed my early years, including my love of the sea. Beginning with a short trip at the age of ten and longer and longer trips during my teens and early 20s, I knew it was the sea that could take me to far-off places that I had heard of and dreamt of. On one trip when I was 25 years old, we were attacked by a French vessel that sunk ours. I managed to grasp a floating board that took me to the southern shore of Portugal. I was nursed back to health, learned languages, studied, married, had a son, learned about the known world, and wondered about the unknown regions.

I developed plans, after considerable study, to sail to some of the unknown parts, namely, to reach the East by sailing west, taking advantage of what I knew of the round world. My proposals were repeatedly refused by several sovereigns until Spanish Queen Isabella, who also originally flatly refused to help, accepted my plans. I prepared to leave Spain in August 1492 after the Queen financed the cost of three ships and a crew of 90 men, leaving the last of the Canary Islands by September 9th.

The voyage was one of the easiest of important voyages, with fair winds, soft air, a serene sky, and an ocean as smooth as a river. But it was taking too long, according to my calculations (which were not accurate). Mutiny was in the air until a crew member shouted, "Tierra! Tierra!" The date was October 12, 1492. It was to be called San Salvador in what would later be called the Bahamas. All of this happened more than 500 years ago; the peoples of the Old World and the New World were now known to each other. In fact, the entire world would be changed-the modern age had begun.

That fateful encounter led to many things-some positive, some tragic. One of the most important was the forging of new, multiracial, multicultural societies in the Americas. Among the negative aspects was the ecological disaster of many who were already in the Americas for hundreds of years as thousands, if not millions, of indigenous Americans, died of unfamiliar diseases and warfare. This all occurred in the wake of a total of four Columbus landings in the Americas and the subsequent populating/conquering of these lands in the ensuing years.

Each centennial year after 1492, I became the symbol of the New World, beginning in 1592. By 1692, my success provided the impetus for additional explorations and inspiration for the settlements by other European nations in the Americas. By 1792, my name developed into a legend in the societies taking root in the New World, a kind of mythic symbol of their perceived good fortune. Additionally, the United States heaped praise upon me: naming of the American capital, the District of Columbia; the naming of cities in many U.S. states; the naming of colleges; and the writing of songs and books, and periodicals with me or my name featured. By 1892, the dam really burst: young America, with its optimism, restless energy, prosperity, romanticism, and the belief Americans had in a special destiny for America, identified with Columbus as glorified by Washington Irving - a man of great and inventive genius, lofty and noble ambition, a visionary of an uncommon kind, etc. Honors abounded, statues and paintings were created, Knights of Columbus was formed, petitions were made to canonize me, coins were struck, stamps were printed, and the nation put the celebration in high gear with parades, floats, fireworks, marches, and many speeches and on and on.

In 1992, celebrations were still planned, and some were implemented, but they were tempered by an increased focus on the negative aspects of my accomplishments. Self-flagellation, mourning, Native American demonstrations, Black Death resuscitation (genocide, ecological disaster in a "land of Paradise") and new debunking of Columbus (me) the man, were focused upon instead of the positive and far-reaching nature of my accomplishments. A book by Kirkpatrick Sale detailed much of the negative- a book that had a considerable impact.

For the first time, there was direct contact among all the continents of the globe and with all the peoples who inhabited them. At once, each society changed its concept of reality and the vision of itself and the universe. That day ushered in the modern age-universal history began on that day, October 12, 1492. And Christopher Columbus, your humble servant, was the key figure. Imposing 21st-century insights and knowledge upon 15th-century actions to deconstruct my era is just poor history. Let us celebrate the beneficial aspects of my life and my era and pledge to improve upon those aspects in which I and others of my time have failed. My legacy is in your hands-will it be of a good fellow or a villain? Will you continue to celebrate Columbus Day, or will I be dumped into the trash heap of history? Thank you for the opportunity to visit you and your era and for me to give a personal account of my record.

Christopher Columbus
(aka George Beelen)

Dr. Cynthia Anderson, YSU President

Singers from Opera Western Reserve singing excerpts from LaTraviata

William Shakespeare was discussed in November by Dr. Dennis Henneman, YSU professor of Communication and Theater. Henneman's use of "the bard's" words, as well as a bit of history of the time, was complemented by five costumed YSU students acting out excerpts, including a sword fight, from Shakespeare's works. We met at Western Reserve United Methodist Church Hall, with a meal prepared and served by church caterers led by Darlene Wells.

William Shakespeare (1564-1616) was an English playwright, poet, and actor, widely regarded as the greatest writer in the English language and the world's greatest dramatist. He is often called England's national poet and the "Bard of Avon". His works consist of some 39 plays, 154 sonnets, three long narrative poems, and a few other verses. Dr. Henneman approached his topic as a person of iconic stature. He read with verve, some of Shakespeare's most famous quotes; can you hear him: "To be, or not to be, that is the question"; "This above all: to thine own self be true, and it must follow, as the night and the day"; "Cowards die many times before their deaths, The valiant never taste of death but once;" "Men at some time are masters of their fate". His works have been translated into every major language and are performed more often than those of any other playwright. They also continue to be studied and reinterpreted, including by Dr. Henneman

Shakespeare was born and raised in Stratford-upon-Avon, Warwickshire, England. He married Anne Hathaway, with whom he had three children. Sometime between 1585 and 1592, he began a successful career in London as an actor, writer, and part-owner of a playing company called Lord Chamberlain's Men. At age 49, he appears to have retired to Stratford, where he died three years later in 1616. Few records of his private life survive, so little is known about his physical appearance, his religious beliefs, his sexuality, and whether others authored some of his works.

Shakespeare produced most of his works between 1589 and 1613. His early plays were primarily comedies and histories, after which he wrote mainly tragedies until 1608, among them Hamlet, Romeo, and Juliet, Othello, King Lear, and Macbeth. In the last phase of his life, he wrote tragicomedies and collaborated with other playwrights. Dr. Henneman spoke briefly about some of the plays: In his summaries, Henneman said, "A Midsummer Night's Dream is a witty mixture of romance, fairy magic, and comic lowlife scenes; The Merchant of Venice contains a portrayal of the vengeful Jewish moneylender Shylock, which reflected Elizabethan views but may appear derogatory today." He also spoke of the wit and wordplay of Much Ado About Nothing, the charming rural setting of As You Like It and the lively merrymaking of Twelfth Night complete Shakespeare's great comedies. Shakespeare's histories include Henry IV and Henry V and the tragedies Romeo and Juliet and Julius Caesar. Dr. Henneman acted out quotes from some of these, giving credence to his own acting ability.

One of the advantages of a play over prose writing is that the actions in the plot can be seen by the audience. In a novel, the author can only describe the action. In the sword fight between Mercutio and Tybalt in Shakespeare's Romeo and Juliet, one hears and sees two of Dr. Henneman's students: Tybalt says, "Boy, this shall not excuse the injuries, that thou hast done me; there-fore turn and draw." And the taunting and sword fighting ensues.

The evening ended with Dr. Henneman reciting one of the sonnets, which were the last of Shakespeare's non-dramatic works: "Shall I compare thee to a summer's day? Thou art more lovely and more temperate; Rough winds do shake the darling buds of May; And summer's lease hath all too short a date."

Dr. Dennis Henneman

YSU students performing excerpts from Shakespeare

Professor Hugh Earnhart spoke of Abraham Lincoln in December. Earnhart related how Lincoln's voice still resonates today, as he shared with us some of the 16th president's life and words. Although heavy snow prevented a few guests and our string quartet from attending, Holy Family Church Hall venue in Poland was pleasant, and The Georgetown caterers' fine cuisine helped to make for a fine evening.

Hugh G. Earnhart was an appropriate speaker to explore the life of Abraham Lincoln. Earnhart is about 6'4'', as was Lincoln, and both have a style that compels one to listen. Earnhart, in complete Lincoln attire, for many years toured the schools and local organizations with his impersonation of Lincoln. He ceased such activity when (in his words) "the outfit got too small". Both are well-read and generally use simple language, often peppered with slang, off-color stories, and jokes.

Abraham Lincoln was born on February 12, 1809, and died by assassination on April 15, 1865. He was a statesman and a lawyer who served as the 16th president of the United States. He led the nation through the American Civil War, the country's greatest moral, cultural, constitutional, and political crisis. He succeeded in preserving the Union, abolishing slavery, bolstering the federal government, and modernizing the U.S. economy. He was born in poverty in a log cabin, reared on the frontier, was self-educated, and became a lawyer, a Whig Party leader, an Illinois state legislator, and a U.S. Congressman from Illinois. In 1854 he became one of the leaders in the new Republican Party and reached a national audience in the 1858 debates against Stephen Douglas-an election which he lost but propelled him into prominence and into the presidency in 1861.

Lincoln's election by a sweep of the North created dissension with the South, who equated his success with the North's rejection of slavery. Southern states began seceding from the Union. To secure its independence, the new Confederate states fired on Fort Sumter, a U.S. fort in the South, and Lincoln called up forces to suppress the rebellion and restore the Union. The four-year-long Civil War was the worst kind of war in that losses on both sides were losses to the nation. Indeed, more than ¾ million deaths resulted. Lincoln pursued the war with the belief that succession was not possible-our Union was constitutionally indissoluble.

Despite the perils of war, he had enacted many measures that strengthened the federal government and even modernized the economy. He managed various factions by exploiting their mutual enmity, carefully distributing political patronage, and by appealing to the American people. His Gettysburg Address became a clarion call for nationalism, republicanism, equal rights, liberty, and democracy. He engineered the beginning of the end of slavery with his Emancipation and his order that the Army protect and recruit former slaves. He also encouraged the border states to outlaw slavery and promoted the Thirteenth Amendment to the U.S. Constitution, which outlawed slavery across the country.

Although a religious skeptic, he was deeply familiar with the Bible, quoting scripture and praising the Bible. His three most famous speeches, the House Divided Speech (before he became President), the Gettysburg Address, and his second inaugural, each contain direct allusions to Providence and quotes from Scripture. Lincoln did believe in an all-powerful God that shaped events, and by 1865, he was expressing those beliefs in other major speeches. By the end of the war, he increasingly appealed to the Almighty for solace and to explain events.

Lincoln's redefinition of republican values has been stressed by many historians. Lincoln called the Declaration of Independence-which emphasized freedom and equality for all-the "sheet anchor" of republicanism. He did this at a time when the Constitution, which tolerated slavery, was the focus of most political discourse. Instead of focusing on the legality of an argument, he focused on the moral basis of republicanism. In the judgment of American citizens, including historians, Lincoln is usually ranked as the best of our presidents. He is remembered and memorialized in many ways. His portrait appears on two denominations of U.S. currency, the penny, and the $5 bill. His likeness also appears on many postage stamps. He has been memorialized in many towns, cities, and county names, including the capital of Nebraska, and two Navy ships have carried his name. Lincoln Memorial is one of the most visited monuments in the nation's capital. Memorials in Springfield, Illinois, include the Abraham Lincoln Presidential Library and Museum, Lincoln's home, as well as his tomb. A portrait carving of Lincoln appears with those of three other presidents on Mount Rushmore, which receives about 3 million visitors a year.

Abraham Lincoln's legacy is international as well as national. His justification for waging war to preserve the Union was to make sure "that government of the people, by the people, for the people shall not perish from the earth". For him, the success or failure of the Union had consequences for the whole world. As the mid-century world's only large-scale experiment in avowed democracy, the United States had to prevail in its war in order to maintain integrity. Lincoln believed that victory would demonstrate to all humanity the viability of democratic government. We enjoyed quite an evening as Professor Earnhart reminded us of the special nature of Abraham Lincoln and how much we are indebted to him.

Professor Hugh Earnhart

Lincoln, the rail splitter

Reverend Brent Allen spoke in January of Jesus Christ at Old North Church in Canfield. Quoting freely from the Bible, he discussed how Jesus remains a "resonating voice" for many in the world. The Old North Praise Band complemented the aura of the iconic figure and the speaker's words about Him. Carolyn Catering prepared a meal that was delicious and abundant. (We always eat very well at our OCA meetings).

Reverend Allen was the pastor of Old North Church at the time he spoke to the OCA. His presentation was of a proselytizing/preaching nature; I guess that's what pastors do. His approach was to talk a little about the life of Jesus but more about some of the major tenets of Christianity and how we should adhere to them. He, of course, did approach Jesus as an iconic figure of the world.

Jesus, also referred to as Jesus of Nazareth or Jesus Christ, was a first-century Jewish preacher and religious leader. He is the central figure of Christianity, the world's largest religion. Most Christians believe he is the incarnation of God, the Son, and the awaited messiah (the Christ) prophesied in the Old Testament. Jesus was a Galilean Jew who was baptized by John the Baptist and began his own ministry. His teachings were initially conserved by oral transmission, and he himself was often referred to as rabbi. Jesus debated with fellow Jews on how best to follow God, engaged in healing, taught in parables, and gathered followers. Tradition holds that he was arrested and tried by the Jewish authorities, turned over to the Roman government, and crucified on the order of Pontius Pilate, the Roman prefect. After his death, his followers believed he rose from the dead, and the community they formed eventually became the early Christian Church.

Christian doctrines include the beliefs that Jesus was conceived by the Holy Spirit, was born of a virgin named Mary, performed miracles, founded the Christian Church, died by crucifixion as a sacrifice to achieve atonement for sin, rose from the dead, and ascended into Heaven, from where he will return. Christians believe Jesus enables people to be reconciled to God. The Nicene Creed asserts that Jesus will judge the living and the dead either before or after their bodily resurrection, an event tied to the Second Coming of Jesus in Christian theology. The great majority of Christians worship Jesus as the incarnation of God the Son, the second of three persons of the Trinity. The birth of Jesus is celebrated annually on December 25th as Christmas. His crucifixion is honored on Good Friday, and his resurrection on Easter Sunday. The widely used calendar era "AD", from the Latin anno Domini, "year of the Lord," and the "BC" before Christ, are based upon the approximate date of Jesus' birth. Christians of the early years designated Jesus as "the Christ" because they believed him to be the Messiah, whose arrival is prophesied in the Hebrew Bible and the Old Testament. In post-biblical usage, Christ became viewed as a name-one part of Jesus Christ. The term Christian (meaning a follower of Christ) has been in use since the 1st century.

The four canonical Gospels (Matthew, Mark, Luke, and John) are the foremost sources for the life and message of Jesus. But other parts of the New Testament also include references to key episodes in His life, such as the Last Supper in 1 Corinthians 11:23-26. Acts of the Apostles refers to Jesus' early ministry and its anticipation by John the Baptist. Acts 1:1-11 says more about the Ascension of Jesus than the canonical Gospels do. In the undisputed Pauline letters, which were written earlier than the Gospels, Jesus' words or instructions are cited several times. The canonical Gospels are four accounts, each by a different author. The authors of the Gospels are attributed by tradition to four evangelists, each with close ties to Jesus: Mark, an associate of Peter; Matthew, one of Jesus' disciples; Luke, a companion of Paul mentioned in a few epistles; and John, another of Jesus' disciples, the so-called "beloved disciple".

The seven "I Am" statements in John might be best understood as falling under and echoing this initial, ultimate claim of Jesus: He is God, and He is the God of Israel. All the Old Testament and God's redemptive acts were pointing to the coming of Jesus as the God-in-flesh, the true and better Israel, and the fulfillment of all the Old Testament types. He is the I Am, the eternal, unchanging, self-existent one, infinite and glorious in every way, and above and beyond all created things. He is God. The "I Am" statements are: I Am the Bread of Life; I Am the Light of the World; I Am the Door or Gate; I Am the Good Shepherd; I Am the Resurrection and the Life; I Am the Way, the Truth, and the Life; I Am the True Vine.

Reverend Allen made references to some of the many accomplishments of Jesus. He was conceived of the Holy Spirit and born of a virgin. He lived a sinless life. He turned water into wine and healed many sick, blind, and lame people. He forgave sins, multiplied fish and loaves of bread to feed thousands on more than one occasion, delivered the demon-possessed, walked on water, calmed the stormy sea, and raised children and adults from death to life. Jesus Christ proclaimed the good news of the Kingdom of God. We are all blessed to know more about this iconic figure of the world.

Reverend Brent Allen and Oliver Musuka

An image of Jesus

In February, Dr. Martha Pallante, in costume, portraying Martha Washington, discussed her famous husband from a wife's point of view and how George Washington was an important voice at America's inception. As a counterpoint to Martha, reminding us of one of America's heroes, Carol Weakland acted in her rendition of "The Scarlet Letter", recounting a sadder chapter of our history. We met at The Georgetown Banquet Center, whose caterers prepared a wonderful "Youngstown Buffet".

Although the iconic figure we addressed at the present meeting was George Washington, we gleaned portions of his life from his wife, Martha. After seven years of marriage to Daniel Custis, he died suddenly in July 1757, making Martha Custis, at age 26, a very wealthy widow with two young children, a 17,500-acre plantation to manage, and responsible for almost 300 slaves. As such, she was a very good prospect; indeed, she was courted by many. George Washington visited Martha Custis twice in March of 1758. Since the two shared friends and acquaintances, it is possible they met before Martha was widowed; however, there is no record of such meetings. George and Martha married on January 6, 1759. It is from the point of view of Martha that we approached George Washington. Martha approached the present OCA meeting with a brief biographical sketch of her husband and homes in on several important pieces of his life.

George Washington was an American political leader, military general, statesman, and Founding Father who served as the first president of the United States from 1789-1797. Previously, he had led patriot forces to victory in the nation's War for Independence. He presided at the Constitutional Convention in 1787, which established the U. S. Constitution and a federal government. Washington has been called the Father of His Country for his many leadership positions in the formative days of the new nation. His first public office was serving as an official surveyor in Virginia from 1749 to 1750. Subsequently, he received his initial training and command with the Virginia Regiment during the French and Indian War. It was here that he learned of and found lacking the military regimen of the British army. He was later elected to the Virginia House of Burgesses and was named a delegate to the Continental Congress, where he was appointed Commanding General of the Continental Army. As his "wife" told us, "he was always humble and reticent about accepting continuing leadership roles. She said that her husband, as a private man, did not speak up much at the political gatherings, nor did he socialize with the officers or enlisted men/conscripts. However, he always was cognizant of his role as one of the privileged and his increased responsibility as a servant of the public."

Washington commanded the American forces in an effort that was not always glorious, but ultimately, with French assistance, it was successful in the end. He was a fighter, but not a tiger; he did often perform heroically. What was particularly noteworthy was his ability to respond to military and civilian concerns: he had to organize into a unified and sustained fighting force consisting of men with short-term participation (3-6 months) and who were reluctant to fight much beyond their individual regions. He had to accomplish this within the parameters of civilian political leadership, who controlled the purse strings. The British had no such person who could walk this tightrope. His armies, with the help of the French, defeated the British at Yorktown in 1781 and signed the Paris Treaty with them in 1783, after which Washington resigned his commission.

Although Washington's desire was to retire to Mount Vernon, he reluctantly acceded to the insistence of those at the Constitutional Convention, where he played a role as a conciliator to become the new nation's first president. Washington was twice elected by the votes in the electoral college. He implemented a strong, well-financed national government while remaining impartial in a fierce rivalry between cabinet members Thomas Jefferson

(Secretary of State) and Alexander Hamilton (Secretary of Treasury). He rejected suggestions to become king or dictator; rather, he preferred "Mr. President". He certainly provided leadership while acknowledging the importance of both liberty and union in making decisions. He displayed common sense, sound judgment, and devotion to the public. During the French Revolution of 1789, Washington proclaimed a policy of neutrality while sanctioning the Jay Treaty with Great Britain.

Though a moral person, Washington owned slaves, and in order to preserve national unity, he supported measures passed by Congress to protect slavery. He later became troubled with the institution of slavery and freed his slaves in a 1799 will. He tried to assimilate Native Americans into the Anglo-American culture but combated indigenous resistance during instances of violent conflict. He was a member of the Anglican Church and the Freemasons, and he urged broad religious freedom in his roles as general and president. At his Inaugural, at the point of saying, "I solemnly swear", he added, "so help me God", then bent forward to kiss the Bible. Upon his death, he was eulogized as "first in war, first in peace, and first in the hearts of his countrymen." He died on December 14, 1799, at the age of 67.

Washington was not like other men to bring his lofty character down to the level of the vulgar passions of common life because "that is to give the lie to the greatest chapter in the uninspired annals of the human race." Nevertheless, "Martha" spoke of her husband's consistent regard for the people by serving them: in his first Inaugural Address, he states: ... "the preservation of the sacred fire of liberty, and the destiny of the republican model of government are justly considered as deeply, perhaps as finally staked on the experiment entrusted to the hands of the American people." He also continued to show his humility and admonished the government to serve the people. In his Farewell Address, he argues that the country should avoid permanent alliances with all foreign nations, although temporary alliances during times of extreme danger may be necessary. He states that current treaties should be honored but not extended. He also recognized the dangers of political parties and warned that attacks by political parties could weaken a nation.

Washington's legacy is secure as one of the most influential in American history. His reputation is impressed upon the American memory, with some biographers regarding him as the great exemplar of republicanism. He became an international symbol of liberation and nationalism as the leader of the first successful revolution against a colonial empire. He is remembered by Washington D.C., the nation's capital; the state of Washington; the Washington monument; dollar bill and the quarter coin; Washington University; thirty states have a Washington county; numerous cities, mountains, lakes, streets, and buildings bear his name; portraits and statutes abound. In 1885, Congress proclaimed Washington's Birthday to be a federal holiday. Biographer Douglas Southall Freeman concludes, "The great big thing stamped across that man is character". Modern historian David Hackett Fischer defines Washington's character with such appellations as: "integrity, self-discipline, courage, absolute honesty, resolve, and decision, but also forbearance, decency, and respect for others."

Martha Washington (aka Dr. Martha Pallante)

Carol Weakland

Ludwig V. Beethoven was the "resonating voice" for our March meeting. Professor Roman Rudnytsky spoke of and performed the music of this iconic figure. As usual, Rudnytsky was brilliant in his rendition of Beethoven's music. The Saxon Club venue and meal were appropriate complements to the evening. The usual standing ovation was given to Roman Rudnytsky, our most frequent performer over the years.

Ludwig van Beethoven, born in 1770 and died in 1827, was a German composer and pianist. He remains one of the most admired composers in the history of Western music; his works rank among the most performed of the classical music repertoire. His works span the transition from the classical period to the romantic era in classical music. His career has conventionally been divided into early, middle, and late periods. The early period, during which he forged his craft, is typically considered to have lasted until 1802. From 1802 to around 1812, his middle period showed an individual development from the classical styles of Joseph Haydn and Wolfgang Amadeus Mozart and is sometimes characterized as heroic. During this time, he began to suffer increasingly from deafness. In his late period from 1812 to his death in 1827, he extended his innovations in musical form and expression.

Born in Bonn, Germany, Beethoven's musical talent was obvious at an early age; he was initially harshly and intensively taught by his father. He later studied under Christian Gottlob Neefe, under whose tutelage he published his first work in 1783. He found relief from his dysfunctional home life with the family of Helene von Breuning, whose children he loved, befriended, and taught piano. At age 21, he moved to Vienna, where he studied composition with Haydn. Beethoven then gained a reputation as a virtuoso pianist and was soon courted by Karl Alois and Prince Lichnowsky for compositions, which resulted in his three Opus 1 piano trios in 1795.

His first major orchestral work, the First Symphony, appeared in 1800, and his first set of string quartets was published the following year. During this period, his hearing began to deteriorate, but he continued to conduct, premiering his Third and Fifth Symphonies in 1804 and 1808, respectively. His Violin Concerto was done in 1806. His last piano concerto (No. 5, opus 73, known as the Emperor), dedicated to his frequent patron Archduke Rudolf of Austria, was premiered in 1810, but not with Beethoven as soloist. He was almost completely deaf by 1814, at which time he gave up performing and even appearing in public. In the years from 1810, increasingly less socially involved, Beethoven composed many of his most admired works, including his later symphonies and mature chamber music and sonatas. His only opera, Fidelio, which had been first performed in 1805, was revised to its final version in 1814. He composed his Missa Solemnis in the years 1819-1823 and his final, Ninth Symphony (Ode to Joy) one of the first examples of a choral symphony in 1822-1824. When it came to the premiere of this massive Ninth Symphony, Beethoven insisted on conducting. The orchestra hired another conductor to stand alongside the composer, who told the performers to follow him and ignore Beethoven's directions. The symphony received rapturous applause, which Beethoven could not hear. Legend has it that the young contralto Carolina Unger approached the maestro and turned him around to face the audience to see the ovation. Written in his last years, his late string quartets of 1825-26 are among his final achievements. After some months of bedridden illness, he died in 1827. Beethoven's works remain the mainstays of the classical music repertoire.

Ludwig van Beethoven is undoubtedly one of the most important and influential composers of Western music. From a young age, he exhibited not only considerable talent, and his attitude toward social norms regarding music. Composing symphonies, sonatas, string quartets, and one opera, Beethoven shattered musical boundaries and set the stage for how musicians and listeners would think about music for the next 200 years, even to the modern day.

Beethoven's legacy is significant in other tangible ways. There is a museum, the Beethoven House, the place of his birth, in central Bonn. The same city has hosted a musical festival, the Beethovenfest, since 1845. The festival was initially irregular but has been organized annually since 2007. The Ira F. Brilliant Center for Beethoven Studies, in the Dr. Martin Luther King, Jr. Library, on the campus of San Jose State University, California, serves as a museum, research center, and host of lectures and performances devoted solely to Beethoven's life and works. The Beethoven Monument in Bonn was unveiled in August 1845 in honor of the 75th anniversary of his birth; it was the first statue of a composer created in Germany, and the music festival that accompanied the unveiling was the impetus for the very hasty construction of the original Beethoven House in Bonn (it was designed and built within less than a month, on the urging of Franz Liszt). Vienna honored Beethoven with a statue in 1880. Also, the third largest crater on Mercury is named in Beethoven's honor, as is a minor planet/asteroid named 1815 Beethoven. His music features twice on the Voyager Golden Record, a phonograph record containing a broad sample of the images, common sounds, languages, and music of Earth, sent into outer space with the two Voyager probes. Genius knows no boundaries!

Ludwig Beethoven

Professor Roman Rudnytsky

To a standing ovation, Reverend Kenneth L. Simon depicted Nelson Mandela at our April meeting. His narrative (interspersed with Mandela quotes) was heartwarming, poignant, and informative, reminding us how relevant Mandela remains. The Harambee Dancers gave additional insight into African music and dance. Anton's Banquet Center was the venue, and their caterers provided an appropriate ethnic meal.

"What counts in life is not the mere fact that we have lived; it is what difference we have made to the lives of others that will determine the significance of the life we lead", are words uttered by Nelson Mandela and words that describe his own life. He worked, despite so many obstacles, to right many wrongs and improved a lot of others. Nelson Rolihlahla Mandela, a South African anti-apartheid revolutionary, political leader, and philanthropist, was born in 1918 and died in 2013. He served as President of South Africa from 1994 to 1999 as the country's first Black head of state and the first elected in a fully representative democratic election. His government focused on dismantling the legacy of apartheid by tackling institutionalized racism and fostering racial reconciliation. Ideologically an African nationalist and socialist, he served as president of the African National Congress (ANC) from 1991 to 1997.

Mandela was born to the Thembu "royal family" in Mvezo, Union of South Africa. Mandela's early life was dominated by traditional customs. He grew up with two sisters in the village of Qunu, where he tended herds as a cattle boy and spent much of his time playing outside with other boys. Both his parents were illiterate, but being a devout Christian, his mother sent him to a local Methodist school. Baptized a Methodist, Mandela was given the English forename of Nelson by his teacher. This was the custom among Africans in those days, undoubtedly due to the British bias toward their education. When Mandela was about nine, his father came to stay in Qunu, where he died of an undiagnosed ailment, which Mandela believed to be lung disease. Feeling "cut adrift", he later said that he inherited his father's "proud rebelliousness" and his "stubborn sense of fairness."

As a young man, he studied English; native language, Xhosa; history, and geography. He embraced Christianity and developed a love of African history, listening to the tales told by elderly visitors and was influenced by the anti-imperialist rhetoric of a visiting chief. Nevertheless, at the time, he considered the European colonizers not as oppressors but as benefactors who had brought education and other benefits to southern Africa. In 1933 Mandela began his secondary education at a Methodist High School in Engcobo, a Western-style institution that was the largest school for Black Africans in his region. He was quite studious but also became active in such activities as long-distance running, boxing, dancing, and gardening. After taking a B. A. degree at the University of Fort Hare, an elite Black university, he studied law before working as a lawyer in Johannesburg. While there, he became involved in anti-colonial and African nationalist politics, joining the ANC in 1943 and co-founding its Youth League in 1944. After the National Party's white-only government established apartheid, a system of racial segregation that privileged whites, he and the ANC committed themselves to its overthrow. He was determined to do what he could to end apartheid "for to be free is not merely to cast off one's chains, but to live in a way that respects and enhances the freedom of others," he argued.

His leadership and involvement led to repeated arrests for seditious activities, and he was unsuccessfully prosecuted in the 1956 Treason Trial. Undeterred, he continued in his quest to undermine apartheid uttering such words as, "The greatest glory in living lies not in never failing but rising every time we fail." Influenced by Marxism, he secretly joined the banned South African Communist Party (SACP). Although initially committed to non-violent protest, in association with the SACP, he led in 1961, a sabotage campaign against the government.

Mandela served 27 years in prison, split between Robben Island, Pollsmoor, and Victor Verster prisons. Amid growing domestic and international pressure and fears of racial civil war, President F.W. de Klerk released him in 1990. Mandela and de Klerk led efforts to negotiate an end to apartheid, which resulted in the 1994 multiracial general election in which Mandela led the ANC to victory and became president. Leading a broad coalition government that promulgated a new constitution, Mandela emphasized reconciliation between the country's racial groups and created the Truth and Reconciliation Commission to investigate past human rights abuses. Economically, Mandela's administration retained its predecessor's liberal framework despite his own socialist beliefs, also introducing measures to encourage land reform, combat poverty and expand healthcare services. These reforms are consistent with his public statements, such as, "Overcoming poverty is not a task of charity; it is an act of justice. Like slavery and apartheid, poverty is not natural. It is man-made, and it can be overcome and eradicated by the actions of human beings." Although opinion polls showed wavering support for both the ANC and the government, Mandela himself remained highly popular, with 80% of South Africans polled in 1999 expressing satisfaction with his performance as president. He declined a second presidential term and was succeeded by his deputy, Thabo Mbeki.

Mandela became an elder statesman and focused on combating poverty and HIV/AIDS through the charitable Nelson Mandela Foundation. He was a controversial figure for much of his life. Although critics on the right denounced him as a communist terrorist and those on the far left deemed him too eager to negotiate and reconcile with apartheid's supporters, he gained international acclaim for his activism. Testament to his fairness, he said: "During my lifetime, I have dedicated myself to the struggle of the African people. I have fought against white domination, and I have fought against Black domination. I have cherished the ideal of a democratic and free society in which all persons live together in harmony and with equal opportunities. It is an ideal that I hope to live for and to achieve. But if needs be, it is an ideal for which I am prepared to die." Adding later, he said: "Thus shall we live, because we will have created a society which recognizes that all people are born equal, with each entitled in equal measure to life, liberty, prosperity, human rights, and good governance." He acted as a mediator in the Pan Am Flight 103 bombing trial and served as secretary-general of the Non-Aligned Movement from 1998 to 1999. Widely regarded as an icon of democracy and social justice, he received more than 250 honors, including the Nobel Peace Prize.

By the time of his death in 2013, Mandela was widely considered both the "father of the nation" and 'the founding father of democracy." Outside of South Africa, he was a global icon, with one reference calling him "one of the most revered figures of our time." Another declared he was a "modern democratic hero." Some have portrayed him in messianic terms in contrast to his own statement that "I was not a messiah, but an ordinary man who had become a leader because of extraordinary circumstances." He is often cited alongside Mahatma Gandhi and Martin Luther King, Jr. as one of the 20th century's anti-racist and anti-colonial leaders. Across the world, Mandela earned international acclaim for his activism in overcoming apartheid and fostering racial reconciliation, coming to be viewed as a moral authority with great concern for the truth. In 2004, Johannesburg granted Mandela the Freedom of the City Award, and in 2008 a Mandela statue was unveiled at the spot where Mandela was released from prison. In November 2009, the United Nations General Assembly proclaimed Mandela's birthday, July 18th, as Mandela Day, marking his contribution to the anti-apartheid struggle. In 2015 the U.N. General Assembly named the amended Standard Minimum Rules for the Treatment of Prisoners as "the Mandela rules" to honor his legacy.

Nelson Mandela, who sought to right the wrongs of his own country, has succeeded in having an extraordinary legacy by tempering his inclination to do ill to those who did ill to him and to his "people". His statement that: "You will achieve more in this world through acts of mercy than you will through acts of retribution", is a fitting succinct definition of this man.

Reverend Kenneth Simon

Harambee dancers

Nelson Mandela

Michelangelo di Lodovico Buonarroti Simoni was the resonating voice of our May meeting, brilliantly and humorously discussed by Buffalo, New York artist and teacher Rosemary Cardoza. The "one-man band" of favorite John Gabriele and the food of Lou Fusillo Catering made this an Italian night to remember. Ms. Cardoza has earned degrees in art education and painting, including a Master of Fine Arts degree from the State University at Buffalo.

Ms. Cardoza began her talk with her own artist's statement: "Life is short, art is long. It's all very simple. Early cave dwellers used charcoal sticks and earth colors to describe the hunt, tribesmen in Africa carved sculptures and made masks, Egyptians built pyramids and painted mummy cases, Greeks and Romans built temples, Native Americans made ceramic pots, and today's third graders make lines with markers and push colors around with a brush. Each artist records the life and times of their culture with whatever means or medium available. Each artist brings their individual state of mind, experience, and emotions to the process. Each artist leaves a footprint on the riverbank. The making of art is not really as precious or esoteric as the critics, and art historians would have us believe. Each of us, in our own way, creates something, and if it touches someone else through color, texture, shape, or form, and causes them to wonder or appreciate, then art has worked its centuries-old magic. Life is short; art is long." What a fascinating introduction to the artist Michelangelo.

Michelangelo di Lodovico Buonarroti Simoni, born in Florence, Italy, in 1475 and died in 1564, was an Italian sculptor, painter, architect, and poet of the High Renaissance who exerted an unparalleled influence on the development of Western art. His artistic versatility was of such a high order that he is often considered a contender for the title of the archetypal Renaissance man, along with his rival and elder contemporary, Leonardo de Vinci. Some scholars have described Michelangelo as the greatest artist of his age and even as the greatest artist of all time.

Several of Michelangelo's works of paintings, sculpture, and architecture rank among the most famous in existence. His output in these fields was prodigious; given the sheer volume of surviving correspondence, sketches and reminiscences, he is the best-documented artist of the 16th century. He sculpted two of his best-known works, the Pieta and David, before the age of 30. Despite holding a low opinion of painting, he also created two of the most influential frescoes in the history of Western art: the scenes from Genesis on the ceiling of the Sistine Chapel in Rome and The Last Judgment on its altar wall. At the age of 74, he succeeded Antonio da Sangallo the Younger as the architect of St. Peter's Basilica. He transformed the plan so that the western end was finished to his design, as was the dome, with some modification, after his death.

In his lifetime, Michelangelo was often called Il Divino (the divine one). His contemporaries often admired his ability to instill a sense of awe. Attempts by subsequent artists to imitate Michelangelo's impassioned, highly personal style resulted in mannerism, the next major movement in Western art after the High Renaissance. Michelangelo, along with Da Vinci and Raphael, are considered the giants of the High Renaissance. Although their names are often cited together, Michelangelo was younger than Leonardo and older than Raphael. Because of his reclusive nature, he had little to do with either of them, and he outlived both of them by more than forty years. He took a few sculpture students and used assistants sparingly and then only for the more menial tasks of preparing surfaces and grinding colors. Despite this, his works were to have a great influence on painters, sculptors, and architects for many future generations. Michelangelo's David is the most famous nude of all time and now graces cities around the world. The dome of St. Peter's influenced the building of churches for many centuries, as well as the civic domes of many buildings and state capitals across America.

Michelangelo was a devout Catholic whose faith deepened at the end of his life. His poetry includes closing lines: "Neither painting nor sculpture will be able any longer to calm my soul, now turned toward that divine love that opened His arms on the cross to take us in." In his personal life, he lived that of a simple man, even as a poor man. He once told Ascanio Condivi, his apprentice: "However rich I may have been, I have always lived like a poor man." Condivi added that Michelangelo "was indifferent to food and drink, eating more out of necessity than of pleasure and that he often slept in his clothes and boots. He was by nature a solitary and melancholy man who withdrew himself from the company of other people.

Ms. Cardoza considered several of Michelangelo's greatest works: David, Pieta, The Last Judgment, and Moses. David is probably his most iconic work and can be seen at Florence's Galleria dell Accademia. The white marble statue, which took two years to create, stands about 14 feet tall and is in the form of a muscled and handsome nude male figure that represents the historical man of David from the Bible in the first book of Samuel; David is a young Israelite shepherd boy who cleverly battles a giant Philistine named Goliath using only a slingshot.

One of his earliest works is the statue titled Pieta. The Pieta is a religious marble sculpture that often evokes feelings of spirituality and emotion. The grand statue is a representation of the Virgin Mary holding Christ in her arms in the sad moments between His crucifixion and burial in the tomb. We are urged to look closely at the expression of the Virgin Mary, who has a look of peaceful acceptance amidst the heartbreak of watching her son die. Pieta can be found in St. Peter's Basilica in Vatican City. It is said to be the only one of his works to bear his signature.

Michelangelo

The Last Judgment, also found in Vatican City, is Michelangelo's famous painting which can be found on the altar wall of the Sistine Chapel. He began this artistic work in the second quarter of the 16th century, and it is said to have taken about four years to complete. The title of The Last Judgment is said to describe the second coming of Christ as statcd in thc Biblc. Thc astounding painting is made even more so by its sheer size, which is 48 feet by 44 ft. The painting depicts a judgment day theme, but the eye travels over a vast array of different scenes, including the joy of the saved, the resurrection of the dead, the despair of the damned, and the angels and saints.

Michelangelo's Moses was originally intended to be an integral part of Pope Julius II's tomb, but it can be seen in the church of San Pietro in Rome. The sculpture was created to portray Moses' reaction to finding the Israelites worshiping other gods shortly after the delivery of the Ten Commandments. Michelangelo is said to have considered Moses one of his most lifelike works, so much so that upon completion of the sculpture, he allegedly hit it on the knee and commanded it to speak.

When one talks about genius, there is little doubt that Michelangelo carries that description. In the process of learning about this 16th-century genius, we also learned something about some of his contemporaries, something about the nature of the man and the nature of the time in which he lived. Genius knows no boundaries.

Rounding out the year in June, Dr. Warren Young, YSU, Professor, Physics, and Astronomy Department, discussed (and at times depicted) Albert Einstein as our "resonating voice". He used a power-point presentation and several props to illustrate Einstein's brilliance and included something of his somewhat normal domestic life. Professor Young recently (at the time of his presentation) retired after nearly 50 years at YSU, serving as chairman for a number of those years. He also ran YSU's planetarium during most of his tenure at YSU. Marcellene Hawk played piano selections, billed as "vamp music" of the 1920s, which was contemporaneous with many of Einstein's important theories. Marcellene is well known in the music community, including performing with the Youngstown Symphony. We met at St. Matthias Church Hall, with catering done by Carolyn Catering.

Albert Einstein (1879-1955) was a German-born theoretical physicist widely acknowledged to be one of the greatest physicists of all time. He is known for developing the theory of relativity, but he also made important contributions to the development of the theory of quantum mechanics. Relativity and quantum mechanics are together the two pillars of modern physics. His mass-energy equivalence formula E=mc2, which arises from relativity theory, has been dubbed "the world's most famous equation." This theory asserted that matter could be turned into energy. Not since Isaac Newton had one man so drastically altered our understanding of how the universe works. His work is also known for its influence on the philosophy of science. He received the 1921 Nobel Prize in Physics for his services to theoretical physics and especially for his discovery of the law of the photoelectric effect, a pivotal step in the development of quantum theory. His intellectual achievements and originality resulted in Einstein becoming synonymous with genius. So, do we refer to him as "genius', genius"?

In 1905, Einstein published four groundbreaking papers. These outlined the theory of the photoelectric effect, explained Brownian motion, introduced special relativity, and demonstrated mass-energy equivalence. Einstein thought that the laws of classical mechanics could no longer be reconciled with those of the electromagnetic field, which led him to develop his special theory of relativity. He then extended the theory to gravitational fields; he published a paper on general relativity in 1916, and in 1917 he applied the general theory of relativity to model the structure of the universe. Dr. Young gave some explanation via power-point of these and other of Einstein's groundbreaking theories.

While Einstein clearly excelled in science and mathematics from an early age, he did not excel at everything. He went to elementary school and later grammar school in Munich, where he felt alienated and stifled by the school's pedagogical approach. He was an average pupil and experienced speech challenges, which permanently influenced his view of education and human potential. Of these experiences, Einstein once reflected: "I believe in standardizing automobiles. I do not believe in standardizing human beings." It was largely in his private time that his passion and inquisitiveness for science and mathematics flourished, as he said: "All that is valuable in human society depends upon the opportunity for development accorded the individual." After finishing his studies in Zurich in 1900, it was again, in his leisure time, while working at the Swiss Patent Office as a young adult, that he developed many of his most influential theories. But he did not retreat from his fellow man, as evidenced by his reminder: "Although I am a typical loner in daily life, my consciousness of belonging to the invisible community of those who strive for truth, beauty, and justice has preserved me from feeling isolated."

Einstein was born in the German Empire but moved to Switzerland in 1895. In 1897, at the age of 17, he enrolled in the mathematics and physics teaching diploma program at the Swiss Federal Polytechnic School in Zurich, graduating in 1900. In 1901 he acquired Swiss citizenship, and in 1903, he secured a position at the Swiss Patent Office in Bern. In 1905, he was awarded a Ph.D. by the University of Zurich. In 1914, he moved to Berlin to join the Prussian Academy of Sciences and the Humboldt University of Berlin. In 1917, Einstein became director of the Kaiser Wilhelm Institute for Physics. He also became a German citizen again. In 1933, while Einstein was visiting the United States, Adolf Hitler came to power. Einstein did not return to Germany because he objected to the policies of the newly elected Nazi-led government. He settled in the U.S. and became an American citizen in 1940. He worked at Princeton University in New Jersey for the rest of his days. There he became a central figure in the fight to curtail the use of the atomic bomb and a strong voice against racism and nationalism. On the eve of World War II, he endorsed a letter to President Franklin D. Roosevelt alerting him to the potential German nuclear weapons program and recommending that the U.S. begin similar research. At one point in his life, he said: " I am by heritage a Jew, by citizenship a Swiss and by makeup a human being, and only a human being, without any special attachment to any state or national entity whatsoever." He did support the Allied Powers in World War II.

Einstein became one of the most famous scientific celebrities, beginning with the confirmation of his theory of general relativity in 1919. Despite the general public having little understanding of his work, he was widely recognized and received adulation and publicity. In the period before World War II, The New Yorker published a vignette in their "The Talk of the Town" feature saying that Einstein was so well known in America that he would be stopped on the street by people wanting him to explain "that theory". He told his inquirers, "Pardon me, sorry! Always I am mistaken for Professor Einstein."

Einstein has been the subject of or inspiration for many novels, films, plays, and works of music. He is a favorite model for depictions of absent-minded professors; his expressive face and distinctive hairstyle (which Dr. Young emulated) have been widely copied and exaggerated. Time magazine's Frederic Golden wrote that Einstein was a "cartoonist's dream come true." He received numerous awards and honors, and in 1922, he was awarded the 1921 (actually awarded in 1922) Nobel Prize in Physics "for his services to Theoretical Physics, and especially for his discovery of the law of the photoelectric effect."

Einstein's name has become synonymous with genius and creativity. Named Person of the Century by Time magazine in 1999, Einstein is a rare icon whose wisdom extended far beyond the realm of science to reveal a man with an almost childlike sense of wonder and a profound love of humanity. A testament to his essence is his statement: "I would teach peace rather than war. I would inculcate love rather than hate." Genius and compassion!

During the course of this year addressing "Resonating Voices of the World" the OCA considered two Americans, two Middle Easterners, two Italians, a German, an Austrian, a South African, and an Englishman. Probably all were geniuses and were members of various religions and cultures, again emphasizing that "genius knows no boundaries."

Dr. Warren Young and wife Sandra

Albert Einstein (aka Dr. Warren Young)

OCA summer board meeting

OCA Officers and Trustees

(seated l to r) Tom Kelly, Tess Trucksis, Betty Beelen, Lita Sevilla, Ann Thompson, Mary Ann Senediak, GDB
(standing l to r) Michael Kurilla, Robert Kohler, Dorothy Palguta-Tesner, Jim Springer

XVII. Resonating Voices of the Valley

The 2011-2012 Ohio Cultural Alliance season was the 25th anniversary of the OCA. The year was an unqualified success averaging 225 people at each monthly meeting. The speakers representing the topic "Resonating Voices of the Valley" were varied and from different time periods and backgrounds. We selected a wonderful array of people who represent a host of racial, religious, ethnic, and cultural backgrounds who have built and maintained institutions that many of us call the "jewels of the Valley." We dealt with some of those people and institutions. In addition to the speakers, the interesting venues, the delicious meals from several different caterers, and the often unique cultural enrichment, the anniversary season offered guest caricature sketches by Dr. Tom Welsch and the display of relevant pictures and memorabilia provided by the Mahoning Valley Historical Society. Special also was the "Happy 25th Anniversary OCA" glass plaque, in the form of the state of Ohio, presented to us by my daughter, Lynn, and her husband, Ron Roman.

We began the year in September with Richard Lander (a long-time docent at the Butler) portraying Joseph G. Butler, founder of the famous Butler Institute of American Art. Executive Director Dr. Lou Zona greeted OCA members, and the young and very talented Nathan Stephens entertained us with piano selections. AVI Food Services provided the meal for the evening.

The following is a transcript of Mr. Lander's talk: Allow me to introduce myself. I am Joseph Green Butler, Jr. I must say I am very flattered to speak to you today as one of the men that made a significant contribution to the Mahoning Valley. To begin, I believe one's ancestors are an important part of a man's life. The history of the Butlers can be traced back to the Twelfth Century. I cannot cover that great amount of time today, so I will begin with the year 1759. It was then my forefathers came from Ireland and settled near Lancaster, Pennsylvania.

My grandfather, Joseph Butler, was born on January 8, 1780. At an early age, he became involved in iron manufacturing, mostly due to the influence of his father, who had erected the first blast furnace in Virginia. My grandfather erected and operated blast furnaces in central Pennsylvania. Grandfather was married twice; his first wife was Easter Green. My father, Joseph Sr., was born May 23, 1814, and given the middle name Green in honor of my grandmother.

My father followed my grandfather into the blast furnace and iron manufacturing business. He erected and operated blast furnaces in central Pennsylvania, becoming an expert blast furnace man, and was often asked to solve problems with other furnaces in the area. It is interesting to note that he erected a furnace in Mercer County (just over the Pennsylvania line from Ohio), and as was the custom in those days to name a furnace after someone, generally a woman, he named it after his wife Temperance Orwig, who lived in the community of Temperance, Pennsylvania.

I entered the world on December 21, 1840. A few months after my birth, my father was offered a position of manager of the company store connected to the James Ward Iron Works in Niles, Ohio. My father accepted the offer and moved us to Niles. At that time, Niles was just a primitive village. There were no electric lights, no rail service, no trolleys, and very few conveniences. The only industry was a grist mill and a rolling mill.

I grew up in Niles. It was there that I received all the formal education I would ever have. The school was a white one-room building sited in the center of Niles. While attending classes there, I became good friends with my classmate William McKinley. McKinley, of course, many years later became the 25th president of the United States. Our friendship lasted until his untimely death in 1901.

At the age of thirteen, I was hired at the company store as a clerk and general duty boy. After some time, I earned a promotion to the position of shipping clerk. I proved myself a good worker, and at the age of twenty-three, I became manager of the James Ward rolling mill. During my years at James Ward, I acquired some knowledge of business practices and iron manufacturing. It was then that I knew I wanted to be an iron master.

My first venture into the iron business was a partnership with David Tod and two others to form the Girard Iron Company. I assumed the responsibility of the sales end of the business. Unfortunately, the company was unsuccessful. I did, however, gain more experience that would become valuable later on.

In 1878 I met John Stambaugh, owner of the Brier Hill Iron and Coal Company. Mr. Stambaugh had learned of the situation of the Girard Company and offered me the opportunity to join his company as general manager. The offer included a higher salary than I had at Girard and interest in earning stock in the company. Brier Hill had a history of success from its start in 1859. I felt I could not pass on the offer and accepted without hesitation.

In the years following, the coal deposits ran out, and the company was rechartered as the Brier Hill Iron Works. It wasn't long until steel became the preferred construction material. The company began production of steel and was then renamed the Brier Hill Steel Company. I was to remain at Brier Hill as director for thirty-seven years.

By the 20th century, I had the privilege of serving as president or director of several companies, most notably The Youngstown Sheet and Tube Company, for many years. Over my business life, I had become associated with great men in the iron and steel business: John and Henry Stambaugh, James Campbell, Thomas Struthers, Henry Wick, and many others. I'm sure these names are familiar to you. Together we made the Mahoning Valley the third-largest steel center in the United States and known around the world.

With wealth, I believe there is an obligation to one's community. Because I felt strongly about this, I became a community leader, starting and supporting community projects and programs, both financially and with my time. Two of the largest are the William McKinley Memorial and the Butler Institute of American Art. Because of my admiration for William McKinley and our long-time friendship, I felt in my heart that there should be a memorial to honor this great man. I decided to take it upon myself to initiate and take charge of a project to bring this about. A project of this size took a great deal of time and labor to complete. All was worth it as all came together, and a beautiful monument now stands in the center of Niles, Ohio, on the very site of his boyhood home. The dedication took place on October 5, 1917; many dignitaries attended this historic event.

I have always loved art and have been collecting paintings for many years of my adult life. In order to display them, I had the third floor of my residence converted into a gallery. Unfortunately, while I was away, a fire broke out and destroyed fifty canvases. Only twelve were spared. Prior to this time, I had started planning for an art museum that would provide a safe and secure place for viewing a collection. I wanted to give exposure to American artists and restricted exhibitions of their works. I considered the project a labor of love. When completed, it had to be a beautiful structure and a credit to the city of Youngstown. At the dedication on October 15, 1919, I presented the Butler Institute of American Art as a gift to the people (of Youngstown).

No account of one's life is complete without including some insight into his private life. As a young man, I was much too busy to enjoy social time. Things changed, however. I was introduced one day to a beautiful and charming young lady. Her name was Harriet Ingersol. I knew at once this was the one I wanted for my life partner. I was successful in winning her hand over several other suitors. We were married in 1866 and settled in Youngstown to a happy marriage and blessed with three children: Blanche, Grace, and Henry. In life, there are happy times and sad times. Two of the sad times were the death of Blanche at the young age of forty-seven and my wife Harriet in 1921, after nearly sixty years of marriage. A few weeks after her death, I was struck by an automobile near my residence and severely injured. Due to the extent of my injuries, I was unable to attend Harriet's funeral, making the loss even harder to accept. In my life, I have always been faithful to my wife and family, loyal to my friends, and honest with business associates. All in all, I have had a wonderful and fulfilling life.

Postscript: Joseph G. Butler died on December 20, 1927, on the eve of his eighty-seventh birthday. Butler left the bulk of his $1,500,000 estate to the Butler Institute. Scarcely more than three decades after his death, Time magazine published a feature story that described the art museum as "booming". In a passage that praised the late industrialist's vision as well as its realization, the magazine's editors wrote: "To set the strictly American tone of the place, he planted a befeathered bronze Indian in front of the building designed by the Manhattan firm of McKim, Mead, and White. With Youngstown University nearby, the two blocks surrounding the museum soon developed into the cultural strip of the U.S.'s third-biggest steel center."

Butler Museum of American Art

Joseph G. Butler (aka Richard Lander)

Nathan Stephens

Dr. Lou Zona

Our October meeting featured Dr. Regina Rees, YSU School of Education, who brilliantly discussed William Holmes McGuffey as she shared relevant material about McGuffey's "Reader" and his life in the Mahoning Valley. Dr. Rees has been an educator for more than 30 years (as of October 3, 2011, the date of her talk), 25 years in Boardman teaching grades 4-12, and currently at YSU in the School of Education. She became interested in storytelling as a way to motivate her students. She became involved with the McGuffey Historical Society when the group established a service that would provide programs about McGuffey to area schools. Dr. Rees has presented stories from the McGuffey Readers at many schools and civic organizations and has written a play about McGuffey and his Readers. Her lively presentation about William Holmes McGuffey and his Readers was informative and humorous. Carol Weakland delivered a dramatic one-woman performance by Henry James, "Turning of the Screw". The meeting was held at the Western Reserve United Methodist Church; volunteers, under the supervision of Darlene Wells, prepared and served the dinners.

William Holmes McGuffey, born in 1800 and died in 1873, was a college professor and president who is best known for writing the McGuffey Readers, the first widely used series of elementary school-level textbooks. More than 120 million copies of McGuffey Readers were sold between 1836 and 1960. Dr. Rees interspersed her narrative regarding McGuffey's life with some readings from his works; she also displayed copies of the Readers and other education memorabilia.

The McGuffey family had immigrated to America from Scotland in 1774 and brought with them strong opinions on religion and a belief in the value of education. William Holmes McGuffey was born the son of Alexander and Anna (Holmes) McGuffey in West Finley Township, Washington County, Pennsylvania, 45 miles southwest of Pittsburgh. He moved to Coitsville, near Youngstown, where he attended public school and also received special tutoring in classical languages. Young William learned to read and write from his mother but studied Latin from a clergyman; he also learned Hebrew and Greek. Instilled in him were regimens of piety and intellectual curiosity that were encouraged at home, school, and from the tutors as foundations for a responsible life. He attended Greersburg Academy in Darlington (near Pittsburgh), Pennsylvania, and graduated afterward from Pennsylvania's Washington College, where he became an instructor. He was a roving instructor, traveling through the frontier of Ohio, Kentucky, and Pennsylvania. He was one of an army of somewhat trained young men who tramped the roads and trails drumming up "subscription scholars." They continually sought full-time or part-time teaching jobs. They were willing to teach in log cabins of one-room schoolhouses. One of the small settlements where McGuffey taught was Poland, Ohio. He had a remarkable ability to memorize and could commit to memory entire sections of the Bible.

McGuffey spent his life striving to instill his strong convictions in the next generation-in his students and his own children. He believed religion and education to be interrelated and essential to a healthy society. In 1829, he was ordained at Bethel Chapel as a minister in the Presbyterian Church. His academic positions included: professor at Miami University and president of Cincinnati College, Ohio University, and Woodward College, all in Ohio. In 1845, he moved to Charlottesville, where he became a professor of Philosophy at the University of Virginia. While McGuffey was teaching at Miami University, he established a reputation as a lecturer on moral and biblical subjects. In 1835, a small Cincinnati publishing firm asked McGuffey to create a series of four graded Readers for primary-level students. He completed the first two Readers within a year, receiving $1,000. McGuffey compiled the first four Readers; the fifth and sixth were created by his brother, Alexander. The fifth was published in 1944, and the sixth was not published until 1957. The series consisted of stories, poems, essays, and speeches. The advanced Readers contained excerpts from the works of great writers such as John Milton, Daniel Webster, and Lord Byron. Pioneer families, who did not have many books, appreciated the Readers. McGuffey's books eventually became the standard books in 37 states and helped influence the literary tastes of 19th-century America.

Two of the best-known schoolbooks in the history of American education were the 18th-century New England Primer and the 19th-century McGuffey Readers. Of the two, McGuffey's was more popular and more widely used.

The approximately 120 million copies of his Readers, sold in about 125 years, places its sales in a category with the Bible and Webster's Dictionary. Since 1961 they have continued at a rate of some 30,000 copies a year. Readers are still in use in some school systems and by parents for homeschooling. McGuffey's Readers were among the first textbooks in America that were designed to become progressively more challenging with each volume. He used new vocabulary words in the context of real literature, gradually introducing new words and carefully repeating the older words. McGuffey believed that teachers should study the lessons as well as their students and suggested they read aloud to their classes. He also listed questions after each story, for he believed in order for a teacher to give instructions, they must ask questions. He desired to improve spelling, sharpen their vocabulary and redevelop the lost art of public speaking. In the 19th century, elocution was a part of every public occasion, and McGuffey was responsible for creating a generation of gifted orators and readers.

McGuffey was remembered as a theological and conservative teacher. He understood the goals of public schooling in terms of moral and spiritual education and attempted to give schools a curriculum that would instill Presbyterian Calvinist beliefs and manners in their students. These goals were suitable for the early 19th-century American republic but not necessarily for the later trend towards nationhood and unified pluralism. Indeed, the content of the Readers changed dramatically by the end of the 1800s to meet the needs of national unity and the dream of an American "melting pot" to include the new immigrants which America welcomed.

McGuffey is one of those familiar names in the Mahoning Valley. McGuffey Road runs from Wick Avenue through the East side and Coitsville Township. On the south side of the road in Coitsville Township is the William Holmes McGuffey Wildlife Preserve, at the location of McGuffey's boyhood home. At one time, there was a McGuffey Plaza and later a Mall on the East side. On the West side, William Holmes Elementary School was recently opened on South Schenley Avenue.

Richard Scarsella, chairman of the William Holmes McGuffey Historical Society and a retired educator, has said that "my proudest achievement is keeping the McGuffey name alive." The local chapter celebrated its 60th anniversary in 2021 and is the last remaining chapter; it once had more than 100,000 members in chapters nationwide. Since its formation, the society purchased the McGuffey homestead, 78 acres on McGuffey Road in Coitsville; acquired National Historic Landmark status for the property; transferred the land (now known as the McGuffey Wildlife Preserve) to Mill Creek MetroParks and donated $15,000 to the Metroparks for the land's maintenance. The society also was instrumental in getting several landmarks named after McGuffey, including McGuffey Elementary School in Youngstown, the McGuffey Bridge on McGuffey Road, and a section of Interstate 680 that's designated the William Holmes McGuffey Memorial Highway. The organization holds an annual dinner as well as a monthly lecture series on topics related to the Youngstown area.

Carol Weakland

McGuffey and his Reader

Dr. Regina Rees

Volney Rogers was our focus in November. Dr. Richard Shale transported us back into the late 19th and early 20th centuries as he skillfully and dramatically discussed just how "resonating" a voice Rogers was and still is in the Mahoning Valley. Trevor Coleman, accompanied by pianist Carole Lynn Fisher, delighted us with operatic selections. YSU caterers prepared the meal, and the site of the meeting was at Fellows Riverside Gardens, Mill Creek MetroParks, which co-sponsored the event.

Dr. Shale has written a book entitled Historic Mill Creek Park (co-authored with Carol Potter) and has spoken extensively about Mill Creek and Volney Rogers. The speech on this particular evening was delivered in Rogers' first-person voice and will be quoted freely. Dr. Shale took us through the story of Rogers' role in creating Mill Creek Park but first provided some facts about his youth and career that led to his interest in such a project.

Rogers was born on December 1, 1846, on a farm in Columbiana. He was one of eleven children, with nine surviving to adulthood. Two brothers became attorneys, two became physicians, and two carried on the farming tradition of his father. He was educated at New Lisbon High School and landed a job with a telegraph company soon after graduating. He moved to Brownsville, Pennsylvania, about 35 miles south of Pittsburgh, to work as a telegrapher. Continuing with this skill, Rogers worked as a telegraph operator in Harrisburg, the state capital, where he learned something of the law profession, then moved on to Waynesboro, Pennsylvania. During his time in Waynesboro, his interest in law grew to the point of abandoning his career in telegraphy and joining his brother Disney in Mt. Gilead, Ohio, who had recently passed the bar and was now practicing there.

Volney's brother, a staunch Republican, was elected as president of the town council, and his partner/father-in-law was elected as a judge, keeping them very busy with their respective political and judicial duties. These duties left them with less time for law practice which helped Volney, who was hired as a law clerk, to organize the office and perform legal research. Brother and judge were excellent tutors who helped Volney as he became a student of law. After two years of study, he was admitted to the bar in 1871. After passing the bar, Volney had to move on as there were already too many lawyers in Mt. Gilead. He contemplated New Lisbon and Canfield but settled on Youngstown, "which I felt was an up-and-coming community." Arriving in Youngstown in 1872, Attorney Volney Rogers rented an office on West Federal Street in Youngstown, a town currently with a population of 8,000 people. After two years, Disney joined him to form a partnership.

Youngstown was becoming a hub in northeastern Ohio. Industry boomed during the Civil War, the coal and steel industries boomed by the 1890s, immigrants were flocking to the city, and it was soon to become the county seat, moving from Canfield. Rogers said, "I was all for it since it would be much more convenient to have the county courthouse a few blocks away instead of in a distant village." By 1874 the battle became quite heated. Youngstown had the votes to send their men to the state legislature, which subsequently succeeded in pushing through a law giving Youngstown the county seat. Canfield continued to challenge the law to no avail. "And so, in the summer of 1876, a parade of about forty wagons collected all of the court records and carried them to Youngstown, where a new courthouse had been erected." So, Youngstown was now the county seat, yet they had no paved roads or electric street lamps. It did have a horse-drawn streetcar running down Federal Street.

By this time, Rogers was settling in: he joined the First Presbyterian Church, was affiliated with the Republican Party, and remained a bachelor. He was elected city solicitor in 1878 and re-elected in 1880. "During these four years, I did my best to organize the city ordinances and index the statutes." His brother, wife, and he lived on West Rayen, but in the mid-1880s, he moved to Howard Street (in the 1890's it was changed to Falls Avenue) south of the Mahoning River. Most Youngstowners lived north of the river, but Rogers liked the solitude and open spaces of the south side. "I could hike down the hill from my house and have a pleasant ramble along the banks of Mill Creek."

It was in the 1880s that Rogers developed interests in public health and in land preservation. "The iron and rolling mills along the Mahoning were turning the river into a cesspool". Clean water and proper sanitation were a problem; typhoid and malaria were a constant problem. "I did what I could to promote clean water, fresh air, and exercise." He enjoyed spending time walking and exploring undeveloped areas of the Valley. He joined the American Civic Association interacting with others who believed "that the health of a city could be materially enhanced by the preservation of public lands within easy reach of its citizens who might wish for a breath of clean air and a drink of clean water while enjoying the natural beauty of the surroundings."

With a population growing by leaps and bounds, a city expanding greatly, and new industry booming, public health was neglected. Such industries as an ice-harvesting operation, DuPont Company storing explosives, and Green's slaughterhouse all adversely affected Mill Creek and the Mahoning River. "Around the summer of 1880, I learned that the timber and quarrying interests had targeted a considerable stretch of Mill Creek for harvesting the trees and the stone", which could render those areas as "spoiled and barren as the banks of the Mahoning River." After learning who owned the property, he arranged for an option to buy the land and turn the land over to Youngstown Township or to a board of park commissioners to be established by law.

"The next problem I faced was that Ohio had no law that permitted the establishment of a township park. And we did not yet have a state park system." He put his legal training to work: he drafted appropriate legislation to create such a park, circulated a petition of support from prominent citizens, took the proposal to Columbus, and assured those from other townships that the law was designed to apply only to one township-Youngstown Township. By the end of February 1891, the Township Park Improvement Act was passed, and the Mahoning County Court of Common Pleas appointed a three-person Board of Park Commissioners with Rogers, Henry Tod, and Robert Mackey as commissioners.

By April 6, 1891, the voters approved by a three-to-one margin the creation of Mill Creek Park and permitted the commissioners to issue bonds to finance the new park. "We surveyed the land and set the boundaries from the mouth of Mill Creek south to a point about a quarter of a mile upstream from Lanterman's Falls. The east and west boundaries were irregular as they conformed to the twists of Mill Creek and included bluffs and ravines on either side of the streambed. The total park area came to about four hundred acres."

Rogers hired his younger brother Bruce as the first park superintendent, eschewing nepotism. Bruce was knowledgeable about landscape architecture, and he became a primary influence in the shaping of the new park. After inviting the famous Frederick Olmsted (who declined) to become the lead landscape architect, Rogers contacted Charles Eliot, who had been a student of Olmsted and was now his partner. Eliot visited the park in 1891 and was most impressed. Rogers shared a quote from Eliot: "So far as natural beauty is concerned, there is no park in the country to compare with Mill Creek Park. It is as if a bit of choice scenery had been taken from the mountains of Switzerland and deposited in a level country." Rogers also hired another leading landscape designer, H.W. S. Cleveland, regarded as second in reputation to Olmsted. He came to Youngstown and made many contributions to the park's design. "These nationally prominent landscape designers helped us to lay out the roads and trails in the park and plan for recreational facilities. We also contracted with the Youngstown Bridge Company to build six steel bridges, two installed in 1892; the other four, including the Suspension Bridge, were built in 1895."

The severe Panic of 1893 worked to the advantage of Mill Creek Park. The commissioners determined to put the unemployed mill hands, carpenters, and stone masons to work, paying the men a dollar a day. During 1893-1894 they "built winding roads with stone curbs, cut trails and lined them with stone walls, developed picnic spots and cleared land to provide scenic vistas. With the modest wages we were able to pay; these workers were able to keep their families from slipping into poverty and starvation." One of the major projects was to remodel the stone building near the old furnace, which had been built in the 1820s as a woolen mill. Under the direction of William Ellis, one of Youngstown's most experienced architects, the old building was totally remodeled and restored and named Pioneer Pavilion "in honor of those early settlers and in 1894 began renting the place for parties and dances."

Rogers' plan called for a number of water features: in 1896, they created the Lily Pond, the Frog Pond, and the Mirror Pond. These were small, but they already had plans for a larger lake which would be designed by a respected engineer from Yonkers, New York, Sherman Gould. He visited the site in 1894, the necessary dam was built in 1897, and the lake was created. Cohasset was an immediate hit with the public, with boats for rent and swimming permitted. In 1904 Rogers and his group began work on another dam, and by 1906, Lake Glacier became the second big lake.

Through his park work, Rogers became acquainted with some very talented people; among them was Julius Schweinfurth, a Boston architect who was hired to design a picnic pavilion. The result was Slippery Rock Pavilion completed in 1911. Rogers said, "I liked his massive rough stone pillars and steep, red tile roof so much that I commissioned him to build us a grand stone arch bridge." The result was the Parapet Bridge completed in 1913.

Rogers said the progress did not come without a struggle. He said city officials came up with "an idiotic scheme to construct in Mill Creek Park two huge sixty-foot dams and a possible third dam that would create immense reservoirs... Under this plan, nearly all of the natural beauty of Mill Creek would disappear-submerged under the deep waters of these ill-conceived reservoirs." Rogers challenged the dam proposal and succeeded at the state level, but city officials put the matter to a local vote. The vote rejected the plan then and again in 1899. Another threat to the park was the city's proposal to run a sewer line down the length of the park. "I filed suit to stop it but lost the case in 1916....I have appealed the sewer case to the Ohio Supreme Court, but I am pessimistic about the outcome.... I fear that it all may be lost." The public sewer ran through the park, contaminating the water and rendering swimming inadvisable in many of the parks once pristine lakes

Rogers (Shale) ended his talk to us, reporting that Rogers was somewhat discouraged by some of these events and took an extended trip to some of the parks out west, "hopefully, the Rocky Mountains and Yellowstone Park will be included." Before he left, Rogers said, "Let me close by encouraging all of you to keep fighting to preserve the park. Go visit the park. Get away from the smoke from the mills and the polluted Mahoning and go for a ramble on one of our fine foot trails. You will quickly conclude as I do that Mill Creek Park is a place that never disappoints an intelligent, appreciative visitor."

Many millions of people from the Mahoning Valley and from near and far have enjoyed the park and have added to it-indeed it is now a regional MetroPark. A local school is named in Roger's honor, and a massive bronze likeness stands at the main entrance of the park. Youngstown Mayor Fred J. Warnock presided over the unveiling when he stated: "We do not erect monuments to selfishness...We erect monuments to those who live for the community and whose high ideal is the welfare of many. That is why we are honoring Volney Rogers today."

Volney Rogers statue at Glenwood Avenue entrance to Mill Creek Park

YSU Trevor Coleman singing operatic selections

Dr. Rick Shale

Dr. Donna DeBlasio, YSU Professor in the History Department at the time of her presentation, discussed the life and times of movie mogul Jack Warner in December. And, of course, we met at the beautiful Powers Auditorium, formerly the Warner Theater built by Jack Warner. Setting the tone, guests were greeted by life-size cardboard cut-outs of Frank Sinatra, Marilyn Monroe, and Marlon Brando, plus popcorn at every table. Music was provided by an instrumental trio led by Dr. Kathryn Umble, YSU School of Music; a film about the Warner Brothers was shown in the Flad Pavilion, and the Mahoning Valley Historical Society had a table of Warner memorabilia. There were also guided or self-guided tours of Powers/DeYor Center. Our meal was catered by Crystal Catering Service.

In the wake of the depression of the 1890s, a Jew from Krasnashiltz, Poland, arrived in the Mahoning Valley with his family of 14. Like so many Europeans, Benjamin Warner had come to the new World seeking relief from autocracy and racism. They followed their brother, Harry, who established a shoe repair shop in the heart of the emerging industrial town. Benjamin worked with Harry in the shoe repair shop until he secured a loan to open a meat counter and grocery store in the city's downtown area. They also opened a store that specialized in bicycle repairs. Jack spent much of his youth in Youngstown. He received his first taste of show business in the burgeoning steel town, singing at local theaters and forming a brief business partnership with another aspiring "song and dance man". During his brief career in vaudeville, he officially changed his name to Jack Leonard Warner. Jack's older brother Sam disapproved of these youthful pursuits suggesting that Jack "Get out front where they pay the actors…. that's where the money is."

In Youngstown, the Warner brothers took their first tentative steps into the entertainment industry. In the early 20th century, Sam Warner formed a business partnership with another local resident and "took over" the city's Old Grand Opera House, which he used as a venue for "cheap vaudeville and photoplays." It failed after only one summer. Sam Warner then secured a job as a projectionist at Idora Park. He convinced the family of the new medium's possibilities and negotiated the purchase of a Model B Kinetoscope from a projectionist who was "down on his luck". The purchase price was $1,000; Jack contributed $150 by pawning his horse.

The enterprising brothers screened a well-used copy of "The Great Train Robbery' throughout Ohio and Pennsylvania before renting a vacant store in New Castle, Pennsylvania. This makeshift theater, called the Bijou, was furnished with chairs borrowed from a local undertaker. Jack, who was still living in Youngstown, arrived on weekends to sing illustrated song slides during reel changes. In 1906, the brothers purchased a small theater in New Castle, which they called the Cascade Movie Palace. They maintained the theater until moving into film distribution in 1907. In the same year, the Warner brothers established the Pittsburgh-based Duquesne Amusement Company, a distribution firm that proved lucrative until the advent of Thomas Edison's Motion Picture Patents Company, which charged distributors huge fees. In 1909 Sam and Jack opened a second film exchange company. Later that year, the Warners sold the family business to the General Film Company for a total of $52,000 (equivalent to $1,500,000 today). The Warners, in just a few short years, were on their way to fame and fortune.

Dr. DeBlasio discussed the various Youngstown sites where the Warner's lived, including Smoky Hollow, where Dr. DeBlasio was also reared. So, Jack Warner, a recent American and Youngstown resident, in little more than a decade, became a major film executive who became the co-head of production at Warner Bros. Studios. In 1920 the four Warner brothers moved to California and established the Warner Brothers Pictures, Inc., one of the giants of the motion picture industry. Jack worked with his brother Sam to procure the technology for the film industry's first talking picture, The Jazz Singer (1927). After Sam's death, Jack clashed with his surviving older brothers, Harry and Albert. Sometime later (in the 1950s) Jack assumed exclusive control of the film production company. Jack Warner's career spanned some 45 years, surpassing that of any other of the seminal Hollywood studio moguls.

Jack's brother, Sam, served as a buffer between Jack and his older brothers. Just before the premiere of The Jazz Singer, Sam died of pneumonia in 1927; his death left Jack inconsolable. In honor of Sam, the remaining brothers built the Warner Theater in Youngstown, heralding the "finest theater ever built". Designed by the architects Rapp and Rapp, the theater was built by a local contractor, the Heller-Murray Construction Company, at the cost of $1.5 million. The balcony featured cantilevered construction to ensure perfect sight lines. Dressing rooms, backstage lounges, and scenery rooms comprised some of the 114 rooms located on five levels. One could wander the long entry foyer to the mezzanine and marvel at wood inlays of Carpathian Elm, Macassar Ebony, Austrian Cherry, English Oak, and Walnut; marble and mosaic tile work; roccoco plaster designs; oil paintings and a number of chandeliers. The theater flourished into the '30s, '40s, and early '50s, but by 1968 the declining movie business forced its closing. The theater was scheduled for demolition but was saved and restored, starting with the efforts of local residents, Mr. and Mrs. Edward Powers. It "lives" with several additions and the efforts of the DeBartolo/York family.

Jack Warner was feared by many and inspired ridicule with his uneven attempts at humor, but he earned respect for his shrewd instincts and tough-mindedness. He recruited many of Warner Brothers' top stars and promoted the hard-edged social dramas for which the studio became known. Throughout his career, he was viewed as a contradictory and enigmatic figure. Although a staunch Republican, Warner encouraged film projects that promoted the agenda of Democratic President Franklin D. Roosevelt's New Deal. He opposed European fascism and criticized Nazi Germany well before America's involvement in World War II. An opponent of communism, he appeared as a friendly witness before the House Un-American Activities Committee, naming some screenwriters who had been fired as suspected communists. Despite his controversial public image, Jack Warner remained a force in the motion picture industry until his retirement in the early 1970s. He died in 1978 at the age of 86.

Jack Warner

Dr. Donna DeBlasio

Muti-talented Dr. Thomas Welsh sketching Warren and Iva Harrell

YSU trio led by Dr. Kathryn Umble

Our focus for January was Henry Stambaugh, whose life and times were described by William Conti, a local architect and President of the Stambaugh Auditorium Association Board of Trustees. Meeting in the beautiful Stambaugh Auditorium, we were also treated to a "backstage" tour of the historic building and were thrilled to hear Dr. Ronald Gould, YSU Dana School of Music, perform selections on the newly restored Skinner organ. Dr. Thomas Welsh continued to do caricature sketches, photos of the Auditorium's history were shown continuously while we were in the ballroom, and Mahoning Valley Historical Society provided a table of Stambaugh memorabilia. Our meal was prepared by YSU Catering.

Henry Hamilton Stambaugh was born on November 24, 1858, one of three sons of John and Caroline Stambaugh. He attended the Youngstown Public schools before attending Greylock Institute and Cornell University. After leaving the university in 1879, he took a job with The Brier Hill Iron and Coal Company. He became secretary, treasurer, and eventually president of the company. Henry followed in the footsteps of his father, who became interested in the development of the iron and coal industry at Brier Hill with David Tod. The business grew and prospered with two large blast furnaces at Brier Hill, large coal fields in Pennsylvania, and valuable iron ore mines in Michigan. In 1912 its properties were merged with others to become Brier Hill Steel Company; Stambaugh became the director and chairman of the board.

In the way of personal life, Mr. Conti told us that Stambaugh lived for many years on Belmont Avenue, the current site of St. Elizabeth's School of Nursing. We were told that "he was deliberate in his judgment, firm in his convictions, very considerate and sympathetic, but forceful in all his dealings with men". He was a lover of dogs and horses, and much of his recreation was enjoyed on the farms near his home. He also took an active interest in the political affairs of Youngstown and the country.

Stambaugh had many business interests and activities, including being a director of many local corporations. He was the director of the Youngstown Sheet and Tube Company, William Tod Company, First National Bank, Tod-Stambaugh Company of Cleveland, The Bessemer Limestone Company, and the Stambaugh Thompson Company. He organized the Realty Guarantee and Trust Company and was the builder of the Stambaugh Building in downtown Youngstown. His activities were numerous: The Community Service Society was formed under his guidance; he was a principal in the founding of the charitable Youngstown Foundation (one of the first gifts to the foundation was his $50,000); he was active in raising $2,100,000 for the Mahoning County War Chest drive during World War I. Some attributed his death on January 4, 1919, to overwork during the war period.

Stambaugh made significant monetary contributions while alive, but it did not end with his death. His generosity by way of his will was widespread with gifts to: The Fresh Air Camp, Youngstown Playground Association, Reuben-McMillan Free Library Association, The Blackburn Home for the Aged, Boy Scouts, The Stambaugh Scout Reservation, The Butler Art Gallery, and 80 acres of land were contributed for playground and park purposes and the Henry H. Stambaugh Golf Course and The Rayen School athletic field. He also remembered many of his friends and relatives in addition to providing funds for the Henry H. Stambaugh Memorial Auditorium (we now know it simply as Stambaugh Auditorium). The street running along the north side of the auditorium bears his mother's name –Caroline.

Conti reported that "His last will and testament left a large portion of his estate to five Trustees to carry out the purpose of building in the City of Youngstown an auditorium for the use and benefit of the people of Youngstown and Mahoning Valley. After a considerable and unavoidable delay, construction began in the spring of 1925 and was completed at the end of 1926." Stambaugh stated that "this building should form a center of culture and progress and should be a fountainhead of inspiration," dedicated to the love he had for the community and its people.

He wished for the building to be a remembrance of the past and its finest traditions, so the people could be enriched. In keeping with his wishes, the classic style was chosen for the building. "One of the main features of the East Ionic portico facing and centered on Fifth Avenue at Park is the sculptures figures in relief on the pediment; it is the work of sculptor Gaetena Ceceri." All exterior stonework is of Indiana limestone. The interior walls are of rusticated limestone, including the main floor of the concert hall. Patterned marble floors are a feature of the lobbies. "Handsome carved oak balcony fronts, proscenium, and panel work together with Corinthian columns flank both sides of the curved balcony to complete the neo-classical style of architecture. The whole of the concert hall is surmounted by the richly coffered ceiling just recently restored." Conti said, "No concert hall was considered complete unless it featured a concert organ, and we have one of the finest," an E.M.Skinner organ, just recently restored. Behind the horseshoe, the balcony is a room with inspirations from Italian sources. Etruscan columns and inlaid oak herringbone make up the patterned floor.

Stambaugh Auditorium was listed on the National Register of Historic places in 1984. Mr. Stambaugh said that the building was dedicated to the entertainment, enjoyment, and education of the Mahoning Valley. This English-American wished for the building to have multiple purposes; Stambaugh Auditorium has indeed hosted a variety of events. Business events and seminars have been held here, as have non-profit fund-raisers. Rehearsals, weddings, graduation ceremonies, proms, and dance competitions make Stambaugh Auditorium the site of choice for many. In addition to local concerts, choral groups, events, and programs, national acts and distinguished speakers have also appeared here, including Chuck Berry, The Beach Boys, B.B.King, Bruce Springsteen, Ray Charles, Buddy Holly, Anderson Cooper, and many more. The Youngstown Symphony had its home here for a while. Henry H. Stambaugh has left quite a legacy in his hometown.

Dr. Ronald Gould

Henry Stambaugh

William Conti

The 19th-century Ohio Governor, David Tod, was our subject for the February meeting. Great-great-granddaughter, Sallie Tod Dutton, shared stories about her relative and his times. Sallie has lived in the Youngstown area her entire life as a teacher, counselor, and member of several boards, including the Tod Homestead Cemetery, Akron Children's Hospital, Juvenile Justice Center of Mahoning County, and the Mahoning Valley Historical Society. Period music was provided by Joe and Darlene Macbean on bagpipe and harp. We met at The Georgetown, whose caterers provided an abundant "Youngstown buffet".

David Tod was a farmer, lawyer, industrialist, transportation pioneer, entrepreneur, visionary, Senator, and Governor. Sallie said, "Most importantly, Tod helped create a renaissance-one that saw rural, early 19th century Mahoning Valley reborn into one of the world's iron and steel capitals." For that alone, Tod's life and accomplishments should be celebrated. But he did much more.

David Tod was born on February 21, 1805, in Youngstown, to a family actively involved in local and state politics. His father, George Tod, born to a Scottish immigrant in Suffield, Connecticut, had located to the Connecticut Western Reserve in 1800. David attended Burton Academy in Geauga County and studied law in Warren, where he was appointed postmaster. Admitted to the Ohio Bar in 1827, he accumulated considerable wealth as a lawyer actively involved in the coal and iron industries of the Mahoning Valley; he went on to become president of the Cleveland and Mahoning Railroad.

Ms. Dutton reported, "Though only 22 years old, his natural ability, integrity, and dignified bearing soon gained him a respectable and remunerative practice. His great force of argument, quick wit, and genial and happy spirit and temperament made him very popular and highly regarded as an able trial lawyer." He quickly repaid his indebtedness for his education and began making payments on the Brier Hill farm that his father agreed to purchase but could not pay for. David bought his parents the first stove they ever had and built them a comfortable house which remained at Brier Hill until 1916 to allow for the development of what is now The Tod Homestead Cemetery. Having acquired title to the Brier Hill farm after his father's death in 1841, he gave up the practice of law in 1843 and relocated to Brier Hill.

David Tod was a man of considerable business acumen, successful as an industrialist and entrepreneur. He helped organize the Pennsylvania-Ohio Canal Company, which opened in 1840. The route began in Akron, moving east through Newton Falls, Niles, Girard, Youngstown, Struthers, Lowellville, and then into the Beaver River in Pennsylvania. It spanned 82 miles, and it helped lift the Mahoning Valley out of rural isolation. At about the same time the canal was opened, Tod began mining coal on his Brier Hill property, where the canal had a stop. Since Youngstown coal was a new product, and the quality of coal varied, Tod had to convince steamboat owners on Lake Erie to try his coal. They were convinced; by the late 1840s, Tod's mines were producing about 160 tons of coal a day. The canal was a success, with 25 boats passing through Youngstown each day. However, Tod realized the future of transportation was not on the water but on the rail.

Tod and some of his investors who helped build the canal began working to bring the first railroad to the Mahoning Valley. These men organized the Cleveland and Mahoning Railroad, which was begun in 1853, with the first train run to Youngstown in 1856. With the death in 1859 of Jacob Perkins, the first president of the railroad, David Tod succeeded him and held the office until his death. The railroad was leased to the Atlantic and Great Western, which later became the Erie Railroad. Tod was also associated with a group of investors who were involved in the manufacture of iron at Akron under the name of the Akron Manufacturing Company. The development of coal, the making of coke, and the opening of the railroad made the Mahoning Valley a more advantageous location for the iron business. In 1859, David Tod joined with his son, relatives, and friends to buy out the Akron Manufacturing Company in 1859 and moved the facilities to Youngstown. This was the beginning of The Brier Hill Iron and Coal Company, which later became The Youngstown Sheet and Tube Company. Other area luminaries to be involved with the company were Henry Stambaugh, William Pollock and Joseph G. Butler, Jr., and three generations of the Tod family. "Tod was becoming a rich man and began listening to the higher call of civic duty," Dutton said.

Simultaneously, David was active in political and military affairs. During the campaign of Andrew Jackson in 1824, Tod became an ardent Democrat and remained so until 1861. In 1827 he was appointed Inspector of the First Brigade, Fourth Division of the Ohio Militia. In 1832 he was named postmaster of Warren, and in 1838, he was elected to the Ohio Senate. In 1840, he was appointed Aide-de-camp to Major General Christopher C. Seely of the Seventeenth Division of the State Militia. In that same year, he stumped for President Martin Van Buren in a losing bid for re-election. Tod, though, was gaining a reputation as a passionate Democrat and a master orator. He ran unsuccessfully for governor in 1844 and 1846. In 1847, President James K. Polk appointed him Envoy Extraordinary and Minister Plenipotentiary of the U.S. to the court of Dom Pedro, Emperor of Brazil.

David Tod's natural ability and common sense, added to his legal training and knowledge of men, enabled him to fulfill his mission to Brazil to the satisfaction of both governments. He put the friendship between the two countries on a solid and firm basis and succeeded not only in healing problems between Brazil and the U.S. but also negotiated a settlement of claims between the two nations totaling about $300,000, which had been in negotiation for thirty years. Tod was largely instrumental in inducing the Brazilian government to break up the infamous slave trade, for which he acquired the goodwill and esteem of Dom Pedro II, the Brazilian Emperor, Millard Fillmore, the current President of the U.S., and Daniel Webster, Secretary of State. Throughout the 1850s, Tod remained a loyal Democrat; in 1858, he ran unsuccessfully for congress as a Democrat. With tensions building between the North and the South, Tod was elected to be vice president of the 1860 Democratic convention in Charleston, South Carolina. Sectionalism tore apart the convention, so a northern faction of the Democratic Party reconvened in Baltimore, with Tod serving as convention president. There, Tod was instrumental in getting Stephen A. Douglas nominated for president. During the campaign, Tod stumped for Douglas and against Republican Abraham Lincoln. However, when Confederate soldiers attacked Fort Sumter in 1861, Tod gave his support to Lincoln.

In 1861, the Union Party, made up of pro-Lincoln Republicans and war Democrats, nominated Tod to be its candidate for governor, which he easily won. He was now one of Lincoln's strongest supporters but got him into trouble with Democratic Party loyalists. But Tod needed help to win the war. He needed men for the Union army, so he spent a lot of his time to boost morale and fill Lincoln's quota for troops. He did everything he could to supply the troops, seek money to improve their conditions, allowed wounded Ohioans to convalesce at or close to home, and even had to deal with the threat of an Ohio invasion. Indeed, there were a few significant threats: in late summer 1862, Confederate General Kirby Smith moved troops from Lexington, Kentucky, toward Cincinnati, which Tod helped to ward off; the next summer, Confederate raider John Morgan and 3,000 of his troops moved north as far as Lisbon, Ohio, where he was finally stopped. Despite his efforts to help keep Ohio safe, he was not re-nominated for another term as governor. Tod never returned to politics even though President Lincoln offered him the job of Secretary of the Treasury.

Upon his return to private life, Tod devoted himself to his family, his coal operations, and to the Cleveland and Mahoning Railroad, the Brier Hill Iron & Coal Company, and the

Mahoning Bank. He took a leading part in local affairs, even assisting in establishing a fire brigade at Youngstown, to which he presented the first fire engine owned by the town. It is still preserved as a relic in the department and bears the name Governor Tod.

Sallie Tod Dutton discussed a number of other interesting nuggets that were part of her narrative:

- David Tod was married in 1832 to Maria Smith of Warren; they had seven children.
- Tod was associated with many of the other leading figures of the Valley, such as Henry Wick, Jacob Perkins, Frederick Kinsman, John Stambaugh, Jr., Henry Stambaugh, William Pollock, and Joseph G. Butler.
- Two of the Tod children were born in Brazil; the last one was named Sallie (all Sallie Tod's spell their names "Sallie").
- David Tod's funeral was held at Brier Hill and was attended by approximately 20,000 people. Eulogies were delivered by Rutherford B. Hayes and James A. Garfield, both of whom later became presidents of the United States.

Sallie argued that "Today, the legacy of Ohio's only governor from the Mahoning Valley is ubiquitous. There is Tod Avenue, Tod Woods School, Tod Hall at Youngstown State University, the former Tod's Children Hospital, and The Tod Homestead Cemetery. V&M Star makes seamless pipe on the site-in fact, on the same building foundation-of The Brier Hill Iron & Coal Co. The Mahoning National Bank of Youngstown, which became Sky Bank, now exists as part of Huntington Bank. Then there is the subtle, even more, significant legacy, namely, the entire industrial development of the Mahoning Valley."

Sallie revealed a family story: "My late father Fred Tod, Jr., often told of a conversation which David Tod had with President Lincoln that has become Tod family lore. David Tod was in Lincoln's office, and the President brought up the spelling of Mary Todd and asked why the governor spelled his name with only one d. The governor said, 'If one d is good enough for God, it is good enough for Tod'". What a legacy of this family that came from Scot ancestry. "Genius knows no boundaries" is what we are reminded of at the Ohio Cultural Alliance.

Sallie Tod Dutton

Governor David Tod

In March, we met at the McKinley Memorial in Niles, Ohio. Michael Wilson, in full-period attire, portrayed United States President William McKinley. A barbershop quartet led by Bob Gussman provided timely music to the delight of our members and guests. Carolyn Catering prepared our wonderful meal. Members were able to tour the building before and after the meeting.

Mike Wilson was the administrator of the Trumbull Soil and Water Conservation District after serving as the CEO for The Home Builders' Association for 14 years. He had begun presenting William McKinley in 1991. His presentations have been given to civic, school, church, and historical groups as far away as Massachusetts. He was a featured performer for the National Travel Writers' Association, was filmed for C-Span giving a front porch speech as part of their series on presidents in 1999, and was approved by the Historical Actors Guild as the official presenter for President William McKinley. His mission was to bring history to life, and indeed, he did. What a treat it was; his presentation was given in period attire, appropriate demeanor, intonation, and even sporting a physical likeness.

William McKinley was born in 1843 in Niles, Ohio, the seventh of nine children of William McKinley Sr. and Nancy. The McKinleys were of English and Scots-Irish descent and settled in western Pennsylvania, where William Sr. was born. His family moved to Ohio when the senior McKinley was a boy, settling in what is now Lisbon. The family trade was iron-making; McKinley senior operated foundries throughout Ohio, in Lisbon, Poland, Canton, and Niles, where President McKinley was born. The McKinley household was steeped in abolitionist sentiment based on the family's staunch Methodist beliefs. The younger William also followed the Methodist tradition, becoming active in the local Methodist Church as early as age 16. He was a lifelong pious Methodist. However, for diversion, he also spent much of his childhood fishing, hunting, ice skating, horseback riding, and swimming.

In 1852, the family moved from Niles to Poland to attend better schools. Graduating from Poland Seminary High School (run by the Methodist seminary) in 1859, McKinley enrolled the following year at Allegheny College in Meadville, Pennsylvania. He remained at Allegheny for one year, returning home in 1860 after becoming ill and depressed. He also studied at Mount Union College in Alliance. Although his health recovered, family finances declined, and McKinley was unable to return to Allegheny. He began working as a postal clerk and later took a job teaching at a school near Poland.

When the Southern states seceded from the Union, and the American Civil War began, thousands of men in Ohio volunteered for service. Among them were McKinley and his cousin William McKinley Osbourne, both of whom enlisted as privates in the newly formed Poland Guards in June 1861. A Republican, McKinley was the last president to have served in the Civil War; he was also the only one to begin his service as an enlisted man and end as a brevet major. After the war, he settled in Canton, Ohio, where he practiced law and married Ida Saxton. In 1876, he was elected to Congress, where he became the Republican Party's expert on the protective tariff, which he argued would bring prosperity. His 1890 McKinley Tariff was highly controversial and, together with a Democratic redistricting aimed at gerrymandering him out of office, led to his defeat in the Democratic landslide of 1890. He was elected governor of Ohio in 1891 and 1893, steering a moderate course between capital and labor interests. With the aid of his close advisor Mark Hanna, he secured the Republican nomination of president in 1896 amid a deep economic depression. He defeated his Democratic rival William Jennings Bryan after a front porch campaign in which he advocated "sound money" (the gold standard unless altered by international agreement) and promised that high tariffs would restore prosperity. Our speaker Mike Wilson was particularly animated in giving us some of McKinley's stump "front porch" speeches.

Rapid growth marked McKinley's presidency. He promoted the 1897 Dingley Tariff in an attempt to protect manufacturers and factory workers from foreign competition and, in 1900, secured the passage of the Gold Standard Act. McKinley hoped to persuade Spain to grant independence to rebellious Cuba without conflict, but when negotiation failed and the sinking of the ship Maine occurred, the Spanish were blamed, and war ensued with the Spanish American War of 1898. The United States' victory was quick and decisive. As part of the peace settlement, Spain turned over to the U.S. several of its colonies: Puerto Rico, Guam, and the Philippines, while Cuba was promised independence but remained under the control of the U.S. Army. The U.S. also annexed the independent Republic of Hawaii in 1898, which soon became a U.S. territory.

Historians regard McKinley's 1896 victory as a realigning election in which the political stalemate of the post-Civil War era gave way to the Republican-dominated system, beginning with the Progressive Era. McKinley defeated Bryan again in the 1900 presidential election in a campaign focused on imperialism, protectionism, and free silver. His achievements were cut short when he was fatally shot on September 6, 1901, by Leon Czolgosz, a second-generation Polish-American anarchist. McKinley died eight days later and was succeeded by Vice President Theodore Roosevelt. As a practitioner of interventionism and pro-business sentiment, McKinley is generally ranked above average as president.

William McKinley is remembered nationally by a mountain named after him (Denali/McKinley Mountain in Alaska), a monument in Canton, McKinley Memorial in Buffalo, McKinley Park and statue in Chicago, McKinley Playground in New York City, McKinley County in New Mexico, McKinley Townships in four states, McKinleyville in California and the $500 bill among others. Locally there are a few streets and buildings carrying the McKinley name. But the one most immediate to us is the National McKinley Birthplace Memorial, the site of our meeting.

The McKinley Memorial Library, Museum, and Birthplace Home is a marble monument with two wings. One houses the McKinley Memorial Library and is a public library. The second wing features the McKinley Museum, with exhibits about the President and an auditorium. The McKinley Birthplace Home and Research Center is located near the Memorial, just down the street. The historic house museum has been furnished for the period when President McKinley was in office. Funding for the national memorial was authorized by Congress and President Taft in 1911; Joseph G. Butler, Jr. began in 1912 a local campaign to raise additional funds. The city of Niles set aside five acres for the location of the facility.

The architect selected by competition in 1915 was McKim, Mead, and White. Their design reflected Greek and Roman themes, from architectural elements to the lettering on tablets and statuary. McKinley's impressive twelve-foot statue stands between two ionic columns and was originally conceived as a bronze monument, but instead, it was decided to carve it from a single thirty-five-ton piece of marble. Bronze busts of men associated with McKinley also grace the interior. They include Theodore Roosevelt, Marcus Hanna, Joseph G. Butler, Jr., Andrew Carnegie, and Henry Clay Frick. The Memorial was dedicated on October 5, 1917. Our speaker said that the Memorial Library is open to the public six days a week, and the Memorial Museum is also open to the public from Tuesday to Friday with no admission.

President William McKinley (aka Michael Wilson)

Barber shop quartet, led by Bob Gussman

President William McKinley

P. Ross Berry was featured in April as Vincent Shivers, via slides and narrative, shared with us how Berry was an early African-American resonating voice. Josh Green and Nikita Jones sang excerpts from the beautiful and poignant musical "Ragtime". The site of this meeting was St. Matthias Church Hall, with a wonderful meal prepared by Carolyn Catering. Shivers studied history at YSU, earning a master's degree, and since then, he has spent many years researching and discussing local African Americans, notably P. Ross Berry.

Shivers said that we have probably passed the Rayen Building on Wick Avenue many times, unaware that it is one of several buildings in Youngstown designed by the Black "practical architect" P. Ross Berry. (The term architect has shifted since the 19th century, so the Mahoning Valley Historical Society refers to Berry as a "practical architect.") Many of the most iconic buildings in downtown Youngstown date from the 20th century, and one of the most prolific local builders made a name for himself in the 19th century-P. Ross Berry.

Plimton Ross Berry was the masonry contractor for many of the most significant buildings in the Mahoning Valley during the late 19th century. Born a free man in Lawrence County, Pennsylvania, he began his career as a bricklayer at the age of 16. At that time, Berry was commissioned by Lawrence County to do brickwork for a new courthouse in New Castle, Pennsylvania. Ten years later, about 1861, Berry and his wife traveled by canal boat with his wife and four children to Youngstown after he was awarded the brickwork contract for The Rayen School (now the Youngstown Board of Education building). Berry trained a cohort of newly freed Black men who came to the Valley after the Civil War and employed them at his foundry. His own brick foundry was noted for its reddish-orange colored brick, an example of which one can see in the Rayen Building. He was also responsible for founding the Brick Mason's Union, Local # 8. His stature in the community was such that a number of white bricklayers worked under his direction, something very uncommon in that era. Berry's influence spread past the Valley and outlasted the buildings he designed through the men he trained. During his forty-year career in Youngstown, Berry became recognized as a master builder of some 65 buildings and, in the process, became a respected citizen of the Valley who was also involved in a number of philanthropic causes.

Berry's accomplishments are all the more noteworthy when one realizes that there were very few Blacks living in the Youngstown area in the late 19th century. According to Irene Stewart, a Black newspaperwoman writing for the Youngstown Telegram in the 1930s, Malinda Knight was the first "colored" resident of Youngstown, arriving in the city about 1831. Blacks came in modest numbers until 1918 when a heavy migration from the South brought many into the city to work in the steel mills. Even though Blacks were often not welcomed by area natives, last in line for the best jobs, and limited in where they could live by restrictive covenants, many left an impressive mark on the community.

While building the original Rayen School, Berry simultaneously built Saint Columba Catholic Church's second church building. Other buildings with the Berry mark included the Youngstown Opera House, the Tod House Hotel, the 1866 jail on Hazel Street, the 1876 Mahoning County Courthouse, William Hitchcock's home, Governor David Tod's residence, and many others. His masonry work included the Homer Hamilton and Company Foundry and Machine Shop and the Dollar Bank Building. During his career in Youngstown, Berry contributed heavily to the growth of religious institutions in the Valley as he was commissioned to build three major churches, including First Presbyterian Church, First Baptist Temple, as well as the previously mentioned Saint Columba.

Intermixed with his narrative, Shivers showed images of many of the buildings he spoke of, as well as several images of Berry and other notables of the era, including his partner Lemuel Stewart. Stewart was a building contractor who moved to the Mahoning Valley after

Berry. The Stewart and Berry families were connected by both friendship and marriage, and their sons continued as builders in the Youngstown area. Berry's own four sons were trained as brick masons and later became union organizers of the Brick Mason's Local # 8.

Berry and other members of the family were the driving force behind the founding of Saint Augustine's Church in 1907. Today, many descendants of the Berry family belong to this church. P. Ross Berry contributed greatly to the building boom that occurred in Youngstown at the turn of the century, not just with bricks and stone, but with a family and descendants who have also made significant contributions to the history and heritage of the Valley. Some of these descendants from near and far gathered recently, for the first time, to honor Berry. The reunion was referred to as "Back Together After100 Years". They toured the Youngstown area taking in some of the "Berry" buildings, and took pictures in front of the Rayen School Building. Berry's great, great-granddaughter, Christine Dwyer Lapcevich from Hamilton, Ontario, said, "We heard all kinds of stories and never got the whole truth. So now we find out who we are and why we look the way we do. It's really wonderful." P. Ross Berry had eight children, among them, gifted musician P. Ross Berry, Jr., who left for Europe to tour with a brass band and married an English woman," explained Bill Lawson, Mahoning Valley Historical Society, Executive Director. He also said, "But it was his son, Plimpton Ross Berry, III that came back to North America. First, he visited Youngstown but then eventually, he ended up in Hamilton, Ontario." Another of the descendants said that she had wanted to be a blueprint specialist and was told at school that they do not teach that to girls. And then, "I find out that my great grandfather was one of the best." Roseejean Turner Hodge, who is 79, grew up in Youngstown and was excited to meet her Canadian cousins. It was as though they always knew each other. After this reunion, local historians asked for help from the varied descendants to gain even more information about the Berry lineage.

Local historian, Howard C. Aley, described Berry as a handsome man, six foot six inches in height. His wife, Mary Long, eventually bore him eight children, four boys, and four girls. Several sons worked in the business, and his offspring included successful doctors, attorneys, musicians, and leaders in their respective communities. Berry worked until age 82 and died on May 12, 1917. He is buried in Oak Hill Cemetery. The P. Ross Berry Middle School was named in his honor but closed as a middle school in 2012. What a legacy from one with humble beginnings and considerable obstacles to success. Was his story and accomplishments a kind of genius? Remember, "genius knows no boundaries."

P. Ross Berry

Vince Shivers sharing film and memorabilia about Berry

Josh Green and Nikita Jones with accompanist

James Malone, Bishop of the Catholic Diocese of Youngstown, was our subject in May. His good friend and fellow priest, Monsignor James Clarke, sensitively shared his recollections of Bishop Malone's joyful and prolific life. The cultural enrichment was offered by the "Wade Raridon Singers", comprised of Dr. Raridon's former students who still wanted to sing publicly. The music was appropriate to the theme of the evening. Dr. Raridon had recently retired from YSU's Dana School of Music. Holy Family Church Hall in Poland was the venue for this meeting, and The Georgetown Caterers traveled to Holy Family to provide the meal.

Monsignor Clarke was the ideal person to speak of the "resonating voice" of Bishop Malone. Monsignor Clarke was active in several capacities in the Diocese during the years when Malone was Bishop, including a number of years as Chancellor. They had a close professional and personal relationship. His narrative prose about his friend and spiritual leader was almost poetic. Monsignor Clarke began his message with a poem entitled "The Dash" by Linda Ellis.

> *"I read of a man who stood to speak at the funeral of a friend. He referred to the dates on his tombstone from the beginning...to the end. He noted that first came the date of his birth and spoke the following date with tears. But he said what mattered most of all was the dash between those years. For that dash represents all the time that he spent alive on earth...and now, only those who love him know what that little line is worth. For it matters not how much we own, the cars, the house, the cash. What matters is how we live and love and how we spend our dash."*

"How did Bishop Malone spend his eighty years of Dash" Clarke mused of the bishop's birth to death-1920 DASH 2000. He spent most of his life here in the Mahoning Valley striving "to know, love, and serve God in this world, and to be happy with God forever in the next." He cherished his life in the Youngstown area and cherished his "Irishness," but he also fiercely advocated ecumenism and diversity. Clarke proceeded to chronicle Malone's life from his first thoughts of entering the priesthood, as a senior at Ursuline High School, to his death at the age of 80. Bishop Malone served in many capacities: "Church shepherd and administrator, pastoral counselor, preacher, speaker, evangelizer, relative, friend (and many other roles besides)", Reverend Clarke noted. After high school, he entered St. Mary Seminary in Cleveland and was ordained a priest at age 25. After ordination, he served as associate pastor at St. Columba, and a few years later (1952), he was appointed diocesan superintendent of parochial schools. During his tenure as superintendent, he initiated a recruitment program for new, young teachers and simultaneously served as director of the newly established "CCD" program in 1956. Fifteen years after his ordination as a priest, Father Malone was named, in 1960, auxiliary bishop of Youngstown at the young age of 39. When Bishop Emmet M. Walsh died a few years later, Bishop Malone was officially installed as the third bishop of Youngstown.

Bishop James Malone

Fortuitously, in 1960, Bishop Malone was privileged to attend all four sessions of the Second Vatican Council from 1962 through 1965. "These extended experiences with the Pope, with bishops from around the world and renowned theologians from world-famous universities, immersed him in the spirit of the Council that changed the Church and his approach to ministry", Clarke reported. He continued, "Bishop Malone brought back to Youngstown that 'Spirit' of the Vatican Council to the clergy, religious and laity alike. In an interview with the Catholic Exponent, Bishop Malone described some of the significant changes in how the Second Vatican Council effected a 'new way' for the parish priests to conduct their ministry. Malone cited how the priesthood was conducted in the '30s, '40s, and '50s: clerical collar, black suit, black hat, black shoes, black coat, and even black automobiles. Conduct between a priest and the laity was always formal. Bishop Malone described his daily parish responsibilities as a young priest as celebrating daily Mass, visiting parish homes, taking census, taking Holy Communion to the sick and shut-ins, hearing confessions, and giving convert instructions.... He explained, 'In 1945, we had no concept of social justice programs, no sense of dissatisfaction with social conditions in our city or nation. We had no notion of racial equality needing to be preached by the Church. We certainly had no notion of social inequality abroad. The Church's interest in the 'world beyond' was to give money once a year to the Propagation of the Faith collection so that we could make pagans into Catholics.'"

"At the same interview, the Bishop noted some of the changes that came out of the Second Vatican Council: 'Priests and bishops now relate to the laity differently. With the 'new vision' of the church...the identity of the layperson and the identity of the priest have become clearer. We now have a more informed and active laity who see themselves living a life of grace, enhanced by the sacraments they receive, and who see the value of their role in the Church as multi-faceted. Bishops and parish priests now see the layperson as one who is also called and gifted and is engaged in the building of the Kingdom of God in the world, in the family, and in many ways that laypersons contribute to the improvement of society.' Bishop Malone argued that 'I tend to be generous in my estimate of the effects of the Vatican Council upon the church in the United States.'"

At the close of the Council, Bishop Malone brought many theologians and experts to the diocese to speak to the clergy, religious, and laity about the new changes and the updated theology. He was also quick to invite members of the Jewish and Protestant faiths to speak and/or participate in talks and workshops to those same groups. The Youngstown Diocese was one of the first dioceses in the country to initiate a Bishop's Advisory Council (now called the Diocesan Pastoral Council) and an Advisory Senate of Priests (now called the Council of Priests). He wanted everyone to know what undergirded the Vatican changes and the philosophy behind them.

Monsignor Clarke reminded us that "Locally, nationally, and internationally, Bishop Malone was well-known for his efforts in interfaith and ecumenical relations with Christians, Muslims, and Jews." Examples of such activity: he was the only American bishop invited to participate in dialogue between the Roman Catholic Church and the World Methodist Council, which convened in Italy; locally and throughout the diocese, he gave many speeches, served on local councils and committees, including inter-faith groups; he developed friendships with leaders of other denominations, including local Jewish Rabbi Sidney Berkowitz and Bishop John Burt with whom he co-chaired the Ecumenical Coalition of the Mahoning Valley in an attempt to "Save our Valley" in the wake of the closing of the local steel mills.

"From his first year as Bishop in Youngstown, Malone was an active member, a willing participant, and an outspoken participant in the National Conference of Catholic Bishops (NCCB)," Clarke reported. He was elected Vice President of the Conference (1980-1983) and then elected President (1983-1986), the first non-cardinal, non-archbishop to be elected to the post. As President, he had several meetings and conversations with Pope Paul VI, Pope John-Paul I, and Pope John-Paul II, as well as with the many offices and officials of the Vatican. Felicity, with words, was among the qualities that commended Bishop Malone to his fellow bishops. A New York Times article stated that "His style reflects much of the informality and directness of Middle Western Catholicism. He mixes easily with his people, aided by an ability to remember names, and places little obvious importance on his hierarchical standing." Colleagues described him as a quiet, progressive leader who stands firmly but not militantly on social issues. It was also reported that "He speaks in complete, complex sentences," one bishop said and added, "It's been a long time since I've heard language used like that. It's like listening to Cicero."

He was president when the U.S. bishops issued their pastoral letters on the Challenge of Peace. (On a personal note, Bishop Malone asked me to give a talk to more than 100 priests and religious regarding the importance of and meaning to our lives of these pastoral letters on peace.) As the bishops drafted their pastoral letter condemning nuclear arms, he was among its most effective and tireless supporters. The response of the media was greeted with almost universal approbation, even adulation on the networks, in the national news magazines, and in the major national dailies. Among other issues addressed during Malone's tenure was the Conference's opposition to the movement of the U.S. Embassy to Jerusalem because, as Malone announced: "such a unilateral move would fail to address the special significance Jerusalem holds for Moslems, Jews and Christians and argued it would present another obstacle toward a Middle East peace." (Of course, we now know that the move was made during the last year of President Donald Trump's administration.) Malone was president of the NCCB also when the pastoral letter Catholic Social Teaching and the U.S. Economy was issued. Clarke reminded us that he was also dedicated, locally and nationally, to social issues.

Bishop Malone did all of this despite the fact that he was diagnosed with abdominal cancer in 1972. In what looked initially to be a bleak prognosis, he was declared cured of cancer after five years of surgery, chemotherapy, and radiation. The remainder of Monsignor's narrative and speech was devoted to the relationship he and the bishop had in good times and to the bishop's death. In just two years into Clarke's priesthood, the bishop invited the young priest to work in the Chancery Offices with him. Clarke shared, "That knot and tangle became the start of our close friendship and the start of a beautiful period in the tapestry of my life." In just four months later, Bishop Malone became a cancer patient. So it was Clarke who spent a great deal of time with Malone at Roswell Park Hospital in Buffalo, New York, spending time with the bishop who thought he was going to die. Monsignor Clarke said, "There was a steady stream of visitors from the diocese, and a flood of get-well cards, letters, and the promise of prayers from Catholics, Orthodox, Protestants, Jews, and Moslems." The bishop came to believe those prayers put him on the road to recovery. Twenty-eight years later, at the age of 80, as he was dying from another kind of cancer, Clarke reminded him similar prayers were being offered for him as he fought this new battle of health problems and setbacks.

Following his first bout with cancer and into his retirement years, one of Bishop Malone's ministries was relating and speaking to other people living with cancer. He was willing to share that he also had emotional and spiritual problems dealing with cancer. His volunteer chaplaincy work with Hospice of the Valley was meaningful to him and for those whom he visited. Clarke shared with us how Malone often stated, "For an 80-year-old man, having been living with cancer since my fifties, I've had, and still have, a great life." Monsignor Clarke was with the bishop just a couple of days before he slipped into the coma just preceding his death when Clarke said he had been listening to Amazing Grace on a CD: "I was moved by the words, 'His grace has brought me safe thus far; His grace will lead me home.' I told Jim, for 80 years, God's grace has kept you safe. God will not abandon you now, especially when God calls you home. He clearly responded, Yes! Praised be God's almighty name. That was the last sentence I heard him speak."

Monsignor Clarke ended his presentation with a few minutes of preaching (he said he was more a preacher than a speaker) about the efficacy of prayer...prayers for people who are sick, prayers for people who are caregivers of the sick. He did this by way of a homily to his parishioners on the occasion of Bishop Malone's death. He thanked them for their prayers for the bishop and for himself as the caregiver. He said he wanted to tell them how their prayers worked. "For example, one of my prayers had been that Bishop Malone would not be alone at the hospital at the time when he passed from life on earth. It was your prayers that enabled me to be there at just the right time. I was with him when he died. I was able to be with him, holding his hand, praying with and for him as he passed. Your prayers are what kept me there for that precious moment."

Monsignor's concluding paragraph ended with: "James W. Malone was a dear friend and bishop who was such a significant part of my life as a diocesan priest. We made and shared a home together for nineteen years. We often traveled together and obviously enjoyed each other's company. Bishop Malone was a talented churchman, a learned man, a loving bishop, and a very important historical figure in the post-Vatican II Church. May he rest in peace and be among those who look after us from the other side of life on earth. Bishop James W. Malone, 1920 DASH 2000. For that dash represents all the time he spent alive on earth, and now, only those who love him know what that little line is worth. For it matters not how much we own, the cars, the house, the cash. What matters is how we live and love and how we spend our dash."

Monsignor James Clarke

What a fitting conclusion to a consideration of a Resonating Voice of the Valley. Was James W. Malone a genius? I don't know, but, in my opinion, he was as nearly a saint as a person could be and was certainly one of the iconic figures of the Mahoning Valley. Here, indeed, was the person like some of us and different from many of us, but we share a common humanity. We in the Ohio Cultural Alliance are privileged to have known him and/or to have learned more about him.

Wade Raridon Singers

We closed our 2011-2012 season in June as William Lawson depicted in costume the life of John Young, founder of Youngstown. H. William Lawson/Bill is the Mahoning Valley Historical Society Executive Director. The Youngstown Connection, a group of talented young people from the Youngstown city schools, treated us to a patriotic program of music and dance. The event was held at the Holy Trinity Serbian Hall in Youngstown, whose caterers served us an abundant and delicious Serbian meal. We were part of a milieu consisting of Scotsman John Young, Serbian cuisine, and American patriotism.

John Young was an American surveyor and pioneer. As a Resonating Voice of the Valley, he is best known as the founder of Young'sTown or Youngstown. His presence, on and off for about six years, was sufficient to shape the early contours of the city, still evident to this day, and to attract one of the key early settlers who helped found the city. John Young was born in 1763 in Petersborough, New Hampshire, the eldest of seven siblings. His parents, of Scottish ancestry, were Dr. John and Elizabeth Smith Young. Dr. John had served in the Revolutionary War. As a restless young man of 20, John left home in 1783 and ended up in Whitestown, New York, where he married Mary Stone White, the daughter of Hugh White, the founder of Whitestown. They, too, had seven children. In 1796, John Young moved with his wife and their son to what would become Ohio while he surveyed the area and settled there soon after. He built a log cabin on the northeast bank of the Mahoning River near what is now Spring Common. John Young was to play a brief but pivotal role in the early development and settlement of the city, which carries his name.

Lawson set the stage for Young's settlement in what was called the Connecticut Western Reserve, which was part of the western land claim of colonial Connecticut. Connecticut relinquished to the U.S. government all western land claims in 1786, except for approximately 3 million acres it maintained as its "Western Reserve". The Connecticut legislature voted to survey the land in their Western Reserve, then to sell those lands. A corporation of 35 Connecticut men formed the Connecticut Land Company in 1795 to secure substantial acreage and facilitate the process of sales to individuals. In 1797, Young purchased a township of 15,560 acres from the Connecticut Land Company for $16,085.16, with the establishment of the city being recorded in 1802.

Lawson explained, "Young must have chosen Township 2, Range 2 because of the advantage of having a navigable river running through it diagonally and the advantage of it being the gateway into the Western Reserve by the southern route." Young and a surveying party made their first visit to the future site of Youngstown, an area that Young considered purchasing. On this first trip into the area, he and his surveyor were reputed to have met up with Colonel James Hillman, who sighted smoke from a fire the Young party had set as he was canoeing up the Mahoning River from Beaver, Pennsylvania. Young persuaded Hillman to join him for a "frolic" (as one source described the meeting) that included an exchange of skins for whiskey. Hillman later became Youngstown's first constable and, during the War of 1812, led a militia that defended the area against Indian attacks. He later served as a representative in the state legislature.

One of the first to buy land from Young and settle in Youngstown was Daniel Shehy in 1796 when he purchased 1,000 acres for $2,000. In late spring 1797, Young, members of the surveying party, and early purchasers and recipients of area lands began settlement. Young cleared several acres of brush around his cabin, which was to be his residence and land office, while the surveying party worked throughout the township. The Hillmans were the first year-round settlers, while Young brought his family to the township in 1799 and lived year-round until 1803. The Young's returned to New York in 1803 when Mary Young was experiencing health problems. But during his time in Youngstown, Young laid out the first plats of the city, including Federal Street, Central Square, North (now Wood) Street, and South (now Front) Street, town lots, and larger farm-size plats. After returning to Whitestown, he was involved in various public works in upstate New York until his death in 1825 at the age of 62.

Howard C. Aley, in his book, A Heritage to Share, shares a letter from a descendent of Daniel Shehy who contends that it was Daniel Shehy, not John Young, that built the first log cabin along the Mahoning and that Young did no more than travel back and forth between New York and Youngstown. There is some evidence of a dispute between the two men over the land purchase, which in the end meant that Shehy acquired only 400 rather than 1,000 acres. The controversy of Shehy's role vis-à-vis Young's role doubtless will continue. What is clear is that Young was involved in the early surveys that gave shape to Youngstown; it was Young who purchased the land and sold it to Shehy and others and for this alone deserves a singular place in Youngstown history as that man who gave the city its name and had the vision of a thriving city on the banks of the Mahoning River.

Lawson/Young ended his presentation with a list of some of John Young's relationships with others who helped make Youngstown: Alfred Wolcott, first surveyor of Youngstown Township; Daniel and Jane McClain Shehy, Irish immigrant who married a Beavertown resident and settled in Youngstown; Abram and Isaac Powers, Beavertown residents who accompanied surveying party in 1796 and bought large tracts of land; Phineas Hill, Beavertown resident who accompanied surveying party in 1796 and bought lands on falls of Mill Creek (Lanterman's Falls); James and Katherine Hillman, who met the Young surveying party on the Mahoning in June, 1796 and who received land if they would settle in Youngstown; George Tod, a lawyer from Suffield, Connecticut who was an early government official of Trumbull County and Youngstown Township; William Rayen, who arrived in 1803 and bought Young's cabin site at Spring Common, which he expanded to a public house and store; Caleb an Hannah Baldwin from Washington County, Pennsylvania who arrived in 1799; William and Henry Wick, who arrived in 1799 and 1802, respectively.

William Lawson portrayed John Young well in his period costume and delivered a narrative of how Young, of Scot ancestry, prepared a town that bears his name. Lawson helped us to imagine how our area emerged as a western society and developed in the late 18th and early 19th centuries.

We ended the Ohio Cultural Alliance's 25th year with a feeling of satisfaction that we addressed topics about individuals and institutions that helped us to better understand the Mahoning Valley and its heritage. In addition, our meals were superb, and our cultural enrichment was enriching.

John Young (aka William Lawson)

The Youngstown Connection

William Lawson and wife Joan

XVIII. Old World Traditions: Lost and Retained

In 2012-2013 we began the Ohio Cultural Alliance's 26th year with the topic "Old World Traditions-Lost and Retained". This topic was addressed to explore how many of the ethnic groups that came to the Mahoning Valley aspired to become Americans yet retained some of their cultures. To some degree, each ethnic group merged with their new American culture but added something new also. The groups that we treated had ancestry from Puerto Rico, Serbia, Italy, England, Africa, Germany, Slovakia, Greece, India, and Croatia. As usual, our speakers were engaging and informative, our meals (many quite traditional and ethnic) were varied and very good, and our cultural enrichment was diverse and entertaining. Highlights also included co-sponsoring an international Serbian dance troupe and a reception to honor the entire cast of Opera Western Reserve's production of The Barber of Seville, which featured former Youngstown Connection member and internationally acclaimed tenor Lawrence Brownlee.

We opened our year in September with Hector Colon as our speaker as he shared with us the traditions of Puerto Rico, as well as other peoples "south of the border". An authentic Hispanic meal was served at Los Gallos Restaurant, and a vibrant mariachi group performed for us. Hector Colon was a Fireman for most of his adult life, becoming the Fire Chief of Youngstown. He was also an active citizen in the area, much of it revolving about Hispanic affairs in the Valley, preserving some of that culture while becoming an American.

Colon began his presentation with some definitions of culture-American culture: baseball, apple pie, and Chevrolet, and how they have impacted our lives. He explained, "A tradition is defined as the handing down of beliefs, statements, legends, information and customs from one generation to another either by word of mouth-things we say or practice and things we do." He said that all of us follow some of the traditions of our forebearers, to a greater or lesser degree, regardless of our heritage. Colon uttered, "Yo soy Puertoriqueno/I am a Puerto Rican."

He proceeded from this point to discuss Puerto Rico, the land of his birth, and its history. His narrative included that the land is part of the West Indies, 35 miles wide and 100 miles long, and is comprised of nearly 4 million people. He told us that Columbus (sailing for the Spanish) arrived on the island and named it San Juan in honor of St. John the Baptist. Some years later, Ponce de Leon explored the island, discovering its beauty and rich ports, renaming it Puerto Rico/Rich Port. Colon offered an image of Spaniards encountering the Tainos Indians, a gentle, friendly people who greeted them, most wearing no clothing. The Tainos fished for shells, used for making jewelry; hunted birds, rodents, and iguana, which they considered a delicacy; ate a root called yucca, which they dried and ground up to make bread; used bows and arrows and clubs for weapons. They also believed in superior immortals that lived in the heavens and that when their ancestors died, they became a protective spirits. And they believed in life after death, so they buried their dead with water, food, and jewelry for their next life. Earthquakes and hurricanes were considered forces of evil. Their culture included painting of their bodies, no written language, but did include dancing and singing about the epics of the past. "That's how they passed on their history, culture, and traditions," Colon revealed.

When the Spaniards arrived, they disdained the native culture and were determined to force the abandonment of those traditions and their way of life. The Spaniards would take care of them, teach them a new religion, and have the Indians do the work, basically as slaves. The Indians did not take up arms against the Spaniards because they believed the Spaniards to be immortal and had superior arms. There were rebellions ultimately, but the superior weapons and new diseases brought by the Spaniards rendered the efforts futile. African slaves were brought to the island to build many of the fortresses and homes and to cultivate sugar cane. Spain gave up its slave trade in Puerto Rico in 1873.

Spain continued to hold Puerto Rico as a colony until the Spanish American War in 1898, at which time it was ceded to the United States. So, a new form of colonialism governed Puerto Rico: in 1917, Puerto Ricans became American citizens with a Bill of Rights and a governor who could appoint their own cabinet. Puerto Rican statehood has been attempted several times, but thus far, neither the Puerto Rican voters nor the U.S. Congress has granted it.

Colon told us that in the late 1940s and the early 1950s, there was an exodus of Puerto Ricans to the U.S., including many to Youngstown. Those coming to Youngstown, as their predecessors from Europe at an earlier time, came to work in the steel mills, providing needed labor. Colon reported that these newest immigrants got jobs, but there were obstacles as they moved toward acculturation and assimilation. A new language, different foods, a different climate, limited access to housing, and plain discrimination made life in this new environment a challenge. Despite these challenges, Hispanics, including Puerto Ricans, have adapted and contributed their own "flavor" of cultures to the area. Hispanics can be found throughout the Valley as steel workers, auto workers, businessmen, lawyers, doctors, educators, and virtually any trade or occupation. Intermarriages with other races are not uncommon. Hector did remind us that there are many aspects to the various cultures that are considered Hispanics, some similar and some dissimilar. Organizations such as Organization Civica y Cultural Americana (OCCHA) and The Sociedad Mutualista Mexicana, among others, keep some of the traditions alive. Most Hispanics retain traditions that are based on religion, such as Three Kings Day, Day of the Dead, and Twelve Grapes of Luck; the Spanish language is generally retained as English is learned, the tradition of Quinceanera for 15-year-old girls is cherished, and Hispanic cuisine is favored and is evidenced in a large number of Hispanic restaurants in the area. Thus, some traditions have been lost, but many others are retained.

Hector Colon

Mariachi band

Our October meeting featured Ann Milkovich, who spoke of her Serbian ancestry and some of their traditions. She emphasized the connection between her Orthodox religion and traditions by discussing practices of fasting, communion, weddings, and saints' days, as well as the important role of foods in these practices. The Church Ladies Guild of Holy Trinity Serbian Orthodox Church prepared typical Serbian fare, and folk dancers (Talija) from Serbia were enormously talented and entertaining.

The first Serbian immigrants to America were part of a tidal wave of the late 19th and early 20th centuries. The exact number of Serbs is difficult to ascertain because they were part of the Austro-Hungarian monarchy and/or lumped together as people from the Balkans. Some did come to the Mahoning Valley to provide labor, as was the case with others from southern and Eastern Europe. Additional Serbians sought political refuge after World War II and into the 1950's-to the 1970s. In the Mahoning Valley, the closely-knit Serbians that arrived centered many of their activities around the church. As more and more Serbians came to the Valley, they gathered and planned for a church where they could participate in Eastern Orthodox services, baptize their children and continue their Christian heritage. Ann Milkovich detailed the origins of Holy Trinity Church on Laird Avenue in Youngstown, the site of our meeting. The congregants started a grade school and organized Saturday programs for the children to learn about the Orthodox faith and to write in Cyrillic, and they were taught folk tales and history via reading and poems. A variety of other activities, both religious and secular, were supplied for the young. And lodges for all were established, the first being St. George Lodge #23, organized in 1905.

The Serbians, as all ethnic groups, faced the difficulties of being newcomers, but before long, they too blended in and made their contributions to the Valley. They made their contributions to the growth, expansion, and development of the Valley by taking part in the economic, educational, political, and cultural identity of the Youngstown area.

The Serbs have many traditions. The Sava is an exclusive custom of the Serbs wherein each family has one patron saint that they venerate on their feast day. In 2021, 22 participants were involved in the Holy Trinity Sava program that offered poems, songs, and recitations. This was a historic milestone for the church since it was their 90th consecutive St. Sava banquet program. Ms. Milkovich said, "that the early Serbian pioneers brought with them their faith and customs which we proudly continue today. The Serbian Orthodox Church uses the traditional Julian calendar; thus, Christmas Day falls on January 7th, shared with the Orthodox churches in Jerusalem, Russia, Georgia, and Ukraine."

Ms. Milkovich told of some of the main holidays, which include Sava, Vidovan, Lazarus Saturday, and Zapis, in addition to Christmas and Easter. A number of saints are also honored: St. George, St. John the Baptist, St. Demetrius, and St. Michael. Over the years, traditional communities began to lose their cohesiveness. As Serbs became part of the greater community, they lost some but not all of their traditions, particularly those associated with the Orthodox Church. As late as the end of the 20th century, Serbian radio programs continued to air in Cleveland, if not the Valley and Serbians continue to this day with their social and cultural groups that serve to promote Serbian beliefs and customs. Holy Trinity Church, for example, holds its Friday Fish Frys, yearly festivals, and hosting Serbian ethnic meals as we did this evening. We also learned that Serbians often follow traditions such as egg decorations and egg tapping at Easter; koleda (groups of young men, masked and costumed going from house to house singing songs and performing acts of magic to summon health, wealth and prosperity for all just before Christmas); honoring guests in a Serbian home with bread and salt and/or a spoonful of a Serbian drink. In a word, some of these customs and others are still practiced by some, if not all, particularly those that relate to their Orthodox beliefs.

Ending our program was the music and dancing of the Talija troupe. Offering the flavor of the Serbian traditions was the Talija Art Company, one of the best representatives of Serbian culture. Established in 1998 in Belgrade, Serbia, the Talija group represents a rich and colorful program, performing folk dances from all regions of the former Yugoslavia. Talija's core repertoire is comprised of the customs and folk tales gathered from these cultures, and the troupe used motion as the element binding the colorful traditions of music and dance together. Talija has about 200 members divided into several groups: senior ensemble, senior children's ensemble, beginners' ensemble, senior musical orchestra, and children's musical orchestra. In groups of about 20, they *travel the world, performing about 400 shows* and special events each year, many of which are on cruise ships. The Ohio Cultural Alliance co-sponsored the group with the Serbian Holy Trinity parish.

Ann Milkovich

Talija dance group

OCA members met at Mt. Carmel Social Hall in November as Vince Camp, Italian activist and host of the Italian Hour on radio, spoke about Italian traditions that have been lost and retained. His humor and knowledge of area Italians was captivating. The Italian meal was delicious, and the musical selections from the Opera Western Reserve's cast of the Barber of Seville provided a capstone for the evening.

The most numerous of the immigrants from southern and eastern Europe that came to America during the late 19th and early 20th centuries were the Italians-some 4 million came during the years 1890-1924. And many came to the Mahoning Valley during that same time period. They found employment in the coal industry and the steel industry. The Niles Fire Brick Company employed hundreds of Italian laborers. The vast majority settled in the Brier Hill and Smoky Hollow areas, near their jobs. Corner groceries, tailor shops, cobblers, and dry goods shops emerged as service enclaves, sometimes referred to as "Little Italy". By 1910 nearly 5,000 Italian-born immigrants lived here, and by 1920, the number had doubled.

They, too, worked to assimilate, yet they determined to preserve some cherished traditions. They formed societies such as the Colombo Club and the Sons of Italy. They established ethnic newspapers and churches, the first being St. Anthony in 1898 and Mt. Carmel in 1913. They also brought with them a passion for art, music, dance, and food. One of the most numerous of the ethnic groups to come to the Valley, the Italians are also among the most visible. Most Italian Americans still identify strongly with their heritage and are proud to display it, although as generations pass, the "Italian DNA" is diluted through time and inter-marriage. Mr. Camp told us, "if there is anything that will help keep their Italian identity alive and relevant, it is by retelling about traditions through stories, recipes, or items such as a pot that 'Nonna' used every day to make sauce or a wine press that 'Nonno' used to press the grapes for winemaking. Most Italian families have a go-to person such as an aunt, uncle, or grandparent who acts as the family historian and tells the youngsters their memories of traditions of the 'early days'." Vince shared some of the other ways traditions are passed down through the church, food, wine, and music.

Many traditions involve religious holidays and the preparation of food. Vince said, "What great vehicles these are to practice traditions and pass down recipes to succeeding generations." It was common for immigrant families to celebrate American holidays while putting their own Italian twist on the food, often including sauce and/or fish, wedding soup, spaghetti, and Italian sausage. Many Italians, to his day, have holiday gatherings in the basement, which houses their bar and a second kitchen. "Generally, I just remember picking at food all day long", Vince revealed.

Most Italian immigrants made wine in Italy, and they continued the practice in their new country. It made economic sense to use native grapes on the backyard trellis, then crush, press, and ferment them into wine. The new immigrants had a reliable, healthful drink that reminded them of home. Vince told a story of one family who said they engage in winemaking every autumn, along with friends and family, to live their Italian heritage vicariously. After the physical work comes to an end, the traditional feast begins. Homemade wine is served, and antipasto is next with homegrown figs, olives, and cheeses. Sausage is then roasted on a grill, pizza is baked in the wood-fired pizza oven, and pasta with the family's sauce and meatballs are served. They said the feast is not complete until the cannoli and biscotti are served with some espresso and maybe a little more wine.

Many of these activities take place in the Church, particularly at Mt. Carmel and St. Anthony's in the Youngstown area. Both churches hold holiday and periodic pasta dinners and sponsor festivals at their churches and at some secular sites (at least six are held in the

Mahoning Valley each year). Columbus Day is revered and celebrated each year, near October 12th.

Italian radio programming has been a staple in the Mahoning Valley for generations. One of the promoters and announcers was our speaker for the evening, Vince Camp. He was the voice of Serenata d'Italia WNIO radio show every Sunday morning, succeeding other distinguished hosts for over 60 years. (Sadly, in 2020, it was canceled.) Local Italian historian Ben Lariccia wrote lovingly of his mother: "Mom would get up early on Sunday morning to start the sauce, the same ragu that almost all our Italian neighbors were making the very same hour. The base had pork and beef browned with garlic in the oil. After she added the tomato sauce, bay leaf, and paste, Mom let the pot simmer until just before we left for church. Then she cut the flame. The pot rested. About two hours later, we'd return to a house full of the aroma of a great meat sauce. As we enjoyed our delicious pasta, an Italian show played on the radio. This was Sunday morning programming for the Italian community." Local Italian radio programming helped to sustain the Italian community and promoted the Italian heritage through songs, stories, and discussion. And our speaker, Vince Camp, was an important part of that promotion.

Roberto Pietraria, a local Italian, reported, "Traditions help to bring families together and celebrate where we came from and honor those who came before us. It's never too late to restart a tradition that your family used to have. I have listened to many 2nd and 3rd generation Italian Americans who remember Nonno making wine in the basement and wisely said they should continue the tradition. I always tell them, 'what's stopping you?"'

Vince Camp

Vince did suggest that while some of the traditions have been diluted over the years and with inter-marriage, one needs just to look around the community to see a significant Italian influence: the large number of Italian restaurants, pizzerias, Italian festivals, plus desserts such as pizzells and spumoni. Traditions also remain in the people who have distinguished themselves in the world of education, industry, business, politics, the arts, and sports. In a word, while some traditions may have been lost, many have been retained.

Western Reserve Opera cast members singing excerpts from Barber of Seville

On November 25, 2012, the Ohio Cultural Alliance held a special meeting to honor the Youngstown Connection, alumnus Lawrence Brownlee and the entire cast of Opera Western Reserve's Barber of Seville. It was held at Stambaugh Auditorium, the home of Opera Western Reserve; a light supper was prepared by Fifth Season Catering.

The Youngstown Connection, at that time in its 25th year, was founded and is directed by Dr. Carol Baird. They had performed their song and dance routines around the community, the State, the nation, and internationally. They have provided our OCA cultural enrichment on many occasions. These young people from the Youngstown city schools have been model citizens with 100% high school graduation rates and an enviable college record also. Many have contributed their artistic talents far beyond high school and college. Perhaps the most noteworthy has been Lawrence Brownlee.

Lawrence Brownlee and Dr. Carol Baird

Lawrence Brownlee was one of the original members of The Youngstown Connection as Dr. Carol Baird, music coordinator of the Youngstown Schools, created the group. After graduating from East High School, Lawrence continued his music education at Anderson University in Indiana and at Indiana University Jacobs School of Music; he studied under Costanza Cuccaro, David Starkey, and Fritz Robertson. His professional debut took place in 2002 as Almaviva in Rossini's The Barber of Seville with the Virginia Opera Company. He has subsequently appeared in Barber of Seville in Vienna, Milan, Berlin, Madrid, Dresden, Munich, Baden-Baden, Hamburg, Tokyo, New York, Washington D.C., San Diego, Seattle, and Boston. He performed in such opera venues as La Scala, London's Royal Opera House, and the Metropolitan Opera House, among others. Lawrence has received many awards and has a large number of recordings to his credit. Brownlee participated in a few selections with current Youngstown Connection members and spoke briefly to the audience. It was a thrill for all of us to see up close this local talent who has done so well.

David Vosburgh, Production Director, whose credits included both opera and Broadway musical, and Susan Davenny Wyner, musical director, who was conductor of the Warren Philharmonic Orchestra, each spoke briefly about their positions with Opera Western Reserve (OWR). The mission of OWR is to produce and present opera performances of the highest quality to audiences in northeast Ohio and western Pennsylvania. OWR made its debut with a fully staged production of I Pagliacci in November 2004 and have presented one every November since. It was a lively and entertaining evening, showcasing an important component of the Mahoning Valley opera.

Brownlee with The Youngstown Connection

English traditions were featured in December as Dr. Peter Norris, YSU, Chemistry Department, shared with us memories and traditions of his homeland, effectively employing power point with narrative and pictures. He said that England celebrates most of the same religious holidays as Americans. He then proceeded to discuss in chronological order the major holidays, beginning with the New Year's celebration. We met at Western Reserve United Methodist Church Hall; their caterers, under the direction of Darlene Wells, catered a distinctive English roast beef meal with all the trimmings. Cultural enrichment was provided by Tapestries of Ohio Madrigal Singers, who entertained us with a modified Boar's Head celebration. Period musical instruments, songs from the 15th-17th centuries, costumes, and drama took us back to early England.

In his introductory comments, Dr. Norris offered geographical, historical, and cultural information regarding England. He spoke also of international engagements, beginning with developing a strong navy which led to exploration and colonization. Among the colonies were those in North America, which held the interest of various European powers of the day. He reminded us that England settled much of the east coast consisting of 13 colonies, with the French and Spanish occupying much of the territory to the west and the south.

"As you well know," he added, "in 1775, the 13 colonies decided to break from England and eventually won their independence, thus beginning the United States of America with English as their first language. Since then, we have mostly gotten along and now have one of the most enduring alliances in the modern world; the so-called 'special relationship' as described by Winston Churchill in his 'Sinews of Peace' address in Missouri in 1946. Churchill was in a unique position to comment since his mother was American and his father, English." Norris made an interesting point in discussing our common language and how "American influence on popular culture has seen 'Americanisms' spread to England, most notably during and since WWII, and 'Britishisms' being adopted by Americans through the influence of popular fiction, music, and cinema."

Dr. Norris chronologically covered significant holiday observances in England, explaining how they are similar and different from the U.S.

- Beginning with the New Year celebration, Norris said they are quite similar in both countries while they party as the old year ends and the new begins. He said that nothing in England quite parallels the countdown at Times Square.
- Valentine's Day is similar in both countries as they swap gifts and cards as a show of affection.
- Mother's Day (Mothering Sunday in England) has similar intents but is held in March in England instead of in May in the U.S. April Fool's Day is followed, but its popularity is waning.
- Summer holidays follow the school year, with many in both countries traveling abroad and locally. The school year begins in the autumn (usually earlier in the U.S.) and "we have a similar system of testing that measures a student's ability at various ages", Norris reported. He added that "The English system 'streams' students at an earlier stage than the USA, with some students being encouraged to prepare for University entrance and others encouraged to follow possibilities in vocational training."
- Halloween, an ancient celebration influenced by Celtic and Christian traditions, is observed in a similar way in England but on a less grand scale than in the U.S.
- November 11th is acknowledged in both countries, but it is called Remembrance Day in England and Veteran's Day/Armistice Day in the U.S.

- Christmas traditions are very similar in terms of religious observation, decorating trees with lights, and exchange of gifts. Norris noted, however, that "we have some differences including a traditional meal of turkey and Father Christmas visits the children versus Santa Claus."
- Some traditions between England and the U.S. are similar but are celebrated somewhat differently.
- Shrove Tuesday is celebrated the day before Lent begins in both countries but "is observed with Pancake races and Mob football in various parts of England...where over 100 players participate" and has been run since 1445 in some regions. A form of the Pancake race has been run in Liberal, Kansas, since 1950.
- St. Patrick's Day is celebrated in both countries, but not with the same fervor as in Ireland and the U.S.
- Harvest Day is the closest thing the British have to American Thanksgiving. On that day, England marks the end of the growing season for which they give thanks with various religious and secular activities.
- Some cultural traditions from England have not been retained in America.
- Rose Nose Day is a modern tradition that began in 1988 as a day set aside to raise money for charity and to have some fun. People are encouraged to don a red clown nose and organize events to raise awareness and money for various causes.
- St. George's Day honors the patron saint of England by flying the national flag and parades. Bonfire Night on November 5th commemorates the abortive attempt by Guy Fawkes et al to blow up Parliament in 1605. These events are somewhat similar to the 4th of July in terms of celebration, but their emphases are quite dissimilar.
- May Day marks a time for a change in England: days are longer, and national elections are typically held in early May.
- June sees the Wimbledon tennis tournament, and the nation celebrates the birthday of Her Majesty Queen Elizabeth the Second with parades and parties.
- The Summer Solstice, which occurs on June 21st or 22nd, and the Winter Solstice, around December 21st, are both observed by gatherings at the ancient monument at Stonehenge in Wiltshire in Southern England. It is believed that the first boulders were laid at the site around 2500 B.C.
- Two other traditions that are lost in America are the British Open and the English summer sport of Cricket-one revered (I suppose Englishmen still are happy to hear of and may follow the British Open) and the other rarely played in the U.S. even though it is somewhat akin to baseball.

Dr. Norris concluded with, "In conclusion, our nations have much more in common than we probably realize, and what differences we do have to make us unique and interesting." This, of course, is the very essence of what we at the Ohio Cultural Alliance are all about: as we learn about others, we find that we have common threads that make up humankind.

Dr. Peter Norris

Ohio Madrigal Singers

Our focus for January was African traditions, as shared by Sarah Brown-Clark, a professor at YSU, a civic leader, and an activist in local politics and in matters relating to the Black community. She reminded us that many of the African traditions were transferred across the Atlantic to the U.S. South, then to the urban areas of the North, most done by oral tradition. Held at the Third Baptist Church in Youngstown, we were treated to a typical African American meal prepared by Marthella Allen, and music of the culture was provided by an exciting gospel choir under the direction of Kris Harper. With the help of jazz pianist and vocalist Howard Howell, they incorporated music rooted in the African American tradition into church service.

African American culture refers to the contributions of African Americans to the culture of the United States, either as part of or distinct from mainstream American culture. To our theme, Professor Brown-Clark addressed some aspects of how culture has been lost from its origins and what has been retained. The distinct identity of African American culture is rooted in the historical experience of the African American people, including the horrific Middle Passage of some 6 million slaves. The culture is both distinct and enormously influential on American and global worldwide culture.

African American culture is rooted in the blend between the native African cultures of West Africa and Central Africa and the European culture that has influenced and modified its development in the American South. Although slavery greatly restricted the ability of Africans to practice their original cultural traditions, many practices, values, and beliefs survived and, over time, have modified and/or blended with European cultures and other cultures, such as that of Native Americans. African American identity was established during the period of slavery, producing a dynamic culture that has had and continues to have an impact on American culture as a whole.

Elaborate rituals and ceremonies were a significant part of African Americans' ancestral culture. Many West African societies traditionally believed that spirits dwelled in their surrounding nature. From this belief, they treated their environment with considerable care. They also generally believed that a spiritual life source existed after death and that ancestors in this spiritual realm could then mediate between the supreme Creator and the living. Honor and prayer were displayed to these "ancient ones", the spirit of that past. West Africans also believed in spiritual possession.

As Christianity started to spread across North Africa, a shift occurred in religion that began to displace traditional spiritual practices from Africa. The enslaved Africans brought this complex religious dynamic within their culture to America. This infusion of traditional beliefs from Africa with Christianity provided a commonplace for those practicing religion in Africa and America.

After emancipation, unique African American traditions have continued to flourish as distinctive traditions or radical innovations in music, art, literature, religion, cuisine, and other fields. Some 20th-century sociologists believed that African Americans had lost most of their cultural ties with Africa. But considerable anthropological research demonstrated that there had been a continuum of African traditions among Africans of the diaspora. The greatest influence of African cultural practices on European culture is found in the American South.

For many years African American culture developed separately from American culture, both because of slavery and the persistence of racial discrimination in America, as well as African American slave descendants' desire to create and maintain their own traditions. Today, African American culture has influenced American culture as a whole while being influenced by that same dominant culture. Yet some of the African cultures remain a distinct cultural body. Brown-Clark related some of the lost and retained traditions that remain in the Mahoning Valley.

Though Africans landed in America with few possessions, they carried their cultures, skills, and spiritual worldviews into the Americas. Wherever African religions took root in the New World, Africans and their descendants changed and adapted their belief systems to local circumstances and influences. Individual circumstances created variations in the way people practiced their faiths, what they believed and what significance it held for their lives.

In some parts of the Americas, religious beliefs emerged in distinct local forms; examples include Santeria in Cuba, voodoo in Haiti, and Candomblé in Brazil. In these places, African deities and African religious customs survived in ways they did not elsewhere in the Americas. Though African religions were largely frowned upon by British authorities, they nevertheless survived and adapted, enabling enslaved to enjoy a degree of freedom in the way they conducted their social and private lives. Some of the slaves and their descendants became Christians; Catholics tended to welcome Africans and convert them simply and with little fuss; Protestant churches tended to insist upon instruction and conversion before baptizing them.

In terms of diet, blends of African, French, and Spanish cuisines covered the colonies and early America. Africa is home to leafy greens, root vegetables, mashed tubers, and beans, among other plant crops. African American cuisine has been called "food to fall in love with" embracing the above cuisines, which resulted in hearty vegetable soups and stews full of spices and aromas poured over boiled and mashed tubers or grains. The African people carried memories through the generations, of their food culture, even with words that bring to mind foods that originated in Africa and are still used today: daddy, buddy, banjo, gumbo, okra, and turnip. One can enjoy some of these delicacies right here in the Mahoning Valley with several caterers, such as Marthella Allen, and restaurateurs, such as Charlie Staples.

Another retained activity is storytelling, as done today by Lynette Miller from Youngstown. After work was done during the periods of slavery, the adults might tell the children stories or oral histories, help them make simple toys, or teach them games. It was during this limited community time that the elders passed along African traditions to the next generation. This has continued in many Mahoning Valley communities to this day.

Africans brought the skills and trades of the homeland, and their expertise helped shape the industry and agriculture of the Americas. West Africans with experience navigating the waterways of their homeland also helped to open the rivers and canals to boat traffic. Seasoned African cattle drivers were also able to apply their skills to oxen teams and livestock, and many were deeply familiar with large-scale rice and indigo cultivation, which was unknown to European Americans. Indeed, signs of African traditional culture can be seen, particularly in the American South, in architecture, art, and handicrafts. Perhaps, the notable Youngstown architect P. Ross Berry had antecedents who had passed down some of the building skills and "tricks of the trade". Yes, some of the traditions of the African culture have been lost, but many have been retained in some form.

Professor Sarah Brown-Clark

Gospel singers under leadership of Kris Harper

German traditions were discussed in February by Professor John Boehm. Having taught German and about the German culture at YSU and elsewhere for many years, he spoke eloquently about German traditions, lost and retained. He addressed matters of religion, education, literature, music, and food. The meal served at the Saxon Club was a truly ethnic German meal, and the music of the German culture was provided by the 40-person Canfield Community Band, directed by Kim Hogan. We enjoyed some rousing "oompah-pah" selections.

As Germans became one of the predominant immigrant groups of the 19th century, it was only natural that they would come to have a powerful influence over the development of American culture. Some German contributions to U.S. life are easy to pinpoint—sauerkraut, for example, or the tuba, or the national fondness for light, fizzy beer. However, the German influence on life in the United States runs much deeper, influencing many of the institutions, traditions, and daily habits that many today think of as being quintessentially American.

Dr. Boehm spoke of the important contributions that German immigrants made in the area of education. They launched the first kindergarten in America; they introduced physical education and vocational education into public schools and were responsible for including gymnasiums in school buildings. Even more importantly, they were among the first to call for universal education. German immigrants also brought a reforming zeal for recreational life, even for Sunday recreation such as Sunday outings. Recreational facilities began to appear in many German immigrant towns, including picnic grounds, bandstands, sports clubs, concert halls, bowling alleys, and playgrounds. German immigrants were also fond of social clubs, singing societies, theater groups, and lodges. Needless to say, many of these recreation facilities are not only retained but also firmly affixed to the America of today.

Germans in the U.S. worked hard to maintain and cultivate their language, especially through newspapers and classes in grade and high schools. German Americans brought their strong support of education, establishing German-language schools and teacher training seminaries to prepare students and teachers for German language training. Culturally and politically transplanted German nationalism was common as the German population grew in America. The development of a foreign language press helped immigrants more easily to learn about their new home, maintain connections to their native land and unite immigrant communities. The Germans were proud of their language, supported many German language public and private schools, and conducted their church services in German. Germans also brought organized gymnastics to America and were strong supporters of sports programs. They used sport both to promote ethnic identity and pride and to facilitate integration into American society. In most major cities in America, Germans took the lead in creating a musical culture with popular bands, singing societies, operas, and symphonic orchestras. The Imperial government in Berlin promoted German culture in the U.S., especially music. A steady influx of German-born conductors spurred the reception of German music in the U.S., while German musicians seized on Victorian Americans' growing concern with emotion. The performance of pieces such as Beethoven's Ninth Symphony established German serious music as the superior language of feeling. The organization of Turner societies also emerged in the mid to late 19th century; these societies became involved in social and sports activities but also started drilling members in militia units at the same time.

World War I changed the relationship German immigrants had with America, at which time their German identification disintegrated. German Americans were increasingly no longer a conspicuous ethnic group, despite the fact that their large numbers throughout the U.S. Public expression of German ethnicity was nowhere proportionate to the number of German Americans in the nation's population.

The transition to the English language was abrupt, forced by federal, state, and local governments and by public opinion, when the U.S. was at war with Germany in 1917-1918. After1917, the German language was seldom heard in public; most newspapers and magazines closed; ethnic churches and parochial schools switched to English.

Of course, one can see that many German traditions are retained; indeed, many have become firmly engrained in American culture. Educational systems, recreation, music, and theater, among others that we now believe are uniquely American, were strongly promoted by German immigrants. Many of the Christian and secular Christmas traditions have been retained by those of German ancestry but are now part of American traditions as a whole- Christmas tree, classic Christmas carols, advent candles, Christmas markets, Santa Claus, and gingerbread houses are the most notable examples. And, of course, Oktoberfest is the largest annual festival in Germany, beginning in late September and into early October has continued in some form throughout the United States, including in the Mahoning Valley. Oktoberfest is known as much for its traditional folk music as it is for its beer drinking. Popular and folk music, marches, and polkas make up the oompah-pah music Germany is famous for.

Some of the authentic German traditions that have been lost are:

- The Schultute, which is a paper bag or a plastic bag in the shape of a large cone, given by parents to their children on the first day of school to help them overcome anxiety. Schultuten are usually filled with various small gifts ranging from candy to items of clothing.
- Tanz in den Mai literally means "dance into May" and is the name of most parties taking place every year on April 30th. This is the night to get rid of evil spirits and celebrate the arrival of spring.
- Tanzverbot means "dancing ban" and is a term that is used to describe the fact that dancing on some holidays is forbidden by state governments. Such bans are mostly linked to Christian holidays such as Good Friday as well as certain memorial days.

The German newspapers, German language church services, and schools are substantially lost, as noted above. But some of the societies, particularly singing societies, remain. In the Youngstown area, the most prominent are the Youngstown Mannerchor and the Saxon Club. Today, the Saxon Club is still very proud of its heritage and is especially so regarding its famous choral group, the Concordia, which presents concerts locally and even in Germany. Perhaps the greatest legacy of the German immigrants to the Valley has been some of the people who have become leaders in the world of industry, business, religion, banking, physicians, contractors, and engineers, among others, and everyday hard-working citizens.

Dr. John Boehm

Canfield Community Band under leadership of Kim Hogan

In March, we met at St. Matthias Church Hall as Loretta Ekoniak shared with us Slovak traditions, many of which appear in her published manuscript about the Mahoning Valley Slovak community. Her verbal images of her ancestors were well received by OCA members. Our ethnic Slovak meal was prepared by Carolyn Catering, and Roman Rudnytsky once again regaled us with appropriate and captivating piano selections.

Ekoniak contends in her book that "Slovak immigrants fleeing poverty in Europe saw a picture of hope and prosperity as they came to the Mahoning Valley...in response to the promise of jobs and good pay in the steel mills. These mills stretched in an almost unbroken chain from Warren, Ohio, through Youngstown and Campbell, and on into Sharon and Farrell, Pennsylvania. From the 1870s, when the first Slovaks came to this area, to the present, there is no part of American life in which these Slovak Americans have not thrived while living the American Dream."

Lansingville is a typical neighborhood in Youngstown, located on the city's far south side that attracted many Roman Catholic Slovaks. This neighborhood developed rapidly as the Market Street Bridge connected the south side and downtown Youngstown. While other European immigrants were also drawn to the area, Slovak Americans became the dominant group in the early 20th century. One of the neighborhood's prominent landmarks is St. Matthias Church. Among the customs that had been developed in the area was the sweeping of their streets and sidewalks once a week.

Most of what follows are gleaned from Ekoniak's book. Folk customs and traditions long affected the life of Slovaks. The birth of these customs is usually rooted in fear of the unknown, an inability to explain events, as well as an attempt to achieve happiness, health, or beauty. These uncertainties were the origin of many superstitions, myths, and legends. Most customs were related to birth and death. As their predecessors were living in close connection with nature, the customs and traditions of the Slovak nation were particularly related to the natural cycle, especially the customs from the pre-Christian period. With the arrival of Christianity, new customs and traditions took hold around Christian holidays. Many of the customs have survived to the present day. For example, the carrying of Morena (in the form of a straw effigy dressed in woman's clothing) symbolizes the end of winter and the arrival of spring. Young girls carried Morena to a local stream, undressed it on the bank, set it on fire, and threw it in the stream. On January 6th boys would go door to door dressed as three Wise Men, singing carols and performing the Twelfth Night play, describing the visit of the three Wise Men after the birth of Christ, following a star. Epiphany marks the end of the Christmas school holidays and the beginning of a new season called Shrovetide, which was always a season of entertainment and feast, and it culminated with a carnival. After Shrovetide, they (as all Christians) observed Lent, a forty-day period of fasting leading up to Easter, the most important Christian holiday.

Special customs are linked to each day of Easter week: on Holy Thursday, they awakened early to bathe in the dew for good health; on Good Friday, they were discouraged from working with anything related to the earth and from eating meat; on Easter Saturday, there were no Mass celebrations until midnight, and on Easter, Saturday food is consecrated in churches and can then be consumed. Young girls decorated Easter eggs for young boys on Monday; the days also include "whipping" and "water pouring"-young boys go from door to door to pour girls with water and gently whip them with a birch rod. In return, the boys receive painted Easter eggs and colored ribbons on their birch rods.

Many Slovak customs are related to the Christmas holiday. In addition to the universal Christmas traditions, Slovaks clean their households, bake honey cakes, and decorate their trees, particularly with sweets for the children. Dinner is composed of Christmas wafers with honey and nuts or garlic; an apple is cut open to form a five-pointed star which means good health. Stuffed cabbage and soup are usually served, followed by fish and potato salad. A tradition of launching lit candles in walnut shell boats has been preserved in some areas. The builder of the boat asks a question about health, employment relationships, etc., then launches the boat and follows its fate. Christmas to NewYears' Day is a time for singing carols and offering good wishes to friends and family.

Other holidays include on December 31st, Sylvester's name day, in memory of Pope Sylvester I. Magical powers were attributed to the night of December 31st-January 1st; during this night, evil forces could do the most harm, but could be warded off by loud noises, including fireworks. May was traditionally called the month of love, with May Day sporting a maypole that was decorated and providing an event for courting. All Saints' Day (All Souls' Day) on November 2nd was a time to visit graveyards and lay wreaths to remember their dearly departed. On December 6th Slovaks celebrate the feast of St. Nicholas as he visits, along with the devil, to give sweets or toys to children who were good and onions or coal to those who were naughty. St. Lucy's Day is on December 13th when people say they could see witches on this day, and it is particularly associated with prophecies about love.

Slovaks are proud of their rich folklore and folk traditions. Each region has a unique character regarding costumes, music, songs, architecture, customs, and dances. Among traditions retained, Ekoniak reminded us of the yearly celebration of Slavic Days in downtown Youngstown. Music and dance and food, and memorabilia all abound at this festive event.

Some traditions are supposedly known only to Slovaks, and many of these have been retained:

- Keeping fish in the bathtub before Christmas
- Taking a tree from the forest to decorate for May Day (as noted above)
- Cold water and birch whips for Easter (as noted above)
- A wedding is not a wedding without a great moderator
- Every meal begins with soup
- Tea can solve any health problem

As noted elsewhere in this section, food is a significant part of all holidays; traditional Slovak food includes (in English): potato dumplings, potato pancakes with flour and garlic fried in oil, fried cheese, and sheep cheese, plain potato pancakes and soups, particularly chicken noodle soup, sauerkraut soup, and bean soup. The traditional Slovak cuisine is handed down from grandmother to daughter to daughter, and all the religious liturgical ceremonies and customs seem to be retained in many of the families. Slovaks have also offered other aspects of their culture to the local community: Slovak folk songs and folk dance, Slovak bands, and Slovak Radio Hour in Youngstown, which originated in 1936 and is still broadcast over station WKTL in Struthers.

Mrs. Ekoniak concluded with her remarks about the resiliency of Slovaks, who assimilated with the broader American cultural traditions but retained many of their social, cultural, musical, and culinary traditions. The multi-cultural interaction, cooperation, and contributions of the immigrant peoples point to the diversity, strength, and truly unique quality of both the Mahoning Valley and our American culture.

Loretta Ekoniak

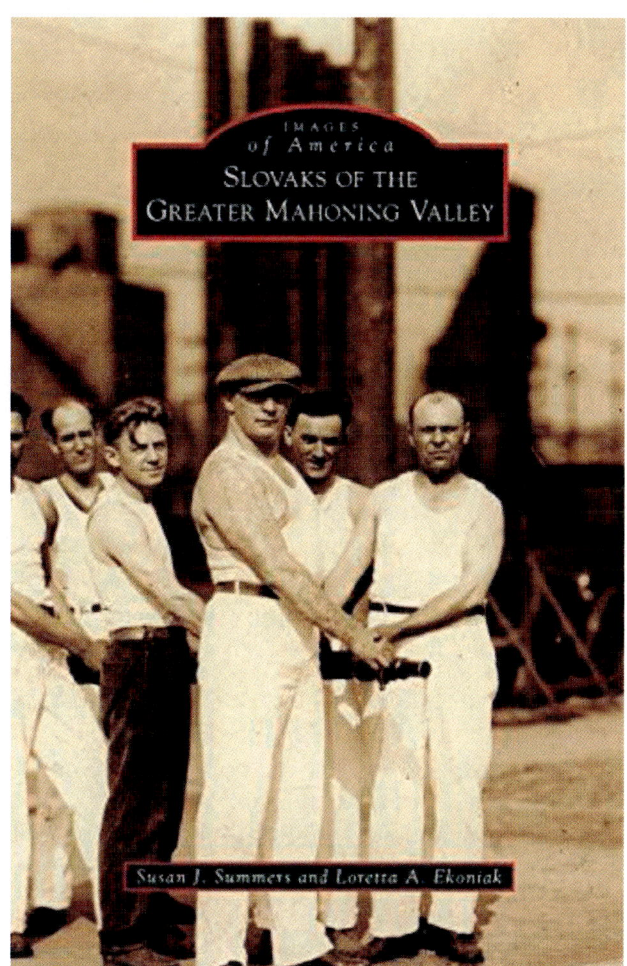

Slovak scene - Title Page of Ekoniak's Book

Greek traditions were the focus of the April meeting. Socrates Kolitsos, active politically and socially in the Mahoning Valley, is particularly active in the Orthodox community generally and the Greek Orthodox community specifically. His strong ties to his church and his ethnic connections are invaluable to his understanding of Greek traditions and to his relating such traditions to us. A sumptuous Greek meal and a young adult Greek dancing group made for an eventful evening. We met at Archangel Michael Greek Orthodox Church in Campbell.

The culture of Greece has evolved over thousands of years and is widely considered to be the cradle of Western culture and democracy. The Greeks introduced such important literary forms as epic and lyric poetry, history, tragedy, and comedy. In their pursuit of order and proportion, the Greeks created the ideal of beauty that strongly influenced Western art. The Greek community in America, including in the Mahoning Valley, value art, beauty, intellect, honor, truth, and hospitality; these values are usually related to the Greek Orthodox Church. Indeed, most of the customs and traditions are of a religious nature, Easter being the most important, with Christmas coming second. Among other important holidays are name days, Saints' Day celebrations, Greek Independence Day, baptisms, and Carnival.

Socrates Kolitsos

Despite some early internal problems among various factions of local Greeks, several strong churches emerged. These churches have had and still do have an enormous influence in the Valley. Among the Greek Orthodox churches that are still active in the Valley are St. John in Boardman, Archangel Michael in Campbell, and St. Nicholas in Youngstown. Their picnics, summer festivals, saint-day celebrations, and festivities have become major local attractions for Greeks and non-Greeks alike. At such festivities, people from all ethnic and religious backgrounds partake of the delicious offerings of Greek cuisine (as we enjoyed on this evening) and become immersed in the spirit of the festivities. It is not unusual to see all groups become moved by the staccato and melancholy strains of the traditional "bouzouki" as they try the intricate steps of Greek folk dancing. Kolitsos said, "a few interesting traditions that are retained, occasionally, if not universally, are the smashing of plates to ward off evil spirits, particularly at wedding receptions and the singing out 'opa' while dancing to express pleasure or good cheer."

Another important component of Greek culture is the family-yesterday and today. Traditionally, the Greek family has been patriarchal but with strong matriarchal underpinnings. Whether the wife and husband are both foreign-born or only one is or perhaps none but of Greek ancestry, there are distinct remnants of Greek culture. The Greek way of life, while assimilated to a considerable degree, still retains elements of their heritage. Even today, the extended family persists, consisting of a nuclear family and ageing parents, and even grandparents.

A third historical thread that runs through the Greek cultural experience is a profound respect for learning coupled with a deep reverence for the Greek language. The historical experience ingrained in the mind of the Greek parent was and is the conviction that whatever education he/she might have lacked, his children would not be deprived of educational opportunity. And, whatever the cost, the sacrifice must be made. In more immediate and practical terms and for the sake of material survival, there was, at the same time, the need to come to terms with the larger American culture.

Another dimension to the Greek experience in the Valley, as well as in America as a whole, has been the pivotal role of Greek American organizations and associations. Two groups that were profoundly important in the intragroup debate over the issue of assimilation were the American Hellenic Progressive Association (AHEPA) and the Greek-American Progressive Association (GAPA). AHEPA sought a more progressive agenda with complete assimilation; GAPA took a more conservative position advocating the preservation of the Greek language and Greek orthodoxy. Both organizations still exist, though it appears AHEPA won the day. Kolitsos also reminded us of the importance of the Greek coffeehouse. "It was a place where one could share his cares, relax, vent his political passions and entertain himself. It was also a clearing house for news regarding those in need, ill, or in trouble and ways to confront the problems. It was also here that business was transacted and planning for the building of churches and the founding of organizations. In the 1920s and 1930s, there were about ten or twelve coffeehouses in Youngstown and more than twenty in Warren." Today there remains one in Campbell and one in Warren.

Greek cuisine locally is the cuisine of Greece and the Greek diaspora. It is common in many Mediterranean countries and is founded upon olive oil and wine, vegetables, fish, and meat, including pork and lamb. (I could testify to its regimen of health by Betty and my stay in Greece for our 50th anniversary and how healthy we were upon our return.) Among the popular foods that have surely been retained locally are such delicacies as moussaka (eggplant or potato-based dished which includes ground meat), papoutsakia (stuffed eggplant), pastitsio (Greek lasagna), souvlaki (gyros), soutzoukakia (Greek meatballs) all of which we usually eat when our OCA meetings are held at a Greek church.

Dr. Louis Cassimatis, the local historian, has written that Greek immigrants have left a proud legacy in The Mahoning Valley. "Their spirit of sacrifice and their faith in themselves and their traditions enabled them and their children to reach the highest pinnacles of American society and enrich American life in the process."

Greek dance group of Archangel Church

In May, Dr. V.Coudray Perni, active in the Indian community as a participant and a speaker in the larger Mahoning Valley community, shared with us the history of the Indian people, some of their culture, and some of their traditions. His stories included unique elements of Indian traditions as well as some of the universal aspects of the people, rendering all of us more nearly alike than different. A beautifully attired Indian dance group performed for us, and samples of Indian food complemented our meal at Georgetown, the site of our meeting.

Kalacakra is a term that Dr. Perni said means wheel of time or time cycles. It is also the name of a series of Buddhist texts and a major practice in Indian Buddhism. Kalacakra also refers both to a patron deity and to the philosophies of the Kalacakra tradition. The tradition's origins are in India and contain teachings on cosmology, theology, philosophy, sociology, myth, prophecy, medicine, and yoga. Dr. Perni spoke of the wisdom of ancient India that addresses the law of the land, non-violence, truthfulness, non-stealing, and non-accumulation. He quoted Mahatma Gandhi, who said, "Happiness is when what you think, what you say, and what you do are in harmony." Dr. Perni continued with more discussion of the history of Indian Buddhism and Hinduism. As Buddhism began to decline around the 12th century, Hinduism stepped in and became the main religion of India. Dr. Perni went into considerable detail, using power point, to explain these developments.

Dr. V. Cordray Perni

Indian influence in the United States is not new. The writings of Emerson and Thoreau paved the way for Sanskrit to be taught at Harvard; the concepts of transcendental meditation, "Yoga" and the idea of re-incarnation are direct influences of Indian philosophies. The legacy of "meditation" is what we all have accepted in the form of relaxation techniques and "Yoga" as breathing exercises to pump more oxygen to our blood stream has been learned and taught in the U.S. Many non-Indians have learned and are learning Indian music and dance and performing them beautifully, as did our dancers on this evening.

Dr. Perni described the stages of life (Ashramas) as follows: "Brahmacharya-the first 20 years of life; Grihastha-the next 40 years that comprise married life and career; Vanaprastha-the next 20 years that represents the detachment from the material world and entering in contemplation and pilgrimage and Sanyasa-the conception of the mystic life to prepare the next life." He proceeded to a discussion of India's contribution to the world, which includes the invention of the number 0; the establishment of the world's first university, begun in Takshila in 700 B.C., where more than 10,500 students from all over the world studied more than 60 subjects; the establishment of Ayurveda, the earliest school of medicine among other firsts.

Though the Indian American emigration to this country and to our area is meager compared to many of the other groups we have addressed at OCA meetings; their contributions have been noteworthy. In the short time they have been here, many have come to meet real needs as practitioners in the medical profession. Others have become professors, including at YSU and Kent State; others are entrepreneurs and consulting engineers, software consultants, and motel owners, most holding at least bachelor's degrees.

Within the last few decades, the Indian immigrants have distinguished themselves as constructive American citizens, acculturating but retaining many of their traditions. They have an active Indian Association of Greater Youngstown, which worked closely with the International Institute of Youngstown during the 1970s and 1980s in bringing their cultural legacy of arts, food, and clothing to Youngstown. The Indian community has built a Hindu Temple in Girard after some years of renting a facility in Austintown, which was the site of an earlier meeting we had when addressing a former topic dealing with India. Many Hindus follow a vegetarian diet that may or may not include eggs and dairy products. Diet of non-vegetarians can include fish, poultry, and red meat (mainly lamb and goat). For slaughtering animals and birds for food, meat-eating Hindus often favor the quick death style of preparation of meat since Hindus believe that this method minimizes trauma and suffering to the animal. The Indian Association arranges food distribution to the poor on the occasion of their Diwali festival, and they have built a water fountain in the Mill Creek Park area where many people walk and jog. A continuing retaining of their heritage of learning and education is the phenomenon of children excelling at schools and colleges.

The cultural enrichment was provided by Dr. Anita Vallabh and several of her students. They divided their presentation into four segments: Ganesha Stuti represents Lord Ganesha, who is the remover of obstacles, widely worshiped at the beginning of ceremonies, events, and rituals for good outcomes; Dhanashree Thillanas are pure dance sequences portraying the ecstasy of movement; Achyutashtakem is a Lord Visnu Stotram describing Lord Krishna in his different forms; and Rajasthani Folk which is one of the prominent forms of folk dance, mostly known for its spins, flowing skirts and fluid hand movements. The fact that such speakers as Dr. Perni and Dr. Vallabh study, retain, and teach others about their culture is a testament to the enduring nature of these relatively new American citizens.

Indian dancers

All in all, many Indian Americans have adopted the Mahoning Valley as their chosen community and try to do as much as they can, according to their talents, to be productive community members.

Dr. Perni and Dancers

We closed the year in June, focusing on Croatia, with Betty Kolmacic Beelen as our speaker. The daughter of Croatian-born parents, author of an article about Croatia, and frequent visitor to the land of her ancestors, she portrayed a visual image of that land and its rich history and traditions, sharing how she learned of her roots and how the culture is celebrated today. A wonderful Croatian meal was prepared by the Croatian Center, Lodge #66 caterers, directed by Nada Bada, and Tamburitza music was provided by two groups led by Libby Fill and Kathy Zadravec. Films and slides of Croatia also filled the room.

Betty Beelen

Mrs. Beelen spoke of the country of her ancestors, knowledgeably and lovingly, indicating in her opening remarks about some of the traditions that have been retained: greeting all with "Dobra nam dosli" (It is good that you have come to us); reminding us of the site of our meeting, "Hrvatska Dom" (Croatian Home); offering a personal welcome with traditional offerings of bread (life's sustenance), salt (life's immortality), and fruit (prosperity) all on a ceremonial towel. She pointed out on a handout of important statistics regarding Croatia, after which she focused on the topic at hand, quoting ethnologist Antun Radic that "Tradition is like the casting in bronze, for all eternity, of the soul of a nation."

Beelen painted verbal images in a nearly poetic manner of a warm breeze coming out of the Mediterranean into the beautiful Adriatic Sea, ending an evening with a blood-red sun setting on the smooth, clear water. She invites us to have a glass of the full-bodied red wine from the Dalmatian coast vineyards, followed by a meal of Croatian potato salad, sarma (stuffed cabbage), kolbassi, breaded chicken, and grilled lamb, followed by Karlovac pivo (beer) and homemade slivovitz (plum brandy). These are among the many types of food and drink available in Croatia as well as in Youngstown, some of which we dined on this evening. And all of this to the melodic and sweet music of the Tamburitza string groups.

Croatia, a small country the size of West Virginia, with a population of about 4 ½ million people, is located along the Adriatic coast. It enjoys a Mediterranean climate, with a spectacular 1100 miles of coastline winding around innumerable bays and inlets, which rise to steep mountainous backdrops, flattening out to pebble beaches along the Adriatic. There are over 1,000 offshore islands, of which about 800 are inhabited. Seventy percent of the land is arable within the Pannonian plain, with the Drava and Sava Rivers running through the plain, making it an excellent region for agriculture. Centrally located is Croatia's capital, Zagreb, a busy modern cosmopolitan city; it is the political, commercial, and intellectual center of the nation. Betty spoke of the enduring struggle of Croatia "to establish and maintain their own identity, defying a legacy of foreign invasion and control, and punctuated most recently by the successful, but bitter, War of Independence in the early 1990s....By virtue of its location and centuries of political affiliation with European countries, Croatians are more culturally aligned with the West and generally consider themselves western Europe rather than eastern Balkan."

Beelen shared that "Our most authentic traditions have their roots in the villages among the peasant culture as opposed to the urban dwellers…whose life was more readily subject to foreign influence. Language and folklore play an important role in preserving

Croatian culture; life experiences are translated into verse, melodies, symbolic rituals, dance, and costumes. Folksongs and poems often attest to the sentiment and regard between family members and especially for Mother."

She continued with the suggestion that "hospitality is the hallmark of Croatian tradition," citing the importance of politeness and following rules of etiquette. Although some of the above have eased, some old customs remain: "newcomers find that initial meetings still tend to be a bit formal and reserved; honorific titles are used, and only close friends and family use first names without being invited. A firm handshake is appropriate while close friends greet each other with an embrace and a kiss on each cheek." Croatians are extremely proud of their culture and are strong nationalists, always remembering their heritage even as they became Americans.

Many of them left their homeland for America, coming in two waves: first, around the turn of the 20th century and again after World War II; they determined to become good Americans, despite their Croatian nationalism. The Croatian immigration to the Valley peaked between1915-1918. Betty said, "Men found jobs in the burgeoning steel industry, saved enough money to send for their families, who upon their arrival here sought out and found other Croatian families and organizations with whom they could share their culture."

Among the organizations that were helpful was the Croatian Fraternal Union (CFU), founded in 1894. With the encouragement of the CFU, hundreds of lodges formed throughout the country, including St. George Lodge #66, the site of our meeting. The Zajednicar, a bi-weekly newspaper published by the CFU, reports relevant news in English and Croatian. A local group that has helped perpetuate the Croatian culture was the all-male Strossmayer Singing Society, likely inspired by the klapa music of their homeland, which features the rich harmony of all-male voices, a'cappella. In 1958 the group dedicated picnic facilities at the Strossmayer Croatian Center in Vienna Township. During the summer months, Croatians assemble for traditional Sunday afternoon picnics featuring lamb roasted on an open barbeque pit, lots of Croatian food and beverages, some kolo dancing (a lively Croatian circle dance) to a Tamburitza group and on special occasions, an outdoor Catholic Mass.

Family is the basis of the Croatian social structure. Betty reminisced, "Perhaps not so common today, but in our family...we celebrated holidays together and spent as many Sundays with them as possible...around the table featuring my mother's famous chicken soup. Kums and kumas (godparents and others close enough to be honored with the title) are often considered extended family members. And name days rather than birthdays were traditionally celebrated within the family." Remembering the dead on joyous occasions is still common practice, as is visiting and adorning grave sites. "Visiting family and friends was a popular activity, and the fine needlework and lace so prized among Croatian women was often the result of hands kept busy during these visits. Doubtless, an activity not retained in today's society, but the needlework and lace produced by these women is still cherished," she added.

The Roman Catholic Church was and still is central to many Croatian families. Family history can often be traced through records of baptisms, confirmations, marriages, and burials; Betty and I were married at Sts. Peter and Paul Church, which was dedicated in 1913. Betty remembered, "As a child, I recall that men sat on one side of the church, women on the other, with children at the front under the watchful eyes of the nuns, customs lost today. On the Saturday before Easter, baskets of symbolic foods such as ham, green onions, horseradish, Easter eggs, kolbassi cheese, wine, Easter bread, and cakes, covered with an embroidered cloth, are still presented for blessing. And the beautiful mid-night Christmas Mass with its procession bearing the Christ child to the manger and the beautiful old Christmas carols is a cherished tradition retained."

Betty reveled in telling of how "Croatians love a good celebration. Christmas, Easter, St. George Feast Day, a baptism, a funeral-all require a good party. But nothing beats a good, old fashion Wedding celebration. Customs have blurred, and arranged marriages are a thing of the past, but occasionally some variant of an old-world tradition can still be found." Betty recounted the fun and humor of a Croatian village wedding filmed on You Tube by an acquaintance, Andrew Norris. "After the ceremony, the group returns to the bride's home for feasting, drinking, dancing, and singing, long into the night and perhaps into the next day, after which the bride and groom depart to his home where they, in days of old, will live with his family." This has not really been retained in America.

Betty continued with a spirited commentary about some of the old country's Christmas traditions. "Sadly, fewer and fewer are still practiced, but their beauty and simplicity merit recalling. The season begins on December 6th and lasts until early January. On the eve of December 6th when each child sets out a pair of polished shoes hoping that St. Nicholas will fill them with candies and other goodies-naughty children will find only a willow switch. On December 13th on the Feast of St. Lucy, the family plants wheat grains in a round dish tied with the Croatian tricolor ribbon. It remains the table centerpiece until the Feast of the Three Kings or Epiphany on January 6th, to be joined by the round, life-shaped Christmas Bread, which is baked on Christmas Eve. Together they symbolize the Eucharistic Christ who gave us eternal life. The father brings in the Yule Log on Christmas Eve, also. The Christmas tree would be decorated with fruit, walnuts, wrapped hard candies, lace ornaments, and a brightly colored Star of Bethlehem. A Manger Scene, first made of paper and a cloth figure, has evolved into elaborately carved displays of wood. Ornaments such as miniature heart-shaped honey spice cakes, an expression of love, complemented with the Christmas red apple, were used as a courting element. While many of these Christmas traditions may have been lost in their purest form, they are still acknowledged in some form, beginning with the tradition of Christmas Day, which is still considered a solemn day to be spent with family. Another that is retained in the 'old world' and occasionally in America is the house blessing by the parish priest sometime during the month of January. With the limited number of priests, this custom has declining adherence."

Betty concluded with, "Alex Haley advised about researching one's roots: 'Find the good and praise it'-well, that's what I tried to do in a small way this evening. There's still a warm breeze coming across the Adriatic, and the moon sends a golden swatch shimmering across the water. That sound of Tamburitza music in the distance has become more distinct, for, as usual, there's a celebration of some kind going on somewhere in the village. If we happened to stroll by, we'd surely be invited to join the festivities with a hearty 'Dobra nam dosli!' But for us, the evening is over. And so we part with a warm embrace, the traditional kiss on each cheek, and a fond 'Laku noc-Doc se vidjemo' (good night, until we meet again.)"

Map of Croatia

"Thank you for accompanying me on this journey to Croatia, the land of my ancestors. I hope you've enjoyed it as much as I have. Hvala (thank you)!" We of the OCA thank Betty Kolmacic Beelen for her journey to Croatia, sharing traditions that are both lost and retained.

Kathy Zadravec (center) & her Group

Libby Fill (center) & her Group

OCA Crowd at St. George Croatian Center,
Lodge #66

The 2013-2014 twenty-seventh year of the Ohio Cultural Alliance continued with the topic "Old World Traditions-Lost and Retained" for a second year. The last year was a success in terms of the number of attendees (averaging 227 at each monthly meeting), the variety of countries explored, the knowledgeable speakers, the cultural enrichment provided, the delicious meals, and the variety of venues. A new feature for this current year was the hosting of a community leader, a "difference maker" who was invited to give a 5- minute presentation about his/her contribution to the community. While with us, they were also able to learn more about the OCA.

We began our year in September with Fred Ghossain as our speaker, who shared with us the personal and general traditions of Lebanon and other parts of the Arab world. April Azhar, in colorful costumes and with considerable grace and ability, demonstrated the tradition of belly dancing. We met at the Embassy Banquet Center in Boardman, where we dined on cuisine with a Middle Eastern flavor. Our first 5-minute presentation was given by Connie Hawthorne, a registered nurse and supervisor at New Destiny Treatment Center, which administers to those with various addictions. Her story was compelling as she shared with us the sadness of addiction and the joy of recovery.

Fred Ghossain presented a fascinating story of his arrival in New York in 1962 after considerable obstacles and anguish. His father emigrated from Lebanon to New York City in 1954, leaving his mother, himself, and three siblings until he could pave the way for them to join him; his mother passed away when he was only five years old. After living with his grandmother for a few years, Fred, as the oldest male and following custom dictates, assumed charge of his siblings though only eight years old himself. The journey of these four youngsters took 16 days from Beirut, Lebanon, to Alexandria, Egypt, to Naples, Italy, to New York City, where his father was waiting for them.

His father never finished high school and had $17.00 when he arrived in Springfield, Massachusetts, in 1954. As a hard worker determined to make a better life for himself and his family, he got a job as a kitchen helper in a Sheraton Hotel, sending most of his money to his family in Lebanon. Ghossain said, "After a few months, the kitchen managers in the hotel saw a lot of potential and eagerness in him as a hard worker and decided to send him to Ithaca, NY culinary school, and he ended up being the head chef in the hotel." After a few years of accumulated vacation time, he traveled to Youngstown to visit a friend from Lebanon. While there, he met Harry Humble, who owned the Hub restaurant in Hubbard, which Fred's father ended up purchasing.

The earliest immigrants from the Eastern Mediterranean were lumped together, making it difficult to differentiate the Lebanese immigrants from the Syrian. Neither of the countries became a nation-state until the mid-20th century as records and statistics were generally combined, all making for a confusing situation. Ghossain remarked, "A land of varied beautiful terrain, Lebanon encompasses coastline, mountain and fertile growing regions such as Bekaa Valley. The population of the country is made up of ethnic groups from every Middle Eastern country, which is reflective of Lebanon's long history." Ghossain suggested that many Lebanese immigrants came to America; others emigrated to other parts of the world. "From their Phoenician ancestors, they have inherited an aptitude for business dealings and fondness for travel. And they usually blend in easily with the societies to which they migrate. But whether at home or abroad, the Lebanese remain intensely proud of their culture and heritage."

Fred continued, "Family is the core of Lebanese social identity, and loyalty to family has traditionally trumped all other allegiances. In Lebanese culture, age is greatly respected, and respect for parents is extremely valued. They also possess a great sense of honor, dignity, humor, and hospitality (it is considered rude not to offer food and drink to a guest). Fathers and eldest males are the heads of the family; shame is avoided at all costs; insults are taken very seriously, particularly to one's name. A person's name and honor are their most cherished possessions. Roles are often defined by gender: women are to be protected; men are undisputed heads of families but take the concerns of other members into consideration."

Ghossain admonished that "Americanization, with its emphasis upon youth, personal achievement, individualization, and independence, has eroded some of these beliefs and practices." The Arab respect for age has diminished, the belief in family honor has lessened, family roles are less gender-defined, hospitality has changed (doors are now locked), people are preoccupied with their own personal concerns, and new immigrants are not helped as much.

Lebanese and Lebanese Americans are deeply religious, with Christianity dominant with Moslems constituting a significant minority. Lebanese belong to one of three Christian rites: the Maronite, the Eastern Orthodox, and Melkite. In the U.S., all three services are sung partly in English, confirmation, and baptism are administered, and use bread soaked in wine for the Eucharist; the marriage ceremony includes the blessing of rings, the crowning of the bride and groom as queen and king, and they share the bread and wine as their first meal together. Arranged marriages are rare, and divorce rates are low.

The occupational profile of Lebanese Americans is very broad; although retail occupations tending to self-employment, managerial and professional positions, such as medicine, law, engineering, and computer science, are well represented. Lebanese cuisine is the Mediterranean: pita bread, hummus, fava bean dip, and rice are staples. Pasta, yogurt, and olives are on most tables. Red meat and chicken are common, but pork is less popular since it is forbidden under Islamic law.

Ghossain ended his remarks with personal experiences of how he used his father as a role model, earned a degree from YSU, married, and raised three children. He recounted how his father, brother, and he found a niche and pursued it. That niche was to start a business making pita and flat breads, using his grandmother's recipe. Starting in their garage, they expanded to a small building on Market Street in Youngstown and finally built their current 16,000 square feet building on South Avenue. They sell their baked products all over the country. They now make healthy Mediterranean foods, including hummus, taboule, kibbee, grape leaves, a variety of vegetarian bean salads, pastries, and a variety of Middle Eastern products and spices.

As an assimilated American with strong Lebanese roots, he concluded: "It has been a great journey, and I'm glad we came to this country. I'm proud of being an American citizen, proud of my family, proud of our church, proud of all hard-working immigrants, especially the Lebanese Americans, and proud of our community."

Fred Ghossain (on left)

April Azhar

Our October meeting featured Rosemary Cardoza, who spoke of her Romanian traditions as we enjoyed a Romanian meal, watched a film of Transylvania and the capital, Bucharest, and toured the Holy Resurrection Romanian Orthodox Church and museum in Warren, the site of our meeting. Our special guest was Tom Humphries, executive director of the Mahoning-Trumbull County Regional Chamber of Commerce, who spoke for 5 minutes about the organization.

Rosemarie Cardozo shared her Romanian traditions, based on considerable research, which resulted in a book about her fellow Romanians in the U.S., which had special emphasis on Romanians in the Salem, Ohio, area. At least 175,000 Romanian immigrants came through Ellis Island during the generation after the 1880s. They came in dribbles before 1900; in large numbers from 1900 to 1924; in smaller numbers after World War II, and others more recently, since the fall of the dictator, Ceausescu, in 1989.

Rosemary Cardoza

Cardoza sketched the history of Romania, saying that the country is in southeastern Europe, bounded by Ukraine, Hungary, Bulgaria, Serbia, and the Black Sea. It is an organic state in the sense that its boundaries often change, and it has developed as a result of interaction with many cultures. It was forged through the blending of the Dacians with the Romans. They were conquered by Germanic invasions from the north of Europe and by Tartars from eastern Asia; then they fell under Hungarian control, after which they came under Russian, Turkish and Austrian rule, and most recently under Nazi and Soviet control. So, Romania became a blend of diverse cultures. The blend can be noted in much of Romanian culture, notably in their churches and many icons representing Byzantine, Gothic, Romanesque and Oriental influences.

The Romanians came to America impelled by both push and pull factors: pushed by depressed economic and social conditions and pulled by the need of the U.S., including the Mahoning Valley, for unskilled workmen. Most Romanian immigrants settled in the industrial heartland of the mid-Atlantic and Great Lakes region, including the Valley. After securing a job and bringing the rest of the family to America, Romanians participated in the acculturation of America while trying to retain some of their own traditions. They became active in the community-at first, largely in their own ethnic community and eventually in the larger society as they easily adapted to the American ways.

Churches were among the most important types of community involvement, with three important churches founded early in the 20th century: Holy Trinity Romanian Orthodox Church on Wilson Avenue dedicated in 1911 (relocated in 1946 to Wick Avenue); St. Mary's Greek Catholic Romanian Church on Prospect Avenue in 1906; and Holy Resurrection Romanian Church in Warren, founded in 1917. They each had women's, men's, and youth organizations. Seven Romanian language newspapers were published at one time or another in the Youngstown area. The last one was the Solia.

The most striking thing about Romanian culture is the strong folk traditions that have survived to this day in the rural communities in Romania; some were brought to the new world. Romanians' rich folk traditions have been nourished by many sources, some of which predate the Roman occupation. Traditional folk arts include wood carving, ceramics, weaving, and embroidery of costumes, household decorations, dance, and richly varied folk music. Although most of these traditions have been lost, remnants of them are retained in some households on holidays and at commemorative festivals and dinners. Music and dance have always represented a lively part of Romanian folklore. Party music is very lively and shows both Balkan and Hungarian influences. Sentimental music, however, is the most valued, and Romanians consider the most important the doina (a sad song either about one's home or about love). The dances are also lively and are practiced throughout Romania by large numbers of professional and amateur groups, thus keeping the tradition alive, at least in Romania (less so in the Valley). Hora is the most famous of group dances, but men's folk dances, such as calusari, are very complex and have been declared by UNESCO to be "Masterpieces of the Oral and Intangible Heritages of Humanity." Both Rosemarie and I have, in past years, done such dancing that is still practiced by smaller numbers at special events, such as at a past OCA meeting when Father Antonescu spoke, and a group from Akron danced.

The cuisine of Romania has the same influence as the rest of Romanian culture. From the Roman times, there still exists the simple placinta (doughnut or pie); the Turks brought mititei (fried meatballs) or perisoare in a soup called ciorba; from the Austrians, there is schnitzel; from the Hungarians, their ornate pastries. Without a doubt, one of the most popular dishes, and could probably be called the national dish, is sarmale (stuffed cabbage), and is often served with mamaliga (palenta or corn meal mush), usually served with tocana (chicken stew). At Romanian events that Rosemarie attends, such a meal is served, often with chicken noodle soup.

Romanians have always loved their adopted land and readily moved into the mainstream of American life. Romanians present the classic rise of an immigrant group. They quickly adopted the American urban life, whether in Youngstown, Salem, or elsewhere, and their acceptance of education as a means of upward mobility facilitated their rapid gain of middle-class status. With the decline of the numbers of Romanians in the Valley, the churches lost attendees, and many of the traditions were lost. However, those churches and organizations that remain still adhere to some of the traditions, particularly in the area of cuisine.

Holy Resurrection Church-Warren

Holy Trinity Church - Youngstown

OCA members met in November to learn of Russian traditions as shared by Dr. Alexander "Sasha" Pantsov, a native of Russia and now an American citizen who teaches at Capital and Ohio State Universities. (He also taught at YSU for one year as a replacement for a colleague on leave.) A talented balalaika ensemble from the Akron area delighted us with beautiful Russian selections. The group consisted of 25 members and was under the direction of Jane Malachany. We met at Old North Church in Canfield; the meal was prepared by Carolyn Catering. Our special 5-minute talk was offered by Dr. Randy Dunn, YSU president.

Dr. Pantsov had previously spoken brilliantly to us about Russian history and Russian emigration to America. His specialties are Russian history, Chinese history, Russian-Sino Relations, and Western European history. He again traced some of the rich history of the Russian people, their customs and traditions, with a little emphasis upon lost traditions.

The culture and traditions of the Russians have a long tradition of achievement in many fields, especially in literature, folk dancing, philosophy, classical music, traditional folk-music, ballet, architecture, painting, and cinema. Russian traditions consist of a very interesting blend of Christian and pagan customs. For many centuries they have determined the rhythm and the lifestyle of the nation-from the clearly written annual calendar to marriage and other rituals. Even non-religious people often enjoy celebrations of national holidays and participate in certain rituals. Pantsov reported, "many of them survive in Russia, but not usually in America. Popular holidays such as New Year, Christmas, Epiphany, and Maslenitsa come with many traditions. New Year is accompanied by making wishes, throwing snowballs, building snowmen and forts, and sledding. Christmas and Epiphany are very religious holidays that are celebrated in the Orthodox Church as family members gather. At Christmastime and many other holidays, it was popular to tell fortunes. Maslenitsa is widely known as Sun and spring festival time; its main traditions are fun, jokes and pancakes. In the old days, Maslenitsa was for remembrance of the dead. Ultimately, it was changed from a time of sadness to a time for fun."

Special Russian dishes include blini (thin Russian pancakes), pelmeni (dumplings), beef stroganoff, syrniki (pancakes of cottage cheese, eggs, and flour), kasha (porridge), borscht, okroshka (cold soup) and pirozhki (puffed pastries with potatoes, meat cabbage or cheese). From observation over the years, some of the local Russian churches serve these foods on special occasions and festivals. Borscht is the most well-known, with every Russian household having its favorite recipe for beet-based vegetable soup.

We were told, previously, by Dr. Melissa Smith of YSU that "culturally, Russians have exerted an influence in the Valley beyond their physical numbers: Russian language is taught at YSU; numerous lecturers have spoken here, and educational travel and student exchanges of faculty and students to Russia is popular. Beyond that, the local classical radio station, WYSU, estimates that 5-10 % of its music is by Russian composers." Additionally, Alexandra Vansuch (of Russian and Slovak descent) has brought a contemporary Russian flavor to the theater scene with collaborative projects with YSU on producing works by Russian women playwrights. Folk arts and culture are represented at regular Russian festivals held at the various Eastern Orthodox churches and at a Russian booth at the Canfield Fair. Traditional foods remain a favorite means of retaining cultural identity. Easter celebrations are connected with the blessing of food baskets at church, dyeing Easter eggs, the preparation of the traditional Easter bread, and the rich dessert, paska. So despite their numbers in the Mahoning Valley (and in Columbus, where Dr. Pantsov teaches), Russians in America have retained some elements of their traditions.

We were reminded of the influence of Russian traditions by the St. Nicholas Balalaika Orchestra from Mogadore, Ohio, who concluded the evening with songs of sadness and solace, humor and dance, as well as melancholic longing and heroic pathos. The close connection with real life is ever present in the music of the Russian people.

Dr. Alexander "Sasha" Pantsov

St. Nicholas Balalaika Orchestra from Akron, under direction of Jane Malachany

Polish traditions were featured in December as Aundrea Cika Heschmeyer related memories and traditions of Poland. Colorful displays and memorabilia adorned the Holy Trinity Serbian Church Hall, which added tangible evidence of Polish culture. Cultural enrichment was provided by Jacek (keyboard) and Dorotea Sobieski (soprano singer), offering beautiful Polish selections, and Larry Kozlowski, who spoke of Polish Christmas traditions as he transformed himself from Santa Claus to the much-revered Saint Nicholas. The area "difference maker" from the community who gave a 5-minute presentation was Sister Isabell Rudge, representing Beatitude House, an Ursuline Sisters project and recipient of today's OCA's "community project".

The culture of Poland is the product of its geography and distinct historical evolution, which is closely connected to its intricate thousand-year history. Polish culture forms an important part of western civilization and the western world, with significant contributions to art, music, philosophy, mathematics, science, politics, and literature. It is theorized that ethnic Poles are the combination of descendants of West Slavs and people indigenous to the region, including Celts, Balts, and Germanic tribes, which were gradually Polonized after Poland's Christianization by the Catholic Church in the 10th century. Over time Polish culture has been influenced by its interweaving ties with many ethnic and minority groups living in Poland. The people of Poland have traditionally been seen as hospitable to artists from abroad and eager to follow cultural and artistic trends popular in other countries. These factors have contributed to the versatile nature of Polish arts. Mrs. Heschmeyer asserted, "many of these traditions have been retained in Poland and even locally in the form of festivals, holiday celebrations, and organizations."

Holidays and ceremonial occasions are widely recognized in Poland and America, including the Mahoning Valley. Namedays and weddings are among the most significant occasions and center on individuals. Common first names are noted in published calendars, along with holidays, so people know when to acknowledge one's nameday. Such celebrations typically feature poultry, cakes, and other party foods. At weddings, the bride and groom are greeted with bread and salt (the essentials of life) upon their return from church. The Christmas season is the traditional time for baking cookies, honey-spice cakes, babka cakes, and cheese-dough apple cakes. The most solemn family gathering is the Christmas Eve supper, called Wigilia. Families gather to share the oplatek, the thin white wafer, followed by a number of meatless dishes, including fish. Paczki (Polish style donuts) are the traditional pastry eaten on Shrove Tuesday and on Fat Thursday (a day when people eat large amounts of sweets and cakes that are afterwards forbidden until Easter Day.) At Easter, the tradition is to consume food blessed at the church on Holy Saturday. One standard item is hard-boiled eggs. During fall harvest festivals, the fruits of the fields are blessed, and cereals and bread made from freshly threshed wheat are eaten as well as placed on graves on All Saints Day.

Overall Polish foods include kielbasa, pierogi (filled with potatoes, cabbage, cheese, or holiday fruits), pyzy (meat-filled dough balls), golabki (meat and rice stuffed cabbage), and soups such as flaki, rosol, grzybowa (mushroom soup) and pomidorowa (tomato soup). And hospitality is key.

Andrea Cika Hechmeyer suggested that "local Polish retain some of these foods, customs, and traditions: pre-Easter blessing of the baskets, celebrating the Polish language in Mass and song, making pierogis a staple of Poles and non-Poles (and spelled a variety of ways), and adhering to Wigilia with family and friends. While a number of grocery stores carry some products which Polish consume, at least one is devoted to traditional delicacies. So, again, as Polish and other immigrants were assimilated into the larger culture, many of the traditions have been retained and are cherished."

Nothing could be more beautiful than the gorgeous voice of Dorotea Sobieski and the incredible transformation Larry Kozlowski made from a delightfully dressed Santa Claus to a bold and colorful St. Nicholas, all while reciting important customs and traditions of the Polish people.

Aundrea Cika Heschmeyer

Larry Kozlowski from Santa Claus to St. Nicholas

Our focus in January was Philippine traditions as described by Dr. Escarlito Sevilla and as pictured in the beautiful and vivid images, he showed on a screen. His wife, Lita, directed a group who performed traditional dances, including the famous bamboo dance. Our special "difference maker" was Suzanne Barbati, executive director of WOW, an indoor, downtown Youngstown facility dedicated to children. We met at Mt. Carmel Church Social Center, with Lou Fusillo Caterers preparing our meal. We also announced a donation of more than $1,000 that our members made to assist the Philippine Red Cross help victims of the recent hurricane and tsunami in their country.

The culture of the Philippines is a combination of cultures of the East and West. Filipino identity was created primarily as a result of pre-colonial cultures, colonial influences, and foreign traders intermixing and gradually evolving together. The advent of colonial rule in the islands marked the beginning of the Philippines as an entity, a collection of Southeast Asian countries under the Spanish Empire. Chinese influence has also been felt throughout Southeast Asia through trade, specifically by the Ming dynasty from as early as the 19th century. The blending of indigenous, colonial, and external influence is very evident in the historic arts and traditions of the country.

The Spanish Empire conquered the islands between the 16th and 17th centuries, resulting in Christianity spreading and dominating throughout the nation and influencing the religion and beliefs of the natives. Then, the Philippines became a U.S. territory for almost 50 years. Influence from the U.S. is manifested in the wide use of the English language and media and in the modern culture and clothing of the present-day Philippines.

The mix of influences is also evident in Philippine traditions and holidays. Filipinos know how to party; the calendar is replete with holidays and festivals. Every municipality has a patron saint whose day is celebrated extravagantly in the homes and in the streets. Residents anticipate the event for months in advance. A feast is prepared, and they go from house to house to taste dishes. The church and plaza are decorated with lights and bunting, and a procession is held with dancing and music. According to the festival, Filipinos dress up in vivid costumes, sporting masks, and headdresses. Fireworks and firecrackers complete the excitement. While not so practiced in America, such activities are discussed and revered at American-Filipino conventions and meetings.

Holidays include Christmas; Rizal Day, which takes place on December 30th making it part of the New Year's Day celebration; Easter; All Saints Eve and secular holidays like Bataan Death March, Labor Day, and Independence Day on June 12th. Sino-Filipinos celebrate the Chinese New Year in Chinatown, Manila, and Muslims enjoy the Islamic feasts for the end of Ramadan and Haj.

Filipinos cook a variety of foods influenced primarily by Indian, Chinese, and indigenous cuisine. The Spanish colonizers brought with them produce from the Americas, such as chile peppers, tomatoes, corn, and potatoes. Rice is a staple and is usually eaten together with other dishes. Other popular dishes include afritada, asada, tapa, empanada mani, paksiw (fish or pork cooked in vinegar and water with some spices like garlic and pepper), kare-kare (ox-tail stew), among many others. Popular snacks and desserts abound chicharon (deep-fried pork or chicken skin), halo-halo (crushed ice with evaporated milk, flan, sliced tropical fruit, and sweet beans) white rice cakes, among others. Lechon is a pork dish (roasted pig) from Spain but also has native pre-colonial origins. It is sometimes called one of the unofficial national dishes and is traditionally prepared throughout the year for special occasions, festivals, and holidays.

As a final word, we were all mesmerized by the bamboo stick dance performed skillfully by a group of local Filipinos. It is a traditional dance, which involved a pair of bamboo poles, and is considered the oldest traditional dance in the Philippines. It is good to see some of the Philippine traditions retained and shared with us in the Mahoning Valley.

Dr. Escarlito Sevilla

Young Philippine students performing bamboo dance

Hungarian traditions were discussed in February by Dr. Stephen Hanzely, YSU Physics, and Chemistry Department. Having been born in Hungary and still maintaining some of the traditions here, he spoke poignantly of some of these traditions and memories. A Youngstown Symphony quartet played beautiful Hungarian melodies to complete the evening. The meeting was held at The Georgetown Banquet Center, whose caterers prepared a meal with some Hungarian elements. Our 5-minute speaker was Bob Hannon, former television personality and current "voice" of YSU football on WKBN radio and currently local United Way Executive Director.

As with most of the countries we have treated in this series, Hungary has experienced fluctuating borders and varied influences. Of its 10 million people, 70% are Roman or Greek Catholics; the rest is a mixture of Protestants, Eastern Orthodox, Jewish, and smatterings of others. 90% of the population is ethnic Hungarian, with the largest minority Roma or Gypsy at about 4%, followed by people of German, Serbian, Slovak, or Romanian ancestry. All of these groups brought their customs, traditions, foods, music, and religious observances with them. Many of these were retained in their original form; others morphed or evolved to reflect the new realities of life. Some were retained even during the emigration to America.

There have been three waves of immigrants from Hungary to our shores: the largest, by far, occurred between the years 1880-1914; next came the so-called DP's or displaced persons during the late 1940s, after World War II; and the third wave arrived after the 1956 Hungarian Revolution. The first group consisted largely of poor peasants and tradesmen; the DPs were mainly middle class, professional people, forced to leave for political reasons; the third group-the, the 1956 refugees-were in their late teens or early 20s, young, energetic, well-educated, and ambitious. (Our speaker was part of this group).

This leads Dr. Hanzely to address the precise theme of this series: traditions lost and retained. In addition to the early groups hastening to acculturate in this new land, Dr. Hanzely asserts "that members of the first two groups have virtually died out, leaving the third group and their descendants to carry on the Hungarian traditions they brought with them." He offered evidence by citing examples of retaining traditions in the Mahoning Valley: a Hungarian radio program on WKTL, Struthers every other Saturday; an annual Hungarian Day celebration around August 20th to honor the founder of Hungary and its first Christian King St. Stephen; an annual picnic at Scenic View near Seven Springs, Pennsylvania; an annual program around March 15th to commemorate the start of the 1848 Hungarian War of Independence; and an annual program around October 23rd to commemorate the start of the 1956 Hungarian Revolution.

Over the years, there were additional efforts to retain some of the Hungarian traditions through the churches and other organizations. Hanzely told of the seven Hungarian parishes that were active in Youngstown during the first half of the 20th century-two Roman Catholic, a Greek Catholic, a Presbyterian, a Hungarian Reformed, and a Baptist, plus the Franciscan Friary on Belle Vista Avenue. "The late 1960s and early 1970s" he said, "also witnessed the emergence of several ecumenical programs organized by the priests and ministers of Youngstown's Hungarian parishes," which also led to a 20-year run of a weekly half-hour radio program of religious and cultural content. Several organizations also strived to perpetuate Hungarian traditions; the largest and most influential was the American-Hungarian Federation of Churches and Societies, founded in 1916. The Federation has functioned successfully "to keep alive Hungarian culture and traditions, to organize and sponsor the commemoration of Hungarian national and religious holidays, and to educate the Youngstown community about the history and heritage of the Hungarian people."

In a personal way, Dr. Hanzely speaks, writes, and reads Hungarian, enjoys listening to Hungarian music, watching old Hungarian movies, eating Hungarian food, and observing Hungarian holidays. Each year he and his wife sponsor a day's worth of programming on YSU's radio station, WYSU, on March 15th, the most important national holiday in Hungary. He confessed, this consummate American, that "When in the company of other Hungarians, I try to observe Hungarian customs and traditions and follow Hungarian etiquette-which, at times, can be awkward, surprising and confusing. It's almost as if one has to assume a different personality."

Dr. Hanzely continued with a discussion of some of the Hungarian customs and traditions, some lost and some retained-some even retained in the Mahoning Valley

- Name Day's are celebrated as well as birthdays. Birthdays are usually celebrated with immediate families; name days are widely known and celebrated.
- Wedding rings or wedding bands are placed on the left hand until the wedding, after which it is placed on the right hand.
- Storks are Hungarians favorite bird, although their national bird is the Turul, a mythical bird associated with the origin of the Magyars (Hungarian people).
- Personal pronouns can be confusing as Hungarians have only one third-person pronoun; there is no he or she.
- Two distinctly different modes of language exist-formal and informal. Such language is important in relations between adults and children, between couples courting, and among friends, and it has implications relating to social hierarchy. All of this may be only symbolic, Hanzely said, "but this collapse of interpersonal hierarchy can be tricky to sustain; couples may even oscillate between the formal and informal."
- In Hungary, church bells are rung vigorously at noon, commemorating Hungary's victory over the Turks in 1456.
- The tooth fairy does not exist in Hungary.
- The first day of the Hungarian week is Monday, and the date is written year, month, and day as 2014, February 3.
- New Year's Day is a time for consuming lentils, which makes people wealthy, along with some form of pork for personal luck and rolling out strudel dough which guarantees long life. One should not eat fish, which will swim away with your luck, or poultry which will make your life fly away.
- Christmas and Saint Nicholas Day are important for religious and secular reasons. The familiar Christian religious traditions are adhered to, but Dr. Hanzely told of more secular traditions: Christmas in Hungary is on December 6th when St. Nicholas visits with his two assistants, one of whom is a good angel who gives gifts to the good children and a mean goblin who punishes bad children and gives them a bundle of twigs (since most children are good and bad, even they get some presents). The parents usually put up an elaborate tree on Christmas Eve; it consists of holiday candies, wrapped colorfully, with chocolate on the outside and flavored jellies on the inside. When decorated, the baby Jesus rings a bell, after which the children rush in to see what gifts the baby Jesus has brought them. A lavish dinner follows, and eating and visiting continue for the 2-day holiday. Hanzely said, "Christmas is the holiday of love and heart."
- Easter is a two-day holiday that follows Christian traditions around the world but with some special twists. Men and boys visit their women, relatives, and friends, greeting girls and women with short poems and dousing them with buckets of water

or sprinkling them with cologne. The women and girls greeted the men with dessert and beverages.

- May Tree is a time for courting where the young man chops down a tree, removes the bark, ties ribbons on the top, and the boy writes a ribbon note to the girl. After a month, the father reads the note and now knows about the boy.
- Halloween in not celebrated but All Saint s Day and All Souls Day are observed on November 1 and 2, respectively.

Dr. Hanzely (as you might expect from a professor) included a test regarding Hungary as well as an interesting sketch of Hungarian wine making, from the favorable climate to the types of wine produced, to the most respected of the wines-the Tokaji wine, from the Tokaji region of Hungary. Dr. Hanzely concluded with, "In Rome, it was the Tokaji wine, which filled the Pope's chalice during Mass. The kings of Poland always celebrated with a glass of Tokaji, and the Russians tsars toasted their foreign dignitaries with wines from the Tokaji region."

YSU Quartet

Dr. Stephen Hanzely

In March, we met to hear Eileen Gilmartin-Turocy, known publicly as TV personality Casey Malone, speak about Irish traditions as they were practiced in her home and perpetuated for many years throughout the community by her late father, County Prosecutor Attorney Vincent Gilmartin. She shared oft-heard audio of a song by her father, complete with a strong Irish brogue. Michael Shaffer and three brothers regaled us with Irish instrumental and vocal selections. Dr. Rick Billak, in a 5-minute address, explained his role as founder and director of the local Community Corrections Association. The meeting was held at St. George Croatian Lodge #66, catered and directed by Nada Bada.

Malone first gave us a brief history of the land of her father and his ancestors. Thought to have been originally the home of hunter-gatherers in prehistoric times, Ireland saw the arrival of the Celts and Gauls around 500 B.C. Normans and Vikings invaded Ireland around the 12th century. Then during the 16th century, the English began a long campaign to conquer and colonize the island. During times of conflict and famine, especially during the Great Potato Famine of 1845, the Irish migrated to other lands, taking many of their traditions with them. In 1921, as a result of the Irish War for Independence from Great Britain, the island was portioned into the Irish Republic and Northern Ireland. Casey believed that through all the upheavals, the Irish adapted to the different influences, making a vibrant culture, some of which was brought to America, including the Mahoning Valley.

Religion has been an important part of Irish society since ancient times. Before Christianity came to Ireland, the ancient Celts followed a druidic religious system. According to tradition, St. Patrick, the 5th-century Christian missionary and bishop of Ireland, arrived around 432 A.D. With the introduction of Christianity, changes in traditions and culture followed. Some of the traditions are age-old, and some are retained to this day. Many of the old Irish blessings are kept alive by people from all over the world and are generally about welcoming, warmth, and turning a negative situation into a positive one. An example is, "wherever you go and whatever you do, may the luck of the Irish be with you."

Along with religion, holidays are an important part of Irish society. These holidays feature a mix of Celtic and Christian traditions, including Celtic seasonal celebrations. Imbolc celebrated on February 1-2, marks the beginning of spring; St. Patrick's Day on March 17th originally celebrated Christianity coming to Ireland but now celebrates all things Irish around the world; Beltane on April 30th-May 1st marks the beginning of summer, and is celebrated with bonfires and decorating homes with flowers; Litha occurs on the summer solstice and is celebrated with bonfires and dancing; Lughnasadh marks the beginning of the harvest season and is celebrated on August 1st, often with feasts of newly harvested crops, music, and games; Samhain, held on October 31st is the Celtic New Year's Eve, which marks the end of the harvest or All Hallows' Eve/Halloween with bonfires, wearing costumes and honoring ancestors; and also Christmas and Easter celebrated similarly in most other Christian countries. With the exceptions of Easter, Christmas, and St. Patrick's Day, most of the other holidays are not celebrated in America.

The Irish have a rich literary tradition of storytelling using myths, fables, poetry, rhymes, and sayings that help explain Irish history and culture. Along with folklore, traditional Irish music has roots in the past. Traditional Irish music includes love songs, drinking songs, dancing songs, funny songs, and ballads with or without instrumental accompaniment. The Irish music is presented abundantly in the Mahoning Valley, as are the Irish step-dancing groups. These groups entertain throughout the year but really "strut their stuff" on and around St. Patrick's Day, which is huge in the Valley. Indeed, Casey Malone has often had an important participating role in the local yearly St. Patrick's Day parade. The music is ubiquitous, the step-dancing is lively, and the beer flows freely. This holiday and the Catholic religion continue to put front and center the presence of the Irish in the Mahoning Valley since they first came to the Valley in the 1840s and afterward.

The first Irish to reach the Mahoning Valley were the Ulster Irish, who arrived in the late 18th and early 19th centuries. Many first settled in Pennsylvania and then migrated into the Valley, looking for economic opportunity. The earliest known permanent Irish presence was Daniel Shehy, who accompanied John Young in 1796 on an expedition to examine a 25-square-mile section of land he was about to purchase from the Connecticut Land Company. Young did not remain, but Shehy bought 1,000 acres and, along with his wife, Jane McLain Shehy, joined a small group of pioneers who formed Youngstown.

The Irish rapidly established a presence in business and safety services, including a number of police and firemen. Despite their humble beginnings, it was not long until they opened a dry goods store, a prosperous construction company, became banking principals, and started a moving and transfer company, even though many Irish worked in the coal, iron, and steel industries of Youngstown.

The Irish, as the earliest group of Catholic immigrants, played a key role in the rise of the Catholic community in Youngstown. Irish Catholics formed the St. Columba's congregation in 1847, building what would eventually be the cathedral for the Diocese of Youngstown. The Ursuline Sisters led parochial education in the city. The first bishop of the Diocese of Youngstown, James McFadden, was an Irish American, as were James Malone and Thomas Tobin. Many sons of Irish families have served as priests; indeed, the matrix for the Catholic Church in the Mahoning Valley was Irish, in the opinion of many non-Irish.

Irish American involvement in cultural, fraternal, and benevolent organizations in the Mahoning Valley is yet another way that the Irish strove to promote and perpetuate their traditions and customs. Some organizations, such as the various local chapters of the Ancient Order of Hibernians (AOH), are part of a national network of Irish cultural preservation and connection with the homeland. It is the oldest Irish Catholic lay organization in America. In mid-19th century America, the AOH aimed to protect Irish immigrants and clergy from attacks perpetuated by nativist-minded Americans who saw the rapid influx of Irish immigrants as a threat to their cultural and economic well-being. Others, such as the Irish American Archival Society, are locally based and focus more closely on preserving Irish traditions in the Mahoning Valley. Former speaker Sally Pallante and current speaker Casey Malone serve the community well in this regard. Whether nationally connected or locally tied, Irish organizations function to connect individuals of Irish heritage and to celebrate all things, Irish.

Besides the Valley AOH chapters, Irish Americans are involved in groups such as the Knights of Columbus, Muintir na h'Eireann, and the Mahoning Valley Gaelic Society, which aims to promote knowledge and appreciation of Irish culture and traditions. The local Irish Heritage Society does similarly. Many of these organizations help to celebrate their Irish heritage in the Valley in St. Patrick's Day parades and cultural events, such as the Festival of Nations held annually at Youngstown State University. Beyond the St. Patrick's Day celebrations, the largest organizational event in the Irish community is the Gathering of the Irish Clans, held as a summertime event. Another annual event is the Mahoning Valley Ulster Project, which brings six Protestant and six Catholic teens from Ireland to the Valley, where they are hosted by a local teen of the same gender and religion. The aim of this experience is to develop friendships and understanding while breaking down barriers of intolerance. These events and organizations, such as the AOH and the Burke School of Irish dance, demonstrate that some of the Irish traditions have been retained and will continue to thrive in the Mahoning Valley. An Irish blessing that also has been retained and is frequently quoted in the Valley is: "May the wind always blow at your back. May the sun shine warm upon your face and the rain fall soft upon your fields. And until we meet again, may God hold you in the palm of his hand."

Eileen Gilmartin-Turocy (aka Casey Malone)

Attorney Vince Gilmartin

Michael Shaffer band

Jewish traditions were the focus of the April meeting. Judy Solomon, architect and part of a prominent Jewish family in Youngstown, offered us a multi-media and multi-participant approach to her thorough look at Jewish traditions. From prayers to songs to memorabilia, she gave us vast insight into the Jewish culture. An authentic Jewish meal was prepared by Kravitz Catering, and a Klezmer band provided wonderfully appropriate music. Interestingly, the event was held at the commodious Holy Family Catholic Church in Poland because of the anticipated large turnout-nearly 310 people. Our 5-minute speaker was Jim Echement, Executive Director of the local Rescue Mission.

American Jews overwhelming say they are proud to be Jewish and have a strong sense of belonging to the Jewish people, according to a major survey by the Pew Research Center. But the survey also suggests that Jewish identity is changing in America, where 22% now describe themselves as having no religion. Increasingly, Jews look upon their Jewishness as more about culture and ancestry than religion. Jewish Americans are not a highly religious group, at least by the traditional measures of religious observance. But many engage with Judaism in some way, whether through holidays, food choices, cultural connections, or life milestones. For instance, many Jews say they often or sometimes cook or eat traditional Jewish foods, and many say they share Jewish culture and holidays with non-Jewish friends, such as a Seder meal or a bar or bat mitzvah. Indeed, the Ohio Cultural Alliance sponsored a modified Seder meal at one of our subsequent meetings.

Ms. Solomon beautifully weaved the story of Judaism. Beginning with the Jewish interpretation of the origins of the religion, Solomon carried her story through the millenniums: Creation (Sabbath), Noah and the Flood, Abraham, Exodus from Bondage in Egypt (Passover), King Solomon's 1st Temple, the significance of the Torah, Ahashuerus and Esther saving the Jews, through destruction of the Jewish Temples, the birth of Jesus and the introduction of Christianity, the Crusades, the Inquisition, the Jewish diaspora, the Holocaust to Judaism in the American mainstream. She had commentaries on each of these significant events (even more) as she told the Jewish story. Throughout her narrative, she showed relevant slides, had members of her family recite scripture at appropriate moments, and even had a member blow the Jewish shofar, which calls the religious to prayer.

Throughout her presentation, Ms. Solomon emphasized the three main beliefs that are the center of Judaism: monotheism, identity, and covenant (an agreement between God and his people). The most important teachings of Judaism assert that there is one God who wants people to do what is just and compassionate, and all people are created in the image of God, and each of them deserves to be treated with dignity and respect. The word that captures the essence of Judaism is Torah, which literally means instruction or teaching, and in its most inclusive definition, encompasses all of Judaism's teachings. And the heart of Judaism is evoked in Leviticus 19:18, the Golden Rule: "And you shall love your neighbor as yourself."

Judaism maintains a pure monotheism; it is very clear that the Torah proclaims only one God of the universe and that we are God's children and, therefore, brothers and sisters. And as God intended a good world, so the crown of His creation was the human being who have the Divine gift of freedom/free will. But He acknowledged man may err/sin; thus, Judaism also embraces repentance. Judaism also teaches that we are all descended from common parentage, and therefore, we are all of one family and unified through our Maker. Judaism stresses deed, not creed. Especially it promotes the sanctification of life. Indeed, Leviticus 19:2 teaches, "Be holy, for I the Lord your God am holy." By this, every act can be raised to a Godly act, and we can become truly human and divine, thus exemplifying the covenant with God. Solomon spent some time talking about events in the course of Jewish life, specifically birth, circumcision, adulthood (a special ceremony of boys, bar mitzvah, and of girls, bat mitzvah), weddings, and divorce.

After considerable commentary about the history of Judaism, Ms. Solomon spent some time discussing some of the holidays and celebrations of Judaism. Among those mentioned were:

- Shabbat - The day of rest and weekly observance of God's completion of creation.
- Rosh Hashanah - The Jewish New Year, a holiday observed with festive meals and a day spent in prayer or quiet meditation.
- Yom Kippur - A day to express atonement and repentance.
- Hanukkah - Eight days of rededication of the Temple of Jerusalem.
- Sukkot –A feast of booths and tabernacles; literally hutlike structures used during the 40 years of Exodus from Egypt.
- Tu B'Shevat - An ecological holiday reminding Jews of their connection to the earth.
- Passover - This commemorates the liberation of the children of Israel who were led out of Egypt by Moses; Seder meals accompany this holiday.

Many of these celebrations are practiced by the Jews of the Mahoning Valley, particularly those who attend their synagogue more regularly. As mentioned above, some of us non-Jews have had occasions to participate in a Seder meal (as the Beelens did with my colleague, Dr. Saul Friedman, and his family) and as we all did at an OCA meeting.

The Valley Jews have come from many countries, particularly from eastern and southern Europe. Regardless of their nationalities, degree of orthodoxy, or secularism, Youngstown's Jews have upheld ethical concepts that form the core of Jewish tradition. From the formation of the first area synagogue, Youngstown's Jews have made piety a priority. Several educational institutions were established to help carry on traditions; concern for Jewish welfare, and care for the aged, young, the poor, and refugees were addressed with the formation of the Jewish Federation. "Much of the credit for a sense of progress and brotherhood must be attributed," Ms. Solomon reported, "to gentiles of good will and to the outstanding Jewish men and women who have enriched this community." Such progress is greater than their actual numbers might suggest. Those that have contributed extraordinarily include the active rabbis, important businessmen (many of whom were enlightened philanthropists, social workers, community leaders, educators, and editors of such journals as the Jewish Times and the Jewish Journal that informed of Jewish news and the passages (weddings, births, graduations, and deaths) which helped to retain some of the Jewish traditions. Many became grocers, tailors, bakers, seamstresses, and craftsmen also.

Dr. Saul Friedman wrote more specifically in a chapter of an OCA-sponsored booklet that "our lives are much richer by the spiritual leadership of Rabbi Sidney Berkowitz that preached to their flocks and added to the ecumenical and religious understanding of the Valley. What would we have done without the Ozerky and Schwebel bakeries, the Tamarkin brothers who created the Giant Eagle chain, Arby's, and Kravitz Deli. We remember William Wilcoff and his association with the Youngstown Sheet and Tube Co. and also Strouss, the Hirshbergs, the Lustigs, and the Livingston, Haber, and Solomon families' thriving businesses. Our lives are certainly richer having attended the Youngstown Symphony concerts under the batons of Franz Bibo, David Effron, and Randy Fleischer, and we have been mightily entertained by the Warner brothers and their work in the film industry." Indeed, the

Jewish legacy in the Mahoning Valley is strong, and many of their traditions have been retained, as Solomon and Friedman reported.

Judith Solomon with Dr. Beelen

Klezmer band

Jewish Shofar

In May, Dr. Charles Sung, a native of South Korea and now a veterinarian in Hubbard, Ohio, shared with us something of South Korean traditions orally and via power point. Beautifully attired in native dress, talented soprano and professor of voice at YSU, Dr. Misook Yun, thrilled the OCA members with vocal selections, some related to South Korea. Doctor Yun is a frequent performer at YSU and with the Opera Western Reserve. She has performed throughout the United States, as well as in Italy, Austria, and her native South Korea. We met at the Saxon Club in Austintown. Our monthly 5-minute speaker was Scott Schulick, outgoing president of the Youngstown Rotary Club, who spoke to us about the history of the Rotary Club and their work in the Mahoning Valley.

Dr. Sung began with a brief history of Korea which began with stone age farmers as early as 4000 B.C., carrying us through their bronze age by 1,000 B.C., iron making by 300 B.C., the disparate kingdoms during the period from 57 B.C. through the 4th century A.D. at which time they were highly civilized and heavily influenced by the Chinese civilization. As Korea developed, albeit struggles among themselves and aggressive neighbors, including the Mongols, they developed a hierarchal society with a king and nobles. They also eschewed Buddhism and embraced Confucianism by the 14th century. Dr. Sung carried us through the Japanese invasions of the 16th century, internal factionalism of the 17th century, followed by the kings clamping down on factionalism in the 18th century. He spoke of the early contacts with the European world in the 19th century, followed by periods of isolationism and then trade with several Asian and Western countries. By 1910 the Japanese turned Korea into a colony to supply Japan with food. Increasingly Japan put more pressure on Korea to adopt Japanese ways as they continued their repressive rule. This ended with the conclusion of World War II when the Japanese surrendered to the Allied Powers.

Moving to post-war history, Sung spoke of the division of Korea into North and South Korea, the subsequent Korean War of the early 1950s, and the significant contrast in the development of South Korea with their economic successes and eventual democratic elections with the repressive, dictatorial and economic failure of the country of North Korea.

The once dominant Confucian culture, with its emphasis on respect for ancestors, age, and seniority, continues to influence the Korean family, their work, and social life but to a lesser degree than in the past. Traditional family life is much involved with rituals marking life-cycle milestones and the observation of holidays and ancestral rites. The most important passages in a person's life, Sung said, are the completion of a baby's first 100 days, one's marriage, and one's 61st birthday. Two of the most important holidays are the Lunar New Year and the Harvest Moon Festival often referred to as the Korean Thanksgiving. Western dress has replaced hanbok (native everyday dress), but they still wear it on special occasions, as Dr. Yun did in her recital.

Food is an important part of Korean cultural identity. In the diets of even the most Westernized urban dwellers, traditional Korean cuisine, which emphasizes grains (especially rice) noodles, tufu, fish and fresh vegetables, continues to occupy a dominant role. Soups are also a common part of a Korean meal. Korea is unique among East Asian countries in its use of metal chopsticks.

Dr. Sung also mentioned some of the Korean holidays, which include Korean New Year's Day, which is celebrated on the first day of the Korean lunar calendar, Korean Independence Day, Memorial Day, Constitution Day, Liberation Day (from Japan) and Mid-autumn Festival as they honor ancestors and ancestral homelands.

Most immigration into the Mahoning Valley arrived in the latter third of the 20th century, responding to business and professional opportunities. Although numbering only about 150 families, they maintain three organizations: The Korean Association, the Korean Church of Greater Youngstown, and the Korean Mission Church, which help to maintain several major Korean holidays: Lunar Fest, Harvest Day, and Independence Day. Sung mentioned that there is a far greater Korean presence in some cities, Atlanta among them.

Dr. Charles Sung

Dr. Misook Yun

We closed the year in June, focusing on the Scandinavian countries, with Beverly Olson, who is of Norwegian ancestry and a lifetime member of the First Covenant Church in Boardman, and Lucy Sharkey, the wife of the current pastor of the same church. The church has been known for its beautiful Lucia celebration. Our 5-minute presenter was Pete Milliken, who spoke about his long tenure at the Youngstown Vindicator. The meeting was held at Western Reserve United Methodist Church, whose caterers, under Darlene Well's direction, prepared and served our meal. The evening concluded with the piano artistry of Roman Rudnytsky, YSU, who performed his own piano translation of a Grieg symphonic work to a thunderous applause and a standing ovation.

Beverly Olson and Lucy Sharkey

As a group, the Scandinavian countries (Sweden, Norway, Denmark, and Finland) constitute among the largest groups of the "old immigrants" to America. Although significant ethnic, language and cultural distinctions exist among these groups, they remain bound by some common characteristics: all immigrated to the U.S. from the cold, northern rim of Europe to lands generally temperate; they shared an attachment to Protestant Christianity; they tended to hard work, intense loyalty to their commitments and economic prudence and they carried a strong egalitarian spirit and disdain for class distinctions with them to the U.S. Cooperative, egalitarian and practical and never showy, seem to have characterized these Nordic countries which seem to have achieved a perfect balance of personal comfort, economic strength, and societal welfare without being acquisitive or excessive.

Most of the Scandinavians who came to the Valley reflected those characteristics and attracted little notice. Fair of skin and hair, they blended easily into the fabric of the community. They, too, found employment in the growing steel industry, in construction, or in a variety of small commercial enterprises. They easily transitioned into the mainstream of American life as they made their contributions to education, religion, and reform movements. Aside from a few church affiliations, Scandinavians have largely disappeared as a distinct ethnic population in the Valley.

Among the traditions and holidays that our speakers addressed were:

- Shrove Tuesday, which occurs the 7th Tuesday before Easter. The celebration is about eating a sweet bread role with almond paste and whipped cream or with jam and vanilla cream.
- Waffle Day on March 25, which is Mary's Annunciation Day or Spring Lady's Day, nine months before Jesus' birth.
- Valborg on April 30th, originally to scare away witches and bad spirits by lighting bonfires. Today it is more about celebrating the arrival of spring.
- Norway's Constitution Day on May 17th, Denmark's Constitution Day on June 5th and Sweden's Constitution Day on June 6th are widely celebrated.
- Midsummer, celebrated between June 19th25th, is the main party of the summer in Sweden, while midsummer (called St. John's Eve) is celebrated on June 23rd in Norway and Denmark.

- Early August is a time to celebrate crayfish season at the Crayfish Party in Sweden.
- Cinnamon Roll Day on October 4th celebrates Swedish baking traditions.
- December 13 is Saint Lucy's Day (Lucia) and is celebrated in Sweden, Norway, and Denmark; it is mostly a secular event (except in Denmark). Saint Lucy has an enduring role as the carrier of light in the dark Scandinavian winters, and people dress in white gowns and sing songs while holding candles. Tradition has it that Lucia is to wear "light in her hair", which in practice means a crown of candles in a wreath on her head. Each of her handmaidens carries a candle, too. The celebration comes from stories that were told by monks who first brought Christianity to Sweden. St. Lucia was a young Christian girl who was martyred, killed for her faith in 304. Our speakers spent considerable time with this celebration since it was such an important activity in their church, the First Covenant Church.
- December 24 is Christmas Eve and is usually deemed much more important than Christmas day. There is a lot of evidence that this fondness for Christmas Eve comes from Scandinavia's Viking heritage. According to the Vikings, a new day starts when the sun goes down on the day before. This idea could be the reason why many Scandinavians start the festivities early on Christmas Eve.

The Valley community generally embraced members of the Scandinavian migrants for their similarities rather than segregate them because of their differences. However, some of their traditions were retained, most notably those of the Swedes, because they represented the largest local contingent and absorbed the Norwegians and the Danes. Scandinavians have made contributions to the social and cultural fabric of the area in the form of a variety of reform and fraternal organizations. The Scandinavian Brotherhood, one of the first of such groups, organized in 1908; others followed, such as the Andre Lodge of the Scandinavian Fraternity of America and the VASA Order of America. Local Swedish immigrants also established two cultural preservation societies: The Swedish Club, which published the Swedish Tribune, and the Swedish Cultural Society. These organizations, plus several flourishing churches, helped to retain some of the Scandinavian churches.

Scandinavian immigrants and their churches and organizations that began their association with the Valley in the heart of the city ultimately moved to the more prosperous areas north and south of the city. Scandinavians remain among the most successful immigrant groups in the Valley. Embraced by older American populations, they advanced quickly through the social and economic strata of the region. However, this success has had a cost; the mainstream has absorbed them, and aside from a few church affiliations, such as the First Covenant Church, Scandinavians have largely disappeared as a distinct ethnic population in Mahoning County.

Once again, we were treated to a successful year of learning, feasting, entertainment, and community building, with our numbers of members and attendees continuing to grow. We continued to respond to community needs by collecting staples and personal grooming necessities to select organizations and continued our 5-minute presentations of community leaders so that we could learn more about them and they could learn more about the OCA.

St. Lucia Day

John Gabriele provided ambiance

XIX. Going Places with the Ohio Cultural Alliance

The theme for this new and expanded year-our, 28th-was "Going Places with the Ohio Cultural Alliance". Programs were offered from September to December 2014; recess in January and February 2015; resumption in March through December 2015. Each speaker addressed a selected country or city of the world, specifically discussing their ethnic composition, their social, cultural, and political composition, some travelogue, and some personal memories.

We began our new OCA year in September with Reverend Monsignor Peter Polando, who shared with us reflections on his most recent visit to the Holy Land, which the Beelens were privileged to be part of his group of pilgrims. Reverend Vit Fiala performed beautifully on his cello, with members showing their approval with a standing ovation. Mt. Carmel's caterer, Lou Fusillo, prepared his usual sumptuous "Youngstown buffet". Our 5-minute presenter was Michael Conway, Executive Director of the Mahoning Valley Economic Development Corporation.

Monsignor Polando began his presentation with a look at the country of Israel. He reported that It is a small yet diverse Middle Eastern country on the Mediterranean Sea that is regarded by Jews, Christians, and Muslims as the biblical Holy Land. Its most sacred sites are in Jerusalem, known as the Holy City, the City of Prophets, and/or the City of Peace. Within the "Old City" of Jerusalem, the dominating Temple Mount complex includes the Dome of the Rock shrine, the historic Mosque, and the Church of the Holy Sepulcher. This Holy Land is a unique and beautiful land, rich with a variety of historical, archeological, and religious sites. One cannot help but be charmed by its sweeping vistas, hospitable citizens, and inspirational images. It is an enchanting mixture of ancient and modern. Yet the history and politics of this small bit of land along the Mediterranean is complex, bewildering, and tragic.

Politically, Israel contains two areas-West Bank and the Gaza Strip- that are under Israel's military occupation, with a modicum of Palestinian control. These Occupied Palestinian Territories (OPT) have been under Israeli military occupation since 1967. Many, though not all, Palestinian Arabs who live in Israel consider themselves Muslims, and an increasing number of Jews have built settlements in the West Bank and Gaza, complicating matters further. Monsignor Polando told us that our major guide on our journey to the Holy Land said he was a Palestinian Arab, a Christian Catholic who had passports from Jordan and Israel.

Arriving in Tel Aviv, our group traveled by bus to Jerusalem, capturing our first view of the city and hearing the first calls to prayer by the Jewish shofar, the Muslim athan/azar, and the Christian bells. Despite huge crowds in Jerusalem, we found most people-visitors and natives alike-hospitable and helpful. But, of course, the most significant and poignant aspect of our journey to the Holy Land was following what tradition tells us were some of the important footsteps of Jesus. (Most of us on this trip were Catholic Christians.)

On the first full day in Jerusalem, we entered the Mount of Olives, where we viewed the Place of the Ascension. The olive groves at the Mount of Olives have been used as a Jewish cemetery for more than 3,000 years and is also the site of several key events in the life of Jesus, including the place where Jesus ascended to Heaven forty days after his resurrection. It is also the site associated with the Lord's Prayer, which features separate slabs that contain the Lord's Prayer in multiple languages. At the foot of the Mount of Olives, we visited the Garden of Gethsemane, where Jesus prayed and his disciples slept the night of his betrayal and crucifixion. Our day included visiting the Church of Dominus Flevit, the Church of All Nations, the site of the Last Supper, and the site of the house of the High Priest Caiaphas, among other sites near the Mount of Olives.

On the second full day, we headed to Bethlehem, starting with the Basilica of the Nativity and the Grotto, venerated as the birthplace of Jesus. This site included a cave chapel and lighted candles among the many visitors (some with flowing garments), making this site potentially hazardous. Next to the Basilica of the Nativity stands the Church of St. Catherine, and located outside this structure is the Crusaders' Cloister and Cave of St. Jerome. Here too, we saw the Chapel of the Innocents, which is said to be the burial place of infants killed by King Herod. Continuing, we visited the Shepherds' Fields, where tradition tells us that an angel announced the birth of Jesus. We ended this day at Ein Karem, the village home of St. Elizabeth, mother of St. John the Baptist, where we toured the Church of St. John the Baptist and the Church of the Visitation.

On the third full day, we traveled to Jericho, one of the oldest cities in the world, continuously inhabited over the last ten thousand years. Over many millennia, Jericho has become a haven for Israelites, Christians, Jews, and Muslims. We viewed the Old City and the Mount of Temptation, said to be where Jesus was tempted by the devil as he fasted for forty days. On his final journey to Jerusalem, we were told that Jesus passed through Jericho, where he encountered Zacchaeus, the chief tax collector, whom Jesus influenced to help the poor and to make restitution to all he had defrauded.

We proceeded to Qumran, an archaeological site on the West Bank where the Dead Sea Scrolls were found. They included manuscripts on papyrus, parchment, and bronze representing writing in Hebrew, Aramaic, Greek, and Nabataean-Aramaic from several hundred years before and after Jesus' life. On we went to take a cable car to the top of Masada, the scene of the epic stand by Jewish rebels at the end of the Great Revolt against Rome nearly 2,000 years ago. The siege of Masada is often referred to as a symbol of Jewish heroism; others see it as a case of Jewish radicals refusing to compromise, resorting instead to suicide. We ended this third day floating and relaxing in the Dead Sea, a lake whose banks are more than 1,400 ft. below sea level.

On the fourth day, we drove to Steven's Gate, where we entered the Old City of Jerusalem, one of the seven gates into the city. We began our tour at the Crusaders' Church of St. Anne and the Pool of Bethesda, the site where Jesus is said to have healed the paralytic man. We proceeded to the Tower of Antonia, where Jesus was said to be taken to stand trial before Pilate, then to the Church of Flagellation, where Jesus was flogged. At Via Dolorosa, we followed several of the Stations of the Cross, which ended inside the Basilica of the Holy Sepulcher, where Jesus was entombed. We ended this day with a visit to the Wailing Wall (Western Wall) in the Old City of Jerusalem. It is the only remains of the Second Temple of Jerusalem, held to be uniquely holy by the ancient Jews and destroyed by the Romans in 70 A.D. We briefly looked into the Israel Museum, where the Dead Sea Scrolls are displayed.

On the fifth day, we traveled to the Jordan River and to the tourist Place of Baptism, where we renewed our baptismal vows. On the sixth day, we took a cruise across the Sea of Galilee from Tiberias to Capharnaum, where we viewed the boat of Jesus Museum, an ancient fishing boat from the 1st century. Capharnaum is the town where Jesus carried out a major part of His ministry. While here, we visited the excavations of St. Peter's house and St. Peter's Church, after which we visited the Church of the Primacy of St. Peter. We walked to nearby

Tabgha, the site where Jesus is said to have fed 5,000 with five loaves of bread and two fish. We proceeded to visit the Mount of Beatitudes, which commemorates the Sermon on the Mount.

On the seventh day, we were bused to Cana of Galilee, where we visited the Franciscan Church of the Wedding Feast; it is here that tradition holds that Jesus changed the water into wine. Monsignor Polando offered Mass here, as he did every day of our trip; he invited the three married couples among us to renew our marriage vows. We were given certificates of renewal by the local Franciscan nuns. We continued to Nazareth, Jesus' birthplace, where we visited the Basilica of the Annunciation, which commemorates Angel Gabriel's announcement of Jesus' impending birth. In the same area, we toured the Chapel of St. Joseph, which was purportedly built over Joseph's carpenter shop, and the Old Synagogue, where tradition holds that Jesus did his early preaching. Afterward, we drove to Mount Tabor, where Jesus is said to have been Transfigured, which was the glorification of the human body as his body underwent a change in form-a metamorphosis- as his earthly ministry was coming to a close.

On the final day, we drove to Mount Carmel in the city of Haifa in the northern part of Israel along the Mediterranean Sea. This bustling port city is the third largest city in Israel; among the major features are the striking Baha'i Shrine and the Stella Maris Monastery and Church. The Baha'i Temple and The Gardens in Haifa, with its gleaming golden dome of the temple and the nineteen terraced gardens, are beautiful to behold and honor the Persian-born Bab, the forerunner of Baha'u'llah, the founder of the Baha'i faith. The name of the 19th-century Stella Maris Monastery refers to an early title accorded Mary, the mother of Jesus. The monastery is the world headquarters and the "Mother Church" of a Catholic religious order of friars and nuns-the Carmelites.

This marks the end of the story of Monsignor Peter Polando and the Beelens, whose words and thoughts are intermingled in this consideration of their trip to the Holy Land. However, it is not the end of the story of the Holy Land of Israel. Now more than 70 years as a nation, but with a history that goes back more than 3,000 years, the country's past and present have experienced tragic difficulties. But the hopes and prayers continue to call for peace. Songs and poems have been written honoring this land. Many have praised it and remain hopeful. Faithful believers around the world pray for peace.

Monsignor Peter Polando

Reverend Vit Fiala

Our October meeting featured the Honorable Harry Meshel, who spoke of Greek traditions and travel, with the evening complemented by Greek cuisine and a travel film about Greece, all taking place at Archangel Michael Greek Orthodox Church in Campbell, Ohio. Our 5-minute speaker was Jackie Burley, Executive Director of Protestant Family Services in Youngstown.

Harry Meshel knew of the importance of one's roots and the pride in those roots, including his own Greek roots. He knew where he came from on his way to becoming a great American. He wanted others to remember their roots also. Harry continuously argued of the importance of the Mahoning Valley for their multiplicity of ethnic groups, which is the strength of the Valley. Remembering one's ethnic background and acknowledging the value of other ethnic groups are both important in the quest to becoming a complete American was always important to Harry.

His contemporaries always knew how important Harry was to the Valley. He served in local government in Youngstown, as state senator, as YSU trustee, and in many leadership capacities in the Valley and the state. Many of us know of his outstanding array of plaques, commendations, awards, and honors given to Harry by virtually all of the social, political, and cultural organizations of the Valley and the State of Ohio. As discussed previously, during a visit to Meshel Hall on YSU's campus, one can view some tangible manifestations of these honors, occupying an entire first-floor wall. These awards have been given to Harry because he has worked hard to promote these organizations and the Mahoning Valley. In whatever capacity he served, he was an intelligent, articulate, and often outspoken advocate for the Valley, indeed, the state of Ohio. Yet, he was a visible leader and a frequent traveler to the native country of his parents-Greece.

Meshel used a film of Greece to show something about the land of his parents and of his own frequent visits. His narrative supplemented the film as he told briefly of their history, their people, their culture, and their geography. He related how Greece has a history stretching back almost 4,000 years and is the birthplace of politics as an art and democracy as a form of government. Its democratic ideals inspired, among others, the framers of the U.S. Constitution. In the 5th century B.C. Greece was composed of city-states, the largest being Athens. By the second half of the 4th century B.C., the Greeks, led by Alexander the Great, conquered most of the then-known world. In 146 B.C. Greece fell to the Romans. In 330 A.D. Emperor Constantine moved the Capital of the Roman Empire to Constantinople, founding the Eastern Roman Empire, which was named the Byzantine Empire or Byzantium. Byzantium transformed the linguistic heritage of ancient Greece into a vehicle for a new Christian civilization. The Byzantine Empire fell to the Turks in 1453, and the Greeks remained under Ottoman control for nearly 400 years. During this time, their language, their religion, and their sense of identity remained strong. By 1821, the Greeks revolted against the Turks, and by 1828, they had won their independence, and the struggle for the liberation of all of their former lands proceeded. Today, the present Greek Constitution, voted in 1975 and amended in 1986, defines the country's political system as a Parliamentary Democracy headed by a President. The religious affiliation is nearly 98% Greek Orthodox.

Greece is located in Southeast Europe and has a population of 10.7 million, with Athens as its capital that features the Acropolis and the Parthenon and with beautiful islands such as Mykonos, Santorini, Crete, and Corfu, which the movie highlighted. Clearly, Greece is a geographically appealing place to visit, with a mountainous mainland and idyllic island beaches. Indeed, Greece is one of the world's most popular tourist destinations. Meshel manifested his considerable knowledge of and emotional feeling for the land of his ancestry. The movie and his narrative made it abundantly clear that Greece, despite its occasional economic problems, is a place many wish to visit, as did the Beelens on the occasion of our 50th wedding anniversary in 2006.

As a postscript, I add that Harry donated a large container of Greek extra virgin oil for us to raffle off.

Honorable Harry Meshel

Greece on the Map

Meshel and Drs. George Beelen and Les Domonkos

OCA members met in November to learn of travel to Germany, as shared by Dr. Warren Young, YSU. Dr. Young is a retired professor after 43 years in the YSU Physics and Astronomy Department, serving as chair for 25 years and director of the Planetarium for 40 years. He has been a frequent traveler to the homeland of his ancestors. The cultural enrichment was provided by the Canfield Community Band, directed by Kim Hogan. They provided appropriate musical selections to the delight of the audience. John Getchey, Executive Director, Eastgate Regional Council of Governments, was our 5-minute speaker. This all took place at the Saxon Club in Austintown, where we dined on typical German food.

Dr. Young has been active in astronomy and science education, writing many articles and papers, teaching college courses, presenting a weekly radio program, conducting astronomy workshops for teachers, and appearing on television programs to explain astronomical phenomena. He has traveled extensively and has sailed throughout the northern and southern hemispheres to point out the wonders of the heavens to thousands of cruise passengers around the world. He has also been an avid skier.

To the point of this current presentation to the OCA, Dr. Young provided each of us with a map to discuss his extensive travel to Germany. His travels took him to most of the major cities, including Berlin to visit the Brandenburg Gate, Frankfurt at night, Dresden rebuilt, Stuttgart, Bonn, Heidelberg, with its famous castle ruins, and Leipzig's Old Town, among others. His images were illuminating. He reminded us of the history of tourism in Germany that, goes back to cities and landscapes visited for education and recreation. From the 18th century onwards, cities like Dresden, Munich, Weimar, and Berlin were major stops on European tours.

After a hiatus during World War II, tourism continued and greatly expanded, as many tourists visited Germany to experience a sense of European history and the diverse German landscape. The country features 14 national parks, 14 Biosphere Reserves, as well as 98 nature parks. The countryside has a pastoral aura, while the bigger cities exhibit both a modern and classical feel. Small and medium-sized cities often have preserved their historical appearance and have old towns with remarkable architectural heritage. Young showed many such scenes in his visual presentation.

The winter sports always appealed to Dr. Young, as indicated above with his skiing history. (He reluctantly ended his skiing participation in his 80's!) He told of the main winter sports regions of the Bavarian Alps and the Northern Limestone Alps, as well as the Ore Mountains, Harz Mountains, Fichtel Maintains, and the Bavarian Forest within the Central Uplands. First-class winter sports infrastructure is available for alpine skiing and snowboarding, bobsledding, and cross-country skiing. In most regions, winter sports are limited to the winter months of November to February. During the Advent season, many German towns and cities host Christmas markets, some of which Young visited over the years. The images he showed were beautiful.

The reconstruction of Germany was a long process of rebuilding after the destruction that resulted from World War II. The country's cities were severely damaged from heavy bombing in the closing chapters of the war, and agricultural production was only about 35% of what it was before the war. The country began a slow but continuous improvement of its standard of living, its infrastructure, its agricultural productivity, and its export capacity, leading to an eventual economic recovery. Tourism followed; Dr. Young and his family were among the tourists.

Travel to the twelve largest cities in Germany more than doubled between 1995 and 2005, the largest increase of any travel destination. This increase mainly arises from the growth of cultural tourism, often in conjunction with educational or business travel. Consequently, the provision and supply of more and higher standards of cultural, entertainment, hospitality, gastronomic and retail services also attract more international guests. Dr. Young has found time to avail himself of these travel opportunities and to share them with us.

Dr. Warren Young

Canfield Community Band, directed by Kim Hogan

The Vatican was featured in December, with the Most Reverend George Murry, Bishop of the Catholic Diocese of Youngstown as our speaker. The poignant tone of the Bishop was continued by the Wade Raridon Singers, who thrilled us with their rendition of several selections they had performed in Rome. St. Charles Church Hall in Boardman was the site of the meeting, and Livosky Catering provided the delicious meal. Our 5-minute speaker was Bill Lawson, Executive Director of the Mahoning Valley Historical Society.

On his second presentation to the Ohio Cultural Alliance, Bishop George Murry spoke knowledgeably about the Vatican, an independent city-state and enclave located within Rome, Italy. He related many interesting facts about the city and some of his memorable moments, including his formal appointment as Bishop of the Diocese of Youngstown. The Vatican City State, also known simply as the Vatican, became independent from Italy with the Lateran Treaty of 1929. It is a distinct territory under full ownership, exclusive dominion, and sovereign authority and jurisdiction of the Holy See, itself a sovereign entity of international law, which maintains the city state's temporal, diplomatic, and spiritual independence. With an area of about 121 acres and a population of about 825, it is the smallest state in the world by both area and population. As governed by the Holy See, the Vatican City State is an ecclesiastical state (a type of theocracy) ruled by the pope, who is the bishop of Rome and head of the Catholic Church, worldwide. The highest state functionaries are all Catholic clergy from all parts of the world. After the Avignon Papacy (1309-1377), the popes live primarily at the Apostolic Palace within Vatican City, although at times, they live in the Quirinal Palace in Rome.

Within Vatican City are the religious and cultural sites that Bishop Murry described. Among them were St. Peter's Basilica, the Sistine Chapel, and the Vatican Museums. They feature some of the world's most famous paintings and sculptures. The unique economy of Vatican City is supported financially by donations from the faithful, the sale of postage stamps and souvenirs, fees for admission to museums, and sales of publications.

Popes gradually came to have a secular role as governors of regions near Rome. They ruled the Papal States, which covered a large portion of the Italian peninsula, for more than a thousand years until the mid-19th century, when all territory belonging to the papacy was seized by the newly created Kingdom of Italy. For most of this time, the popes did not live at the Vatican. The Lateran Palace, on the opposite side of Rome, was their usual residence for about 1,000 years. From 1309 to 1377, they lived at Avignon in France. On their return to Rome, they chose to live at the Vatican. They moved to the Quirinal Palace in 1583 after work on it was completed under Pope Paul V (1605-1621), but on the capture of Rome in 1870, he retired to the Vatican, and what had been their residence became that of the King of Italy. After a considerable conflict between the Italian kings and the popes, the acrimony was resolved in 1929 when (as stated above) the Lateran Treaty between the Holy See and the Kingdom of Italy was signed, establishing the independent state of Vatican City and reaffirming the special status of Catholic Christianity in Italy.

The territory of Vatican City includes St. Peter's Square, distinguished from the territory of Italy only by a white line along the limit of the square, where it touches Piazza Pio XII. St. Peter's Square is reached through the Via della Conciliazione which runs from close to the Tiber River to St. Peter's. This grand approach was constructed by Benito Mussolini after the conclusion of the Lateran Treaty.

Bishop Murry described the solemnity of the pope's pronouncements from the window of the Papal Palace of Castel Gandolfo, actually meeting the pope, the magnificence of the Sistine Chapel, and the procession through the main doors of St. Peter's. The Beelens were thrilled to process through those doors when we visited Rome in the year 2,000 as part of the group led by then Bishop Thomas Tobin and Monsignor Michael Cariglio.

Once again, this brilliant Jesuit was accorded a standing ovation by the OCA members. Sadly, he died a few years later after a long illness.

Bishop George Murry

Scene of Vatican

Our focus in March was Turkish travel and traditions as described by Dr. Birsen Karpak, Professor of Management at the YSU School of Business, who showed and narrated colorful images of her native land. Turkish string music, Turkish dancing, a sampling of exquisite Turkish carpeting and artifacts, and a Turkish meal completed a most enjoyable evening. The meeting was held at Western Reserve United Methodist Church in Canfield, but the meal was prepared by Anatolia Cafe from Cleveland, Ohio. Stan Boney, a veteran local WYTV/WKBN newsman, was our 5-minute speaker relating to us some of the joys and trials of his profession.

Dr. Birsen Karpak

Dr. Karpak has had an enviable history in the teaching profession at YSU and elsewhere. She has secured grants from the National Science Foundation, and NATO has conducted various institutes and has received numerous awards in research and teaching. She also enjoys integrating her research into her teaching. To the point of our current theme, Karpak has extensively traveled and has organized Istanbul Study tours since 2006.

Dr. Karpak told us and showed us that Turkey is a richly historical land with some of the best cuisine, beautiful beaches and mountains, and the great city of Istanbul. From the ancient port city of Ephesus to the soaring Byzantine dome of Aya Sofya, Turkey has more than its fair share of world-famous ruins and monuments. A succession of historical figures and empires, including the Romans, Byzantines, and Ottomans, have all left their mark on this former stopover along the legendary Silk Road. Experiencing their legacy could take one, Karpak relates, "from the closeted quarters of the sultan and his harem in Istanbul's sprawling Topkapi Palace to the romantic and mysterious Lycian ruins on Mediterranean beaches".

Turkey is a country bridging Europe and Asia. Turks form the vast majority of the nation's 83 million people, and Kurds are the largest minority. Turkey's capital is Ankara, while its largest city and financial center is Istanbul. Turkey is a regional power and a newly industrialized country with a geopolitically strategic location. Its economy, which is classified among the emerging and growth-leading economies, is the 20th largest in the world. It is a charter member of the United Nations, an early member of NATO, the IMF, and the World Bank. Its government is a unitary presidential constitutional republic.

Turkey's diverse landscapes, from Aegean olive groves to eastern steppes, provide a lyrical setting for its many great ruins. The country's most magical scenery is to be found in Asian Anatolia, where beautiful vistas are provided by the vertiginous Mediterranean coastline, Cappadocia's otherworldly "fairy chimney" rock formations and wavy valleys, the alpine pastures of Kackar Mountains and golden beaches such as the long Patara Beach. We were told that lasting impressions come from the views of mountain-ringed Lake Egirdir or from the hilly hinterland on the southwest coast's many peninsulas.

Turkey offers activities to suit every temperament, from outdoor adventure to cultural enrichment. Watery fun includes diving, windsurfing, rafting, and canyoning in mountain gorges, kayaking over Kekova's sunken ruins, and traditional cruises on the Mediterranean and Aegean. We saw in Dr. Karpak's images paragliding flights and hot-air balloons riding over Cappadocia. Dr. Karpak offered an invitation: "For a fresh angle on stunning Turkish scenery, we could trek to highland pastures or walk part of the Lycian Way Trail." " In town," Karpak teased, "we could soak in a hammam, which contains three chambers: a hot room to steam, a warm room to scrub, and a cooler room to relax or take a culinary tour and sample Turkey's delicious specialties-ranging from meze on a Mediterranean harbor to a pension breakfast featuring ingredients fresh from the garden. For the sociable and family-oriented Turks, gathering and eating well is a time-honored ritual. So, we were urged to dig into olive oil-lathered Aegean vegetables, spicy Anatolian kebabs, and other delicious entrees as we drink a tulip-shaped glass of Turkish cay (tea) and contemplate some baklava for dessert."

Turkish Tea Setting

China was the topic, in April, of Drs. George and Maggie McCloud. They have visited China on innumerable occasions and initiated cultural exchanges between Youngstown State University and various Chinese cities. Chris Yambar, a local artist, provided evidence of his artistic talents and comic relief related to some of his artistic characters. The site of our meeting was The Embassy, whose caterers prepared a meal with some Chinese cuisine. We had two 5-minute speakers: Jim Cossler of the Business Incubator and Carole Bopp, a representative of Hope House, one of the recipients of our monthly charity distribution.

Drs. George and Maggie McCloud

Dr. McCloud joined the faculty at YSU in 1997. During his tenure at the university, he was Dean and Provost of the College of Fine Arts, then Special Assistant to the President for Development and Public Relations, Special Assistant to the President of University Advancement, and was the Vice President of University Advancement. While Dean of the College of Fine and Performing Arts, he was instrumental in developing the SMARTS program and was the founder of the Summer Festival of the Arts. He was also a former commentator for the radio show, Looking Out on YSU. Dr. McCloud knew the importance of the ancient world culture and the economic power of China and was instrumental in introducing the faculty and students of YSU to the arts of China through cultural exchange programs. At an earlier OCA meeting, he did a series of readings (see above) with a drama student. He even acted, wrote, and produced while in graduate school and while at the University of Michigan, some years before he came to YSU.

In the early summer of 2008, a group of students from William Patterson University of New Jersey and YSU spent three and a half weeks on a carefully crafted study tour of China. In a work that Dr. McCloud co-authored, he offered first impressions of the students as they attempted to make sense of the complexities of China, using visual arts as the lenses through which to focus their experiences. The intellectual leader of this enterprise was Professor Zhiyuan Cong, who had worked in the rice fields during the Chinese Cultural Revolution and later was educated at Nanjing Arts Institute and eventually became a professor of art at William Patterson University. McCloud revealed that "As colleagues, we discovered shared ideas regarding learning." When McCloud moved on to YSU, he continued to work on travel study projects. Discussions ensued for two years before he actually offered courses at our university and took students to China. McCloud's colleague Dr. Cong, who is a painter, printmaker, historian, and teacher, is able to combine these arts and render a unique understanding of Western and Eastern culture. McCloud was helped by Cong to provide a picture of Chinese tradition that sometimes contrasts with accepted pedagogy in American education. McCloud said of Cong that "He created a rich backdrop for research and reflection...introducing our students to arts administrators, faculty and students along with visits to museums, universities, historical sites, artist demonstrations, and lectures."

During the remainder of his time with us, Dr. McCloud discussed the importance of tourism in China and showed us images of some of his students at important sites, ancient cities, and historic towns. Tourism in China is a growing industry that is becoming a significant part of the Chinese economy. (This author led a group to China in 2004 and could attest to the large number of tourists from all parts of the world.) The rate of tourism has greatly expanded over the last few decades since the beginning of reform and "opening-up".

The emergence of a newly rich middle class and an easing of restrictions on movement by the Chinese authorities are both fueling this travel boom. China has become one of the world's largest outbound tourist markets. (Again, the Beelens have seen this in our travels, too.)

In the many visual images that Dr. McCloud showed, we visited vicariously Xi'an, the city that has unearthed thousands of terracotta soldiers that were created to frighten invaders; renowned historic cities/towns such as Chongqing, Wuhan, Shanghai, Beijing, Chengdu, Suzhou, (the Venice of the East). He showed pictures of famous sites such as the Grand Canal of China; the Great Wall of China; the Silk Road; the Forbidden City; the Summer Palace and the Temple of Heaven in Beijing; the Three Gorges along the Yangtze River, and many others, most of them with his students. Sadly, within the next year, Dr. George McCloud passed away. He was a credit to the University and an inspiration to the many students whom he touched.

Chris Yambar concluded the evening with examples of his contributions to Bongo comic books, including The Simpsons, Sponge Bob Square Pants, and Popeye. It was one of Yambar's own creations, Mr. Beat, a cartoon beatnik character that brought him to the attention of the creator of the Simpsons. Yambar's humor and his delightful presentation were infectious as he presented his narrative and some of his actual work. His art touched a lot of emotions, as he made fun of himself and others through his comedic artwork. His Pop Art is in galleries and private collections nationwide. Sadly, Chris died suddenly in 2021.

Chris and Maureen Yambar

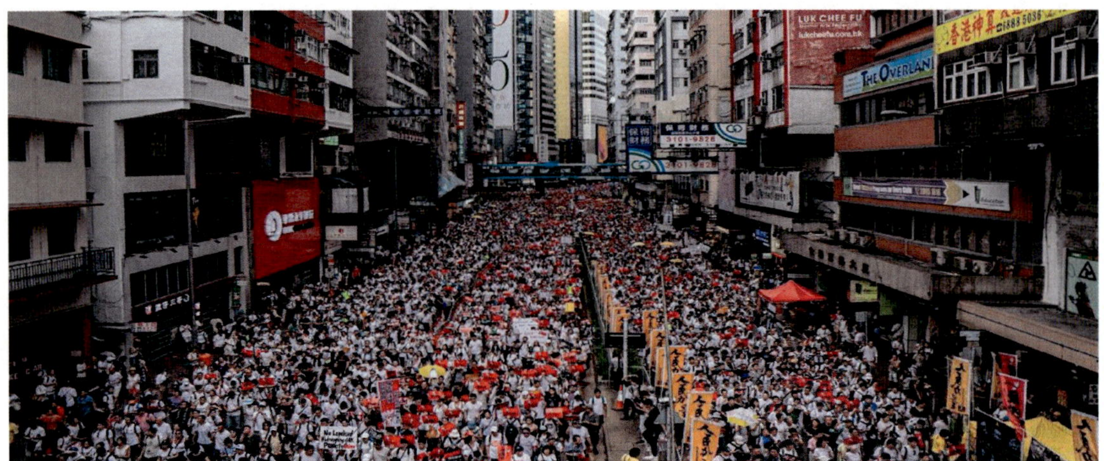

Crowd in China

In May, we traveled vicariously to St. Petersburg with speaker Reverend Kathryn Adams, a frequent traveler to that Russian city. Her missions to Russia (which we addressed in a previous OCA meeting) have taken on a legendary tone, yet she also shared at the current meeting many of the tourist aspects of her travels. Dr. George Kalbouss, whom we engaged through the Ohio Humanities Council, discussed the relationship of popular Russian songs to American songs. We met at Western Reserve United Methodist Church Hall in Canfield, whose caterers, under the direction of Phyllis Harmon, prepared and served a wonderful meal. Dr. Rashid Abdu, well-known to OCA members, offered the 5-minute presentation about the Joanne Abdu Breast Care Center.

Reverend Adams accepted our invitation to speak about some of the important attractions in the city of St. Petersburg, the second largest city in Russia, formerly known as Petrograd and later Leningrad. As Russia's Imperial capital, and a historically strategic port, it is governed as a federal city. St. Petersburg is known as the "cultural capital of Russia," receiving over 15 million tourists in 2018. It is considered an important economic, scientific, cultural, and tourism center of Russia and Europe. It is home to some federal government bodies and is a seat for the National Library of Russia, as well as home to the headquarters of the Russian Navy and the Western Military District of the Russian Armed Forces. The Historic Center of Saint Petersburg and Related Groups of Monuments is home to the Hermitage, one of the largest and most beautiful art museums in the world, the Lakhta Center, the tallest skyscraper in Europe, and was one of the host cities of the 2018 FIFA World Cup and the UEFA Euro 2020.

Reverends Kathryn and Russ Adams

The 18th and 19th-century architectural ensemble of the city and its environs is preserved in virtually unchanged form. St. Petersburg has retained many of its pre-revolutionary buildings, as modern architectural "prestige projects" tended to be built in Moscow; this largely prevented the rise of mid-to-late 20th-century architecture and helped maintain its 18th and 19th-century appearance. St. Petersburg is inscribed on the UNESCO World Heritage list as an area with 36 historical architectural complexes and around 4,000 outstanding individual monuments of architecture, history, and culture. The city has 221 museums, 2,000 libraries, more than 80 theaters, 100 concert organizations, 45 galleries and exhibition halls, 62 cinemas, and around 80 other cultural establishments. Every year the city hosts about 100 festivals and various competitions of art and culture, including more than 50 international ones. The musical life of St. Petersburg is rich and diverse, with the city playing host to a number of annual carnivals. Ballet performances also occupy a special place in the cultural life of the city. Reverend Adams assured us that she has only sampled this abundant cultural life of St. Petersburg and will share only a few that she sampled with us.

Among those that Adams mentioned and described were:

- The Hermitage/Winter Palace was founded when Empress Catherine the Great started acquiring works of art in the late 1700s, but the museum did not open until 1852. Today it's the second-largest museum in the world. The Hermitage technically occupies six buildings, although the main part of the museum is housed in the Winter Palace, which served as the home of the Russian emperors until 1917.

- Peter and Paul Fortress was originally a fortified area meant to protect the state from foreign attack. Constructed in 1703, the fortress never saw any actual combat, but it did serve as a prison and execution quarters during the Bolshevik Revolution. Today it is part of the State Museum of the History of St. Petersburg.
- Mariinsky Theater is among the top theaters in the world. This huge building is home to the Mariinsky Ballet, Opera House, and Orchestra. Some of the best works have been premiered here, the likes of Tchaikovsky, Mussorgsky, Glinka, and Rimsky-Korsakov.
- Peterhof Palace was built by Peter the Great, who was inspired by the French Palace at Versailles. The Palace includes nearly 4 hectares of land, with upper and lower gardens and the famous Cascade Fountain.
- The Church of the Savior on Spilled Blood, more formally known as the Cathedral of the Resurrection of Christ, is a memorial to Tsar Alexander II, who was assassinated there. This church is different from other St. Petersburg religious landmarks in that its baroque and neoclassical appearances incorporate elements of medieval architecture. Likewise, the Cathedral has a fantastic mosaic collection, which includes biblical scenes and ornamental patterns.
- The Golden Triangle is bordered by the Dvortsovaya embankment of the Neva River, Nevsky Prospect, and Fontanka River. Reverend Adams told us that within this Golden Triangle, one could see the Palace Square, with the Hermitage, St. Isaak's Cathedral, Church on Spilled Blood, Field of Mars, Summer Garden, and Michailovsky Garden.
- St. Isaac's Cathedral's shining golden globe, even at a far distance, is a marvelous sight; its museum contains a lavish interior that gives some indication of the life of the Russian royalties.
- Eliseyev Emporium is a large retail and entertainment complex located on the famous Nevsky Prospekt. It is one of the most striking examples of St. Petersburg Art Nouveau architecture, considered controversial when it was built in1902-1903.
- At the conclusion of our St. Petersburg tour Dr. Kalbouss, using a piano, discussed the relationship between Russian and American songs. In a knowledgeable yet humorous way, he gave examples of songs that were popular in Russia and then became Americanized and American songs about Russia and its culture that were never intended for Russian audiences. All OCA members left the meeting humming Russian/American melodies that they had just heard.

Dr. George Kalbouss

Scene of St. Petersburg

San Salvador, where Christopher Columbus first landed in America, was Dr. Ron Shaklee's focus in June. His knowledge of the area is significant as he has studied the island and held classes for YSU students there for nearly two decades. Filipe Gonzalez Trio provided Latin music, and Carolyn Catering prepared an appropriate meal. This meeting was held at St. Michael's Social Hall in Canfield. The 5-minute speaker was Eileen Novotny speaking of the work of the Ursuline Sisters of the Diocese of Youngstown.

San Salvador, also known as Watling's Island, is an island and district of the Bahamas widely believed to be the island where Columbus first landed in the New World in October 1492. He named it San Salvador after Christ the Savior, as he was working on behalf of the Spanish to surpass the Portuguese, who had established trade routes around the Horn of Africa. Columbus' records indicate that the native Lucayan inhabitants of the territory, who called their island Guanahani, were "sweet and gentle" people. Over the years, others have occupied the island and have alternative sites of Columbus' first landing. Regardless of who occupied the island and which of the islands in the Bahamas was the first landing, this area has been studied often. More than 1,000 students and researchers work from the Bahamian Field Station every year as a base of operations for studying tropical marine geology, biology, and archaeology. The island is home to many shallow-water coral reefs, where snorkelers can observe hundreds of fish species without the use of scuba equipment. Today, thanks to its many sandy beaches, the island's main industry are tourism. Wouldn't this be a very agreeable place to study, do research, and to get a great tan while on the beach?

Among the people engaged in studies of this region is Dr. Ronald Shaklee, who was appointed to the YSU Department of Geography in 1988. Prior to accepting this position, Dr. Shaklee held teaching positions at Missouri University and Mississippi State University, at which time he was introduced to the teaching and research facilities at the Bahamian Field Station on San Salvador Island. Upon arrival at YSU, he instituted a Bahamian teaching and research program at the University. Except for 2020, when the global pandemic effectively shut down international travel, YSU students have visited San Salvador every year since 1988. Through his efforts, faculty members in Archaeology, Biology, Geology, and Mathematics have been introduced to teaching and research opportunities in the Bahamas. Over 1,000 YSU students have been introduced to field instruction and research on San Salvador Island through Honors Tropical Ecology seminars and classes in Geography, Archaeology, Biology, Geology, and Mathematics. In 1991, The College of the Bahamas Gerace Research Center and Youngstown State University entered into an Affiliation Agreement. This Agreement serves as the longest continuous active agreement between YSU and a partner international institution. Additionally, dozens of Bahamian students have been afforded the opportunity to study at YSU.

Shaklee's publications have been focused on the Bahamas and the Caribbean. He consistently involves students in his research efforts. The results of student research conducted on San Salvador are routinely presented at university and professional conferences held at regional, national, and international levels. Dr. Shaklee's publications include: "In Columbus' Footsteps: A Geography of San Salvador Island, The Bahamas and San Salvador Weather and Climate." His numerous research articles deal with historical weather conditions in the Bahamas, Bahamian environmental issues, Bahamian tourism, and the cartographic evolution of the Bahamas Archipelago over time. He has even published a children's book, "The Misadventures of Maria the Hutia", a book that addresses mankind's impact on threatened tropical environments.

One of Dr. Shaklee's scholarly works is "Cultural Landscape Change at San Salvador: 1984-2011" which he presented at the 14th Symposium on the Natural History of the Bahamas.

Shaklee said that his paper charted cultural landscape changes that have occurred in San Salvador since 1985. The main purpose of the photographic record that he compiled during his first visit was for personal use as a memory prompt. At that time, he had no reason to believe he would return to the island on a regular basis. His work, then, was a personal photographic record of the landscape changes during the period since 1985. His conclusion: "In a digital age, images of any locale can be recorded far more easily...than was possible ...by print and slide film. They can also be shared instantly for global distribution. A far more comprehensive study of change at San Salvador is possible if others...contribute to an electronic repository of historic images of the island." Dr. Ronald Shaklee has contributed significantly to YSU and his students, as well as to the Bahamian region, most notably San Salvador.

Dr. Ronald Shaklee talking to member Ruth Fletcher

Filipe Gonzalez Trio

Our July meeting dealt with the African country of Cameroon, with Dr. Victor Wan-Tatah, a native of that country and a retired YSU professor, as the speaker. Dressed in typical native Cameroon attire, Dr. Wan-Tatah shared many aspects of the culture, traditions, and attractions. Cultural enrichment was presented by Dr. H.W. Martin of Dayton University, who discussed the phenomenon of African literature being passed down by oral experience. The meeting was held at Antone's Banquet Center in Boardman. Our 5-minute speaker was Colleen Kelly, who reported on her work at the Youngstown Incubator and its mission to "jump-start" the economy of the Valley.

Dr. Wan-Tatah, after a long tenure at YSU's Philosophy and Religious Studies Department, has attained Emeritus status in retirement. He had been active in the department and the University, including activity in the Black Studies Program. His publications include a monograph entitled "Religion and Politics in Presidential Elections". His divinity degree from Harvard and continuous study were helpful in researching and writing the work. As a native of Cameroon and his continuous interest in that country, we invited Dr. Wan-Tatah to give us some insight into that African land.

The Republic of Cameroon is sometimes identified as West African and other times as Central African due to its strategic position at the crossroads between West and Central Africa. We were amazed when Dr. Wan-Tatah indicated that its nearly 25 million people speak 250 native languages. Early inhabitants included the Sao civilization and the Baka hunter-gatherers in the southeastern rainforest. Portuguese explorers reached the coast in the 15th century, and Fulani soldiers founded the Adamawa Emirate in the 19th century, but Cameroon became a German colony in 1884. After World War I, it was divided between France and the United Kingdom as League of Nations mandates. For the remainder of the 20th century, certain Cameroon forces fought for independence until the country succeeded and renamed itself the United Republic of Cameroon.

The official languages of Cameroon are French and English; its religious population is predominantly Christian, with a significant minority practicing Islam, with others practicing traditional faiths. Large numbers of Cameroonians live as subsistence farmers. The country is often referred to as "Africa in miniature" for its geological, linguistic, and cultural diversity. Its natural features include beaches, deserts, mountains, rainforests, and savannas. Its cities with the largest populations are Douala on the Wouri River, its economic capital and main seaport; Yaounde, its political capital; and Garoua. Cameroon is well known for its native music styles, particularly Makossa and Bikutsi, and for its successful national football (soccer) team. It is a member state of the African Union, the United Nations, the Commonwealth of Nations, the Non-aligned Movement, and the Organization of Islamic Cooperation.

Among the many activities Wan-Tatah recommended:

- Hop in a 4wheel drive and motor through the Central Highlands to see vibrant, verdant valleys and breathtaking waterfalls, and hope to see the striking orange and purple skylines at dusk.
- Find colonial architecture in Foumban, a culture-rich town of buildings from Cameroon's period of German colonization. Also, one can see a beautiful Sultan's Palace and nearby the Musee de Palais, and the Musee des Arts.
- Go on a gorilla safari in Lobeke National Park from an especially built night watchtower; equally exciting and easier to spot are elephants, buffalo, and the giant forest hog. At Ndjidah National Park, in the far north, one can see lions, elephants, buffalo, and the chance to spot the rare black rhinoceros.
- Scale an active volcano at Mt. Cameroon, which is a popular destination for mountaineers interested in a 3–4day trip.

- Wade waist-deep through Korup national Park, Africa's oldest and most biologically diverse rainforest offering a wide variety of primates, including the short-tailed drill monkey.
- Learn about the local fauna at Limbe, a pleasant port town that boasts beautiful botanical gardens. Today, conservation is at the heart of the scent-filled gardens, which offer trails and insights into Cameroonian botanic culture.

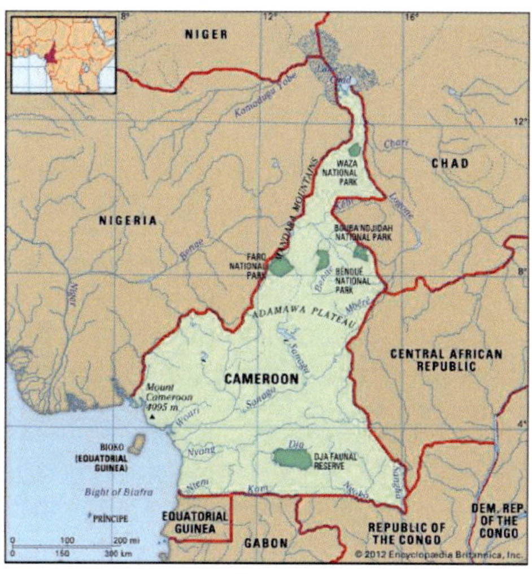

Map of Cameroon

Dr. Wan-Tatah's excitement about his native land is palpable, and wishes some members would try something a little different from exclusively Western travel.

Dr. H. W. Martin, professor of English and Poet-in-Residence at the University of Dayton, concluded the evening with a fascinating talk about how the sermon, the spiritual, the work song, the blues, gospel jazz, and popular ballads, and folk tales, operate to keep African-American literature alive.

Dr. H. W. Martin, Dr. G. D. Beelen and Dr. Victor Wan-Tatah

The city of Paris was the topic in August. Frequent traveler Barbara Krauss, WYSU radio host and leader of many worldwide tours, took us vicariously to this beautiful city, offering valuable tips on understanding their culture. The meeting was held at the Holy Trinity Serbian Orthodox Church Hall, whose caterers prepared a wonderful meal (not French, though.) The cultural enrichment was provided by Steve Papas and Tony Valenzenzi, who played appropriate melodies on their guitars.

Barbara Krauss was a voice and piano graduate from the Dana School of Music at YSU and has always had a love of languages, witness her accurate pronunciation of composers and vocalists on WYSY radio as their classical music announcer and producer. As a frequent traveler to France, Krauss believes that the country of France and the language are inseparable. Indeed, she first fell in love with the language and then the country. About 20 years ago, she was sent to a training conference in Paris to learn the ropes about conducting tours. She was skeptical at first about embracing Paris "as a bastion of romance and culture", but after the conference and after brushing up and improving her French for a few years, Barbara not only learned the language but fell in love with it and with France.

She learned more and more about the language and the country, which enabled her to suggest to her American travelers how to ingratiate themselves with the French rather than to be boorish. She spoke of certain ways that a Frenchman knows how to identify an American: "lack of knowledge of French (or even trying), informal attire, gum chewing, baseball caps, constant smiling, lack of decorum (boisterous) are among the tell-tale indications." Mrs. Krauss also spoke of greeting a Frenchman, providing a flow chart to help the non-French person to figure out what form of address to use. In providing these suggestions, Barbara offered them to be helpful: "Rather than focus on what separates us, I'd like to tune into why we find each other so interesting...for the French are as intrigued by us as we are of them."

The history of bread is "actually the history of France", Barbara argued: "it was after all the shortage of bread in those tempestuous summer months of 1789 that led directly to the French Revolution." Her own interest in baking bread led her to a discussion of the French love of and consumption of bread. They consume a great deal of it (more than most cultures) and have "strong and personal alliances with their bakers and will go out of their way to buy from their favorite." Yet most French citizens are slim owing to their penchant for walking and biking. And they generally do not snack.

Mrs. Krauss spoke of the educational system and the great emphasis placed upon learning instilled in their children at a very early age. Education is free but very competitive. It is offered in three stages: primary school, secondary school, and high school. She said, "Primary and secondary education is free, neutral, secular, and compulsory between ages 6 and 16. After that, placement in a university is based upon test scores that are difficult and competitive because when placed, the costs are free or nominal."

Barbara said that the French also "adore their vacation time." "Paris usually empties out in August, with most people on the road heading south to the country. The regular work week is 35 hours, not 40, and summer vacations are long." Barbara has found the French people to be hospitable and friendly, contrary to the belief of some. "But," she admonishes, "a mannerly way of asking questions is very important as is deportment of the one who is asking. Almost without fail, the French have returned respect with respect, kindness with kindness, and humor with humor."

Although Barbara spent most of her presentation speaking about the people of Paris, she ended on a note of commenting on a few Paris landmarks: "There are, of course, some of the world's most famous landmarks in Paris, including the Louvre...which was once a royal palace and fortress. It dominates the Right Bank of the river Seine...and is some 550,000square feet. Its origins date back to the medieval period, and its present structure has evolved in stages since the 16th century. It was the actual seat of power in France until Louis XIV moved to Versailles in 1682, bringing the government with him. The iconic Pyramid that now graces the front of the Louvre was designed by I.M Pei, the same architect who designed the glass pyramid structure for the Rock and Roll Hall of Fame in Cleveland. The Pyramid was commissioned for the 1989 bicentennial of the French Revolution and was completed in 1993 with the addition of the 'inverted pyramid' below it. This is one of the most popular sites in the world, with nearly 10 million visitors per year." "The river Seine," Krauss continued, "...represents a sort of culture divide in Paris, with many shops and centers of haute couture on the right and libraries, bookstores, and universities on the left. In French, penser means 'to think,' and depenser means 'to spend'...Paris is a city where legends like Coco Chanel and Ernest Hemmingway could feel equally at home."

Barbara indicated after her formal presentation, and some of us know from our own visits to Paris, that there are many other not-to-be-missed sites, some of which appear below:

- The Eifel Tower is one of the symbols of Paris, offering stunning views, built in 1888 and standing almost 300 meters high.
- Musee d'Orsay is famous for housing the largest collection of impressionist and post-impressionist masterpieces-Matisse, Monet, Cezanne, Degas, Van Gogh, and Rodin, among others.
- Arc de Triomphe at one end of the Champs-Elysees, commissioned by Emperor Napoleon I, commemorates the military power of France.
- Cathedral Notre-Dame of Paris is a Gothic architectural masterpiece that has adorned Paris since 1163 and, as we know, suffered severe damage just a few years ago.
- Sacre-Coeur is a famous basilica that sits on the highest peak in Paris, Montmarte.
- Luxembourg Gardens contains a palace and gardens commissioned in the early 17th century by Marie de'Medici and is among the most beautiful display of flora.
- Place de la Concorde is the largest square in Paris and is where Marie Antoinette and Robespierre were beheaded.

Barbara concluded her presentation with the suggestion that one should investigate, wander Paris-even get lost. She said, "So my advice is: if you really want to get the feel of a place, allow yourself the freedom of uncertainty. What you'll find is a connection to a place that you will not find sticking close to a group, a tour guide, or a city map.... Happy travels."

Barbara Krauss

Eiffel Tower

Steve Papas and Steve Valenzenzi

Cuba was Dr. George D. Beelen's topic in September. He traced the history and traditions of the country and related experiences from his own two visits. Several members of the Fred Astaire Dance Studio performed a few typical Cuban dances. The meeting was held at Holy Family Church Hall in Poland, and the food was prepared by Madure's Catering from New Castle, Pennsylvania, and was truly a Cuban feast. The 5-minute presenter was Deryck Toles, director of the program, Inspiring Minds, which addresses the problems of youth.

Only 90 miles from the shores of the United States, Cuba is unknown to most Americans, rendering it an almost mysterious and exotic land. Today, Cuba is a political dinosaur state engendering fear and despair but set in a tropical Hispanic paradise whose land and character exude hope and possibilities. Upon arrival at Joe Marti International Airport, one's initial impression is that Cuba is inefficient, drab, and run-down. However, as one settles in, there are other experiences to be had. Walking through lush urban parks in Havana (the capital), dining at open-air restaurants, hearing the pulsating sounds of salsas, mambos, and cha-cha-chas, and smelling the Cuban delicacies wafting through the humid air are intoxicating. Both of my trips to Cuba consisted of around 15 people and were sanctioned by the U.S. Government.

The state socialism of today's Cuba is a product of many ideological forces. It is Hispanic, nationalistic, capitalistic, and communistic, all together or one at a time, depending upon the event and the wishes of El Jefe, Fidel Castro, or now a handpicked successor. In true Latin style, the people are generous, hospitable, family-oriented, gregarious, and resilient. The qualities were exhibited by our guides, service people, and ordinary citizens.

In Havana's Old Town, we walked the major plazas-Plaza de la Cathedral, Plaza de Armas, Plaza Vieja, and Plaza de San Francisco. Along the way, we saw many urban parks with children using the playground equipment, teens and young adults playing baseball, and males of all ages admiring the 1953 Pontiacs, 1956 Chevrolets, and 1950's vintage Cadillacs. Other modes of transportation were large buses, holding up to 350 passengers; coconut carts, holding one or two, standard buses; bicycles, tricycles; and horse-drawn carriages. In addition, we saw exotic natural beauty and a wonderful array of architecture, representing 16th-century baroque, 17th-century Cuban baroque, Moorish-style baroque, neo-classical, Italian Renaissance-inspired, Gothic, and modern. Buildings were in various stages of restoration, but many were in a sad state of disrepair. Notable among the restored were several tourist hotels built by Europeans, primarily. One that was not restored much was Hotel Riviera, built by a mob boss, Myer Lansky, in the 1950s. While it no longer includes the casino, much of the ambiance and furniture seems stalled in the 1950s.

Traveling to museums showcased the varied history of the land: the Palacio, which was the seat of government for Cuba's colonial governors; the Capitolio, built in 1928, was modeled after the U.S. Capitol; the Castillo de la Real Fuerza (Castle of the Royal Forces), considered to be the oldest stone fortress in the Americas; and several museums that emphasize the continuing nationalistic thread that runs deep in the Cuban soul.

Cubans pay homage to Christopher Columbus at Colon Cemetery and in different parks to Jose Marti, Carlos Manuel de Cespedes, and Antonio Maceo, among other heroes in early attempts at independence. And, of course, there are abundant reminders of the current Revolution (1958-present): Revolutionary Square, Ernesto "Che" Guevara, and others, but not of Fidel Castro; plenty of Revolutionary propaganda at the Museo de la Revolucion, including tanks used at the Bay of Pigs invasion and Granma, the cabin cruiser Fidel and eighty-one other revolutionaries used when they landed in 1956 to start the Revolution.

Restaurants and bars, both large and small abound; some are open to all, others only for tourists. In recent years some have opened private restaurants called paladores. Music, indeed, the arts generally, are ubiquitous. On a single day, we heard folkloric music at a restaurant, an opera (La Traviata) at the Gran Teatro, and jazz music at a small cabaret. Another evening we were treated to a performance by the popular Buena Vista Social Club at the Hotel Nacional.

Art is everywhere-in public facilities, at hotels, in restaurants, and in a growing number of commercial establishments. Dance is a staple in Cuba. Gabriel Marquez called Cuba "the most dance-oriented society on earth". In the cabarets, or on the ballet stage, or in the streets, music and dance envelop the visitor. Walking along the Paseo del Prado, a boulevard (laid out in the 17th century) lined with trees and statues, wrought-iron lamp posts, and coral rock benches, one can see, at any given moment, young and old talking, dancing, engaging in fencing lessons, playing chess, reading and flirting.

Along the famed Malecon, we saw similar examples of a city that works. Laid out in 1901, this sea wall is Havana's most recognizable feature. The curving wall stretches about four miles and protects mini-mansions with their Moorish-domed windows, mosaic iron balconies, stone buildings, and heavy carved doors. From a distance, they look impressive; up close, their former brilliance has been worn away by salt, heat, high-humidity hurricanes, and neglect. Yet, the Malecon is always teeming with activity.

Religion is not dead in Cuba. As in other Latin American countries, Roman Catholicism exists beside or is a mixture of other practices brought by African slaves and Catholic priests. Our visits to Catholic churches and to the Colon Cemetery showed Catholics practicing their faith. However, the island's most popular religion, Santeria, originated in Africa. It is a mixture of African Yoruba and Catholicism. Every September 8th, the Virgin's Feast Day is celebrated with both a Catholic Mass and a Santeria ritual in a blending of the two religions.

Although most of our tour focused on Havana, we did travel to the Vedado and Miramar districts, just outside of Havana. These were the upscale residential districts prior to the Revolution, but today lack the glitter and grandeur of the early 20th century. Traveling farther west on our way to Pinar del Rio, we saw the lush growth and natural beauty of the countryside, rural communities, and farm towns. One of the many noteworthy stops was at a tobacco farm, which was a natural complement to our tour of a cigar factory in Havana. We also visited a model socialist community built on the ruins of a 19th-century coffee finca (farm), a local school at Las Terrazas where fundamental education was taking place. Little wonder, their literacy rate is about 98%. Continuing west, we traveled to the spectacular Vinales Valley, which is purported to be among Cuba's most majestic landscapes. The lush verdure, studded with the famous flat-topped rock formations (mogotes) offered breathtaking views overlooking the valley. The western part of Cuba comes close to being a real tropical paradise. On an earlier trip to Cuba, we traveled east to such cites as Matanzas, Santa Clara, Cienfuegos, Camaguey, and Santiago de Cuba, at the far eastern end of the island, where we saw a marvelous example of a Caribbean carnival.

Among the departures from the Cuban desire to be free of U.S. neo-colonialism are the reverence for Ernest Hemmingway, whose home we visited; the love of the American automobile, even those fifty-plus years old; and the acknowledgment since 1993 of the strength of the U.S. dollar, the most acceptable medium of exchange in that socialist land.

So, what conclusions can we arrive at regarding contemporary Cuba's Revolutionary state, with elements of Latin culture, nationalism, capitalism, and communism? It is a country of natural beauty, urban amenities, 98% literacy, basic health care for all, low-cost housing and jobs for everyone, and a remarkable resilient people-a potential model to many third-world countries. Yet this same country is replete with cities whose building stock is crumbling or needs to be painted, with an economy in shambles, no free press, few consumer goods, and considerable political repression. It has been said that Cuba today "is like a 1950's Cadillac-held together by American design, Russian built pieces and Cuban imagination and resilience."

GDB speaking of Cuba

Fred Astaire dancers

In October, we met to hear Dr. Y.T. Chiu speak about travel to Tibet. He is an area plastic surgeon who graduated in 1962 from The National Defense Medical Center located in Taipei, Taiwan. His recent visit gave currency to this remote country; the images he showed were striking, and his narrative told us about some of Tibet's traditions and culture. Dr. Joseph Kromholtz, YSU, Dana School of Music, provided beautiful violin music. The meeting was held at The Georgetown Banquet Center, whose caterers provided a sumptuous meal, if not ethnic. Our 5-minute presenter was Sister Jerome Corcoran, who commented on her latest initiative, "Sister Jerome's Poor".

Dr. Chiu was born in Hong Kong, moved to China during World War II, then to Taiwan. In 1962 Dr. Chiu immigrated to the Youngstown area and made varied and significant contributions to the Valley, among them a nine-year term as YSU Trustee, a long-time member of the Boards of the Youngstown Symphony, Butler Art Museum, the Rotary Club, and the Mahoning Valley Historical Society. He has traveled extensively, including to Tibet, which he spoke of to the OCA members.

Tibet is a region in East Asia covering much of the Tibetan Plateau, spanning about 970,000 square miles. It is the traditional homeland of the Tibetan people as well as some other ethnic groups and is now also inhabited by considerable numbers of Han Chinese and Hui people. Located in the Himalayas, the highest elevation in Tibet is Mount Everest, earth's highest mountain, rising more than 29,000 ft. above sea level. Dr. Chiu showed images of these mountains and of some people scaling them.

Chiu narrated, along with images, something of the history of the Tibetan people. The Tibetan Empire emerged in the 7th century, but with the fall of the Empire, the region soon divided into a variety of territories. After centuries of conflicts, divisions, and consolidations, Tibet fell under Chinese rule following the Battle of Chamdo in 1950; most of the territories were eventually incorporated into the Chinese provinces of Sichuan and Qinghai. The current borders of Tibet had been generally established in the 18th century but are now under increasing Chinese control. Tibet was occupied and incorporated into the People's Republic of China, and the previous Tibetan government was abolished in 1959 after a failed uprising. There are tensions between Tibet's current political status and dissident groups that are active in exile. Tibetan activists in Tibet have reportedly been arrested and/or tortured.

The economy of Tibet is dominated by subsistence agriculture, though tourism has become a growing industry in recent decades; Chiu's presentation included many images of tourists from his group as well as from other groups of tourists. The dominant religion we were told by Dr. Chiu is Tibetan Buddhism. In addition, there is Bon, which is similar to Tibetan Buddhism, and there are also Tibetan Muslims and Christian minorities. Tibetan Buddhism is a primary influence on the art, music, and festivals of the region. Tibetan architecture reflects Chinese and Indian influences. Staple foods in Tibet are roasted barley, yak meat, and butter tea.

Tourist attractions in Tibet, to a large extent, are shaped and defined by distinct altitudes, varied topography, and climate on the Qinghai-Tibet Plateau. To most of the international and domestic tourists, the biggest draw of Tibet tours is to be able to personally experience life in the spiritual realm of Tibetan Buddhism, enjoy the sublime life of alpine scenery and see as much as one can about Tibetan folk culture and customs. The capital city and spiritual center, Lhasa, is ideally situated for an initial tour; it has a history of 1,300 years. The historic city is filled with prestigious Tibetan monasteries, palaces, and temples and exciting religious and secular life. Chiu reported that, "We saw images of some of the must-see attractions in Lhasa: Potala Palace, the most iconic palace of Tibet, which is also known as the winter palace and residence of former Dalai Lama; Jokhang Temple, the spiritual heart and holiest religious site in Lhasa; the Great Three Gelugpa Monasteries, i.e., Drepung Monastery (the biggest of the monasteries); Sera Monastery (where to see a dramatic monk debate); Ganden Monastery (where to see the most beautiful view of the Lhasa Valley); and heavenly Namtso Lake, which is the largest saline lake in Tibet. Dr. Chiu said there are varied trips to Tibet, depending upon one's toleration of high altitudes and depending upon the time you have." Dr. Chiu concluded by saying, "The trip to Tibet was a memorable and inspiring experience."

Dr. Y.T.Chiu

Dr. Joseph Kromholtz on violin

In November, we "traveled" to Venice with Al Bright, YSU Professor Emeritus of Art, and Dr. Virginia "Dee" Banks Bright, Infectious Disease Specialist, both of whom have spent time in that city. Although the focus dealt substantially with the art of Venice, we learned of many of the city's treasures. Music was provided by an accomplished young pianist Nathan Stephens performing in the beautiful Butler Museum of American Art. AVI Catering provided the meal.

Each of the speakers is an extraordinary professional in their own right, but they complemented each other as they spoke about travel to Venice: Dr. Banks is an infectious disease specialist affiliated with multiple hospitals in the Youngstown and Pittsburgh areas. She received her medical degree from Case Western University School of Medicine and has been in practice for more than two decades. Professor Al Bright was (he died in October 2019) an American artist and art educator. He became the first African American full-time faculty member at his alma mater, Youngstown State University, and was the founder and director of its Africana Studies program from 1970-1987. His art work has been displayed in many museums around the nation, including the Butler Institute of American Art, in his native Youngstown.

Built on more than 100 islands and devoid of cars, Venice is a walker's paradise, even to get lost in, as Barbara Krauss suggested to us, with her trips to Paris (see above). Even when crowds reach their maximum, a stroll down the Floating City's winding passageways reveals the city's abundant charm. The architectural splendor of Doge's Palace and St. Mark's Basilica in Piazza San Marco reign supreme, while the Grand Canal splits the city in two. The floating city is renowned for its Gothic art and architecture.

Due to its location on the marshy Venetian Lagoon, the entire architecture of the city is designed intelligently, making it unique from any other style of architecture in Europe. Originating in the 14th century, Gothic architecture has three different types, including Byzantine and Islamic influence, secular Gothic, and religious Gothic. Dr. Banks said, "As you walk around this beautiful city, you can appreciate the many types of architecture that have gone into some of Venice's most recognizable buildings throughout the centuries. It's this architecture that partly makes Venice so unique and different." Although Modernism had not been well received, attitudes changed after the disastrous flood in 1966. People put aside their difference and agreed to make changes to the city and its architecture in order to save it. Since then, with the help of UNESCO, Venice has completed more than 1,500 restoration projects, striving to maintain a harmonious mix of the old and new architecture.

Among the attractions Al and Dee featured were:

- Doge's Palace was built by the powerful families that ruled the Venetian Empire from this fantasy palace; it was built in 1340 and became a museum in 1923.
- St. Mark's Basilica is the crown jewel of Venice; it is an ornate cathedral that blends elements of Gothic, Byzantine, Romanesque, and Renaissance architecture and is also known for its striking domes.
- St. Mark's Square (Piazza San Marco), one of the most famous squares in Italy, is the geographic and cultural heart of Venice.
- Grand Canal is the bustling "main street" of the city built on water, and it is lined with sumptuous Venetian palaces and crowded with gondolas, water taxis, and public ferries.
- Murano is one group of Venice's many islands which has been at the center of Venice's glassmaking industry since 1291.

- Rialto Bridge was the first to span Venice's Grand Canal between its two highest points. The original 12th-century wooden bridge was replaced in 1592 by a stone structure.
- Marco Polo's Palace Home is in a quiet corner of Venice; the Venetian Palace is believed to be Marco Polo's former residence. This image, as well as the others listed, captured a great deal of life in Venice.
- While Dr. Banks and Professor Bright thrilled us with the architecture of Venice, they also showed images of many artists and their works, for which Venice is famous. Some of the famous Renaissance painters' works who defined Venetian art as we think of it today appear all over the city in the museums and galleries, of course, but also in the many little churches, which also boast incredible works of art. Among those mentioned were:
- Giovanni Bellini was one of the forerunners of the Venetian School and was known for his adept realism and color-handling. One of his works adorns the altar of the Church of San Zaccaria Altarpiece since 1505.
- Titian was arguably the most important painter of the Venetian School. He was incredibly versatile, equally skilled at landscapes, religious and mythological scenes, and portraits, like the famously erotic vision of the goddess of love, Venus of Urbina, done in 1538.
- Tintoretto prolifically produced altarpieces and canvases, such as his work The Miracle of St. Mark Freeing a Slave, done in 1548.
- Veronese produced his work The Wedding at Cana during 15621563, which is massive (22 by 32 ft) and is on display, not in Venice, but at the Louvre.
- Canaletto's scenes of Venice were collected in Venice and throughout Europe with his work Canal of San Marco with the Piazza San Marco, done in the 1730s, among the most famous.
- Francesco Guardi, with his work Capriccio with Bridges Over a Canal, the most famous, features his spirited brushwork and sparkling canals, is viewed by many to have influenced the Impressionists a century later.
- Needless to say, Al had considerable to say about each of these works. Our speakers say they are always thrilled to visit Venice and soak up the ambiance—and even get lost.

Professor Al Bright

Dr. Dee Banks Bright

Butler Executive Director Dr. Louis Zona

Butler scene

Our final meeting of this extended season ended in December when we featured Iceland, as long-time OCA member Dorothy Palguta Tesner shared her experiences of her recent visit. Her images were intriguing as she urged members to give this little country a try. We met at the Western Reserve United Methodist Church Hall. The Canfield Community Band, under the direction of Eric Babel, provided a stirring finish to this memorable 28th OCA program.

Dorothy Tesner is among the very first to be involved in the OCA. She and several educators were on a recent tour of Mexico with me, at which time we were urged by people like Pepin Hernandez Laos (see above) to initiate a multicultural organization that ultimately became the Ohio Cultural Alliance. Ms. Tesner also served on the OCA Board and as secretary for the entire 30 years of our existence. She is also a former educator and a world traveler, from a safari in Africa to much of Europe and to Iceland, her current topic.

Iceland is a Nordic island country in the North Atlantic Ocean and the most sparsely populated country in Europe. The capital and largest city is Reykjavik, and the surrounding areas in the southwest of the country are home to over two-thirds of the population. Iceland is volcanically and geologically active. The interior consists of a plateau characterized by sand and lava fields, mountains and glaciers, and many glacial rivers that flow to the sea through the lowlands. Iceland is warmed by the Gulf Stream and has a temperate climate, despite a latitude just outside the Arctic Circle. Its high latitude and marine influence keep summers chilly, and most of its islands have a polar climate.

Ms. Tesner invited us "to explore a unique and bizarre country" that is "quite accessible, being 4 ½ hours from New York City." Each year the number of tourists is greater than the overall population of 330,000. Tourism is vitally important to Iceland's economic success as it provides the locals "with job opportunities and accounts for a large percentage of its gross domestic product." As the economy is stimulated by tourists, the government has more funds to build convenient transportation access, which benefits both tourists and locals. Reykjavik, the capital, is home to two-thirds of the population. Tesner said, "It is a cosmopolitan city with chic hotels, 170 restaurants, upscale shops, museums, concerts, festivals, freeways, a multitude of bars and is considered a 'hot spot' of Europe."

After the Norwegian chieftain Ingolfr Arnarson became the first permanent settler in Iceland in 874, the country experienced immigration from other Nordic countries. Following a period of civil strife, Iceland came under Norwegian rule in the 13th century; in 1397, the Nordic countries united under the Kalmar Union. Iceland struggled for independence, succeeding in 1918 and founding a republic in 1944. Until the 20th century, Iceland relied largely on subsistence fishing and agriculture until the industrialization of the fisheries and Marshall Plan aid following World War II brought prosperity, helping Iceland to become one of the wealthiest and most developed nations in the world. Iceland has a market economy with relatively low taxes as well as the highest trade union membership in the world. It maintains a Nordic social welfare system that provides universal health care and tertiary education for its citizens. They rank high in economic, democratic, and social stability, as well as equality, ranking among the highest in the world in median wealth per adult and in development. And Iceland runs almost completely on renewable energy.

Dorothy admonished us, "In order to appreciate and really experience Iceland, you need to have a passion or at least an interest in nature and geology. If volcanoes, lava fields, geysers, waterfalls, glaciers, ice caves, and thermal spas excite you and if you can tolerate weather that changes 5 times a day, then this might be a splendid destination. Temperatures range from the '30s to the '50s. Actually, it's milder than New York City because of the Gulf Stream. The weather is volatile with driving rain, fog, intense sun… and only 4-5 hours of daylight in the winter." Among some other interesting features of Tesner's talk were that many tongue-twisting words were hard to pronounce and also the unusual nature of last names: married women do not change their names, the use of gender suffixes, and phone books are alphabetized by first names. However, the use of English has been widespread since 1999.

She spoke of traveling the Ring Road in a counterclockwise direction. Short tours could include some spectacular sights. Going east, Dorothy narrated and showed images of some of these sights:

- Gullfoss (Golden Falls) is the most iconic massive waterfall. She said, "you are guaranteed a rainbow on a sunny day." A sign read. "Watch your children; we cannot rope off everything."
- A geyser which is a geothermal area that once spouted as high as 262 feet but is now just a calm, steamy vent. "People tried to encourage eruptions by throwing soap and rocks into it", to no avail.
- "Strokkur is close by and very accommodating, spouting every 5-10 minutes, anywhere from 30-115 feet".
- Skalholt is a Catholic settlement that once was the most wealthy, influential, and populated of Catholic settlements.
- Thingvellir is "not to be missed," Dorothy advised, "since it is the most significant historical site where the Parliament first convened in 930 and met through 1798." It was also famous as a symbol of the nationalistic movement for independence from Denmark, which was finally achieved in 1944.
- Volcanoes abound in Iceland, numbering about 200. Tesner related that "Many of these volcanoes are sub-glacial, often the most dangerous, because the weight of the ice cap creates a pressure cooker.... In the spring of 2010...Eyaajallojokull, off the southern coast, erupted for about 6 months, causing havoc with air traffic and canceling flights as far away as Europe." Another famous volcano is Surtsey, which actually created a new island in 1963 through a series of deep-sea eruptions, as magma fought its way out of the sea bed to build the new land.
- Blue Lagoon is the most popular tourist attraction. Tesner said that "it is not a natural thermal spa. It was formed by the runoff from the neighboring power plant, which pumped blazing hot mineral-rich water into a lagoon which was dug into a lava field." The color comes from algae, silica, and other minerals, which are touted to be beneficial for a variety of health purposes.
- The Pearl is a futuristic glass dome that sits atop enormous tanks storing tons of geo-thermally heated water for the city.
- Other points of interest that Dorothy spoke of were whale watching; the Northern Lights (Aurora Borealis), and the Skaftafell Ice Cave in Vatnajokull National Park and Myrdalsjokull Glacier Park to see disappearing glaciers.

Among other "fascinating and bizarre" experiences, Dorothy cites dining in Iceland. "For the adventuresome," she recommended, "the Puffin (a fishy tasting bird), Minke Whale (a cross between beef and tuna, serve raw to rare), How Karl (putrefied shark) and Skyer (a whipped whey that is something like yogurt, crème frieche and soft serve enhanced with berries.)" It was an adventure that Tesner described to us by way of her fascinating narration and captivating images. A fitting conclusion to our final program for 2015.

"Going Places with the Ohio Cultural Alliance" took us to all parts of the world: Europe, Asia, Middle East, Africa, and Central America, with a concentration on countries, cities, and islands. The number of attendees ranged from just under 200 to a high of 276 for this year, which ran from September 2014 to December 2015. The OCA enjoyed another banner year.

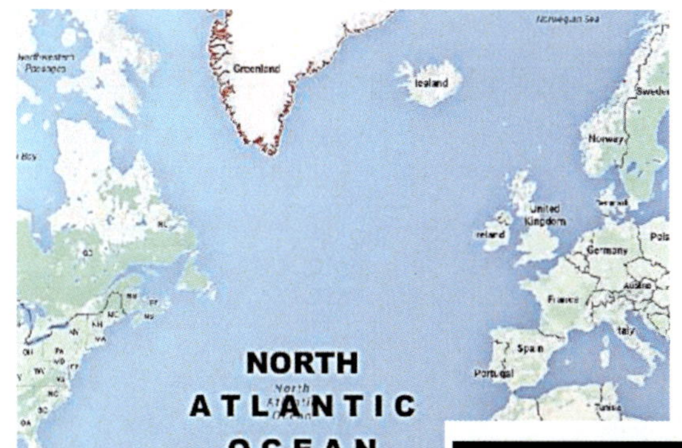

Iceland on a map

Reverend Kathryn Adams and Dorothy Palguta Tesner

Blue Lagoon is the most popular tourist attraction.

XX. Faith in the Mahoning Valley

The theme for the OCA's 29th year (2016) was "Faith in the Mahoning Valley". We began a new schedule with programs offered monthly from March through December. For this year, the Ohio Cultural Alliance collaborated with the Mahoning Valley Association of Churches (MVAC), which celebrated its 100th year in 2016. We discussed many of the religions of the Mahoning Valley, focusing on the elements of history, heart, and heritage of their respective traditions.

The OCA/MVAC held its first joint meeting in March when Sudhakar V. Rao, MD, addressed the theme, "Faith in the Valley: Hinduism." Cultural enrichment was provided by a group of Indian dancers from Akron. We met at The Georgetown Banquet Center in Boardman and enjoyed a meal that included some Indian elements. Our 5-minute speaker was Guy Burney, Executive Director of The Community Initiative to Reduce Violence (CIRV) in Youngstown.

Dr. Rao is a pediatric cardiologist, a professor at Northeast Ohio Medical University and at Ross University School of Medicine, an active scholar, a Hindu priest, a community leader, and a beautiful lecturer. His presentations have been to many interfaith groups, which made him a perfect presenter for the OCA, considering our current theme of "Faith in the Mahoning Valley". He did not disappoint.

Dr. Rao spoke of his own faith of Hinduism as he indicated how similar its tenets are to the other major religions of the Valley. He described Hinduism as a diverse system of thought marked by a range of philosophies and shared concepts, rituals, cosmological systems, pilgrimage sites, and shared textual sources that discuss theology, metaphysics, mythology, Vedic yajna, yoga, agamic rituals, and temple building, among other topics. The Indian religion of Hinduism is a way of life that is the world's third-largest religion, with over 1.2 billion followers.

Rao began with key beliefs of Hinduism, which include "truth is eternal", "Brahman is truth and reality", "the Vedas are the ultimate authority", "everyone should strive to achieve dharma", "individual souls are immortal", and "the goal of the individual soul is moksha".

Prominent themes in Hindu beliefs include the four Purusarthas, the proper goals or aims of human life: namely, dharma (ethics/duties), artha (prosperity/work), kama (desires/passions) and moksha (liberation/freedom from the passions and the cycle of death and rebirth). Hinduism prescribes eternal duties, such as honesty, refraining from injuring living beings (Ahimsa), patience, forbearance, self-restraint, virtue, and compassion, among others. Hindu practices include rituals such as puja (worship) and recitations, japa, meditation (dhyana), family-oriented rites of passage, annual festivals, and occasional pilgrimages. Along with the practice of various yogas, some Hindus leave their social world and material possessions and engage in lifelong Sannyasa (monasticism) in order to achieve moksha (freedom/liberation).

Using considerable images and power point, Dr. Rao told us something about the various Hindu texts, which are classified into Sruti (heard) and Smrti, (remembered), the major scriptures of which are the Vedas, the Upanishads, the Puranas, the Mahabharata, the

Ramayana, and the Agamas. There are six astika schools of Hindu philosophy. Scholars regard Hinduism as a fusion or synthesis of Brahmanical orthopraxy with various Indian cultures, having diverse roots and no specific founder. He also reported that currently, the four largest denominations of Hinduism are Vaishnavism, Shaivism, Shaktism, and Smartism. Sources of authority and eternal truths in the Hindu texts play an important role, but there is a strong Hindu tradition of questioning authority in order to deepen the understanding of these truths and to further develop the traditions. Hinduism is the most widely professed faith in India, Nepal, and Mauritius. Significant numbers of Hindu communities are found in Southeast Asia, the Caribbean, Europe, and Africa, and North America, including a significant presence in the Mahoning Valley. Dr. Rao exuded compassion and empathy throughout his presentation, ending with "why can't we just get along"? The Indian dancers were lively, disciplined, and ornately dressed. What a concluding complement to a wonderful evening.

Dr. Sudhakar V. Rao

Indian dancers from Akron

The OCA/MVAC held its second joint meeting in April, addressing the theme "Faith in the Valley: Judaism and Early Christianity," with Rabbi Joseph Schonberger and Father George Balasko as our speakers. We met at Temple El Emeth in Liberty, Ohio, with Kravitz Catering arranging a modified Seder meal. Members of the Jewish youth community treated us with dialogue and music appropriate to a Seder meal. Our 5-minute presenter was Ms. Penny Wells, Youngstown director of Sojourn to the Past, a catalyst for leadership development among city school students to help make a difference in the schools and the community at large.

Father Balasko is the co-creator of Jewish/Christian Dialogue with the late Rabbi Samuel Meyer of Temple El Emeth. Through his many ecumenical programs, Balasko is highly regarded in the Jewish community. For more than 20 years, he has served as host and producer of the Jewish/Christian Dialogue network television series, which airs in several markets around the world. As an interesting note (but not necessarily relevant to this evening's presentation), Father Balasko is also known for his work in originating, adapting, writing, and producing the first Polka Mass.

An example of his education series is "Torah Studies for Christians", hosted by Jewish/Christian Studies of Youngstown and the B'nai B'rith Guardian of the Menorah at Villa Marie Education and Spirituality Center. Working closely with the biblical text, participants explored the methods and insights of the sages of the Jewish tradition, their love for the Torah, their eye for detail, their incisive questions, debates, and creative storytelling (midrash). In this way, participants deepened their appreciation of a Torah tradition that is the core of Jewish life, which formed Jesus as a Jew, and which is the root of the biblical heritage of Christians.

Rabbi Schonberger, the spiritual leader of Temple El Emeth, hosted the meeting and was the co-presenter with Father Balasko. Together they discussed Judaism and early Christianity, much as Balasko and Meyer had been doing for a number of years, but this evening in truncated form. During their presentation, we were reminded of the early development of Christianity. Jewish Christians were the followers of a Jewish religious sect that emerged in Judea during the late Second Temple period (1st century A.D.) The Nazarene Jews integrated the belief of Jesus as the prophesied Messiah and his teachings into the Jewish faith, including the observance of the Jewish law. The name may derive from the city of Nazareth or from prophecies in Isaiah. Jewish Christianity, we were reminded, is the foundation of early Christianity, which later developed into Christianity. Christianity started with Jewish eschatological expectations, and it developed into the worship of a deified Jesus after his earthly ministry, his crucifixion, and the post- crucifixion experiences of his followers.

Our presenters told of the many areas of commonality between Judaism and Christianity, such as monotheism, a God that is mighty and good and is our Creator who reveals His word to man and answers our prayers. They told of the split that took place during the first centuries CE. The First Jewish-Roman War and the destruction of the Second Temple in 70 CE were the main events, but the separation was a long-term process.

A delightful bonus was the young peoples' recitation and singing that accompanied the Seder meal. One additional surprise was issued by Rabbi Schonberger, who said to me, "George, I have another special conclusion to the evening." He led us into the sanctuary to introduce us to an exceptionally talented and inspirational musical combo that played Klezmer music and a host of uplifting numbers that left us fairly floating out of Temple El Emeth. What an evening this was.

Seder meal

Father George Balasko and Rabbi Joseph Schonberger

Surprise appearance by a Klezmer group

The OCA/MVAC held its May meeting with Reverend John Mulqueen, addressing the theme "Faith in the Valley: Catholicism." We met at St. Nicholas Church Hall in Struthers with the meal prepared by Loretta's Catering. Cultural enrichment came in the form of beautiful music provided by Reverend Vit Fiala performing on cello. Our 5-minute presenter was Heidi Daniel, Executive Director of the Youngstown and Mahoning County Libraries.

Father Mulqueen is a retired Roman Catholic priest ordained in 1962. He has served as a Catholic high school religion teacher, pastor, and missionary. He spent several years in El Salvador with the Maryknoll Missionaries. He holds both a Master's and Doctor of Divinity degrees.

Father John Mulqueen

Father Mulqueen began his presentation with words that are essential to the Catholic faith: "Catholic, the word-universal, open and inclusive; Apostles' Creed-1st century-'I believe in the holy Catholic church'; Nicene Creed-4th century, 'I believe in one, holy, catholic and apostolic church". Over 2,000 years, many people have called themselves Christians and have recited these creeds, but changes have also occurred during this period of time: in the 11th century, there was a division within Christianity between the East and the West; from the late Middle Ages, there was a conviction that the church needed reform; the most definitive efforts of reform occurred in the 16th century with Luther and Calvin; from this point on Catholic usually meant Roman Catholic; many of the reform churches continued with the ancient creeds, but catholic was spelled with a lower case c. His point is that Christianity is not static.

After a brief look at the history and settlement of the Mahoning Valley, Mulqueen discussed the establishment of the Catholic churches in the Valley, beginning with St. Mary's in Warren in 1837. He reported that 11 Catholic churches were built along the Mahoning River valley. Most were generally composed of pretty strong ethnic congregations, but more importantly, in the 19th century, they were territorial (one was expected to attend the church in your territory). This changed at the beginning of the 20th century when most of the Roman Catholic churches were national (ethnic). He said that eight Byzantine parishes and Maronite parishes were established, all having different cultures but some positive relationship to Rome. In his prepared text, Father Mulqueen listed these early churches and their dates of founding.

He continued with a discussion of the various types of Catholic churches: the territorial, national, Byzantine, Maronite, Ruthenian, Ukrainian, and Romanian, and some of the variations in their worship, i.e., national parishes had the Mass in Latin (until the Vatican Council), but hymns were in the native languages; Byzantine churches celebrated the Mass in their native language and had a marked cultural difference in prayers and forms, and had their own church law, plus a more complicated issue that was the question of married priesthood, permitted in some Catholic rites, but not others.

Father Mulqueen also addressed the parish Catholic schools, which evolved/devolved from the 19th-century proscription that every Catholic parish have a Catholic school with every parent to send their children to Catholic school, to the mid-20th century and beyond, which witnessed the significant decline in Catholic schools. He wondered out loud where we are in the Catholic Church: while the basic ministries of the church continue, i.e., worship, to know the Word, outreach for the common good, and administration/stewardship, he also cited the decline in priests, nuns, and deacons; the decline in church attendance and subsequent consolidations of parishes. He admonished us with several closing remarks that although there is light in the Church, there is also darkness: "We've learned to enough to hate, not quite enough to love." He is not certain what our future is, but his hope is that the ecumenical spirit continues to bring us together to worship the Lord and do works of mercy. His concluding words: "We may not need more theologians but more martyrs, a daunting task." We left the meeting in a contemplative mood.

The music of Father Vit Fiala enhanced the mood and suggested the light rather than the darkness.

OCA May, 2016 crowd

The June meeting featured Reverend Constantine Valantasis, pastor of St. Demetrius Greek Orthodox Church in Warren, who addressed the theme "Faith in the Valley: Orthodox". It was held at Archangel Greek Orthodox Church Hall in Campbell, whose caterers prepared a sumptuous Greek meal. Cultural enrichment was provided by a Balalaika group directed by Jane Malachany. Our 5-minute speaker was Maraline Kubik, who spoke of Sister Jerome's Program for the Poor.

Reverend Valantasis was born in Youngstown and reared in Campbell, Ohio, and the son of the author's classmate in high school. He is a graduate of Hellenic College/Holy Cross Greek Orthodox School of Theology in Brookline, Massachusetts. He was ordained Deacon in 1988 and a Presbyter in 1990. He has served in North Ridge, California, and in Massillon, Ohio, before coming to St. Demetrius in 2010. We learned that Reverend Valantasis is a practitioner of kung fu/martial arts. Whether he is wearing a black cassock or a black belt, Reverend Valantasis sees no conflict between his Christian beliefs and his martial arts philosophy. In fact, participation in martial arts since he was a youngster has enhanced his spiritual life, he said. He argued that it is part of his Christian discipline and it helps him to relax.

Reverend Constantine Valantasis

The Greek Orthodox churches are descended from churches that the Apostles founded in the Balkans and the Middle East during the first century A.D., as well as from the maintenance of many ancient church traditions. Orthodox churches, unlike the Catholic Church, have no single Supreme Pontiff or Bishop but hold to the belief that Christ is the head of the Church. However, they are each governed by a committee of Bishops called the Holy Synod, with one central Bishop holding the honorary title of "first among equals." Reverend Valantasis explained that Greek Orthodox churches are united in communion with each other, as well as with other Eastern Orthodox Churches. The Orthodox embrace a common doctrine and a common form of worship, and they see themselves not as separate churches but as administrative units of a single Church. They are notable for their extensive tradition of iconography, for their veneration of the Mother of God and the Saints, and for their use of the Divine Liturgy on Sundays, which is a standardized worship service dating back to the 4th century A.D.

The current territory of the Greek Orthodox churches more or less covers the areas in the Balkans, Anatolia, and the Eastern Mediterranean that used to be a part of the Byzantine Empire. The majority of Greek Orthodox Christians live within Greece and elsewhere in the southern Balkans, including Albania, but also in Jordan, the Palestinian territories, Iraq, Syria, Lebanon, Cyprus, Anatolia, Eastern Turkey, and the South Caucasus. In addition, due to the large Greek diaspora, there are many Greek Orthodox Christians who live in North America and Australia.

In a written summary of St. Demetrius, we learned of their interpretation of Greek Orthodoxy, a summary of which follows:

- We believe what the Bible tells us that we have all sinned and the wages of sin is death, but the gift of God is eternal life through Jesus.

- God, in His own time and in His own way, will bring the world to its appropriate end. According to His promise, Jesus will return personally and visibly in glory to the earth; the dead will be raised, and Christ will judge all.
- About the Church: The Church is the Body of Christ, the Family of God, the Bride of Christ, a habituation of God through the Holy Spirit, given the assignment of fulfilling the Great Commission by Jesus, who is the Head of the Church. Every person who is born of the Spirit is an integral part of the Church and becomes part of the Body of Christ.
- About separation of the Church and state they believe that each local church is self-governing and must be free from interference by any external ecclesiastical or political authority; that every human being is ultimately responsible to God in matters of faith and life and that each person is free to worship God according to the dictates of his/her conscience. We further believe that governments are established by God; that Christians, as good citizens, should be subject to governing authorities insofar as possible, recognizing our greater allegiance to God and His kingdom in matters wherein human authorities conflict with clear, biblical mandates.

The talented Balalaika group provided memorable music that was both lively and beautiful to end the evening.

On an additional note, attendees of OCA meetings have, over the years, toured several Orthodox churches, including Archangel Michael church, the site of this meeting and Romanian Orthodox churches in Youngstown and Warren.

Balalaika group

The July meeting focused on "Faith in the Valley: Islam" featuring Dr. Ikram Khawaja and Mrs. Randa Shabayek. We met at The Embassy Banquet Center in Boardman, whose caterers prepared a substantially authentic ethnic meal. The Youngstown Connection, under the direction of Dr. Carol Baird, once again provided our cultural enrichment. Our 5-minute presenter was Carol Potter, Executive Director of the Better Business Bureau.

Dr. Khawaja who has spoken to the OCA previously has also participated in writing for two of our publications. He is a retiree of YSU having served as a professor and chair of the Geology Department, dean of the School of Arts and Sciences, provost and interim president of YSU. Khawaja is a native of Pakistan, Shabayek is a native of Egypt and both are active members of the Islamic community of the Valley. Mrs. Shabayek is also the former president of the Islamic Society of Greater Youngstown. Both talked about how Islam has more in common with the other major religions than differences.

Shabayek explained the principles and basic teachings of Islam which revolve about the five pillars. This includes five daily prayers, declaration of their faith, fasting during Ramadan, the importance of charity and pilgrimage to Mecca at least once in their lifetime. She reiterated through short stories and messages in the Quran that Islam is a peaceful religion and that there are many misconceptions surrounding the faith. Concerning female clothing she argued that Islamic women who are drop-dead gorgeous feel more comfortable showing only their eyes to avoid becoming the center of attention. "A woman should wear it because their beauty is for themselves and their families," she said. "We cover the whole body except for the hands and the face. It's not just the look that's important, but also what's in the heart. It's what's inside." She related that scarves were worn in biblical days as a sign of modesty for men as well as women. "It's been a part of Christianity for such a long time. Jesus' mother wore it", she said.

She added, "according to Islamic teachings, the hajj pilgrimage is a spiritual journey that cleanses the soul and wins absolution. A Muslim who performs the hajj washes away all sins and returns home free of sin, much like a newborn. The pilgrimage to Mecca...is required once ...for all Muslims who are able and can afford the trip. Mecca is in Saudi Arabia, south of Mount Arafat. Muslims can travel there any time for their pilgrimage." Mrs. Shabayek said she and her husband have already made their pilgrimage. However, they could return in the name of someone else who isn't able to make such a trip. She did say that when they travel, her head scarf draws attention, especially since 9/11. Nonetheless she will continue to wear it because it is part of her religion.

Dr. Khawaja reiterated some of the ideas embodied in Islam: The uniqueness of the One and only God; the revelations of the teachings and commandments of God to Prophets which make the way of peace of the whole universe and all humankind; the day of judgment which inaugurates the afterlife. "Islam establishes a code of conduct which outlines human responsibilities to God, to oneself, to the family and to humankind." Faith and practice are two basic components of organized religions. In Islam, there are five articles of faith: Belief in one God; Belief in God's angels; Belief in God's Books and Holy Qur'an as His last book; Belief in God's prophets (pbut) and Mohammed (pbuh) as His last and final messenger and Belief in life after death.

Dr. Khawaja also disabused us of commonly held impressions unsupported by facts: Muslims are predominantly Arabs; Islam is outside of the Judea-Christian tradition; early conversion to Islam was through the use of force; women have inferior status in Islamic culture and Islam teaches hatred of Jews. He argued that toleration and coexistence are expressed throughout Islamic teaching. Our two speakers spoke knowledgeably and poignantly about their chosen religion. They also were excellent spokespersons for the relatively small local

Islamic community, most of whom are professionals, active in their three or four local religious facilities and active in the Youngstown area community.

Dr. Ikram Khawaja

Mrs. Randa Shabayek

Islamic food

In August the OCA/MVAC joint meeting addressed the topic "Faith in the Valley: From a Fractured Church to Ecumenical Cooperation" with Reverend C. Edward Weisheimer as our speaker. We met at St. Michael's Church Hall in Canfield and Madure Catering prepared the meal. Cultural enrichment was provided by the Penn-Ohio Singers who regaled us with religious melodies, barbershop music and a mix of other songs. Our 5-minute presenter was Patricia Syac, Executive Director, of the Youngstown Symphony.

Reverend Weisheimer has received a Master of Divinity degree from Yale Divinity School and Doctor of Divinity degree from Christian Theological Seminary. He was ordained in 1965 in the Christian Church, Disciple of Christ. He has served in many ministries in Illinois, Indiana and Ohio, including as Senior Minister, Central Christian Church in Youngstown. His volunteer services cover a multitude of areas: Ecumenical Coalition in Youngstown, Interfaith Home Maintenance, Food Warehouse, Affordable Housing for Seniors Program, Director of the United Church Homes and Dialogue on Racism, most in the Youngstown area. His credentials for interfaith involvement are vast and varied.

Reverend Weisheimer has seen a fractured church among the Christian community but has been more optimistic in recent years as ecumenism has become more of a reality nationally and internationally. Ecumenism is the movement to promote Christian unity. He reminded us that Jesus founded one, holy catholic and apostolic church. Catholic with an upper case "C" is used for the proper noun naming the Catholic Church. In the creed catholic is spelled with the lower case "c" to mean ecumenical, universal, or all over the land. Ecumenism is needed because despite the will of God, we the people get divided up when individuals and groups don't hear God saying and doing the same thing to each and all of us. Ecumenism reminds us that Jesus founded one church.

When divisions rise to a level that compromises the unity of the church, an ecumenical council can be a gathering that clarifies and corrects who we are and what we are teaching in the name of Jesus. An important ecumenical council, the Second Vatican Council, was convened in 1962 and closed in 1965. "On a local level such ecumenism is celebrated by way of the Mahoning Valley Association of Churches, with increasing vigor", Weisheimer noted. The Mahoning Valley Association of Churches is made up of congregations from Columbiana, Mahoning and Trumbull counties. MVAC works to be a witness to Christ's call that His followers would be one. By working cooperatively, in the church and the community, they seek to bring about the realm of God on earth. Their mission reads that "We value diversity, racial harmony, justice and respect as we strive for reconciliation within the Church and beyond." More about MVAC and their activity was covered in a subsequent meeting.

A second special meeting of the OCA Board was held in August to arrange for a formal termination of the Ohio Cultural Alliance as an autonomous organization. We agreed that all good things come to an end. We had good run for 30 years. We said we would continue with our September, October, November and December meetings, continuing our theme of Faith in the Valley" and plan and hold a final meeting in February 2017.

Reverend C. Edward Weisheimer

Penn-Ohio Singers

The OCA/MVAC September meeting featured Reverend Lewis W. Macklin who addressed the topic "Faith in the Valley: The Local Black Baptist Church." We met at Western Reserve United Methodist Church, with the meal catered by Carolyn Catering. Cultural enrichment was provided by Reverend Kenneth Simon and members of his congregation. Our 5-minute presenter was Harry Meshel who spoke of the Youngstown Labor and Industry Museum (Steel Museum) in Downtown Youngstown.

Reverend Macklin is the lead pastor of Holy Trinity Missionary Baptist Church in Youngstown, is very involved in the community and has received a host of awards for his contributions. Reverend Macklin graduated from Wilson High School, Youngstown State University with a B. A., a Master of Arts from the Southern Bible Seminary and Institute in Augusta, Georgia and a doctoral degree from the same institution. In addition to the ministry, he has served as president of local boards and as chairperson of district organizations. He has been recognized for community leadership by the YSU Office of Diversity, co-convener of the Reverend Martin Luther King Planning Committee, chairman of the American Wellness Walk of the Mahoning Valley and he serves as chaplain for the Youngstown City Police Department.

Although there are a host of Black churches in Youngstown, Reverend Macklin concentrated primarily on Holy Trinity, suggesting that there are many similarities among them. Holy Trinity has a rich history and legacy of pursuing matters of social justice. In fact, the "Mother of the Civil Rights Movement", Rosa Parks, spoke at Holy Trinity in 1957. After several locations during their 70+ years, Holy Trinity relocated in 1992 to their current location at 505 Parkcliffe Avenue in Youngstown. In June 1997 the church extended a call to Reverend Lewis who previously served as youth pastor at New Bethel Baptist Church.

Reverend Macklin said the Black churches as well as most religious institutions' membership have been in decline. Despite all the preaching, teaching, singing, dancing, revivals and conferences church attendance continues to decline. He said he implores his congregation to work harder with ideas and deeds. Each individual can do something as in 1 Corinthians 3:7-9 we read, "It's not important who does the planting, or who does the watering. What's important is that God makes the seeds grow… The various efforts of faith organizations and their leadership should be seen as a complement to sacred and secular responses to promote peace, foster unity and quell incidents of violence within our city," he said.

Reverend Macklin spoke of the various activities he and his congregation have participated in: NOW Youngstown, National Night Out, Come Revive Youngstown (CRY), Community Initiative to Reduce Violence, Fathers' Day Prayer Event and Kingdom Reign International Ministries, among others. He said, "We cannot let negativity attempt to charge the atmosphere…How can I offer tangible support." He offered a prayer for resolving conflicts and seeking peace among others by asking God to lead us to a path to peace which ends with: "May I find humility in You, and may I be the first to forgive, to make amends and to move forward in a healthy way. You have placed me among others, and I pray that I would glorify You through all my actions and conversations. Help me to see others the way You see them and give me an extra measure of grace and patience today as I keep the faith." Among the aspects of the worship service of the Black churches one can glean: clap our hands and voice shouts of praise; pray in the spirit; sing choruses and scriptures, as well as hymns; dance; sing in the spirit; have musical instruments as part of worship service; stand and sing unto the lord; lift our hands; have the whole church pray at once. These parts of the worship are an integral part of the service and the enthusiasm is palpable. As a personal observation I would note that Black congregations remember "to dress to honor the Lord." Reverend Macklin is an exemplary example of the clergy who prays and acts. The evening ended with a prayerful, joyous and lively musical presentation by Reverend Kenneth Simon and members of his congregation of New Bethel Baptist Church of Youngstown.

Reverend Lewis W. Macklin

Reverend Kenneth Simon gospel singers

The October meeting of the OCA/MVAC addressed the topic "Faith in the Valley: Old North Church (Mega Churches)" with Dr. Nick Gatzke, Senior Pastor. We met at Old North Church, with The Praise Band of Old North providing the cultural enrichment. Carolyn Catering prepared the meal. Our 5-minute presenter was Kathy Cook, President of Mercy Health in Trumbull County.

Dr. Reverend Nick Gatzke is Senior Pastor of Old North Church in Canfield after serving as Senior Pastor of Osterville Baptist Church in Cape Cod, Massachusetts. He received his education and training at Moody Bible Institute (B.A.), Gordon-Conwell Theological Seminary (M.Div.) and the London School of Theology (PhD). His primary responsibilities at the church include preaching and teaching the Bible, vision casting, leading the staff team and working with the elders in providing leadership, oversight and spiritual care for the church.

Reverend/Dr. Nick Gatzke

Old North Church was founded in 1936 in Canfield. Through the years it has seen thousands of people experience life change as they have come to faith in Jesus through the message of the Gospel. Today, Old North consists of a body of believers that ranges across multiple generations and comes from a variety of backgrounds, professions and communities in this region. Old North Church is a Baptist Church that is part of Converge World Wide and enjoys ministry partnerships with a variety of churches and organizations in this region and across the globe. While Old North Church is technically not a megachurch in numbers of members, it is large and has many missions and functions.

The largest churches in America continue to grow, but that growth extends beyond increasing worship service attendance. In the United States there are approximately 1,750 Protestant megachurches with regular attendance of 2,000 or more according to a recent Hartford Institute for Religion Research. The average attendance at megachurches has grown 34% since 2015. These large churches are increasingly expanding their influence beyond the sanctuary. Many have opened a new campus of their church and many have multiple sites. In addition to larger congregations spread across more campuses, megachurches are also growing more ethnically diverse. The latest studies do indicate that there are some areas of decline, particularly in average seating capacity in the megachurches and worshippers attending somewhat less frequently.

Choice and diversity of programs are hallmarks of the megachurch. Some have suggested that they resemble shopping malls in their wide array of consumer-driven ministerial offerings. This provides the entire membership with a continuous supply of appealing choices that fit their tastes. Worship is one of the central drawing cards that anchor the church. The worship service is a high quality, entertaining and well-planned production, which include skits, special musical numbers, interpretive dance and videos. Megachurches hold prayer service, Bible studies, singing services and perhaps healing or charismatic praise services. Many have Saturday evening youth-oriented services or beginner courses in basic Christianity. The diversity offered extends even to the choice of the style, form and time of a worship event that best fits one's needs and tastes.

Old North Church may not be as large as most megachurches, but they do have a large physical plant, housing rooms for all age groups and all types of worship. They, too, emphasize diversity in membership, elaborate musical celebrations, including the worship accompaniment of The Praise Band which features musical instruments and choral numbers. Reverend Dr. Gatzke explains, "Old North offers ministries for children that are newborn all the way through high school and college. There are adult bible study groups that meet. No matter the age, it is an opportunity for the entire family to grow." Reverend Gatzke ended his presentation with, "My greatest joy in ministry is seeing how God changes lives through the preaching of scriptures. Having personally experienced an ongoing relationship with God, I get really excited when I can help others as they engage in a fulfilling relationship with God. The Lord is working in this way at Old North and it makes it an exciting place to be."

Old North Church Assembly

The joint meeting of the OCA/MVAC in November addressed the topic, "Faith in the Valley: Wither MVAC and Faith in the Valley" with Reverend/Dr. Robin Woodberry and Dr. Thomas Sauline as speakers. The lively cultural enrichment was provided by Judy Conti's senior dancers. The meeting was held at the Saxon Club, with their caterers providing the meal.

The Mahoning Valley Association of Churches (MVAC) is an autonomous body governed by delegates from congregations, denominational bodies and organizations who are members. It is a local manifestation of ecumenical ministry which seeks to cooperate with both regional and national expressions of ecumenism. It includes congregations from Columbiana, Mahoning and Trumbull counties. We were told that they work to be a witness to Christ's call that His followers would be one. By working cooperatively in the church and the community they seek to bring about the realm of God on earth. They state in their mission statement that they value diversity, racial harmony, justice and respect as they strive for reconciliation within the Church and beyond.

Both speakers were optimistic that MVAC, now in its 100th year, can and shall continue its missionary work for at least another 100 years. As executive director, Reverend Woodberry is responsible for carrying on the duties of the MVAC's mission, programs and functions. She has a history of serving. Her mother, the Reverend Regina Thornton, was a long-time minister in Warren after being ordained in 1979. Woodberry said," I grew up with her preaching at church. She was a role model who inspired me. I saw the service she provided to people in the community, noting that her mother was a trailblazer for women in the ministry."

Woodberry was licensed in ministry in 1995 and ordained in 2005 in the Baptist church. She earned her Doctor of Ministry degree from Southern Bible Institute and Seminary in Augusta, Georgia. She has served as assistant pastor at New Bethel Baptist Church in Youngstown, where she oversees church administration and the youth and children's ministries and assists the senior pastor in carrying out all pastoral responsibilities such as preaching, teaching, weddings and funerals. She is also preparing to be ordained into the Episcopal Church so she will be able to preach for that denomination as well. She was named executive director of MVAC in 2014. While her job is part-time, Reverend Woodberry said she often speaks to different groups and is a guest preacher at churches of different denominations. She said there is a lot of multitasking between being a pastor and also working with various community groups and organizations.

Reverend/Dr. Robin Woodbury

Woodberry has also been active in the community, including with Church Women United Youngstown Area, the Interdenominational Ministerial Alliance and facilitates a partnership between MVAC and the Alliance for Congregational Transformation Influencing Our Neighborhoods (ACTION). She said she focuses on the oneness that Jesus spoke about for all denominations. A recent example of the work of the MVAC is a program called Carols and Caring: Holiday Hope for Healing, especially for those affected by drug addiction and their families.

Dr. Thomas Sauline who helped facilitate the series of programs hosted by OCA and MVAC has also been vital to the MVAC, from the Catholic perspective. He has been a lay ecclesiastical minister for over 30 years as Catholic high school catechist, Parish Director of Religious Education and consultant for religious Education in the Diocese of Youngstown and has served as executive director of the MVAC. He holds a B.A. degree and a Master of Biblical Studies from the Athenaeum of Ohio and a Doctor of Ministry from St. Mary's Seminary and Graduate School of Theology in Wickliffe, Ohio. He participates in the development of various programs of the MVAC; indeed, his work in the community and his work helping to craft the year-long programs of the OCA and MVAC helped in the celebration of the MVAC's 100-year anniversary. Sauline is actively involved in ecumenical ministries, serving on the board of the MVAC and co-chairing the Lutheran-Catholic Dialog. He is diocesan liaison for the Loyola Institute of Ministry Extension program and instructs facilitators in "Treasured Gifts from God", the diocesan child protection in-service program.

In specific response to the theme of "Wither Faith in the Valley" Sauline said "Faith in the Valley has a hopeful future because people of good faith and their congregations are working together for Christian unity' and they are building relationships with people of other faiths. To the statement building Christian unity Sauline referred to Jesus' Last Supper prayer "that they may all be one", to Bishop George Murry's statement "in the cross of Jesus Christ every barrier to Christian unity has been broken," to the OCA and Schaff lecture series, the Youngstown Mayor's prayer breakfasts as examples of efforts to effect Christian unity. He referenced various local actions for building relationships with people of other faiths, i.e., addressing racism with honesty and forgiveness, advocating for better schools, electing leaders who are faith witnesses, employing everyone with a livable wage, healing addicted families, making health care accessible for everyone, providing adequate housing, promoting non-violent resolution of conflict and taking responsibility for the safety of our communities.

Dr. Tom Sauline

Dr. Sauline also spoke of the leadership of Pope Francis in his October 13, 2016, meeting with representatives of the German Lutheran Church at which time Pope Francis said, "we can continue our ecumenical path with confidence, because we know that, beyond the many questions that still separate us, we are already united. What unites us is much more than what divides us." These and other pronouncements by the Pope and the German Lutheran representatives are all hopeful signs. Both of our speakers are enthusiastic about the future of the Mahoning Valley Association of Churches and by local, national and international acts and actions of cooperation and unity. Sauline concluded with a quote from an address Pope Francis made at a meeting with the Sheikh and representatives of the different religious communities of Azerbaijan in 2016, "In this night of conflict that we are currently enduring, may religions be a dawn of peace, seeds of rebirth amid the devastation of death, echoes of dialogue resounding unceasingly, paths to encounter and reconciliation reaching even those places where official mediation efforts seem not to have borne fruit."

Judy Conti Senior Dancers

GDB Jr. Dancing with Senior Conti Dancer

The final meeting of the series "Faith in the Valley: Whither Christian Faith and Interfaith in the World", held in December, was presented by Reverend Joseph T. Hilinski, Ecumenical Delegate, Diocese of Cleveland and pastor at St. Barbara Parish in Cleveland, Ohio. We met at Mount Carmel Social Hall in Youngstown with a sumptuous meal prepared by Lou Fusillo Catering. Cultural enrichment was provided by pianist extraordinaire Roman Rudnytsky, one of our most frequent guest performers. Father Hilinski explained that he has a very unusual portfolio for a Roman Catholic priest, in that his work as a Catholic pastor and as director for the office of continuing education for priests, deacons and lay ministers would put him in the mainstream of the Catholic Church; his work as Director of Interfaith Affairs gave him a broader perspective other Catholic priests might not have. He said his life and faith were considerably impacted by getting to know the religious groups and their members in the Cleveland area.

Father Hilinski stressed the relationship of culture and society to religion in many societies. He referred to Islamic Archbishop, Michel Sabba, Patriarch of Jerusalem, who described a situation that "puts religious identity and choice in a social context so different from the American scene. Religion is not a personal choice primarily-religion and religious life has a strong social and cultural dimension; it is reinforced by identification with a very real social group, and upon that group one finds his or her survival. One does not just join a church or religion. Family, roots, history and tradition weigh heavily. This is the context for most of the world not only in Muslim areas but also Hindu, Buddhist and many in Africa." Hilinski argues that freedom of religion in our context and in theirs is very different. While different, he also notes that in some ways our world is not so different. "Let's face it", he said, "many of those who are still in our churches are products of an acculturation of a religious life in our families and ethnic groupings." He said, "this is not necessarily bad and his family's Polish culture and ethnic identity has brought me much in the way of my faith and making it part of my life. I have grown in appreciation of my faith but I am not Catholic because I am Polish. And yet that identification of culture, ethnic identity and religiosity for some is so intertwined that it is all mixed together. That is true even for us in the USA."

Father Hilinski said that even different religions take different approaches to the question of culture, ethnic identity, and religion. "Judaism is a religion, but a Jew is not defined by the religion of Judaism. The Jew takes his or her identity from belonging to the people of Israel by the birth of Jewish parents...we should not make the mistake of considering that all Jews in Israel are religious and that many would be, to our eyes and ears, simply secular but they are Jews." He gave an interesting quote of a charismatic figure of the Middle East, Archbishop Elias Chacour, who said in a recent interview, " I am a Palestinian, a proud Palestinian, a Palestinian Arab. My mother language is Arabic. I am also a Christian. I am a Palestinian Arab Christian-and a citizen of Israel." Hilinski noted how confusing this could be to those who think that all Palestinians are Muslims and bloodthirsty - people born to violence. Archbishop Chacour said that he aims to prove that there is a way to create unity with respect for diversity that can coexist in the Holy Land. (As a note from the author: on my trip to the Holy Land with Monsignor Polando we had a guide who identified his background identically.)

Hilinski continued, "The issue of how religions see themselves connected to each other can bring a sense of commonality, but it also might create tensions of difference." He cited the story of the two children of Abraham-Ishmael and Isaac, which is the story of Jews and Arab Muslims-Arabs claim Ishmael as their ancestral connection to Abraham as the Jews claim Isaac as theirs. And what about the Christians, Hilinski wondered, where do we go with this question of our relationship to these other religions? He continued by noting that we seriously reflected on this matter "when the Second Vatican Council ventured into this question of how we are related to all other religions."

Hilinski proceeded with "some sobering thoughts:" 2000 years of missionary work of Christians has yielded about 1/3 of the world's population and of those, ½ are Catholic and ½ are divided up among Orthodox and various Protestant groups. After Christianity, the next largest bloc of religions is Islam with about 17% (actually Islam and Catholic Christians are about the same in numbers); Hinduism about 13%; Buddhism about 6% and Judaism about .4%. He continued by saying Americans often confuse our religious situation with the world, which in our case is about 82% Christian, 10% other religions and 8% no religious preference, with the latter growing.

He then asked and attempted to answer how the Catholic Church looks at the 2/3 of the human race that are not Christians and what it sees. The Catholic Church is "out there proclaiming the message of Christ and are engaged in missionary work throughout the world, but should not forget that Islam is also a missionary religion." He said, "The Catholic Church believes that the human being must freely embrace the Christian faith and not be coerced as had been the case at some times and in some places in the past. But the Second Vatican Council took a big leap with proclaiming: 'This Vatican Council declares that the human person has a right to religious freedom.'" The Church had to give up its old ways of force and believe that the Christian truths will win out.

Father Hilinski spent a majority of his remaining time in sketching the importance and impact of the Second Vatican Council. He reported that the bishops came from areas of the world where Catholics were not in the majority: Africa and Asia where there were more Hindus and Muslims and from Europe where secularism was growing. They acknowledged that here was great vibrancy in these religions and that Judaism also has remained strong and vibrant in many areas. The bishops made a number of observations about the reality and efficacy of these religions around the world. Among these observations were: the people of the world are aware of these other religions; humanity forms but one community; religions seem to answer some very basic common questions that human beings have about life, whether religious or not, i.e. the problems that weigh heavily on people's hearts are the same today as in past ages; there is a religious sense among human beings at a primitive level in the hearts of all, i.e. the Catholic Church now sees in different people a certain awareness of a hidden power, sometimes a supreme being and even more of a Father; the Catholic Church for the first time addresses itself on its view of other religions, particularly Hinduism and Buddhism.

Hilinski reported that the Second Vatican Council issued two key summary statements on the attitude of the Catholic Church to religions of the world, i.e., the Catholic Church rejects nothing of what is true and holy in the various ancient religions and that the human person has a right to religious freedom as they seek truth. Father Hilinski proceeds to a discussion of the importance of dialogue by asking "What is the working attitude we should have to other religions?" Quoting the Vatican Council, "The Church…urges its sons and daughters to enter with prudence and charity into discussion and collaboration with members of other religions." This includes spiritual, moral, social and cultural truths. Again, from the Vatican Council writings, "In faithfulness to the divine initiative, the Church too must enter into a dialogue of salvation with all men and women." Quoting further "First-God is in dialogue with each human soul; Second-we believe that through us as Catholic Christians, God is in dialogue with them; Third-we also realize that through them, God is in dialogue with us." All can learn from others' religions.

Dialogue was an important message of the Second Vatican Council, as was the address of Father Hilinski to the Ohio Cultural Alliance. He said that there are many forms of interreligious dialogue: the dialogue of life; the dialogue of action; the dialogue of theological exchange; and the dialogue of religious experience. Hilinski made another important point about dialogue which is to compare ideal with ideals. He said," Do not compare our ideals with their practice...Every religion has some skeletons in their closets." He admonished us that while every historic religion embodies many good things and many truths, each has also acted against or violated their own strictures, including those of Catholic/Christian faiths.

Father Hilinski concluded with "would that we could see all the practitioners of world religions in a dialogue of life and holy competition in elevating the most noble and compassionate dimensions of the human race." What a fitting concluding remark to end the regular programming of the 30-year run of the Ohio Cultural Alliance whose mission has been to promote world peace and understanding by interacting with peoples from other cultures.

Revered Joseph T. Hilinski

Roman Rudnytsky

GDB, Rev, Hilinski, M. Senediak, Rev. Ray & wife Sue, R. and S. Rudnytsky

Best Cake Ever!

XXI. Farewell Meeting

On February 6, 2017 the Ohio Cultural Alliance held its final meeting. We met at the Tyler Center of the Mahoning Valley Historical Society (MVHS) with Carolyn Catering providing a wonderful multiethnic meal. We looked retrospectively at our 30 years and considered our legacy. Many wore ethnic costumes with the MVHS displaying several ethnic items of dress; Dr. Tom Welsh did caricature drawings of several members; George D. Beelen Jr. showed two movies that he prepared over the years-one featuring the OCA's first 20 years and the second featuring the last 10 years. And we said our good-byes.

Saying goodbye to people who care for each other is very difficult. In life, we meet many persons at many events at different places, and we get connected with each other, but at times we have to say goodbye to them. At that time, we feel empty and brokenhearted. But we strived to make this evening a happy and memorable occasion. I read a statement at the meeting that reads: "Don't cry because it's over; smile because it happened." In 30 years, we engaged in a learning experience for all of us. What we have done is to look at people like us and different from us, with an overriding theme that genius knows no boundaries. Over the years, OCA members have examined and studied cultures, heritages, traditions, religions, and ethnic aspects of about 50 countries, hosting about 300 meetings. Each meeting consisted of a brief business meeting (and a little Beelen philosophizing), a talk based upon the theme for the year, relevant cultural enrichment, and a meal that was often ethnic, based upon the country addressed that evening. And we met at varied venues, public and private, throughout the Valley.

Among additional activities of the last ten years of OCA history were the monthly collection of personal items and non-perishable foods to be contributed by members to be given to various charitable groups in the Valley and the invitation to our meetings of "difference makers" in the community to give a 5-minute talk regarding their respective roles/contributions to the Valley. Thus, OCA members learned about them and their organizations, and they learned about the Ohio Cultural Alliance. Arguably the largest group in the Valley that meets monthly (10 meetings per year), we were building community. Among the other ways that we built community among ourselves in the OCA and in the larger Mahoning Valley are the following activities:

- Generic "prayer of thanks" before each meeting
- Occasionally ask each member to invite someone (at no cost) to the meeting that is different from them, such as different sex, religion, race, age, etc.
- Shake hands with someone in the audience that you do not know; identify and greet them
- Invite each person to include in their reservations milestones in their lives: birthdays, anniversaries, promotions, retirements, achievements, etc.
- Include in reservations answer to "question of the month"; first to respond earns a free meeting
- Nametags were issued to all attendees

- Hold special summer meetings for officers and board members, usually at an ethnic restaurant
- 50/50 raffle at each meeting
- Display huge world map to encourage each attendee to know where each country that we discuss is located

We have over this 30-year period enhanced our minds, our palates and our auditory systems. Have we made a difference? Have these experiences mattered? Have we dealt with enough issues that are universal? Have we learned to challenge some of our own suppositions and "truths"? Are we now more inclusive? Are we now more understanding? Are we now more tolerant? Are we more compassionate? We certainly did try.

William Lawson, the MVHS Executive Director, said that the "MVHS celebrates the people of the Mahoning Valley, something to which the OCA also was devoted". It is for this reason that the OCA has become part of the MVHS. In an effort to continue the OCA's legacy of cultural awareness, the OCA contributed $25,000 and President Jim and Ellen Tressel added another $5,000, to the YSU Foundation for an endowment that will provide a YSU student intern who will work at MVHS to further the work of the OCA. Lawson called such interns "the lifeblood of our organization", saying they are an integral part of working with the historical society's numerous collections. In 2019 this new iteration of the OCA (with a new name-Mahoning Valley Cultural Alliance) sponsored three initial meetings and planned five additional meetings for 2020. Sadly, the pandemic of 2020-2022 has put any subsequent meetings on hold. Our hope is that we can resume in the not-too-distant future.

One of those happy with the OCA's work was Dr. Khalid Iqbal of Liberty, Ohio, a pediatrician who came to the area about 40 years ago from his native Pakistan. He said, "Opening oneself to discovering more about other cultures lays the groundwork to see that they have more similarities with one another than differences, especially when it comes to upholding virtues such as honesty and integrity."

With the end of 30 years of OCA we have received many validations for our efforts-efforts of the Officers and the Board of Directors and all involved in any way to make it work for 30 years.

- "OCA will be remembered as a noble, original concept well thought out and well planned...What a wonderful opportunity it gave members to meet people they would not otherwise meet and have a chance to hear new ideas, new thoughts, and other voices. What an honor to be invited to enter distinguished buildings, sacred churches where we were served good, different foods." Ann Trefethern
- 'We have traced the ethnic roots and examined the historical contributions of the multiplicity of cultures, religions, customs, people, food, literature, art, and music around the globe and in the Mahoning Valley." Michael Kurilla
- "Thanks for the memories. What a ride we have all had these 30 years." "Many thanks for your noble efforts...and astonishing execution during these OCA years in trying to make the world a better place." Tom and Margie Kelly
- "I'm always amazed at the interesting themes and quality of the speakers, entertainment, and food." Terry Gallagher
- "The OCA is a model of the ecumenical friendships...The 2018 OCA events have enriched my ecumenical and interfaith relationships." Dr. Tom Sauline

- "I think the OCA is providing a needed avenue for expanding the development of friendship and pride in our community." Reverend C. Edward Weisheimer
- "Thanks for everything; it's been a wonderful education and cultural enlightenment." Tom and Carrie Ramos
- "I am disappointed that no one has stepped up to take the lead. The organization is very needed in Youngstown." Attorney Carl Nunziato
- "Congratulations on your 30-year OCA success." Chris and Maureen Yambar
- "Thank you for all the wonderful years." Thomas and Elaine Welsh
- "Thank you for the so many years that the OCA has served our community." Rosemarie Kascher
- "Thanks for keeping us well-informed and entertained." Bob and Joan Gallitto
- "Well done, good and faithful OCA servants." Anita Brabant
- " I want to congratulate you on the incredible success of the OCA. I'm glad that so many people were able to experience it." Gina Marinelli
- "Thank you for the many years ...making so many people educated and happy." Jeanne Foley
- "Thank you for the wonderful, enlightening programs of OCA...Our love of history will be continued by visits to the Tyler History Center (MVHS)." Margaret Skripac

GDB and his wife, Betty, with plaque from children GDB Jr., Gary Beelen and Lynn Roman

From left, Robert Kerpsack and Margaret Skripac chat with George Beelen, a retired Youngstown State University professor, at the Tyler History Center during the final meeting of the Ohio Cultural Alliance.

Iqbal explained.

In addition, opening oneself to discovering more about other cultures lays the groundwork to see that they have more similarities with one another than differences,

Also during the farewell dinner, guests watched a half-hour film that Beelen's son, George D. Beelen Jr., produced that encapsulated many of the OCA's accomplishments over its 30-year span. Shown

Venice and Iceland; and the organization's recent collaboration with the Mahoning Valley Association of Churches, which looked at many of the world's faiths.

Another highlight of the

Youngstown Vindicator Article featuring Dr. R. Kerpsack, M. Skripac and GDB

GDB and his Sister, Joanne Coppola

Dr. Rashid Abdu

Betty Beelen and Granddaughter Lauren Beelen

GDB Talking to Local Media

Premiere of the 4th and Final OCA Video

YSU President Jim Tressel

The Vindicator

Farewell *and* hello

Appeals court weighs Trump's travel ban

Kasich budget proposal includes cuts to shrinking school districts

Vindicator headline for OCA Final Meeting

Farewell crowd filled the Tyler Center

XXII. Acknowledgements

Founding and leading the Ohio Cultural Alliance for 30 years and chronicling its history have been labors of love. I have written what I believe to be an accurate summary of our origins, our development and our programming. In this work I have tried to focus on important thoughts and deeds presented, as well as I can recollect them, using files from each meeting, notes from some of them and actual hard copies from some of the speakers. Admittedly, the work is somewhat uneven, given the abundance of material regarding some topics and subjects and the paucity of material for other topics and subjects.

Although the major ideas of the Ohio Cultural Alliance purport to be fresh, as suggested in the subtitle of our work: "Peace and Understanding through Local Engagement", it is also derivative. That is to say, I believe that locally we had programming that gives evidence that all peoples have genius (and scoundrels) as we but have learned about people like us and also about those who are different from us. It is derivative in the sense of my using material from the speakers, with some supplementing from texts, monographs and the internet. The strengths of the work are attributable to all of the participants; the weaknesses are mine.

History is vital to my life. Developing some understanding of all history and all peoples and all cultures really makes me tick. Learning history-the people, the times, the issues, etc. is fun, it's basically humanistic, it can give us personal strength and it is frequently up-lifting. But most importantly it gives us perspective and it helps us to better understand and deal with our here and now. Among recent books that have encouraged me are Steven Pinker's "The Better Angels of Our Nature" and "Enlightenment Now: The Case for Reason, Science, Humanism and Progress" where Pinker deals with how much better off our world is today, the beginning of the 21st century. In the "Better Angels" he deals with declining violence in the world and in the "Enlightenment" he shows how, since the Enlightenment, we are not only less violent, but we are smarter, richer, more curious, and enjoy more open societies, more tolerance and have many more reasons to live.

In his inspiring book, "The Soul of America", Jon Meacham reassures us that the good news is that we have come through darkness, distraction, strife and disenchantment many times in our history, but time and time again, Abraham Lincoln's "better angels" (used in his 1st Inaugural Address) have found a way to prevail. He advises us, as "better angels", to enter the arena, resist tribalism, respect facts and deploy reason, find critical balance and keep history in mind. He insists that we place our times in context, in perspective.

The approach we have taken with the Ohio Cultural Alliance and thus, with this book, are basically an upbeat attitude, despite acknowledgement of problems. We believe that as a civilized society we are assigned to learn about each other and to learn from each other, as part of this civilized existence. The history of humankind attests to the advantages of membership in civilized society, despite inherent inequalities and all the constraints on freedom such membership entails. The Smithsonian Institution issued a relevant quotation recently: "Let us use history to inspire us to push a country forward, to help us believe that all things are possible and to demand a country lives up to its ideals." And in our 30 years the Ohio Cultural Alliance carried out this activity, this history, painlessly, with verve as we appealed to our senses: we used our minds, our eyes and our taste-with the speakers, the entertainment, the food and the travel-to varied sites for our meetings and travel actually and vicariously. Often, the meetings touched our hearts also.

Many people have been responsible for the continuing success of the Ohio Cultural Alliance: the Officers and Board Members (32), the speakers (196), providers of cultural enrichment (176), caterers (64), sites (77), charitable group recipients (over eight years-23), 5-minute "difference maker" speakers (over three years-27). Each of them is listed below.

Officers and Board Members (over the years)

- President, George D. Beelen
- Vice President, Mary Ann Senediak, Reverend Gary Schreckengost, Martin Greggo, Becky Merideth
- Treasurer, Dorothy Palguta Tesner
- Secretary, Betty Beelen, Sandra Young, John Catoline
- Historian, Ann Thompson, Sandra Young
- Administrative Assistant, Betty Beelen, Gloria Dragus, Mary Bellotto, Bonnie Harris
- Generic Prayer Reflection, Reverend Jim Ray and alternate Warren Harrell

Board Members, Warren Harrell, Michael Kurilla, Tom Kelly, Theresa Trucksis, Ruth Fletcher, Regina Rees, Wilma Stubbs, Robert Casey, Don Barry, Juanita Roderick Latham, Ron DiTullio, Robert Henderson, Ann York, Louis Cassimatis, James Springer, Fern Kelly, Robert Kohler, Lita Sevilla, Frank Feeley, Hector Colon, in addition to those who have served as officers. Each of these people had special tasks that they performed, such as greeting attendees at meetings, publicity, selling 50/50 tickets, helping with finding speakers, cultural enrichment performers, sites, caterers, meeting photographer and other duties as assigned.

While all of the above have performed valuable assistance over the years, several have contributed significantly and over a long period of time:

- Mary Ann Senediak has been vice president for most of OCA history and had presided when I was out of town.
- Dorothy Palguta Tesner was an original member of the OCA and had served as treasurer from the beginning.
- Son, George D. Beelen, Jr., had served significantly in producing and directing four films for the OCA: "The Peopling of the Mahoning Valley" and three that visually chronical the history of the OCA. This present OCA history was considerably enhanced by his forethought of archiving thousands of OCA images in our 30-year history and placing appropriate images throughout – work that was time-consuming and skillful
- YSU secretaries Mary Bellotto and Bonnie Harris, who provided typing assistance in the early years, and my sister -Gloria Dragus, who helped with mailing for a few years.
- Michael Kurilla and David Costello, among the brightest students that have come through our YSU History Program (baccalaureate and master's degrees), served as my major proofreaders for the entire manuscript.
- Sandy Young and Ann Thompson diligently recorded for 20 of our 30 years a scrapbook of our history using photos, articles, notices and comments resulting in a comprehensive visual history of those years.

- Finally, the OCA would not have been able to continue for 30 years had it not been for the continual and vital work of my wife, Betty Beelen. Her work with the overall planning, the creating of a mailing matrix and yearly brochures, the communication with speakers, sites, caterers, providers of cultural enrichment, etc. are some of the ways that she helped to keep the OCA a vital and ongoing part of the Mahoning Valley.

All of the above have served the Ohio Cultural Alliance and/or the writing of this manuscript in innumerable ways; I am thankful for the assistance of each of them in more ways than they could realize.

XXIII. Appendices

A. Topics and Countries (and number of times)

African-American/African (10)
Amish
Arabs (3)
Argentina
Asians (2)
Australia
Austria, OCA/UNA
Black Protestant
Brazil
Cameroon
Canada
Carpatho-Rusyn
Catholicism (5)
China (3)
Commonality of Philosophies/Religions
Costa Rica
Croatia (5)
Cuba
Czechoslovakia/Slovakia (5)
Dominican Republic
Egypt
Episcopalianism
France (7)
Germany (8)
Great Britain/England (4)
Greek Orthodox (11)
Hispanic (5)
Hungary (6)
Iceland
India (5)
Ireland (8)
Islam (3)
Italy (11)
Japan (3)
Judaism/Israel (8)
Lebanon
Lebanon, OCA/UNA
Liberia
Malaysia
Mega-Protestant
Methodist
Mexico (3)
Middle Eastern (2)
Native American
Pakistan
Philippines (3)
Poland (6)
Protestant
Puerto Rico
Romania (4)
Russia/Ukraine (9)
San Salvador
Scandinavian (6)
Serbians (3)
Slavic
South Korea (2)
Spain
Switzerland
The Oneness of Humankind
The Oneness of the Universe
The Other Europe
Tibet
Turkey (3)
USA (4)
Wales (3)
Zimbabwe

B. Yearly Brochure 1997 - 1998

1997-98 Program

EXPRESSIONS OF CULTURE: THE ARTS IN OTHER NATIONS

George McCloud, Ph.D.	Sept. 17	Kick-Off (Butler Institute)
Maria Jukic Leskur	Oct. 6	Croatia (St. George Lodge)
Flo DiRienzo Schneider	Nov. 3	Italy (St. Lucy Hall)
George Kulchytsky, Ph.D.	Dec. 1	Ukraine (Ukranian Orthodox Center)
John Boehm, Ph.D.	Jan. 5	Germany (Saxon Club)
James Kiriazis, Ph.D.	Feb. 2	Greece (Archangel Michael Hall)
Joan Ready	March 2	Ireland (St. Christine Hall)
Saul Friedman, Ph.D.	April 6	Jewish Tradition (Ohev Tzedek Temple)
James Tavalario, Ph.D.	May 4	Poland (Krakusy Hall)
Professor Al Bright	June 1	African Tradition (Third Baptist Hall)

OHIO CULTURAL ALLIANCE

Pepin Hernandez Laos' portrayal of the quetzal bird, an ancient Mayan symbol, dropping the seed of peace which is bound for the hearts of humankind to effect worldwide understanding.

Ohio Cultural Alliance, Inc
George D. Beelen, President
P.O. Box 561
Canfield, OH 44406

Address Correction Requested

TO:

NONPROFIT ORG.
U.S. POSTAGE PAID
YOUNGSTOWN OHIO
PERMIT NO. 57

OHIO

CULTURAL ALLIANCE

OHIO CULTURAL ALLIANCE

The **Ohio Cultural Alliance** (OCA), based in Youngstown, Ohio, was formed during 1987. The OCA participates along with other cultural alliances throughout the world to promote world peace and understanding by interacting with peoples from other cultures. The hope is that such contact will effect understanding and empathy which will lead to peace in our time.

The OCA is an incorporated, tax-exempt organization. Monthly meetings, September through June, consist of a brief business session, a 30-40 minute program, an ethnic meal and some type of relevant cultural enrichment, and an up-date on projects both in-place and planned. During the last several years, these meetings have attracted an average of 150 people. Elected officers for 1997-98 are:

President	— George D. Beelen
Vice President	— Mary Ann Senedak
Secretary	— Sandra Young
Treasurer	— Dorothy Palguta-Tenner
Trustee	— Anne York
Trustee	— James Springer
Trustee	— Fern Kelly
Trustee	— Ann Hall
Trustee	— Robert Kohler
Trustee	— Theresa Trucksis
Trustee	— Thomas Kelly

The OHIO CULTURAL ALLIANCE is partially funded by theInternational Institute Foundation of Youngstown, Ohio.

RETROSPECTIVE

The Ohio Cultural Alliance has explored a number of exciting themes since its inception in 1987. Among them have been "Common Threads in a Diverse World," "Celebrating Life in a Troubled World," "The Making of America: A Land of Hope," "Doing Business with Another Culture," "The Family in Another Culture," and the 1996-97 theme, "Health and Medical Care in Another Culture."

OCA kicked off the 1996-97 year with a two-day (September 30-October 1) Health Care Workshop entitled "Traditional Medicine and Complementary Therapies: The Best of All Worlds" held at Youngstown State University. An outstanding array of local specialists addressed traditional medicine and such complementary therapies as hypnosis, acupuncture, chiropractic, humor, massage, psychotherapy, art, yoga, Tai Chi, imagery, pet, and Hospice. Internationally acclaimed author, lecturer, and physician, Dr. Larry Dossey was our featured speaker. In his keynote address and in several other presentations Dr. Dossey focused on the efficacy of prayer in healing and discussed how we can create a lasting partnership between faith and medicine. Our largest assemblage of nearly 300 people attended the September 30th OCA dinner meeting held at the Ukrainian Orthodox Center.

In November, the OCA met at the Saxon Club to hear Ohio State Senator Robert Hagan speak about the Canadian health care system. An OCA favorite, YSU professor Roman Rudnytsky performed piano selections to the delight of those in attendance.

The December focus was health care in France with Salim El-Hayek, MD, who received his medical education in France, as our speaker. Allan Mosher, Ph.D., of YSU's Dana School of Music, sang French songs and selection from French composers. Eberth Catering served a French dinner, with the Ursuline Mother House as the meeting site.

Dominican Republic was featured in January with Federico Cano, MD, as our speaker. His slides and the rhythmic merengue, performed by professional dancers Mr. and Mrs. Kenneth Scavnicky, added the cultural dimension to our evening.

Well-known opthamologist Dr. Kong T. Oh, originally from Malaysia, spoke of health and medical care in his native country in February. To complement Dr. Oh's presentation, a group of dancers led by Mark Lee provided the cultural enrichment by performing the traditional "Dragon Dance."

In March, the OCA met at the Maronite Center to hear four Lebanese medical doctors and a nurse-midwife engage in a comprehensive discussion of health care and medicine in Lebanon. St. Maron's Youth Dancers provided the cultural enrichment, and a six-course Lebanese dinner was prepared by the Ladies Guild of the church.

"Health and Medical Care in India" was the topic addressed in April by the immediate past president of the Mahoning County Medical Society, Chander Kohli, Md. Using slides to embellish his text, Dr. Kohli shared insights regarding his native land. Miss Pavana Bhat, a senior at Lisbon High School, performed authentic dances from the land of her ancestors.

The Philippines was our focus in May. Discussing health care and medicine in his native land, Ecarlito U. Sevilla, MD, offered fascinating insights using slides to complement his presentation. As an added attraction, Dr. Sevilla was joined by his wife, Leta, and by Rea McClain in several native dances performed with native costumes and music.

The final meeting of the season was held in June at YSU and dealt with several Asian countries, primarily Japan and Korea. Speaker for the evening was Dr. Henry Yoo, an area veterinarian and health care management consultant. Cultural enrichment was provided by Anna Korchmaros and her cultural group performing Japanese dances complete with costumes and props.

OCA's two special projects for the year were the Health Care Workshop, "Traditional Medicine and Complementary Therapies: The Best of All Worlds" and the printing of our third publication, "An Ethnic Encyclopedia: The Peopling of the Mahoning Valley." Both were unqualified successes which proved to be fitting capstones to the first decade of our existence.

In response to our membership, our monthly "travel adventures" will once again take us to various meeting sites throughout the Mahoning Valley as we consider our **1997-98 OCA Program, "Expressions of Culture: The Arts in Other Nations."**

Plans are in motion for yet another ambitious and exciting project, the preparation of a film entitled, "The Peopling of the Mahoning Valley." We will continue our exploration of actual and vicarious travel possibilities with The Friendship Force. In addition, we have begun to develop a mutually beneficial association with our neighbor and kindred organization, Cleveland's Intercultural Community Council.

From the OCA By-Laws: *"The OHIO CULTURAL ALLIANCE exists for the purposes of the cultural and educational enrichment of its participants and their communities through meaningful exchanges of ideas and persons. It is envisioned that these exchanges* [illegible] *between philosophical traditions, the arts and sciences, sports, business, and the professions may be discussed freely and candidly. The sole purpose and end result of the "Alliance" is meant to be the promotion of peace and understanding among peoples."*

For more information contact:
Dr. George D. Beelen, President
Ohio Cultural Alliance, Inc.
P.O. Box 561
Canfield, OH 44406

C. Samples of Monthly Notices

DR. GEORGE BEELEN PRESIDENT
322 BENTON AVENUE
AUSTINTOWN, OHIO 44515

April 16, 1993

Dear Friend:

The Ohio Cultural Alliance will hold its next meeting at **6:00 p.m. on Monday, May 3**. We will meet in the Chestnut Room, Kilcawley Center, Youngstown State University.

Join us as we explore the various Asian migrations to the United States and to the local area. Our speaker is Dr. Yih-Wu Liu, YSU professor of Economics, who holds a Ph.D. from Southern Illinois University. Dr. Liu has had continuous contact with Taiwan (his native land) and other Asian countries.

To complement Dr. Liu's talk, a Chinese youth group will perform and sing ethnic dances and songs.

The ethnic meal will consist of:

Chinese cabbage salad with scallions and ginger dressing
Beef with pea pods
Marinated chicken with ginger-orange sauce
Vegetable stirfry

Steamed white rice
Fried bananas with coconut
Rolls
Coffee, tea, punch

Do plan to attend and learn about the Asian experience in the U.S. and something about their history, their food and customs. The cost for the entire evening is $10.00. (For those with paid-up memberships, for 1992-93, the evening is no cost--one per $15.00 membership.) Please make your check payable to the Ohio Cultural Alliance and mail it today; please call 742-1603 or let us know by mail if you, by virtue of your paid-up membership, are attending free. Mail your reservation today to:

Dr. George D. Beelen, History Dept.
Youngstown State University
410 Wick Ave.
Youngstown, OH 44555

The deadline for the reservation is **Thursday, April 29.** See you soon for another chapter of the exciting sage, "The Making of America, A Land of Hope."

Best regards,

George D. Beelen

George D. Beelen
President, OCA

GDB/mb

DR. GEORGE BEELEN PRESIDENT
322 BENTON AVENUE
AUSTINTOWN, OHIO 44515

an integral part, cultural heritage informs the present and guides the future."
. . . Alixa Naff

May 17, 1993

Dear Friends:

The Ohio Cultural Alliance will hold its next meeting at **6:00 p.m. on Monday, June 7 at the Maronite Center**, 1555 South Meridian Rd. This is a community-wide event jointly sponsored by the OCA, U.N. Association, St. Maron Church, Coalition for Peace in the Middle East and the Arab Community Center. A very large crowd is expected.

This program is the 20th and final in a series of the Ohio Cultural Alliance: "THE MAKING OF AMERICA, A LAND OF HOPE." The subject for June 7 will be **"Arab Immigration to the U. S. and Arab-American Contributions."** Special guest speaker will be **Alixa Naff**, Curator of the Arab-American collection at the **Smithsonian Institution**. Dr. Naff has traveled throughout the U.S., Canada and the Middle East in search of the emigrant/immigrant story and worked with the late Albert Hourani of Oxford and Harvard. Dr. Naff is the author of Becoming American: The Early Arab Immigrant Experience.

The Ladies Sodality of St. Maron will prepare an authentic Lebanese feast:

kibbee (lamb baked with cracked wheat, onions and pine nuts),
tabouli (parsley salad with cracked wheat, tomatoes and olive oil)
hoummos-bi-tahini (chick pea and sesame seed paste dip)
f'tyer (spinach pies)
laban (plain yogurt)
chicken and spiced rice
Arabic bread
ba'lawa for dessert

Additionally, a local Palestinian-Lebanese dance group will perform. The evening will conclude with a very special benediction to take place in the St. Maron Church sanctuary as the Antonine Sisters sing in Arabic and Syriac (ancient west Aramaic).

Cost for the entire evening is $10.00. Checks should be made payable to Ohio Cultural Alliance and mailed to:

Dr. George D. Beelen, History Dept.
Youngstown State University
Youngstown, OH 44555

Deadline for reservations is Thursday, June 3rd. PLEASE RESERVE AS SOON AS POSSIBLE. For further information, you may also contact Ray Nakley at 759-6977.

Best regards,

George D. Beelen

George D. Beelen
President, OCA

742-3452

P.S. We are now accepting $15.00 dues for our 1993-94 year with the theme "Doing Business in Other Cultures."

DR. GEORGE BEELEN PRESIDENT
322 BENTON AVENUE
AUSTINTOWN, OHIO 44515

"We pray for children who want to be carried and for those who must, for those we never give up on and for those who don't get a second chance. For those we smother ... and for those who will grab the hand of anybody kind enough to offer it."
-Ina J. Hughs, Charleston, South Carolina

February 12, 1993

Dear Friend:

The Ohio Cultural Alliance will hold its next meeting at 6:00 p.m. on Monday, March 1st. We will meet at the Holy Trinity Serbian Orthodox Church Hall located at 53 Laird Ave, Youngstown, Ohio (take Mahoning Ave. to Steel St.; travel one block on Steel to First St. which will run into Laird).

Join us as we explore the Serbian migration to the United States and to the local area. Our speaker is Mr. William Nikolin, former diplomat in Belgrade, who will share the Serbian immigrant experience with us.

To complement Mr. Nicholin's talk the Holy Trinity choir will sing traditional melodies for us.

The meal will consist of :

Roast chicken	Apple struedel
Serbian pilaf	Palachinke
Vegetable	Rolls & butter
Salad	Coffee/tea/punch

Do plan to attend to learn about Serbian experence in the U. S. and something about their history, their food and customs. The cost for the entire evening is $10.00. Please make your check payable to the Ohio Cultural Alliance and mail it today (how about right now!) to:

Dr. George D. Beelen
History Department
Youngstown State University
410 Wick Ave.
Youngstown, OH 44555

The deadline for the reservation is Thursday, February 25th. See you soon for another chapter of the exciting saga, "The Making of America, A Land of Hope."

Best regards,

George D. Beelen

George D. Beelen
President, OCA
Professor of History

GDB/mb

DR. GEORGE BEELEN PRESIDENT
322 BENTON AVENUE
AUSTINTOWN, OHIO 44515

"One of the things that is important for our institution is to make international connections. How do our programs connect with the ethnic groups in our community? How can we include international options in our programs? How do we connect back to homelands . . . ?

Dr. Les Cochran, President, YSU

November 19, 1992

Dear Friend:

The Ohio Cultural Alliance will hold its next meeting at 6:00 p.m. on December 7, 1992. We will meet at Holy Trinity Ukrainian Catholic Church, Byzantine Rite, located at 525 W. Rayen Ave., Youngstown, Ohio.**

Join us as we explore the Ukrainian/Russian migration to the United States and to the local area. Our speaker is Dr. George Kulchytsky, YSU professor of history, Ukrainian native and active participant in Ukrainian-American affairs locally, nationally and internationally.

To complement Dr. Kulchytsky's talk, Professor Roman Rudnytsky of YSU's Dana School of Music, and world-renowned pianist, will perform for us selections from Ukrainian/Russian music.

The meal will be typical of Ukrainian/Russian cuisine and will consist of the following:

Chicken Kiev	Russian mixed vegetables with sour cream	Carrot cake
Veal Stroganoff	Tossed salad w/Russian dressing	Punch
Pierogi	Pumpernickel bread	Coffee
Caucasian rice w/fruit		Tea

Cost for the entire evening is $10.00. Please make your check payable to the Ohio Cultural Alliance and mail today to:

Dr. George D. Beelen
History Department
Youngstown State University
410 Wick Ave.
Youngstown, OH 44555

The deadline for the reservation to reach me is Friday, December 4. See you soon for another chapter of the exciting saga, "The Making of America, A Land of Hope!" Come also to meet YSU's new president, Dr. Les Cochran, who believes we must work much more closely with the ethnic groups of our community.

Best regards,

George D. Beelen

George D. Beelen
Professor of History
President, OCA

**** Please note change of site.**

GDB/mb

DR. GEORGE BEELEN PRESIDENT
322 BENTON AVENUE
AUSTINTOWN, OHIO 44515

"The world stands
on three things
truth
justice
humility."
. . . Pirke Avot

October 22, 1993

Dear Friend:

The Ohio Cultural Alliance will hold its next meeting at 6:00 p.m. on Thursday, November 5, 1992.** We will meet at Ohev Tzedek Temple located on 5245 Glenwood Ave., Boardman, Ohio.

Join us as we explore the Jewish migration to the United States and to the local area. Our speaker is Dr. Saul Friedman, Professor of History at Youngstown State University and noted author, lecturer and Emmy award recipient for several excellent videos. To complement Dr. Friedman's talk, Lawrence Ehrlich, cantor, will sing and we will tour the temple itself.

The meal will be typical of Jewish cuisine and will consist of the following:

Chicken soup with matzo balls	Dessert
Roasted chicken quarters	Rye bread
Farfel with mustrooms	Tea/coffee
Glazed carrots with pineapple	Punch

Cost for the entire evening is $10.00. Please make your check payable to the Ohio Cultural Alliance and mail it today to:

Dr. George D. Beelen
History Department
Youngstown State University
410 Wick Ave.
Youngstown, Oh 44555

The deadline for the reservation to reach me is **Tuesday, November 3.** See you soon for another chapter of the exciting saga, "The Making of America, A Land of Hope."

Best regards,

George D. Beelen

George D. Beelen
President, OCA

** Please note change of date.

GDB/mb

DR. GEORGE BEELEN PRESIDENT
322 BENTON AVENUE
AUSTINTOWN, OHIO 44515

As people of many cultures and races,
may our voices speak together
of hope and welcome to all.
May our hands lift high the torch
of new life and solidarity.
May our hearts yearn
for justice and truth.

From a Fifth Centenary Prayer

August 25, 1992

Dear Friend:

The Ohio Cultural Alliance is happy to announce the commencement of its sixth year. Enclosed please find a brochure, which includes pertinent information regarding the OCA (past accomplishments and future programs), plus a form which I ask you to send back to me by return mail to insure your status with OCA and to make reservations for our next meeting.

Our opening meeting for this year will be held at **Youngstown State University** on Monday, September l4, l992 at 6:00 p.m. (Chestnut Room, Kilcawley Center). Our focus will be the Czechoslovakian migration to the United States and to the Mahoning Valley and our speaker is Michael Kurilla who is of Slovak ancestry and an active member of Holy Name Church.

Cultural enrichment will be provided by Steve Garchar (and orchestra) who will play polka music to which we can dance or listen. The ethnic meal which will be prepared by YSU chefs from ethnic recipes will consist of:

Mixed Salad — Pierogi
Potato Soup — Sauteed Carrots
Stuffed Cabbage — Coffee, Tea
Kolachi

Do try to attend this first meeting of the l992-93 OCA year; it promises to be a great one. The total cost for the evening will be $l0.00. Please make your checks payable to the Ohio Cultural Alliance and send them to us in the envelope provided. The deadline is Friday, September 11th; mail it today. See you soon.

Best regards,

George D. Beelen

George D. Beelen, President

Enclosures

D. Speakers (Pages)

E. Cultural Enrichment (and number of times)

Art

Jazz Group and Prof. Al Bright (2)

Dance

Always Dancin'Group

Anna Korchmaros Dancers

Avala Serbian dancers

Azhar, April-Belly Dancer

Bamboo Dance-L.& L. Sevilla (2)

Bhat, Pavana-Dance and Slides

Ceyhan, Pinar-Folk Dance

Chinese Singers/Dancers

Conti, Judy- Senior dancers

Fred Astaire dancers

Greek dancers (5)

Greek Dancers-Akron

Harambee Dancers (2)

Howland Dancers

Irish Step dancers (3)

Lebanese Dancers

Lin, Anita-Dancer

OCCHA Teenage Dancers (2)

Pakistan- Dance, song, fashion

Palestinian-Lebanese Dancers

Perni, A.-Indian Dancers (3)

Philippine Bamboo Dancers

Pittsburgh Slovakian dancers

Prato, Angela-Belly Dancer

Pringle, Mark-Dragon Dancers (3)

Red Hawk Dancers

Romanian Dancers-Akron

Scavnicky, Ken-Dancers (2)

Scottish Dance Group

Shirana-Belly Dancer

St. John Greek Dancers (2)

St. Maron's dancers

Talija Serbian dancers

Tango dancers

Thomas, Dr. Julie

Ukrainian dancers (2)

Youngstown Connection (7)

Yun, Dr. Misook (3)

Zivili

Media

Africa-Films and Artifacts

Brazil-film/slides/music

China-Slides

Egypt-Slides

England-Slides

Europe-Slides

Film-Is. of Hope Is. of Tears

France-Slides

Greek Film

India-Slides

Japan-Movie

Kabuki film

Mexico-Images

OCA film

Pakistan-Slides and Video

Romania-Video

Scandinavia-Slides

Sentinels of Silence-Film

South Korea-Slides

Music

Bag Piper

Balalaika Group (2)

Bannon, Betty (6)

Barry, Don-Organ

Bodnar, George-Pan flute

Bright, Prof. Al -Jazz Group (2)

Canfield Comm. Band (3)

Carpatho-Rusyn melodies

County Mayo

Cutshaw, Todd-Piano

Dana String Quartet

Dolovy, M. (6)

El Dabh, Halim - Drums

Esparra, Porfirio -Guitar

Fiala, Reverend Vit-Cello (2)

F. Fowler, YSU

Garchar, Steve-Polka Band

Gabriele, John (4)

Gonzalez, Felipe-Music (5)

Gould, Dr. Ronald-Organist (4)

Greek Music

Guitar and Bouzouki

Hallewell, Mary-Organist

Hawk, Marcellene-Piano

Holy Name Choir/Polka Band

Holy Trinity Serbian Choir

Klezmer Band

Kromholtz, Dr. Joseph, YSU

Libby Tamburitza (3)

Lyda, Mark-Piano

Mancino, John-Piano

Mariachi quintet

McIntosh, A.-Keyboard Blues

Minogue, J.& B.-Irish Ballads

Ohltmans, Dr.Carolina-Piano

Old North Praise Band (2)

(Music cont.)

Pantales, Teddy-Guitar

Papas, Steve -Guitar

Perkins, Dr. Ted-2 Horns (2)

Rollin, Drs. Robert and Gwen-Piano/Violin (3)

Rudnytsky, Roman (17)

Sepesy, Alex-Harmonicas

Sepesy, Teresa-Harmonicas

Seraphim Singers (2)

Shaffer, M. -Irish Band

Simon, Rev. Kenneth + New Bethel Choir

Sobieski, Dr. Jacek and Dorotea (3)

Solich, Tom-Piano

St. Mathias Choir

Stephens, Nathan (3)

Struthers Comm. Show Choir

Style of Five-Russia

Tamburitza group (3)

Turkish Music

Umble, Dr. Kathryn Umble

Valenzisi, T.-Guitar

Veal, Julian-Guitar

Violin/Piano/Singers-Seder Meal

Wade Raridon Singers (4)

Wilcox, Dr. John-Violin

Yo. Symphony Quartet (2)

YSU Dana quartet

YSU Early Music Ensemble

YSU Horn Trio

YSU Jazz Group

Other

Tapestry of Ohio

Chris Yambar (Comedy)

Program

Flute, dance, dress-Tom NetzYSU Planetarium

Literature

Maureen Collins (Poetry)

Jocelyn Dabney (Storyteller) (2)

Margaret Lishe (Storyteller)

Dr. H.W. Martin (Storyteller)

Dr. George McCloud (Drama) (2)

Mill Creek-Carol Potter

John Tamblien (Poetry)

Carol Weakland (2)

YSU 5 Students (Shakespeare)

Song

Antonine Sisters Hymns (2)

Sophia Brooks

Dana Singers Duo

L. Ehrlich (Cantor)

Atty. Vincent Gilmartin

Josh Green (Vocals)

George Kalbous (Piano/Singing)

Kosovo Men's Choir

Jamie Marich (Guitar/Song)

J. Matranga (Opera)

Jennifer Davis-Mosher (Opera) (4)

Allan Mosher (Opera) (8)

O. & M. Musuka (Hymns)

New Bethel Church (Choir)

Ohio Western Reserve Singers

PENN/Ohio Barber Shop

Philips Chapel Gospel Group

Tours

Al Khair Mosque

Archangel Michael

Arms Museum

Butler Museum of Art (2)

Mt. Carmel Church

Ohev Tzedek Temple

Steel Museum

(Song cont.)

Dr. Rosemary Raridon (2)

Dr. Wade Raridon (2)

Saxon Concordia Chorus (3)

Spiritual and Gospel Choirs (2)

St. John (Campbell) Men's Choir

Third Baptist Choirs

M. Tosh (Opera)

Wade Raridon Singers

YSU Gospel Group

Dr. Mei Zhong

F. Sites (and number of times)

Al Khair Mosque
Antones (4)
Archangel Michael (8)
Arms Museum (2)
Bethel Lutheran
Butler Art (6)
Canfield High School
Casa Ramirez
Croatian Lodge 66 (8)
Embassy (3)
F. R. Gardens-Mill Creek (5)
First Presbyterian (2)
Georgetown (14)
Golden Hunan
Grand Buffet (2)
Holy Family, Poland
Holy Res. Rom., Warren
Holy Trinity Romanian
Howard Johnson - Indian
Hungarian Presbyterian
Immaculate Heart of Mary
Indian Comm. Center, Aust.
Jade Court (2)
Jewish Community Center
Krakusy Hall (2)
Los Gallos Restaurant
Mahoning Country Club
Maronite Center (6)
McKinley Memorial
Mr. Anthony (2)
Mt. Carmel Center (13)
National Shrine of Lebanon
New Bethel Baptist
Ohev Tzedek (4)
Old North Church, Canfield (3)
Our Lady of Hungary
Pilgrim Collegiate
Poland Methodist
Poland National Sacred Heart (4)
Powers Auditorium
Saxon Club (19)
Serbian Hall (8)
St. Ann
St. Charles (2)
St. Christine (2)
St. John Episcopal (4)
St. John Orthodox Bd. (3)
St. John Russian, Campbell (3)
St. Joseph, Austintown
St. Lucy, Campbell (3)
St. Mathias (12)
St. Michael, Canfield
St. Nicholas Banquet Center
St. Nicholas Church Hall, Struthers
St. Nicholas Greek, Youngstown (2)
St. P. & P. Ukrainian (5)
St. Patrick Youngstown
St. Patrick, Hubbard (4)
St. Rose of Lima (2)
St. Stephen Hungarian
Stambaugh Aud. Marble Rm. (2)
Steel Museum
Tabernacle Baptist
Temple El Emeth (2)
Third Baptist (4)
United Meth., Liberty
Ursuline Mother House (4)
Vienna Presbyterian
Western Reserve United Methodist (12)
Youngstown Club (4)
Youngstown Playhouse
YSU (12)
YSU Chestnut Room (2)
YSU DeBartolo Hall (5)
YSU DeBartolo Stadium Club (2)
YSU Outdoor
YSU Planetarium

G. Crowds at Various Venues

H. Caterers (and number of times)

Antone's Catering (6)
Embassy (4)
Monica's Catering
Rachel's Catering
Al Khair members
Allen Catering Third Baptist
Anatole's Rest. Cleveland
Anna Williams Third Baptist
Archangel Michael Catering (9)
AVI Catering
Caesar's Catering
Carlos Ramirez (2)
Carolyn Catering (13)
Chrystal Catering
Croatian Lodge Caterers (7)
Debbie Sheridan Amish
Eberth Catering (23)
Frankie's Hubbard
Georgetown (16)
Golden Hunan
Grand Buffet
H. Johnsons Indian Palace
Holy Res. Rom. Orth. Warren
Indian members
Jade Court
Jeannie Lott-Thomas
Kravitz Catering (3)
Lilac Catering
Livosky Catering (10)
Loretta's Catering
Los Gallos
Lou Fusillo (13)
Madure Catering
Mah. Country Club
Maronite Mrs. Nakely (5)
Mike Vargo Lebanese
Mr. Anthony's Catering
New Bethel Catering
Ohev Tzedek Sisterhood
Ohev Zedek Ladies Guild
Our Lady of Hungary members
Peppers Catering II
Poland National Sacred Heart (5)
Robyn Catering
Saxon Caterers (21)
Serbian members (7)
St. John Bd. Sisterhood
St. John Episcopal members (3)
St. John Philoptochos Society
St. Lucy Catering
St. Nicholas members
St. P & P Ukrainian members (5)
St. Patrick Ann Lawson
St. Rose of Lima members
Third Baptist Catering
Turkish food members
United Meth. Liberty
Veta Necara (Romanian)
Winston Catering
Western Reserve United Methodist (11)
Yo. Area Jewish Federation
Youngstown Club (3)
YSU Catering (23)

I. Food has always been an integral part of our meetings

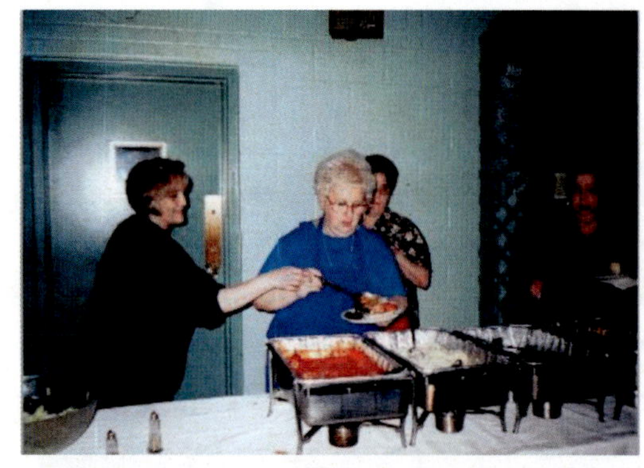

J. Recipients of OCA food contributions (8 years)

Beatitude House (3)

Dandridge Nursing Home (3)

Dorothy Day (3)

Ed Port

Fish Samaritan House

Gleaners (14)

Habitat for Humanity

Heart Ministries

Heart Reach

Hope House (2)

Park Vista

Philippine Red Cross

Protestant Family Services (2)

Rescue Mission (5)

Salvation Army (5)

Second Harvest

St. Columba Food Pantry (9)

St. Lucy's Food Bank

St. Vincent de Paul (9)

Toys for Tots

United Methodist Community Center

Ursuline Sisters

YMCA (2)

K. Difference Makers (3 years)

Bob Hannon

Derek Toles

Dr. Rashid Abdu

Dr. Rick Billak

Eileen Novotny

Guy Burney

Heidi Daniel

Jackie Burley

Jim Echement

John Getchey

Michael Conway

Penny Wells

Pete Millikan

Scott Schulik

Sister Isabelle Rudge

Sister Jerome Corcoran

Stan Boney

Susan Barbati

Tom Humphries

Colleen Kelly

Kathy Cook

Connie Hawthorne

Maraline Kubik

Carol Potter (BBB)

Harry Meshel

L. YSU Presidents who have spoken to the OCA

Dr. Neil Humphrey

Dr. Leslie Cochran

Dr. David Sweet

Dr. Cynthia Anderson

Dr. Randy Dunn

Jim Tressel

"YOU CAN NEVER TELL WHEN YOU DO AN ACT
JUST WHAT THE RESULT WILL BE,
BUT WITH EVERY DEED, YOU ARE SOWING A SEED,
THOUGH THE HARVEST YOU MAY NOT SEE.
EACH KINDLY ACT IS AN ACORN DROPPED
IN GOD'S PRODUCTIVE SOIL;
YOU MAY NOT KNOW, BUT THE TREE SHALL GROW
WITH SHELTER FOR THOSE WHO TOIL."
Ella Wheeler Wilcox

Made in the USA
Monee, IL
24 March 2023

e9c99562-4b70-483c-ab98-613c11e26916R01